CHILDREN LEARNING MATHEMATICS

A COGNITIVE APPROACH TO TEACHING

EMMA E. HOLMES

California State University, Fullerton

PRENTICE-HALL, INC., ENGLEWOOD CLIFFS, NEW JERSEY 07632

Library of Congress Cataloging in Publication Data

Holmes, Emma E.
    Children learning mathematics.

    Includes bibliographies and index.
    1. Mathematics—Study and teaching (Elementary).
2. Cognition in children.   I. Title.
QA135.5.H585   1985   372.7   84-17676
ISBN 0-13-132481-0

Editorial supervision and interior design: Serena Hoffman
Cover design: Wanda Lubelska Design
Manufacturing buyer: Barbara Kelly Kittle

PRINTED IN THE UNITED STATES OF AMERICA

10 9 8 7 6 5 4 3 2 1

ISBN 0-13-132481-0 01

PRENTICE-HALL INTERNATIONAL, INC., *London*
PRENTICE-HALL OF AUSTRALIA PTY. LIMITED, *Sydney*
EDITORA PRENTICE-HALL DO BRASIL, LTDA., *Rio de Janeiro*
PRENTICE-HALL CANADA INC., *Toronto*
PRENTICE-HALL HISPANOAMERICANA, S.A., *Mexico*
PRENTICE-HALL OF INDIA PRIVATE LIMITED, *New Delhi*
PRENTICE-HALL OF JAPAN, INC., *Tokyo*
PRENTICE-HALL OF SOUTHEAST ASIA PTE. LTD., *Singapore*
WHITEHALL BOOKS LIMITED, *Wellington, New Zealand*

CONTENTS

PREFACE

Children Learning Mathematics: A Cognitive Approach to Teaching gives guidelines and practical suggestions for relating cognitive theories of learning to teaching elementary school mathematics. Cognitive theories describe learning as a process of organizing ideas, creating meaning, and retaining knowledge. To enable teachers to use these ideas in teaching elementary school mathematics, this book discusses cognitive principles of instruction, explains methods to guide learning, gives lesson examples, and describes many learning activities for classroom use.

Chapter 1 gives four principles of a Cognitive Model for Guiding Learning of Elementary School Mathematics. These principles deal with encouraging cognitive (mental) processes, stressing concepts and generalizations, emphasizing intrinsic motivation, and providing for individual differences. Procedures to implement the principles are also described. One section discusses the theories of prominent cognitive psychologists to give background for comprehending the model.

Chapter 2 relates the model to planning, evaluating, and organizing for instruction in elementary school mathematics. It gives a topic plan outline and a lesson plan outline as well as examples of lesson plans. A topic plan example is given in Appendix III.

Chapter 3 discusses the learning and teaching of problem solving. Because developing problem-solving abilities is a major objective of instruction, suggestions for guiding the learning of problem solving are given early in the book so that they can be related to material presented in other chapters.

Chapter 4 describes introducing number concepts to young children. It also discusses children's initial school experiences in learning about space and measurement.

Chapters 5 through 12 describe a cognitive approach to teaching the traditional topics of elementary school mathematics: base and place value, basic facts for the four operations, computation with whole numbers, fractional numbers and ratios, computation with fractional numbers, decimals and percent, geometry, and measurement. These chapters give procedures, sample lessons, games, and activities to guide children to learn mathematical content. Although the mathematics involved in children's learning experiences is often briefly outlined, these chapters deal mainly with pedagogy.

Chapter 13 discusses the use of the calculator and computer in learning and teaching elementary school mathematics. These machines can make important contributions to learning. This chapter gives suggestions for using them as resources, particularly in the upper grades.

Chapter 14 is a summary of ideas presented in all the chapters. It relates the Cognitive Model given in Chapter 1 to the ideas discussed in the other chapters.

There are study questions at the end of each chapter. Answering these questions will give readers opportunities to relate and retain the chapter material.

Four appendices provide useful supplementary material. Appendix I is a table describing assessment activities that are adapted from Piagetian tasks. Appendix II is a table of grade placement of topics traditionally taught in elementary school mathematics. Appendix III, as noted, is a topic plan example. Appendix IV lists suppliers of learning materials.

My students have found that cognitive approaches help children become excited about mathematics and learn the subject well. These students also report that a cognitive orientation has given new meaning and satisfaction to their work with children. I expect you will have similar experiences.

I wish to thank the following reviewers of the manuscript for their helpful suggestions and criticisms: William E. Schall, State University of New York at Fredonia; Mary Anne Fowler, Northeastern Illinois University; David Fitzgerald, Northeastern State University; and Therese Kuhs, University of South Carolina. My thanks, too, to my Prentice-Hall editors, particularly Bob Lentz, Serena Hoffman, Susan B. Willig, and Shirley Chlopak, Susan's assistant, for their valuable contributions in the preparation of the manuscript. And special thanks to Myral Shields, my typist, for her patience and cooperation.

I am also very grateful for the encouragement of my husband, Robert T. Holmes.

Emma E. Holmes

CHILDREN LEARNING MATHEMATICS

1 A COGNITIVE MODEL FOR GUIDING LEARNING OF ELEMENTARY SCHOOL MATHEMATICS

The teachers were back at Lowell School for the fall orientation, and Sally Kramer was looking forward to her meeting with Jim Yates. She had assumed the principalship of Lowell School the first of August, and all month parents had been asking that their children be assigned to Jim Yates's fourth grade. She wondered why they often said, "Jim Yates is a great math teacher!" As she walked into Jim's room, she thought, "Now I'll find out!"

After a few friendly exchanges, Sally broached the topic. "Jim, I've heard that you are a super math teacher. How do you teach?"

Jim laughed. "Sally, that's the wrong question. The question is, how do children learn mathematics?"

Surprised—and intrigued—Sally shot back: "O.K.—I'll ask it: How do they learn math in your class?"

Jim's deep interest was apparent as he answered. "Children learn by *making sense* out of what goes on in a math lesson. Children must create their own ideas. If they can't figure out what's going on, they make something up, hoping it will be O.K.—or else they quit and do nothing. The learning experiences we provide must help learners *understand* mathematical concepts. If they understand, remembering isn't so hard."

"Give me an example," replied Sally.

"Let's go to the chalkboard and I'll explain."

At the chalkboard, Jim wrote:

$$4 \times 9 = 35$$

"When a child writes this," he declared, "a teacher should ask, 'Why is that child making this mistake?'"

Sally interrupted: "Not enough practice."

"No," replied Jim, "not enough meaning. If you understand the multiplication facts, you know a product ends in 5 only if a factor is 5."

"I'll go along with that," said Sally. "But how do you teach meaning? And don't they ever drill?"

Jim took up her first question thoughtfully. "To help children develop *meaning*, a teacher provides experiences that foster mental manipulations—cognitive processes, the psychologists call them. Children learn by mentally relating old and new experiences; they must do mental things, like comparing, classifying, or inferring. For example, with those multiplication facts, children in my class would have many opportunities to look for patterns. They would observe that when a factor is 5, the product ends in 5 or 0; when a factor is 2, the product is never an odd number; and so forth.

"You also asked, 'Don't they drill?' Of course, almost everyone needs rehearsal. But practice should be an activity the learner views as necessary after a series of lessons for developing meaning. The child, with teacher guidance, decides what steps must be taken to attain immediate recall. I stress that drill is the learner's responsibility. I emphasize personal responsibility for both comprehending and reviewing. Of course, they are still children, and I give a lot of guidance and support, but I often tell them that they control their own learning.

Then I arrange lessons so that they have many opportunities to make decisions about learning activities."

"What are your lessons like?" asked Sally.

"The children get many opportunities to use what they already know to make sense out of the new materials. For example, if they are studying multiplication, like 34 × 42, it is important for them to remember that they know how to multiply 30 × 42 and 4 × 42. After we have discussed their prior learnings, they are quick to notice that the new procedure is probably a combination of these previous learnings. I ask a lot of questions to guide them in the process of forming new concepts and rules. I tell them that my questions will help them recycle what they know to produce something new."

"Neat," said Sally. "But don't you use concrete materials? I thought that was the way to begin."

"The children work a lot with concrete and pictorial materials. They either create ideas or verify them using objects, pictures, or diagrams. However, many of my fourth graders have developed some logical thought processes, like classifying. For example, I can ask them to sort exercises into those they have studied and those that are new to them. The work children have done in the primary grades with concrete and graphic materials has contributed to their mental development and also enabled them to build fundamental number ideas. I ask them to use their thinking abilities whenever possible. Whether they are using concrete, pictorial, or symbolic materials, they must process the material cognitively—that is, mentally. To get this point across to them, I say to the boys and girls, 'You have to toss ideas around to learn.' "

Sally smiled. "You've given me some ideas to toss around. I like your approach. It makes sense to think about learning before teaching."

Jim Yates's ideas are shared by many teachers who believe that teaching elementary school mathematics should be based on cognitive theories of how children learn. Such ideas about teaching are the focus of this book. Every chapter emphasizes the theme: *Teaching is helping children grasp the meaning of mathematical ideas.*

Later in this chapter the ideas of cognitive psychologists regarding how children learn will be briefly reviewed. First, however, an overview of a cognitive approach will help readers understand the orientation of this text. Therefore, the Cognitive Model for Guiding Learning of Elementary School Mathematics will next be described. Procedures to implement the model will be discussed after the review of theories of learning.

Four principles for teaching based on how children learn make up the Cognitive Model:

1. Encourage the use of cognitive processes.
2. Stress learning concepts and generalizations.
3. Emphasize intrinsic motivation.
4. Provide for individual differences.

PRINCIPLES OF THE COGNITIVE MODEL

Encourage the Use of Cognitive Processes

Learning mathematics involves thinking mathematical ideas. Mathematics deals with patterns and relations. It is abstract, not concrete. To form mathematical ideas, children must use cognitive processes, such as comparing and inferring. They must mentally manipulate mathematical content.

The teacher's role is to encourage children to use cognitive processes. The teacher must avoid thinking for the child. For example, in guiding children to form number concepts, the teacher often asks children to produce equivalent sets. When children create examples of sets with the same number, they are actively engaged in a problem-solving experience that requires thinking about mathematics. The teacher does not form equivalent sets and ask learners if the sets have the same number, since such a question only requires children to verify the teacher's thinking.

Table 1-1 gives six categories of cognitive processes for learning elementary school mathematics. Examples illustrating how to encourage each cognitive process are included. As shown, the six categories are: receiving, interpreting, organizing, applying, remembering, and problem solving.

Receiving is being alert to stimuli. The cognitive process in this category is attending. **Interpreting** is using prior learning to make

TABLE 1-1. COGNITIVE PROCESSES FOR LEARNING
ELEMENTARY SCHOOL MATHEMATICS

Category	Cognitive Processes	Description	Example
Receiving		*Being alert to stimuli.*	
	Attending	Maintaining awareness of; perceiving; observing.	Please watch what I am writing.
Interpreting		*Using past experience to understand present experience.*	
	Translating	Restating in another mode of expression (concrete, pictorial, or symbolic) or in another form of a mode; labeling.	Show these fractions on the number line: $\frac{3}{4}$; $\frac{4}{3}$; $\frac{2}{5}$.
	Comparing	Noting likenesses and differences; discriminating.	How are 2×3 and 3×2 alike and different?
	Classifying	Grouping by critical or distinguishing attributes; categorizing.	Which sums go together? $3 + 1$; $2 + 3$; $4 + 1$; $2 + 2$.
		Arranging elements or categories by levels of increasing (or decreasing) inclusiveness: hierarchical classification.	Classify the following: circle, rectangle, polygon, hexagon, square, and ellipse.
	Ordering	Placing in a series in terms of an increasing or decreasing attribute or characteristic; sequencing.	Put these numbers in order: .7; .09; .83; .17.
Organizing		*Forming and structuring ideas.*	
	Relating	Connecting in terms of some qualitative or quantitative property; associating in terms of perceived or defined attributes or processes; transforming.	How are addition and multiplication alike?
	Questioning	Asking for clarification; noting inconsistencies; inquiring.	A pupil says: "I don't know why dividing by a decimal gives a larger number for a quotient than the dividend."
	Inferring	Using reason to abstract concepts, principles, patterns, or rules from particulars.	What do you notice about: $80 \div 20 = 4$; $40 \div 20 = 2$; $60 \div 30 = 2$? What is the pattern?
		Using reason to move from concepts or principles to examples or to conclusions; if/then reasoning.	If $5 + 5 = 10$, what is $5 + 6$?

TABLE 1-1 (cont.)

Category	Cognitive Processes	Description	Example
	Summarizing	Condensing subject matter; noting main ideas; outlining.	Let's review what we learned today about rectangles.
Applying		*Using ideas in new situations.*	
	Predicting	Foretelling; stating consequences; estimating.	Estimate to the nearest hundred: $43 \times 22 = N$; $19 \times 21 = N$.
	Evaluating	Concluding on the basis of evidence that criteria have been met; checking a solution; judging.	Use repeated subtraction to check: $12 \div 4 = 3$.
	Hypothesizing	Postulating a relationship.	How many addition facts have a sum of 8?
	Testing	Devising and carrying out a plan to verify a hypothesis.	Write the facts of 8 to check how many facts have a sum of 8.
Remembering		*Deliberate effort to retain.*	
	Rehearsing	Reviewing and organizing actions and ideas with intent to recall later; practicing.	Talk to yourself about the properties of triangles.
	Imaging	Using visual or auditory representations of objects and events; mental picturing; drawing.	Close your eyes and make a picture of five boats. Think what "five" means.
	Retrieving	Bringing to mind; recovering ideas; focusing on past experience; using rules.	What do you know about regrouping of ones in addition?
Problem Solving		*Finding solutions to unresolved situations.*	
	Combinations of cognitive processes		What number between 25 and 50 is divisible by 4 and a multiple of the sum of $5 + 6$?

present experience meaningful. It is comprehending. The subcategories of interpreting are translating, comparing, classifying, and ordering.

Organizing means forming and structuring ideas. It includes the cognitive processes of relating, questioning, inferring, and summarizing.

Applying is using ideas in a new situation. It includes predicting, evaluating, hypothesizing, and testing.

Remembering is defined as a deliberate

effort to retain. The subcategories are rehearsing, imaging, and retrieving.

Problem solving is a mental activity combining cognitive processes to find a solution to a perplexing condition or situation.

Using any cognitive process in learning elementary school mathematics involves memory of experience. Learning is a process of creating meaning by integrating new experience with what is known.

To encourage the use of cognitive processes, teachers plan activities designed for learning a particular cognitive process, such as ordering, or for employing cognitive processes in studying mathematical content. Receiving, interpreting, and remembering are stressed with young children. School beginners are guided to observe and listen (attend) and to create "mind pictures" (images). Young children also compare, classify, and order as they carry out activities which require investigating concrete objects and exploring relations among properties of objects or sets. They solve problems related to life events.

Older children are assigned tasks that require more organizing and applying. They are also guided to use problem-solving steps that involve understanding the problem, planning a solution, carrying out the plan, and evaluating the solution.

Teachers are alert for opportunities to encourage children to use appropriate cognitive processes in learning elementary school mathematics. Many learners do not know how to use mental processes to incorporate ideas. Teachers must guide them in learning these processes. Therefore, readers need to become very familiar with the cognitive processes described in Table 1-1. Suggestions for guiding learners to employ cognitive processes are given in all chapters.

Stress Learning Concepts and Generalizations

Concepts and generalizations make up the content of mathematics. If teaching stresses concepts and generalizations, children can understand and apply mathematics more readily than if teaching emphasizes facts and rules learned by rote.

A **concept** is an idea representing a class of objects or events which have certain characteristics in common, called *critical attributes*.

A concept is given a label and is defined in a specified way. Examples of concepts possess the critical attributes and are designated by the concept label. Concepts are represented by concrete objects, graphic materials, or symbols.

An example of a mathematical concept learned by elementary school children is the idea *square*. The concept is learned by young children as they attend to and compare the attributes of square and nonsquare objects or drawings and intuitively classify the concept examples as square and not square. Finally they infer the concept *square*, remember the word *square*, and use the concept to label other square objects they encounter. Several years later they will learn a definition of a square: a plane, simple, closed figure with four sides equal in length and four right angles.

Concepts are related to form higher-level ideas called **generalizations**. Generalizations can be rules or mathematical principles. Examples of generalizations learned in elementary schools are the *computation rule* for long division and the *commutative property of multiplication* ($a \times b = b \times a$). Generalizations are constructed by inferring from examples of the generalizations or from prior learnings.

Concepts and generalizations exist in our minds and are constructed as we mentally process experience. Teachers cannot directly teach concepts and generalizations; they can only provide experiences that enable learners to *create their own* concepts and generalizations. Teachers who understand that learners form their own ideas view mathematics instruction as a process of guiding learners rather than a process of transmitting information to children. To guide learning, teachers frequently ask children thought-provoking questions. They also often assign learning activities that require children to engage in cognitive processes other than rehearsal and retrieval.

Learning concepts and generalizations takes time. Readiness precedes the construction of an idea, and the understanding of a concept or generalization is enriched over a number of months or years. For purposes of teaching, it is useful to think of the learning of concepts and generalizations as a three-phase process: (1) developing prerequisite understanding; (2) constructing the concept or generalization; and (3) extending and consolidating conceptual knowledge. Taken together, these three phases will be called the **learning-teaching sequence.** Using the three-phase learning-teaching sequence to guide children in their study of concepts and generalizations is a major theme of this book. Procedures to implement the sequence are given later in this chapter. Other chapters relate the sequence to the topics of elementary school mathematics.

Developing prerequisite understanding is building readiness for learning a concept or generalization. Prerequisite understanding can be an intuitive (immediate) awareness of an idea. It is often learning from work with objects or pictorial materials. For example, knowing that joining two sets results in another set is an intuitive understanding for learning addition of numbers. Prerequisite understanding can also be previously learned mathematical ideas that contribute to the formation of other concepts and generalizations. For example, knowledge of base 10 and place value is necessary for understanding addition computation with whole numbers.

Constructing a concept or generalization is forming an idea by relating past and present experience. The process involves inferring from examples or from prior learning, naming the idea, describing it, and, when appropriate, stating a formal definition or rule. Pupils are often asked to produce or work with examples to demonstrate that they have formed an idea. Constructing a concept of division would be: working with objects to form the idea that division of numbers relates to the separation of a set into subsets each with the same number, using the word "division" correctly, and showing the meaning of division with materials (Figure 1-1). Working with examples of a generalization can involve using a rule—for example, constructing a rule for division with divisors greater than 10 includes finding quotients using the steps in the algorithm.

6 divided by 2 equals 3
(How many 2s equals 6? 3 2s)

FIGURE 1-1. Diagram to show the meaning of division.

Extending and consolidating conceptual knowledge is the next phase of the learning-teaching sequence. During this phase, learners extend understanding by studying content that is related to ideas recently constructed and consolidate knowledge by reviewing and rehearsing to insure retention.

Extending understanding is deepening meanings. Ideas are enriched and expanded. Learning experiences for extension include producing new examples of concepts or generalizations, investigating properties of the operations, and reexamining computation rules. The insights pupils develop often aid recall. For example, learning that addition is commutative ($4 + 3 = 3 + 4$) can prompt memory of addition facts.

Problem solving is an important aspect of extending conceptual knowledge. To solve problems, learners must comprehend ideas and relate them to problematic situations. Understanding is extended in the problem-solving process. An example is extending understanding of fractional numbers by solving the problem: Give as many addition sentences as you can in which each of the two addends is a fractional number and the computed sum is between $1\frac{1}{2}$ and $1\frac{7}{8}$. What do you notice about your solutions? To solve the problem requires skill in computation as well as comprehension of addition of fractional numbers.

Activities designed to insure consolidation of knowledge help pupils attain performance objectives and remember mathematical ideas. Children achieve immediate recall of facts, work with computation rules, develop skill in using computational shortcuts, and review previously learned material. Whenever possible, activities contribute both to extending and consolidating knowledge.

The extending and consolidating phase of conceptual learning is of importance because it enables learners to build knowledge structures, grasp the interrelatedness of mathematical ideas, and develop competency in performance. Teachers plan thought-provoking and motivating activities for this phase of the learning-teaching sequence.

Emphasize Intrinsic Motivation

Motivation is a drive to reach certain goals. The sources of motivation are external and internal. **External sources** can be individuals to please or rewards to attain. For example, if children are extrinsically motivated, they often exert effort to get good grades in order to win praise from a teacher or a parent. **Internal sources** of motivation involve interest in mathematics and a desire to achieve. For example, children who are intrinsically motivated will expend energy to figure out a puzzle or to get a perfect score on a test because attainment of these goals is personally satisfying.

Both extrinsic and intrinsic motivation contribute to learning mathematics. However, teachers emphasize intrinsic motivation for several reasons. Intrinsic motivation is self-regulated and can lead to persistence in accomplishing tasks. It can also be more reliable than extrinsic motivation because it is under the control of the learner. Intrinsic motivation is often intertwined with knowing and therefore is a powerful drive for understanding.

Intrinsic motivation is related to several forces in children's lives: expectancies, a warm and supportive model who values achievement, challenging and curiosity-arousing experiences, an awareness that effort is related to achievement, and interaction with peers.

Expectancies are goals learners set for themselves. They define what children will strive to accomplish and the time they will give to achieve a goal. Expectancies are related to achievement. Learners tend to perform so that they will achieve at their level of expectancy. For example, children who want to achieve in mathematics attend to instruction. Those who desire to compute without error are careful in their work.

In general, elementary school children have a need to be competent and to master real-world tasks. Achievement leads to personal satisfaction and pleasure. Teachers help learners both set and attain goals of learning mathematics to enable children to feel competent.

Children imitate the *models* around them, especially if those models are warm, caring, and supportive of their efforts. Pupils identify with those important to them and adopt their values. For example, teachers who prize mathematics can be influential in forming the attitudes of children toward mathematics.

Interest can be stimulated by *challenging and curiosity-arousing activities*. Finding solutions to mathematical problems and puzzles is an enjoyable activity for many learners. Motivation is generated by thought-provoking questions. Games are also motivating.

Intrinsic motivation is related to the belief that *effort affects achievement*. Children who believe they can make a difference are more industrious than those who feel that achievement is due to external factors, such as luck. Boys and girls who assume responsibility for learning mathematics are more likely to achieve than those who attribute success and failure to forces outside themselves.

Peers make important contributions to the development of elementary school children. *Interacting with peers* at school can be pleasurable and motivate learning. Group learning experiences can generate interest in mathematics as well as provide opportunities for children to learn from each other.

Teachers know that learning is enhanced or impeded by the motivations children bring to the study of elementary school mathematics. They give careful attention to ways to direct motivation. Later in this chapter and in other chapters, suggestions are given for influencing the motivations of learners.

Provide for Individual Differences

Awareness of differences in learners is the first step in providing for the educational needs of all children in mathematics classes. Children differ in their achievement and in the processes they use to learn mathematics. They also differ in attitudes.

Mathematical achievement involves both conceptual understanding and computational skill. Children with different achievements bring different levels of knowledge to the learning of material new to them. They differ in readiness to learn.

Pupils differ in their abilities to process ideas mentally. Some are able to grasp mathematical relations quickly; others take many more experiences to comprehend the logic of fundamental ideas. For example, some children easily grasp the notion that addition and subtraction are related; others work with addition and subtraction for a long time before they understand that the two operations are inverse. Mathematically gifted children can also solve problems that other children are incapable of solving.

Children differ in the kinds of learning experiences needed to construct mathematical knowledge. Some need many concrete experiences to form ideas. Other children can use pictures as profitably as objects. Some children can easily manipulate symbols.

Children bring different attitudes to the study of mathematics. Some children are stimulated by mathematical ideas. They are challenged by problem solving. Other children have little interest in mathematics. The abstractions are difficult for them to grasp, and they often experience failure. They can develop attitudes of helplessness: Whatever I do, it's not good enough. I can't learn.

To help all children learn mathematics, teachers consider the special instructional requirements of learners who are mathematically gifted, of those who make good progress, and of those who grasp ideas slowly, do not remember easily, and can quickly experience frustration in their study of mathematics. Guidelines for providing for these individual differences are related to the model and its implementation. They will be given later in this chapter.

The four principles of the model were constructed from the views of major cognitive learning theorists. These ideas are summarized in the next section to give readers an understanding of the foundations of the model.

COGNITIVE THEORIES OF LEARNING

Theories of learning explain how learning occurs but do not describe guidelines to promote mathematics learning in the elementary school. To be useful to teachers, learning theories must be stated as principles for teaching. The Cognitive Model for Guiding Learning of Elementary School Mathematics is a set of such principles reflecting the theories of cognitive psychologists. The model will give teachers more specific direction for their work with children than can be gained from theoretical material. However, a study of cognitive theories of learning can deepen and enrich an understanding of the model and contribute to its usefulness. Therefore, this section briefly reviews the theories of the five cognitive psychologists whose ideas have contributed very importantly to the development of the model: Jean Piaget, Jerome S. Bruner, David P. Ausubel, Richard R. Skemp, and M. C. Wittrock.

Jean Piaget

Jean Piaget's contributions to a cognitive approach to teaching have been many. However, they do not deal directly with teaching but rather focus on the nature of knowing and the thought processes of learners.

Piaget claims that knowing is essentially a process of adaptation and organization. **Adaptation** involves assimilation and accommodation.

Assimilation is incorporating new experiences into cognitive (mental) structures. Assimilation enriches understanding. A learner's knowledge is broadened by the assimilation, or taking-in, process. **Accommodation,** on the other hand, is the process of changing cognitive structures. Through accommodation learners modify their ideas and create new concepts. **Organization** of cognitive structures is intertwined with assimilation and accommodation. As adaptation occurs, cognitive structures become more integrated and coordinated.

When assimilation is not possible because cognitive structures are too limited to incorporate a new experience, **disequilibrium** occurs. Disequilibrium sets in motion the process of accommodation, which insures that cognitive structures are modified or changed to provide for assimilation of an experience. Disequilibrium is the main motivational factor in learning. Awareness of inconsistency or incompatibility of ideas triggers disequilibrium. Motivation for Piaget is thus intrinsic and develops out of a situation that is not sensible to an individual. Learners seek a state of equilibrium to insure meaningfulness.

Piaget's **stage theory** of development is useful in explaining children's thought. Four periods have been identified by Piaget: Sensorimotor, preoperational, concrete operational, and formal thought.

The **sensorimotor period** begins at birth and continues until a child is about two years old. During this period learning is in terms of sensory stimulation and motor actions. Infants begin life with reflexive behaviors. These are coordinated and new behaviors result. Continued integration of behavior results in new actions. Gradually intentional, anticipatory, and experimental actions become evident. Of special significance is the development of **object permanence**; from about the eighth month a child becomes increasingly aware that an object that is not present does in fact exist and can be sought and found. In general, during the sensorimotor period, children become aware of themselves and the world of people and objects. Their learning, however, relies on sensorimotor experiences.

The second period of development, the **preoperational period**, extends generally from age two to age seven. The major achievement during these years is the ability to use images and symbols. Language, an especially useful symbol system, develops during this period. Images and symbols free thought from action; language contributes to the development of knowledge. However, the thought of preoperational children is still quite limited.

The major cognitive limitation of children during this period is that they cannot think operationally; that is, they cannot manipulate symbols to produce logical thought sequences. This limitation is rooted in children's centered and irreversible thought. **Centered thought** considers only one aspect of a situation. **Irreversible thought** cannot move back and forth, relating "before" and "after." Centered and irreversible thought are evident in the preoperational child's responses to tasks devised by Piaget to assess thinking abilities. Many of these tasks are described in Appendix I.

The thought of preoperational children is perception bound. They think about what they see. They do not conceive of processes or relations. They think about what is observed and do not make logical transformations of data.

Preoperational children are also egocentric; that is, they cannot take another's point of view. They are at the center of the world and they believe that their thoughts are shared by others.

The **concrete operational period** extends from about age seven to age eleven. Thus, during most of the elementary school years, children exhibit concrete operational thought, which is characterized by logical reasoning about ideas that can be represented in the real world. Children in this period can think logically about concrete experience. They can classify and order objects and events. Of major importance is their ability to **conserve** or grasp the idea that certain properties of objects remain invariant (for example, number, length) though other properties have been changed (for example, space, arrangement).

Decentered and reversible thought underlie the abilities to conserve, classify, and order and to understand mathematical concepts. During the concrete operational period, thought becomes decentered and reversible. **Decentering** is taking several aspects of a situation into account and relating them appropriately to solve a problem. **Reversible thought** is two-way thinking; for example, understanding addition and subtraction as inverse operations depends on reversibility.

In the concrete operational period children become less egocentric. They can take another's point of view and thus greatly extend their understanding of the world.

The **formal thought period** begins at about age eleven. During the next few years young people become able to deal with ideas not represented in the real world. They can think about thoughts. They understand ratios and proportions. They form hypotheses and begin to solve intellectual problems systematically. Their thinking becomes more scientific and abstract.

In summary, Piaget's theories emphasize that thinking develops from pupils' interreactions with materials and becomes more logical as children grow older. Children's meanings are constructed and thought processes change by active involvement with objects and ideas. These concepts form the underpinnings of the Cognitive Model for Guiding Learning of Elementary School Mathematics.

Jerome S. Bruner

Jerome S. Bruner is a major cognitive theorist who has also given attention to the theory and practice of teaching. Bruner (1966) says human beings face the task of creating a model of the world to use in dealing with life's experiences. This model of reality is constructed by using three **modes of representation:** enactive, iconic, and symbolic. These modes roughly parallel Piaget's periods.

The **enactive mode** refers to learning from actions. The **iconic mode** is characterized by the use of images in understanding the world. The **symbolic mode** involves representing reality by the use of language. From early childhood to adolescence, language develops from a simple tool for designating objects to a powerful vehicle of thought in which words are used to deal with the conditional and the hypothetical. According to Bruner, language is highly significant in learning, for it aids communication and abstraction. Language makes possible the acquisition of knowledge and efficient problem solving.

Bruner believes that in learning children need experiences in the enactive and iconic modes as well as in the symbolic mode. He claims that even after learners grasp abstractions, they use their store of images in problem solving.

According to Bruner, *concepts* and *principles* are the keys to understanding. They make it possible to go beyond an immediate situation to a more general view of experience. Conceptual learning provides the learner with a structure of knowledge which makes subject matter easier to comprehend, remember, and apply. Knowledge of general principles can also contribute to students' interest in subject matter.

Bruner advocates the learning of principles by inductive or inquiry methods. He urges teachers to present examples to learners and guide children in the discovery of major conceptual content.

Bruner gives considerable attention to *motivation* in learning. He states that the will to learn is required for learning to take place in the artificial atmosphere of the school. The will to learn is cultivated by enlisting the natural energies of children. These natural energies or intrinsic motives are expressed in curiosity, a drive for competence, identification with models, and interaction with others to reach common goals. Bruner believes that educators must use these intrinsic motives to nurture children's will to learn, because intrinsic motivation is more dependable than external rewards for insuring that children will attend to their own learning.

In regard to *reinforcement*, Bruner notes that learning depends upon establishing a learning expectation or criterion and receiving information to determine whether the criterion was met. Knowledge of results is crucial in learning. However, the knowledge of results must be useful to the learner or it will not be used. That is, the learner must understand how it is related to his or her learning.

At first the teacher provides feedback, but the learner must be helped to take over this function. Learners must become self-sufficient. Otherwise they are always dependent on the presence of a teacher.

Bruner also discusses *readiness* to learn. He notes that readiness consists of simpler ideas taught to children that enable them to attain more advanced ideas. Related to his concept of readiness is his proposal for a particular curricular design, the **spiral curriculum**. Significant ideas are introduced to children in their early years in forms they can understand and are then reintroduced throughout the years of their schooling in increasingly more complex and abstract forms.

In summary, Bruner believes learners master subject matter using three modes of representing experience: enactive, iconic, and symbolic. He feels learning is enhanced by helping students grasp the conceptual framework of

a subject and by fostering intrinsic motivation. He believes learners should grow in their ability to generate their own feedback. He stresses that readiness for learning is dealing with subject matter in forms appropriate to learners' intellectual development. All these ideas are prominent in the Cognitive Model for Guiding Learning of Elementary School Mathematics.

David P. Ausubel

David P. Ausubel's theories refer to the learning of verbal material. Ausubel (1968) says learning is a process of gaining meaning. For students to learn, the learning material must be potentially meaningful, and learners must have meaningful learning sets.

Potentially meaningful material is organized so that it can be logically related to a learner's cognitive structure. Generally this is done by relating new materials to more general ideas or by extending or modifying previously learned material.

A **meaningful learning set** is a disposition to make sense of experience and avoid rote learning. A learner must actively mingle ideas: comparing and contrasting, relating, reorganizing, questioning, and reconciling discrepancies. The learner's task is to integrate material into his or her cognitive structure. The teacher is responsible for the meaningful presentation of material; the learner is responsible for engaging in meaningful learning.

Ausubel advocates beginning lessons with **advance organizers**, introductory materials at more general and abstract levels than the materials to follow. Advance organizers provide a structure into which subsequently presented material can be incorporated. This is a deductive approach, stressing the presentation by the teacher of broad, inclusive concepts to which other ideas are related in the process of learning.

Ausubel believes that there are differences in the way children learn based on their developmental stage. He states that the learning of young children will be less abstract than that of adolescents, and he suggests the use of concrete materials that illustrate ideas to aid the thinking of children in the elementary school.

The Cognitive Model for Guiding Learning shows, in general, the influence of Ausubel's ideas that learning is a meaningful process and, in particular, his emphasis on the importance of mental manipulation of ideas by learners.

Richard R. Skemp

Richard R. Skemp is both a mathematician and a cognitive psychologist. Skemp (1971) says mathematics is a *system of concepts* that becomes organized at higher and higher levels of abstraction. To understand mathematical concepts, learners must assimilate them to their mental structures. According to Skemp, it is not possible to assimilate concepts unless they are communicated by means of *examples*. In working with young children, teachers provide physical examples for learners to use in forming mathematical concepts. Skemp says sensory and motor experiences must precede paper-and-pencil work in the study of fundamental ideas. In the learning of higher-order concepts, examples must still be used. He believes definitions alone are inadequate to insure understanding. The examples used in the learning of higher-order concepts are lower-order concepts already assimilated by students.

He emphasizes that for students to advance in the study of mathematics they *must* have mentally available the contributory concepts for each new level of learning. Rote learning does not make concepts available. In fact, rote learning impedes further learning, for at some point the learning of mathematics by rote breaks down and learners can go no further because learners have not built mental structures for assimilating mathematics. Skemp urges teachers to avoid rote learning in their students by evaluating students' understanding. This can be done by noting how students deal with new but related mathematical situations, not by observing students' skills in mechanical computations.

Skemp acknowledges that routine manipulations are necessary in mathematics but says such activity is to be distinguished from mechanical manipulations. In routine manipulations learners can, at any time, pause and give meaning to their work. In mechanical manipulations learners are engaged in meaningless tasks and could not give meaning to their work even if they wished to do so.

The Cognitive Model for Guiding Learning reflects Skemp's emphasis on meaning, his stress on the learning of concepts, and his advocacy of an approach to learning concepts that emphasizes a study of examples by students.

M.C. Wittrock

M.C. Wittrock (1979) developed his own model for instruction from cognitive theories. It is based on the premise that learners construct their own meaning in the course of instruction. Wittrock's model has three levels of instructional procedures that relate to learners' aptitudes:

1. When teachers ascertain that learners are not meaningfully processing information, they make explicit the relations between previously learned material and new information. This is done by use of verbal or imaginal devices that highlight the organization and specific details of the material.

2. When teachers ascertain that learners are meaningfully processing material when asked to do so, they use oral and written activities to insure that learners generate relevant relations in a verbal or imaginal mode.

3. When teachers ascertain that learners spontaneously generate appropriate relations, they direct learners' attention to higher-level concepts, significant issues, and to complex interactions.

Wittrock's model reflects his belief that *learning is a discovery process*: learners, themselves, must uncover significant relations between past experience and new information. They must assume responsibility for cognitive activity and produce mental elaborations or cognitive transformations, such as classifications, inductions, deductions, imaginal devices (such as drawings), summaries, and reports. Instruction, according to Wittrock, is stimulating learners to use their cognitive processes in the learning act.

In the course of instruction, Wittrock suggests teachers must also give attention to *individual differences* in processing information and to the *motivations* that individuals bring to learning situations. He tells teachers to take into account learners' cognitive styles, such as field-dependence or field-independence. (**Field-independent learners** are likely to be self-directed and individualistic; **field-dependent** learners are sensitive to their surroundings and to people.) He notes that what individuals attribute their successes and failures to is related to motivation. He urges teachers to influence learning by helping students accept that they are in control of their lives and can achieve success in learning by effort and hard work. He claims that teachers are responsible for planning activities and interactions that stimulate learners to engage in appropriate elaborations. Learners are responsible for the active processing of information and for attending to learning tasks.

Wittrock's ideas are integrated into all four principles of the Cognitive Model for Guiding Learning of Elementary School Mathematics. In particular, his emphasis on learners' creation of meaning and their responsibility for producing mental elaborations and his stress on individual differences in learning are major themes of the model.

This section has reviewed the theories of five cognitive psychologists—Piaget, Bruner, Ausubel, Skemp, and Wittrock—whose ideas were woven together to construct the Cognitive Model for Guiding Learning of Elementary School Mathematics. While each theorist has approached the study of learning from his own perspective, each emphasizes that learning is a mental process involving the construction of meaning.

INSTRUCTIONAL PROCEDURES

The four principles that make up the Cognitive Model are general guides to teaching. To influence practice, they must be implemented by the use of appropriate teaching procedures. Two types of procedures are used: managerial and instructional. **Managerial procedures** for teaching include planning, evaluating, and organizing; Chapter 2 describes these procedures. This section describes instructional procedures to implement a cognitive approach to teaching.

Instructional procedures are communication techniques. Teachers employ four instructional procedures to guide the learning of children: telling, modeling, questioning, and questioning methods. All four apply to *oral communication* with learners. Telling, questioning, and questioning methods are most appropriate for use in *written materials*. The instructional procedures are discussed in turn.

Telling

Teachers present their knowledge to children when they tell and explain. They tell children the meaning of symbols (for example, "=" means equals or the same as) and give explanations that describe or define concepts and generalizations (for example, addition of numbers is related to joining sets). Knowledge children cannot retrieve is stated by teachers to aid pupils' recall.

To insure that learners understand what they are told, teachers relate telling to meaningful learning activities and often prompt pupils to use cognitive processes in their explanations (for example, tell yourself how ">" and "<" are alike and different). Teaching is also adapted to differences in learners' abilities to assimilate explanations.

Children receive explanations from sources other than their teachers. A child's answer to a teacher's question is an explanation for others in the group. Children explain to each other when they study together. Written material includes explanations to promote learning elementary school mathematics.

Telling can also convey ideas about motivation. Teachers explain appropriate expectations for learners. Children tell each other their attitudes—positive or negative—toward mathematics. Children hear from parents how they should feel about mathematics.

Modeling

Teachers serve as models when they talk and act in ways that convey to learners the nature of desirable mathematical behaviors. For example, teachers explain and demonstrate how to use protractors. They model cognitive processes, as in translating fractional-number ideas to number-line diagrams (Figure 1-2). Children model for each other: a child can model problem solving by thinking a problem solution "out loud." Learning from models is learning by imitating. Behaviors cannot be imitated, however, unless they are simple enough to be internalized.

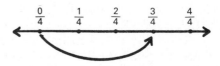

FIGURE 1-2. Number line showing $\frac{3}{4}$.

Modeling is effective for encouraging intrinsic motivation as well as demonstrating certain mathematical performances. Children observe teachers and others they admire setting goals, persevering, and enjoying mathematical puzzles; often they themselves begin to exhibit these behaviors. However, to develop interest in mathematics, children must also achieve success and experience a sense of accomplishment.

Questioning

Question-asking is the most effective instructional procedure because it requires children to participate actively in learning experiences. Three types of questions are used in oral or written communications with learners: direct, mirror, and open. They are used as children study mathematical ideas represented by objects, diagrams, and symbols.

Direct questions guide learners to make *specific responses*. Direct questions ask learners to recall information. They guide rehearsal and help learners retrieve ideas useful in constructing new knowledge. Direct questions can take the form of requests to employ cognitive processes. Assignments frequently state a cognitive process to be used in completing the task, as, compare these numbers.

Direct questions can guide pupils to examine expectations and to relate effort to achievement. For example, a teacher can ask: How soon should those in your group expect to be able to recall the one hundred multiplication facts? . . . How will you reach your goal? . . . What plans will you make?

Mirror questions direct back to learners what they have said so they can *examine their responses*. These questions are used when children give a hint about what they know. For example, when Alice cannot respond correctly to 7 × 8 = ?, a teacher first inquires directly: "What fact do you know that includes 8 as a factor?" If the child responds, "Five," then to help Alice clarify her response, the teacher asks the mirror question: "You know 5 × 8?"

Mirror questions can help children discuss motivations. For example, when Ted comments that math is hard, the mirror question, "You think math is hard?" can encourage Ted to explain his reason for this attitude. He may say math is hard because the facts are hard to remember. From this response the teacher receives information useful in guiding Ted to recall facts as well as develop a positive attitude toward mathematics.

Mirror questions are used instead of direct questions because they appear to many children to be less threatening. To be effective in guiding learners, however, they must be asked with sincerity and genuine concern for children and their ideas.

Open questions encourage learners to structure experience from their *own perspective*. These questions give learners leeway in responding.

Responses to open questions tell teachers the meaning of an experience for children. Knowing what children understand enables teachers to evaluate learning and to help pupils use prior knowledge to construct concepts and generalizations.

Open questions often begin with such inquiries as: "What do you notice?" "What do you mean?" or "What do you think?" For example, a teacher can ask young children to make observations about the attributes of beads by asking, "What do you notice about these beads?" The children respond that the beads are red, blue, big, little, square, round, and the like. The teacher can use these responses in subsequent questioning to guide children to classify the beads.

An open question that probes for the reasons behind a response is often called a *justification question*. Justification questions are always asked when administering Piagetian tasks because awareness of a child's reasoning helps a teacher determine the developmental level of the learner. Justification questions often begin with the word "Why."

Open questions can initiate lessons to promote interest in mathematics. For example, a fifth-grade teacher can ask, "Why do you think fifth graders should (or should not) use hand-held calculators?"

In all questioning, teachers remember to wait for children to respond. They provide time for thoughtful consideration of a question and its answer. Teachers pause five to seven seconds after asking a question before giving a follow-up to an unanswered question.

Questioning Methods

Direct, mirror, and open questions are used together in systematic ways, called methods, to guide the learning of elementary school mathematics. There are two questioning methods: inductive and deductive. These two methods are a major vehicle for implementing the principles of the Cognitive Model. The questioning sequence in each method encourages children to employ cognitive processes to create meaning. At each phase of learning concepts and generalizations, the methods guide pupils to relate past and present experience. Intrinsic motivation is fostered by the thought-provoking questions that characterize the methods. Both methods can be adapted to meet individual learning needs. They provide a flexible design for group lessons, for working with only one child, and for the preparation of independent study materials.

The sequence of questions comprising the **inductive questioning method** guides children to construct concepts and generalizations by making *inferences from examples* meaningful to them. The examples are concrete, graphic, or symbolic representations of an idea. Examples are produced by learners or presented by the teacher. Initially three or four examples are used. Questions guide children to observe critical attributes or patterns in the examples and to abstract ideas from the observations. This method is appropriate for use with children of all ages but is used especially with young children. An inductive sample lesson is given in Box 1-1. A lesson plan that illustrates the use of the inductive method is given in Chapter 2. Many examples of lessons based on the inductive method are also given in later chapters.

The **deductive questioning method** is a sequence of questions guiding learners to form ideas by *reasoning from prior knowledge*. Children are helped to draw conclusions, state implications, produce examples of concepts and generalizations, and develop rationales for rules. The questions asked guide learners in the process of if/then reasoning. This method is used when learners can make deductive inferences. Box 1-2 gives a sample lesson. A lesson plan using the deductive questioning method is given in Chapter 2. Other chapters also give lesson examples for the deductive questioning method.

Instruction employing either the inductive or deductive questioning method includes telling and modeling when necessary to enhance pupils' cognitive processing of ideas. The reader will observe instances of telling and modeling in the lesson examples in many chapters and should note how these procedures contribute to the learning process.

Instructional procedures are adapted to provide for individual differences in learners. Guidelines for teaching mathematics to children who differ in achievement and cognitive processing of experience are given in the next section.

PROVIDING FOR INDIVIDUAL DIFFERENCES

Teachers who have been able to help every child learn mathematical concepts and generalizations during a school year experience a sense of satisfaction and achievement at the end of the year. Their success is the result of knowing how to guide the learning of children with differing abilities and how to manage teaching so that appropriate learning opportunities are provided for all children. In this chapter instructional guidelines for working with the mathematically gifted and with children who learn mathematics slowly are described. In the next chapter managerial procedures that relate to providing for individual differences are discussed.

Guiding the Learning of the Mathematically Gifted

The mathematically gifted not only learn mathematics more quickly than other children do, but they are able to grasp relations and solve problems that less gifted learners cannot comprehend. They often seek challenges and enjoy problem solving.

The instructional program for the mathematically gifted provides for learning more challenging mathematics than is ordinarily offered in the elementary school as well as for the study of concepts and generalizations in the traditional curriculum. Instruction also takes into account the advanced cognitive abilities of the mathematically gifted. Six guidelines will be useful to teachers as they work with the mathematically gifted.

1. Emphasize learning activities that require learners to use organizing (relating, questioning, inferring, and summarizing), applying (predicting, evaluating, hypothesizing, and testing), and problem-solving cognitive processes.
2. Encourage the use of concrete and diagrammatic material to verify ideas as well as to develop certain intuitive understandings.

BOX 1-1. *SAMPLE LESSON: USING AN INDUCTIVE METHOD TO INTRODUCE THE COMMUTATIVE PROPERTY OF ADDITION*

1. Boys and girls, you know many addition facts. Today we will find out something very interesting about these facts. What we learn will help you remember facts and learn new facts.

2. Please use the counters in the math kits that are on your tables to show the meaning of the fact questions I will write on the chalkboard. Keep all your work in front of you, please. (Teacher writes on chalkboard:

    $$4 + 1 = N \quad 1 + 4 = N\,)^*$$

    Look at the facts carefully and show them with the counters. . . . †

3. What do you notice? (The numbers are the same, but turned around. The answers are the same. The counters are just turned around, too.)

4. Let's do some more examples. I will write pairs of facts on the chalkboard. Think about the facts. Show them with counters. Notice what is going on. (Teacher writes:

    $$\frac{2 + 3 = N \quad 3 + 2 = N}{3 + 1 = N \quad 1 + 3 = N\,)}$$

5. What did you notice with these examples? (The answers are the same. You can see that the counters are just opposite. The numbers are turned around, too.)

6. What have we found out about addition facts? (You can change the order of the numbers, but you won't change the answer.)

7. Yes, that is called the order rule. Let's use this rule. Please make $2 + 1 = N$ into another fact question. ($1 + 2 = N$.)

8. Good. I will pass paper for you to use to write the fact questions that go with those I write on the board. Please write the sums as you do your work. (Teacher writes:

    $$2 + 4 = N \quad 1 + 5 = N\,)$$

9. Let's talk about what we have done. Joan, tell us about the first example. ($2 + 4 = 6$. I used that to write $4 + 2 = 6$. I just turned the numbers around.) Good. . . .

10. Let's review what we have learned. (You can make another fact by turning the old fact around.) Yes, we can use the order rule to change the order of the numbers in an addition fact. You can turn the numbers around, but the answer is the same. This rule will help us learn new facts. Just think what you know! You can make up new facts all by yourself!

---

*In all sample lessons, parentheses enclose teacher actions or pupils' responses.

†In all sample lessons, three dots (. . .) indicate pupils are working independently or that similar dialog continues.

*BOX 1-2. SAMPLE LESSON: USING THE DEDUCTIVE METHOD
TO GENERATE ADDITION FACTS*

1. You are really learning your addition facts. Today we will learn how to make new facts from old facts. Knowing this will also help remember facts.

2. Let's begin with: What is the sum of 5 + 5? (10.) (Teacher writes 5 + 5 = 10 on the chalkboard.)

3. Now let's think about 5 + 6. (Teacher writes fact question on chalkboard.) How is it different from 5 + 5? (Five is now 6.) Is 6 greater than or less than 5? (Greater.) How much greater? (One greater.)

4. How much greater than 5 + 5 is 5 + 6? (I bet the sum is 11.) Why? (5 + 5 = 10. 5 + 6 is 1 bigger. That makes the sum 1 bigger. That's 11.) (11 is shown as sum of 5 + 6.)

5. Very good thinking, Angie. Please make some tallies on the chalkboard to show us your thinking.

$$(\text{/////} \quad \text{/////}$$
$$\text{/////} \quad \text{//////})$$

Tell us about your diagram. (These tallies show that 5 + 6 is 1 greater than 5 + 5. You can see 1 more tally in the second row. So the answer is 1 more than 10. That's 11.)

6. O.K. Let's study some more facts to see how they go together. I'll write pairs on the chalkboard. You know one fact in each pair. Figure out the other sum by thinking how the fact questions are different. (Teacher writes:

$$\begin{array}{cc} 2 + 8 = N & 3 + 8 = N \\ \hline 7 + 3 = N & 7 + 4 = N \end{array})$$

If you wish, check your sums by making tallies.

7. What have you found out? (I know 2 + 8 = 10, so 3 + 8 is 11, 3 is 1 greater than 2. . . .)

8. Very good thinking. You can also use this comparing method to help remember addition facts. I'll write a fact you know on the board. Think how it can help you with other addition facts you know. (Teacher writes 4 + 4 = 8.) (It can help remember 4 + 5 = 9. I think it can help remember 4 + 3 = 7, because it is just 1 less.)

9. Splendid! The comparing method works when one number in a fact question is 1 greater or 1 less than in another fact question and the other number is the same in both.

10. Let's look at this idea with other facts. . . .

11. Your study paper for today has addition fact questions you know. Please make other addition facts from the ones on the paper. They can be facts you know or new facts. Work with a partner if you wish. Tomorrow we will discuss what you have done and learn more about the method. You caught on to this method quickly! You should feel proud.

3. Stress the deductive questioning method.

4. Provide opportunities for learners to choose challenging problems and puzzles or advanced topics to study in mathematics classes or during free time.

5. Suggest that gifted learners work cooperatively with other gifted learners to solve intriguing problems or to complete special projects.

6. Help gifted learners set high expectations for achievement.

Specific suggestions are given in the following chapters for guiding the learning of the mathematically gifted. Teachers will also find suggestions in professional journals, such as the *Arithmetic Teacher*.

Guiding the Learning of Children Who Learn Mathematics Slowly

Children who learn mathematics slowly can find the study of mathematics interesting and rewarding if their special educational needs are taken into consideration in teaching. These children should not be expected to study all the topics of the traditional elementary school mathematics curriculum. For example, computation with decimals will probably be introduced in junior high school rather than in the elementary grades. However, children who learn mathematics slowly can succeed in learning many whole- and fractional-number ideas, geometric concepts, and measurement applications. They need appropriate instruction, success experiences, and a caring teacher. The guidelines teachers use to enable these children to construct ideas are:

1. Provide many opportunities for using interpreting (translating, comparing, classifying, and ordering) cognitive processes.

2. Assign many different, novel, and motivating activities for remembering (rehearsing, imaging, and retrieving).

3. Insure that prerequisite understanding has developed before introducing a new concept or generalization. Emphasize developing intuitive awareness by using many concrete and graphic examples in the study of concepts and generalizations.

4. Use telling and modeling procedures often with children who grasp mathematical relations slowly. Insure that telling and modeling will cue learners to use cognitive processes to internalize mathematical ideas.

5. Help children learn to choose appropriate aids to use in solving problems. Stress real-life problems.

6. Guide children who learn mathematics slowly to participate with other children in appropriate activities. (Measuring projects and rehearsal games in which chance plays a major role in winning are examples of group activities in which children of differing abilities can work cooperatively.)

7. Help learners develop confidence in their ability to succeed in learning some mathematical ideas. Guide them to set realistic goals for achievement. Help them learn to relate achievement to effort. Insure many success experiences.

A variety of activities based on these guidelines will be suggested in many chapters. However, children who learn mathematics slowly also need patient teachers who are enthusiastic about the progress they are making. Supportive teachers as well as appropriate learning experiences influence the achievement of children who learn mathematics slowly.

SUMMARY

A Cognitive Model for Guiding Learning of Elementary School Mathematics was described in this chapter. The model has four principles:

1. Encourage the use of cognitive processes.

2. Stress learning concepts and generalizations.

3. Emphasize intrinsic motivation.

4. Provide for individual differences.

These principles are based on the ideas of Piaget, Bruner, Ausubel, Skemp, and Wittrock. These cognitive theorists stress that learning is a process of creating meaning by mentally manipulating experience. Past and present experience are related. There are three modes of representing experience: enactive, iconic, and symbolic. Teachers influence the cognitive processing of experience by various interventions, which we have called instructional procedures.

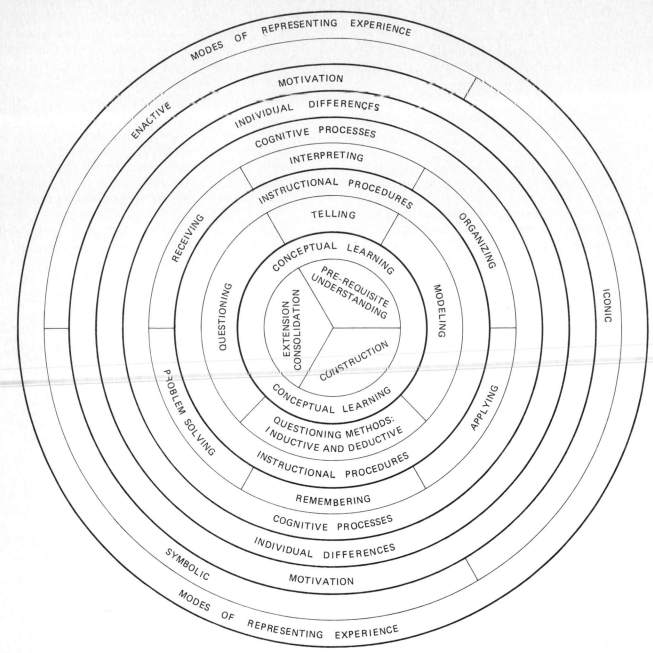

FIGURE 1-3. The learning-teaching process of the Cognitive Model for Guiding Learning of Elementary School Mathematics.

The outcome of learning is the construction of concepts and generalizations by learners. The theorists also note that motivation and individual differences affect the learning process.

These ideas are shown graphically in Figure 1-3, a diagram to represent the learning-teaching process. The diagram enables the reader to view the learning-teaching process as a whole and grasp the interrelation of the principles of the Cognitive Model for Guiding Learning of Elementary School Mathematics. The outer band shows the three categories of representing experience: enactive, iconic, and symbolic. The next two inner bands represent the factors—motivation and individual differences—which must be given consideration by teachers if they are to promote the learning of all children. The next band shows the six categories of cognitive processes which are involved in creating mathematical meaning: receiving, interpreting, organizing, applying, remembering, and problem solving. Instructional procedures used to promote learning—telling, modeling, questioning, and questioning methods—are given in the adjacent band. The outcome of the learning process—conceptual learning—is represented in the inner region. The three phases of learning concepts and generalizations—prerequisite understanding, construction, and extension and consolidation—are included in this part of the diagram.

STUDY QUESTIONS

1. Note an experience you have had recently that involves numbers or geometric concepts (for example, discussing housing costs, figuring sales tax, buying paint and painting a room). Recall your thinking as you participated in the events. Which cognitive processes did you employ? Share your ideas with another student in your class.

2. Review the three-phase sequence for learning and teaching concepts and generalizations. How does it relate to cognitive theories, particularly those of Piaget, Bruner, and Skemp?

3. What are your expectations for studying this text? List them. Discuss your expectations with at least one other person. As you work with the material in the following chapters, observe if these expectations are motivating. Also decide if your expectations were fulfilled.

4. Give at least two children of the same age several Piagetian tasks outlined in Appendix I. Compare their responses. What significance do you attach to the ways they differ and do not differ in responding, particularly to the justification questions?

5. Consider a mathematical concept learned in the elementary school. What would it mean to learn that concept in the enactive mode? The iconic mode? The symbolic mode? Discuss your ideas with another teacher or teacher-in-training.

6. In a small discussion group, share elementary mathematics class situations in which it would be appropriate to ask mirror questions.

7. Observe experienced teachers of elementary school mathematics at two grade levels. Identify inductive and deductive questioning methods used by these teachers. (Remember that a deductive method is not a telling method.) What differences did you observe in the methods used by these teachers? Why?

8. Outline in writing your own views of learning and teaching elementary school mathematics. Have you incorporated any ideas from cognitive theorists by studying this chapter? Why? Or why not?

REFERENCES

Ausubel, David P., *Educational Psychology: A Cognitive View.* New York: Holt, Rinehart & Winston, 1968.

Biggs, Edith E., and James R. MacLean, *Freedom to Learn.* Reading, MA: Addison-Wesley (Canada) Ltd., 1969.

Bruner, Jerome S., *The Process of Education.* Cambridge, MA: Harvard University Press, 1961.

————, *Toward a Theory of Instruction.* Cambridge, MA: The Belknap Press of Harvard University Press, 1966.

Davidson, Patricia S., and Marion I. Walter, "The Laboratory Approach," in *The Slower Learner in Mathematics*, Thirty-fifth Yearbook of the National Council of Teachers of Mathematics, ed. William C. Lowry, Washington, D.C.: The National Council of Teachers of Mathematics, Inc., 1972.

Flavell, John H., *The Developmental Psychology of Jean Piaget.* New York: D. Van Nostrand Company, 1963.

Gagné, Robert M., "Some Issues in the Psychology of Mathematics Instruction," *Journal for Research in Mathematics Education*, 14, no. 1 (January 1983), 7-18.

Klausmeier, Herbert J., Elizabeth Schwenn Ghatala, and Dorothy Frayer, *Conceptual Learning and Development: A Cognitive View.* New York: Academic Press, Inc., 1974.

Klausmeier, Herbert J., and Chester W. Harris, *Analyses of Concept Learning.* New York: Academic Press, Inc., 1966.

Johnson, Martin L., "Identifying and Teaching Mathematically Gifted Elementary School Children," *Arithmetic Teacher*, 30, no. 5 (January 1983), 25-26, 55-56.

Levin, Joel R., and Vernon L. Allen, eds., *Cognitive Learning in Children: Theories and Strategies.* New York: Academic Press, Inc., 1976.

Minuchin, Patricia P., *The Middle Years of Childhood.*

Monterey, CA: Brooks/Cole Publishing Company, 1977.

The Nuffield Foundation, *I Do and I Understand*. New York: John Wiley & Sons, Inc., 1967.

Piaget, Jean, and Barbel Inhelder, trans. Helen Weaver, *The Psychology of the Child*. New York: Basic Books, Inc., 1969.

Pulaski, Mary Ann Spencer, *Understanding Piaget: An Introduction to Children's Cognitive Development*. New York: Harper & Row, Publishers, 1971.

Rohwer, William D., Jr., Paul R. Ammon, and Phebe Cramer, *Understanding Intellectual Development: Three Approaches to Theory and Practice*. Hinsdale, IL: The Dryden Press, 1974.

Schulz, Richard W., "Characteristics and Needs of the Slow Learner," in *The Slow Learner in Mathematics*, Thirty-fifth Yearbook of the National Council of Teachers of Mathematics, ed. William C. Lowry. Washington, D.C.: The National Council of Teachers of Mathematics, Inc., 1972.

Skemp, Richard R., *The Psychology of Learning Mathematics*. New York: Penguin Books, Ltd., 1971.

Wittrock, M. C., "The Cognitive Movement in Instruction," *Educational Researcher*, 8, no. 2 (February 1979), 5-10.

Woolfolk, Anita E., and Lorraine McCune-Nicolich, *Educational Psychology for Teachers*, 2d ed. Englewood Cliffs, NJ: Prentice-Hall, Inc., 1984.

2 MANAGERIAL PROCEDURES: PLANNING, EVALUATING, AND ORGANIZING

The managerial procedures—planning, evaluating, and organizing—are carried out to insure that instruction is effective. Without good management, instruction is haphazard and conceptual learning is not given adequate attention. Inconsistencies occur in expectations and in classroom routines. Children flounder and learn less than they are capable of learning. Therefore, competent management of instruction has high priority in teaching elementary school mathematics.

In this chapter guidelines for planning, evaluating, and organizing are discussed. The Cognitive Model for Guiding Learning of Elementary School Mathematics is the basis of the discussion.

PLANNING

Planning is stating what will be accomplished and how it will be achieved. Teachers make plans for learning and teaching major topics in elementary school mathematics. They plan the lessons they will conduct and the study activities to be pursued independently by learners. This section describes determining purposes and choosing learning activities; topic plans and lesson plans are also discussed.

Determining Purposes

Purposes of instruction in elementary school mathematics are given in terms of goals and objectives. **Goals** are broad aims, such as learning about fractional numbers. **Objectives**

are less broad and can be very specific, such as the pupils will draw and name at least four geometric figures. In planning, consideration is given to goals and objectives for mathematical content, learners' cognitive processes and motivations, and meeting individual differences.

Content goals and objectives stress knowledge of the structure of elementary school mathematics. Understanding of concepts and principles is emphasized. Learners are encouraged to construct meaning by relating mathematic ideas. For example, the inverse relation of multiplication and division is explored by learners to understand division facts.

Subject-matter goals and objectives relate to the curriculum for a grade level that has been adopted by a school or a school district. Curricula differ, but in general they incorporate the traditional subject matter of elementary school mathematics. Major areas are: Sets and Numbers, Base 10 and Place Value, Basic Facts (Addition, Subtraction, Multiplication, and Division), Computation with Numbers Greater than 10, Fractional Numbers, Computation with Fractional Numbers, Decimals, Geometry, Measurement, and Problem Solving. New curricula often include such units as Using the Hand-Held Calculator. A table showing topics and appropriate grade levels for instruction is given in Appendix II.

Planning to teach the concepts and generalizations of elementary school mathematics involves considering objectives for each phase of the learning-teaching sequence: (1) developing prerequisite understanding, (2) constructing the concept or generalization, and (3) extending and consolidating conceptual knowledge.

1. When prerequisite understanding is to be developed on an intuitive level, objectives stress learning in the enactive and iconic modes. Learners work with concrete and graphic concept examples. Objectives stress learner descriptions of these experiences in nonmathematical language—that is, words and phrases familiar to children. If prerequisite understanding involves mathematical ideas from another topic, objectives deal with examination of previously taught subject matter.

2. When concepts and generalizations are to be constructed, objectives refer to the mathematical language and symbols used to describe the new learning, to identifying and producing examples in one or more modes, and to using rules to perform routine manipulations.

3. When conceptual knowledge is extended, objectives state aims, such as constructing examples in a systematic manner (if appropriate to the new learning), describing relations among ideas, and solving problems. Learners are expected to deepen and use their knowledge in different situations. Objectives for consolidation include pupil retention of ideas, the development of skill in writing symbols and in making geometric figures, and proficiency in computation.

Goals and objectives for the processes of learning are less often given in curricula guides than those for content, with the exception of problem-solving processes. A cognitively oriented approach to instruction, however, includes planning for learners to engage in all cognitive processes discussed in Chapter 1. Cognitive-process objectives state mental transformations pupils use to learn mathematics. For example, pupils will order fractional numbers to extend understanding of these numbers. Cognitive-process objectives often deal with problem solving.

Process objectives are matched with learners' levels of cognitive development. Younger children will be expected to perform less complex and detailed cognitive transformations than older learners. However, instructional goals include helping all children perform at higher levels of thought than they spontaneously exhibit.

Goals and objectives for the development of learner motivation deal with: helping learners set and achieve expectancies for learning; involving pupils in planning; guiding learners in interpreting evaluation; and arousing interest in mathematics. Objectives for developing motivations are more difficult to state than content objectives. Nevertheless, teachers are always aware that human interactions have affective dimensions which cannot be neglected, and they give serious consideration to learners' motivations.

Goals and objectives to provide for individual differences are derived from the guidelines given in Chapter 1 for teaching the mathematically gifted and for teaching children who learn mathematics slowly. Objectives for gifted learners insure they will have opportunities to appreciate the structure of mathematics as they explore patterns and relations. They are also helped to extend their interest in the subject. As these learners need little rehearsal, objectives should deemphasize the remembering processes. Objectives can relate to learning topics not in the traditional curriculum, such as probability.

Objectives for learners who learn mathematics slowly deal with attending to instruction and opportunities to use interpreting processes. Translating among modes of learning is especially important for these learners. Telling and modeling are always related to activities for creating meaning. Objectives for conceptual learning are adapted to learners' abilities to form ideas. Remembering processes are stressed.

Instructional objectives for content, process, and motivation are stated behaviorally and conceptually. **Behavioral objectives** are purposes given in terms of the performances learners will be able to exhibit at the conclusion of instruction. The behaviors relate to meanings children have acquired. Behavioral objectives state exactly what learners will do. They give observable and measurable behaviors. The verbs used in behavioral objectives include words such as *show*, *name*, and *compute*. **Conceptual objectives** are aims given in terms of knowledge, abilities, and attitudes. They state objectives in a general way. The verbs used in conceptual objectives include words such as *know*, *understand*, and *infer*. Examples of the two kinds of objectives are given in Box 2-1.

Both behavioral and conceptual objectives have a place in cognitively oriented instruction. Behavior objectives deal with specific performances of learners. They help teachers emphasize well-defined behaviors. They also directly

---

BOX 2-1. EXAMPLES OF OBJECTIVES FOR BASE-TEN CONCEPTS

Behavioral Objectives

1. Pupils will count by ones for any thirty numbers between one and one hundred.

2. Pupils will use standard numerals to describe seven sets of bundles of ten objects and single objects representing numbers in base ten.

3. Pupils will count by tens forward and backward for at least ten numbers, all less than one thousand.

4. Pupils will show pleasure in their abilities to count, such as smiling when counting is completed.

Conceptual Objectives

1. Pupils will grasp the meaning of numbers to one thousand.

2. Pupils will count in base ten by ones, tens, and hundreds.

3. Pupils will understand grouping in base ten.

4. Pupils will develop awareness of relations in the base-ten numeration system, as they use concrete, graphic, and symbolic materials.

5. Pupils will infer patterns in counting to the extent possible.

6. Pupils will be proud of their counting abilities.

---

relate evaluation to learning. Conceptual objectives, on the other hand, help teachers look beyond specific performances to a variety of behaviors that can show that learners have constructed concepts and generalizations or developed skills. Conceptual objectives give perspective to instruction. They provide a framework for considering behavior as a demonstration of the meanings learners have acquired. While behavioral objectives help teachers focus on certain behaviors of children, conceptual objectives enable teachers to view the learning process as broader than acquiring the performances selected for inclusion in behavioral objectives. Thus, behavioral and conceptual objectives supplement each other.

Instructional objectives are not only for the use of the teacher. Pupils are told the instructional objectives to be attained by completing learning tasks. Whether the activity is teacher-directed or carried out independently by children, its purpose is discussed with learners. If they are aware of instructional objectives, children can more readily guide their efforts toward attainment of objectives.

Choosing Learning Activities

Teachers are responsible for choosing the learning activities to be carried out under their direction or independently by children studying alone or together. Learning activities are the means for attaining purposes. They are selected from pupils' or teachers' books and designed by teachers. Each chapter of this textbook gives activities to advance children's mathematical learning.

Teacher-directed activities are a part of lessons and insure sequential development of ideas. Independent study activities are carried out by learners with no direct teacher guidance. They provide learners opportunities to interpret, organize, rehearse, or apply material, to engage in problem solving, to develop good work habits, and to study cooperatively.

Criteria for choosing learning activities are derived from the four principles of the Cognitive Model for Guiding Learning of Elementary School Mathematics. Criteria for selecting activities related to each principle are listed in Table 2-1.

TABLE 2-1. CRITERIA FOR SELECTION OF LEARNING ACTIVITIES DERIVED FROM THE COGNITIVE MODEL FOR GUIDING LEARNING OF ELEMENTARY SCHOOL MATHEMATICS

Principles of Cognitive Model	Criteria for Learning Activities
Encourage cognitive processes	Insure that activities provide for pupils to engage in all cognitive processes. Structure activities as problems whenever possible.
Stress learning concepts and generalizations	Relate materials to the phase(s) of instruction currently in progress:
	Emphasize concrete and graphic materials to develop *intuitive* understanding. Use all modes of learning to *review related subject matter.*
	Provide for activities in all modes of representation when teaching for *concept formation,* but insure that learners can use symbols.
	Use creative, open-ended, and problem-solving activities to help learners *extend* understanding. Stress all modes of learning. Stress symbolic mode in *consolidation* activities. Teach memory aids.
Emphasize intrinsic motivation	Select and design unusual and curiosity-arousing activities. Use games and puzzles. Make some activities "fun."
Provide for individual differences	Insure that activities match learner's level of achievement and cognitive development.
	Activities should be challenging and motivating for learners, whatever their developmental level.
	Provide frequent work with concrete and graphic materials for young children and those who learn mathematics slowly.

The criteria for learning activities emphasize that children should have manipulative experiences in kindergarten and the primary grades to develop intuitive understanding of mathematical ideas. Action experiences are necessary because young children learn by abstracting from their actions. After work with objects, children represent their ideas with pictures and use symbols.

Older children also use concrete and graphic representation of mathematical ideas in their learning. Often experiences with objects and diagrams enable older learners to verify ideas attained by cognitively manipulating mental representations of experience. Older children are helped to "think mathematics" whenever possible. Nevertheless, some children in the postprimary years need to explore concepts and generalizations through action and images before mentally processing ideas without concrete or graphic aids.

All chapters give activities for learners. Some activities will be designated as appropriate for gifted children and some for those who learn mathematics slowly.

A number of general suggestions apply to activities selected or prepared by teachers for pupil use without teacher direction. Such activities usually relate to the topic currently being studied and involve extension or consolidation. However, independent study activities can deal with relearning of material previously studied. Intuitive understanding of concepts can also be the focus of assignments.

Independent study activities should often be games. Chance as well as knowledge should frequently play a role in winning a game. However, a "winner" is not required in all games played.

Problem solving is an important independent study activity. Beginning in the primary grades, pupils should solve problems several times a week. Teacher-directed discussion of problems solved is a frequent follow-up to problem-solving assignments.

Pupils should learn how to evaluate independent work. They are expected to develop habits of checking problem solutions and calculations. They can use the answer sheets supplied by the teacher.

The same objective can often be attained by different independent study activities. The most motivating activity should, of course, be chosen.

Topic Plans and Lesson Plans

Planning topic instruction and lessons is necessary for beginning as well as experienced teachers. While topic and lesson plans are generally more detailed when teachers begin their careers, all competent teachers make plans.

A **topic plan** deals with a significant idea in elementary school mathematics, such as properties of geometric figures. It outlines teaching a major concept or generalization and subordinate concepts. It includes mini-lesson plans that implement the three-phase sequence presented earlier.

A topic plan has the following sections:

Topic title

Topic objectives

Prerequisites and assessment of prerequisites

Final evaluation

Materials

Supplemental objectives

Sequence of episodes: Mini-lesson plans

A topic plan is prepared for a period of two or more weeks of daily instruction. Once written, a topic plan can be used with different groups with adaptations for learners' special instructional needs. An example of a topic plan for introducing the basic multiplication facts is given in Appendix III.

The subject matter of a topic is the emphasis of a series of lessons. Lessons are verbal and written exchanges among a teacher and pupils to foster learning. Lessons stress discussion. The outline of a lesson plan is given in Box 2-2.

A **lesson plan** begins with a statement of the lesson *objectives*. Objectives are written for content and process. The lesson objectives may be given behaviorally or conceptually. A lesson should focus on *one* subject-matter objective, which is related to one or more topic objectives. One or two major process objectives are given. If the lesson objective is to help pupils learn processes, such as problem solving, no content objective is stated.

The *preparation* section follows the objectives. It gives the comments and questions teachers will use to insure that learners are ready to learn. This section states what a teacher will say to guide learners to be attentive, communicate the objective for the lesson, motivate, and help learners retrieve relevant previously learned material.

The third section of a lesson plan is the *development* section. It describes the study material pupils will use and indicates how the instructional procedures will be employed in connection with activities for learners. An inductive or deductive method is often used in this section. However, the development section can employ telling, modeling, and the three types of questions not sequenced as methods to reach an objective, particularly a cognitive process objective.

As described in Chapter 1, an inductive method guides pupils to construct ideas from studying examples they understand; an inductive plan is given in Box 2-3. A deductive method helps learners attain new knowledge by using if/then reasoning in an informal manner; a deductive plan is given in Box 2-4.

The development section usually begins with requests for pupils to use interpreting processes. Learners are asked to translate, compare, classify, or order ideas to aid in understanding new material. When teachers ascertain that learners have performed one or more of these mental transformations, they stress organizing processes: relating, inferring, or summarizing. Children are also often asked if they have questions about the ideas discussed.

The applying process, evaluating, is included in the development section, whenever appropriate, to help learners develop habits of checking their ideas. Predicting, especially estimating, is often included in this section. A few

BOX 2-2. A COGNITIVELY ORIENTED LESSON PLAN OUTLINE

1.   Objectives (content and process)
2.   Preparation
    2.1.   Insure pupils are attentive.
    2.2.   Discuss with learners the main objective of the lesson.
    2.3.   Arouse intrinsic motivation. Help learners set expectations for success in meeting the objective. Note need for effort.
    2.4.   Review with learners related prerequisite knowledge, as appropriate to lesson.
3.   Development
    3.1.   Present—or direct learners to generate—the study material for the lesson.
    3.2.   Use instructional procedures, mainly inductive and deductive methods, to stimulate:
        3.2.1.   Cognitive processes.
        3.2.2.   Construction of meaning.
        3.2.3.   Internalization of content.
    3.3.   Revise communications with learners when their actions and comments indicate they are not meeting objectives (cognitive and affective).
4.   Closing
    4.1.   To determine how pupil learning relates to objectives, obtain feedback by:
        4.1.1.   Observing and questioning regarding lesson content.
        4.1.2.   Asking learners for their self-evaluations.
    4.2.   Give learners feedback.
    4.3.   Make assignments or give options for independent study, if follow-up work is needed.

BOX 2-3.   COGNITIVELY ORIENTED LESSON PLAN
USING THE INDUCTIVE METHOD

Teacher's Name   Age / Grade of Math Group

  John Smith   8-9   3rd

1.   Objectives
    1.1.   Content: Learners will use a rule for obtaining products mentally when factors are a number less than ten and a multiple of ten.
    1.2.   Process: Learners will infer patterns in examples and construct rule for mental multiplication, using past learning of renaming numbers greater than ten to understand new task.
2.   Preparation
    2.1.   Let's turn to our math lesson. Today we are going to do mental multiplication using numbers greater than ten, like $3 \times 20 = 60$. Think to yourself: I can learn this today if I try.
    2.2.   You will feel very proud when you can use your brain to get answers in this kind of multiplication!

2.3.   We will be working with numbers greater than 10, so let's take a few minutes to review renaming large numbers. What is 8 tens? 10 tens? 15 tens? 12 tens? What kind of thinking did you do to rename these numbers? Why?

3.   Development

3.1.   I have written four math sentences on the board.

$$1.\ 4 \times 20 = 80$$
$$2.\ 2 \times 70 = 140$$
$$3.\ 3 \times 50 = 150$$
$$4.\ 3 \times 30 = 90$$

3.2.   Study each sentence.* Look at the factors. Look at the product. What do you notice? What goes together? . . . Can you think about getting the product in steps? What would you think first? . . . Next? Try using the steps to find $5 \times 30 = N$. . . . We agree the product is 150. Let's make a rule for getting products like these mentally. (Statements of rules may differ.) . . . Yes, think the basic fact and then think times 10. Rename as tens or hundreds. (Write the rule on the board.)

3.3.   Think the answer for $4 \times 40 = N$. Tell us how you thought about it. . . . Yes, we can think $4 \times 4 \times 10 = 16 \times 10 = 160$. We begin by renaming tens as ones times ten. (Discuss: $7 \times 20 = N$; $3 \times 20 = N$; $2 \times 80 = N$. Write $7 \times 20 = 7 \times 2 \times 10 = 14 \times 10 = 140$, and so on, on the board.)

4.   Closing

4.1.   Look at the sentences I have written on the board. You have been finding the products by thinking. You have not used paper and pencil. What kind of numbers are factors in these sentences? Let's say our rule for doing this kind of mental work; don't look at the board!

4.2.   Let's help each other review what we have learned. Ask your neighbor a multiplication question like we have studied today. Then have him or her ask you one. Be sure to think the answer before you ask the question! (Teacher rotates and listens to pupils test each other, to obtain feedback.)

4.3.   Let's work together again. How are we doing? What have we learned? How can we remember what we have learned?

4.4.   I don't think you will forget how to do this kind of mental work. You really learned it quickly. How do you feel about that?

4.5.   Tomorrow we will study our rule using materials.

*With some groups the teacher may find it necessary to have a discussion of each equation rather than ask the group to examine the set to find a rule.

lessons deal with hypothesizing and testing. Developing problem-solving processes is frequently the focus of the development section.

The final section of a lesson plan is the *closing*. It describes how to help learners relate what they learned to the objectives set at the beginning of a lesson and how to obtain feedback evaluation. This section also gives learners' assignments or options for independent study when follow-up to the lesson is appropriate.

Lessons are planned to relate to each other to meet the objectives of topic plans. The lesson plans in Boxes 2-3 and 2-4 would be part of the topic plan "Beginning Multiplication Computation."

In the discussion of planning, several references were made to evaluating. The next section of this chapter describes evaluating learning of elementary school mathematics.

BOX 2-4.   COGNITIVELY ORIENTED LESSON PLAN
USING THE DEDUCTIVE METHOD

Teacher's Name	Age / Grade of Math Group
John Smith	8-9 3rd

1. Objectives
    1.1.   Content: Learners will use a rule for obtaining products mentally when factors are a number less than ten and a multiple of ten.
    1.2.   Process: Learners will infer rule for mental multiplication using prior learning and informal if/then reasoning.

2. Preparation
    2.1.   Let's turn to our math lesson. Today we are going to do mental multiplication using numbers greater than ten, like $3 \times 20 = 60$. Think to yourself: I can learn this today if I try.
    2.2.   You will feel very proud when you can use your brain to get answers in this kind of multiplication!
    2.3.   Let's take a few minutes to review. Remembering what we have learned will help us with the new rule. Yesterday, you recall, we learned to think products like $2 \times 2 \times 10 = 40$. (Teacher writes on the board:

$$2 \times 2 \times 10$$
$$3 \times 2 \times 10$$
$$4 \times 2 \times 10 \ )$$

Please think the products. . . . Explain your thinking. . . . We also know how to name tens as the product of ones and ten. (Teacher writes on the board: 40 60 30 20.) Please give each number as ones times ten. . . . Explain your answers. . . .

3. Development
    3.1.   I'll write a math sentence on the board for us to study to learn a new rule. (Teacher writes $4 \times 20 = N$.) Think how this example is like what you know. Look at examples written on the chalkboard to recall what we have just reviewed. You can use what you know to figure out how to find $4 \times 20 = N.^{*}$ . . .
    3.2.   Yes! We can rename 4×20, $4 \times 2 \times 10$. Why? . . . What is the answer?
    3.3.   O.K. Now think others I'll write on the board:

$$2 \times 30 = N$$
$$3 \times 30 = N$$

What are the products? How did you think the products? . . .
    3.4.   Good! Now let's talk about a rule. . . .
    3.5.   Yes, the rule is: Think the tens number equal to ones times ten. Think the basic fact. Think the basic fact times 10. Rename the product in tens. I'll write our rule on the board.

3.6.   Let's use the rule to find other products:

$$2 \times 40$$
$$2 \times 20$$
$$2 \times 70$$
$$3 \times 50$$

3.7.   Let's discuss what we have done. How are the last two a little different from the first two? . . . (Pupils revise rule.)

3.8.   I believe you can do any now! Let's try a few more to help keep the rule in mind. (Write on board: $3 \times 70 = N$; $8 \times 20 = N$.)

4.   Closing

4.1.   Look at the sentences I have written on the board. You have been finding the products by thinking. You have not used paper and pencil. What kind of numbers are factors in these sentences? Let's say our rule for doing this kind of mental work; don't look at the board!

4.2.   Let's help each other review what we have learned. Ask your neighbor a multiplication question like we have studied today. Then have him or her ask you one. Be sure to think the answer before you ask the question! (Teacher rotates and listens to pupils test each other, to obtain feedback.)

4.3.   Let's work together again. How are we doing? What have we learned? How can we remember what we have learned?

4.4.   I don't think you will forget how to do this kind of mental work. You really learned it quickly. How do you feel about that?

4.5.   Tomorrow we will study our rule using materials.

*If pupils need further guidance, the teacher can say: You know how to multiply mentally with three factors when one is 10. How could we rename this product as three factors, with one factor, 10? Or say: It will help us to rename 20. How can it be renamed with 10 as a factor?

EVALUATING

Evaluating gives information to teachers and pupils about the levels of children's learning. This information is used in two ways. First, the results of evaluation enable teachers to plan instructional objectives so all children can use present learning to develop new mathematical knowledge. Evaluation enables teachers to provide for individual differences in learning elementary school mathematics. Second, evaluation gives information to teachers and learners about the attainment of lesson and topic objectives. It helps determine if expectations have been met. It enables teachers to judge the effectiveness of instruction. Both teachers and children should be able to experience success in their accomplishments as a result of evaluation.

This section discusses types of evaluation and some general considerations related to evaluating the learning of elementary school mathematics.

Types of Evaluation

Three types of evaluation enable teachers to carry out their instructional responsibilities of insuring that all children make progress in learning mathematics: assessment, feedback evaluation, and final evaluation.

Assessment looks at learners' achievement of the prerequisites necessary for the study of particular subject matter. In cognitively oriented instruction, assessment reveals learners' knowledge and levels of cognitive functioning. Assessment gives guidance to teachers in making decisions about content objectives, cognitive processes, and modes of instruction (concrete, graphic, or symbolic) to emphasize with individuals or groups. Thus it enables adaptation to individual differences. Assessment is part of the instructional phase developing prerequisite understanding. It is carried out by questioning, with pupils giving oral or written responses.

Feedback evaluation provides information to teachers and learners regarding the progress learners are making at all phases of the learning-teaching sequence. Teachers need to know if pupils are assimilating ideas by employing cognitive processes effectively. If not, instructional plans are revised. Learners also need to know how they are doing. Children cannot develop feelings of competency if they are not aware of their progress.

To obtain feedback during each instructional phase, teachers observe and judge what children are saying and doing. They decide whether or not learners are constructing meaning from instruction and growing in mathematical thought. Feedback evaluation is **informal**, relying on observation, and **formal**, involving written or oral activities designed for evaluation.

Learners receive feedback from teachers and are helped to develop strategies for assessing their own learning and thus to provide feedback to themselves. Learners are also guided to relate feedback to their expectancies of attaining lesson or long-range objectives.

Feedback evaluation is included in all lessons. It can also be derived from follow-up to a lesson. Whenever possible, independent study activities include feedback to learners.

The third type is **final evaluation**. It mainly determines if content and problem-solving objectives have been met when instruction in an area has been completed. If feedback has been obtained for lessons and pupil activities, and if subject matter has been retaught whenever necessary, final evaluation should demonstrate that the objectives of instruction have been met.

Final evaluation of subject-matter learning is usually in the form of paper-and-pencil tests at the end of the study of one or more topics. Final evaluation of most cognitive processes and of motivations is usually less formal than that of attainment of subject-matter and problem-solving objectives. Observation of their reasoning and problem-solving processes will provide clues regarding pupils' use and development of cognitive processes. Observation of learners' perseverance and their interest in mathematical games and puzzles will give indications of their motivation to study mathematical topics.

General Considerations

In designing evaluation of learning, it is necessary to decide whether a learner's achievement will be judged against a criterion defining attainment of objectives or compared with the achievement of others. In cognitively oriented instruction, evaluation is in terms of a learner's *attainment of objectives*. Pupils are *expected* to attain objectives.

Records are made at the beginning and end of each month, semester, and year or at the end of each topic studied. Teachers and learners analyze these records to determine progress and accomplishments. Relearning is undertaken when necessary.

Oral and written evaluation questions are used in the three types of evaluation; questions ask learners to recognize, recall, or produce information (Box 2-5). **Recognition questions** are usually easiest because they require deciding only which of several given responses is correct. **Recall questions** require retrieval of information or procedures. **Production questions** ask learners to generate ideas, solve problems, or give reasons for their answers; recall, of course, plays a role in learners' responses. Open questions requiring learners to explain answers are especially important in cognitively oriented instruction because they help teachers understand how learners are thinking about the content.

Evaluation of learning often requires children to engage in high-level thinking to complete tasks not encountered previously. Children are asked to adapt what they have learned to applying and problem-solving exercises. Bloom's *Taxonomy of Educational Objectives: Cognitive Domain* can give suggestions for writing evaluation exercises for different levels of cognitive behaviors. The categories are: knowledge, comprehension, application, analysis, synthesis, and evaluation.

Final evaluation is usually summarized in **grades** given to pupils and parents. Grades are often letters representing a level of learning attained, such as "S" for "satisfactory." Grades are derived from scores on tests given at the end of the study of a topic or subject-matter area. Tests should relate to instruction and reflect provision for individual differences. A performance criterion of 80%–89% is considered to show satisfactory progress; 90%–100% indicates mastery of subject matter. Teachers help

---

BOX 2-5.   *EXAMPLES OF EVALUATION QUESTIONS*

Recognition Questions

1.   Mark the set showing 7:   . . . .
2.   Circle which are greater than 12:   14   12   11   15
3.   Label these figures using the words *rectangle, triangle,* or *not given*:

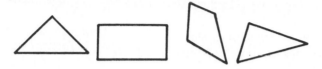

Recall Questions

1.   Define a circle.
2. $40 \times 28 = N.$
3. $\frac{2}{3} + \frac{3}{4} = N.$

Production Questions

1.   Give 5 addition names for 8.
2.   Use arrays to show $4 \times 3 = 3 \times 4$.
3.   Write 3 exercises for addition computation with renaming of tens and find their sums.

---

learners exert effort so that at least satisfactory progress can be demonstrated. If pupils show unsatisfactory progress at the end of a period of study, they are given help to relearn material, especially if knowledge of the subject matter is necessary for further progress.

Subsequent chapters give suggestions for the three types of evaluation. Since a cognitive approach to learning emphasizes mastery of subject matter and development of cognitive processes, evaluation exercises must be an integral part of instruction.

ORGANIZING

Organizing for instruction includes grouping children for learning and scheduling instructional periods. This section discusses some of the options available to teachers when they attend to these two aspects of the managerial task of organizing.

Grouping

Grouping children for learning usually involves dividing a class into several smaller classes for teacher-directed lessons or independent study. Grouping accomplishes a number of purposes:

1.   *Attending to individuals:* Children need to interact with their teacher in teacher-directed lessons to sustain thought and interest in the subject matter. This is possible only if the group is small enough for the teacher to communicate with each learner.

2.   *Providing for common background and prior learnings:* When children have all attained key prerequisites, the teacher can proceed with confidence that each child can relate past and present experience to achieve a new integration of knowledge.

3. *Insuring that each child will have many opportunities to work with ideas and materials when the learning activity is an oral activity or game:* Being a member of a large group gives each child very few opportunities to participate in oral activities; a small group makes this possible.

4. *Providing for children to discuss ideas with each other to improve their comprehension:* Children often help each other learn in small groups.

5. *Using social motivation to energize learners:* Group work on problems can be stimulating and motivating.

There are several *ways to group*. The procedure most frequently used is to test children for their level of achievement and to group them on the basis of similarities in achievement. In grouping, however, attention should also be given to level of cognitive development.

Children who work together easily or who choose to work together can be grouped for work on special projects. This type of grouping is satisfying to children and may be highly motivating. Special projects include preparing bulletin boards, making presentations that require research of historical mathematics topics, and interviewing class members.

An important aspect of teacher-directed lessons and independent study is cooperative learning. **Cooperative learning** involves grouping children in pairs. A team of two study together. Cooperative learning is especially appropriate for working with examples of content studied in larger groups and for problem solving. Cooperative learning is very motivating. It also gives learners opportunities to clarify ideas by talking to each other.

Standards must be set for group work so that children will know what is expected and all learners can study without interruption. Age-appropriate standards are set in class meetings, frequently reviewed with children, and maintained during mathematics lessons to help learners develop mature work habits and experience satisfaction in adhering to group rules.

Scheduling

The objective of scheduling is to insure that learners have instruction directed by their teacher and opportunities to study independently. *Teacher-directed lessons* give learners guidance in forming concepts and generalizations. With young children, daily instruction under a teacher's guidance is recommended. With older children, teacher-directed lessons can occur only three or four times a week.

To deepen understanding, children must also have opportunities to manipulate ideas on their own. Children need to work alone to coordinate and fuse ideas. Learners should have time each day for *independent study*.

Teachers should schedule two or three groups for instruction. With three groups, three teacher-directed lessons of approximately twenty minutes each can be scheduled each day of the week. When children are not working with a teacher, they are engaged in independent study activities. However, this plan is varied from time to time to provide for different study arrangements. These give learners experiences working with children other than those in their regular mathematics groups and in settings different from the usual teacher directed lesson format. An entire class can be grouped into teams of three or four pupils for special activities: playing games, researching mathematical topics, or engaging in problem solving. Some learning objectives are met by instructing the class as a whole. For example, a measurement project in which children work in teams to measure objects inside and outside the class using meter sticks would involve all children in the class. Generally, however, small-group instruction is necessary to meet individual learning needs. Sample schedules for groups at three different grade levels are given in Table 2-2.

At the beginning of each mathematics class period, children are told the *work requirements* for the period. With older children, the schedule for the week may be posted. Times for teacher-directed lessons and for independent study together with the names of the children involved are announced and usually posted. Assignments for children working without teacher guidance are given. Routines are established for distributing study material so pupils can begin work promptly. Monitors usually help the teacher distribute and collect learning materials. The teacher's efforts are directed toward establishing an environment for effective learning. Children are encouraged to feel pride in contributing to the maintenance of such an environment and to feel satisfaction in the progress they make when cooperation and concern for others are shown.

TABLE 2-2. EXAMPLES OF SCHEDULING AT THREE GRADE LEVELS

	Kindergarten	Third Grade	Sixth Grade
Monday	3 groups,* *teacher-directed* activities and *independent study:* observing and producing patterns (use objects).	3 groups,* *teacher-directed:* multiplication—representing products or patterns in products; *independent study:* using rods or squared paper to show facts or patterns in products; studying facts. (Two days.)	3 groups,* *teacher-directed:* representing and writing equivalent decimal fractions; *independent study:* own math book pages or bulletin board depicting decimal fractions we use and meaning of decimals. (Two days.)
Tuesday	Same as Monday with new activities for learners.		
Wednesday	3 groups,* *teacher-directed:* problem solving; *independent study:* jigsaw puzzles, design blocks, or stringing beads in patterns.	3 groups,* *teacher-directed:* problem solving; *independent study:* diagram problems and write problems; cooperative learning one day. (Two days.)	2 groups,* *teacher-directed:* problem diagrams and writing equations (one-step or two-step); *independent study:* choose problems for solution and write problems. (Two days.)
Thursday	*Whole-class* outdoor activity: jumping, clapping, and hopping using patterns given by child or teacher.		
Friday	3 groups,* *teacher-directed:* problem solving; *independent study:* same as Wednesday	Groups of 3 or 4 play games of own choice for reviewing basic facts of addition and subtraction; teacher gives individual instruction.	Groups of 3 or 4 play games, work on math puzzles, or complete week's assignments; teacher gives special help, as required on book pages or solving two-step problems.

*Level of instruction relates to learners' levels of prior attainments; activities differ in kind or complexity to meet individual differences in learning.

SUMMARY

In this chapter the two aspects of planning were discussed: determining purposes and choosing learning activities. The planning of instruction for elementary school mathematics topics and lessons was also described. The nature of evaluation was examined. Organizing was discussed in terms of grouping for instruction and scheduling groups for teacher-directed lessons and independent study.

Planning, evaluating, and organizing are the managerial aspects of teaching. They insure that pupils will have related learning experiences, gradually acquire self-direction in studying mathematics, and feel satisfaction in achieving learning goals.

STUDY QUESTIONS

1. Write five conceptual objectives for teaching mathematics in the elementary school. Rewrite them as behavioral objectives. What do you see as the advantages of each type of objective?

2. Write a lesson plan using an inductive procedure. Share your plan with another student. Critique each other's plan using the characteristics of an inductive plan and the model in this chapter as your standards.

3. Repeat the activity in Study Question 2, this time writing a plan using a deductive procedure.

4. Begin a file of mathematics games. Make a card for each game, giving its purpose and the cognitive processes pupils will employ in playing it.

5. Visit an elementary school classroom. Observe how the children are grouped for instruction. Share your observations with another student.

REFERENCES

Barnett, Carne, with Sharon Young, *Teaching Kids Math.* Englewood Cliffs, NJ: Prentice-Hall, Inc., 1982.

Bloom, Benjamin S., ed., *Taxonomy of Educational Objectives: The Classification of Educational Goals. Handbook I: Cognitive Domain.* New York: David McKay, 1956.

Burns, Marilyn, *The I Hate Mathematics! Book.* Boston: Little, Brown and Company, 1975.

Crosswhite, F. Joe, and Robert E. Reys, eds., *Organizing for Mathematics Instruction.* 1977 Yearbook of the National Council of Teachers of Mathematics. Reston, VA: The National Council of Teachers of Mathematics, Inc., 1977.

Good, Thomas L., and Jere E. Brophy, *Educational Psychology: A Realistic Approach.* New York: Holt, Rinehart & Winston, 1980.

Junge, Charlotte W., "Adjustment of Instruction (Elementary School)," in *The Slow Learner in Mathematics*, Thirty-fifth Yearbook of the National Council of Teachers of Mathematics, ed. William C. Lowry. Washington, D.C.: The National Council of Teachers of Mathematics, Inc., 1972.

Maletsky, Evan M., "Aids and Activities," in *The Slow Learner in Mathematics*, Thirty-fifth Yearbook of the National Council of Teachers of Mathematics, ed. William C. Lowry. Washington, D.C.: The National Council of Teachers of Mathematics, Inc., 1972.

Molina, Norma M., *Mathematics Games for Classroom Use.* Morristown, NJ: Silver Burdett Company, 1980.

Seymour, Dale, and others, *Aftermath 1*, rev. ed. Palo Alto, CA: Creative Publications, 1971.

———, *Aftermath 4*, rev. ed. Palo Alto, CA: Creative Publications, 1971.

Sobel, Max A., and Evan M. Maletsky, *Teaching Mathematics: A Sourcebook of Aids, Activities, and Strategies.* Englewood Cliffs, NJ: Prentice-Hall, Inc., 1975.

Waters, Margaret M., "Strategies for Teaching Children Gifted in Elementary School Mathematics," *Arithmetic Teacher*, 27, no. 5 (January 1980), 14-17.

3 LEARNING AND TEACHING PROBLEM SOLVING

Real and simulated problems require that we make decisions about how to cope with puzzling situations. Problems arise when we do not know what to do but believe something must be done. To solve problems, we use previously acquired knowledge, often in creative ways, to restructure a situation so that it is comprehensible and manageable.

A major objective of the study of elementary school mathematics is the development of problem-solving abilities. The National Council of Teachers of Mathematics states in *An Agenda for Action: Recommendations for School Mathematics of the 1980s* that problem solving should be the focus of instruction. Children's mathematical learning should enable them to solve number and space problems that arise in daily life, in school subjects, and later in job-related activities.

The cognitive approach to learning is often referred to as a problem-solving approach. Learning occurs in response to disequilibrium. It involves the construction of new knowledge. This is problem solving in a broad sense. Problem solving in a narrow sense requires deliberate effort to recall and reorganize what is known in terms of the requirements of a problem situation. The broad sense is stressed throughout this text. The narrow sense is emphasized in this chapter. Problem solving will be discussed in terms of types of problems, instruction for problem solving, and providing for individual differences in problem solving.

TYPES OF PROBLEMS

Problems are classified as routine and nonroutine or as applied and nonapplied (Table 3-1). **Routine problems** require the recall of procedures for their solution. Solutions must be designed for solving **nonroutine problems**. Often the solutions for nonroutine problems have not been studied by children; to solve these problems, children must construct nonstandard procedures. **Applied problems** describe real problematic situations. **Nonapplied problems** involve numerical and space relations.

The two classes can be combined into four categories: routine/applied, routine/nonapplied, nonroutine/applied, and nonroutine/nonapplied. Teachers use the four categories in choosing problems for instruction to insure that all types of problems are studied by pupils. The following discussion describes the four types. Box 3-1 gives examples.

Routine/applied problems relate to real or contrived life experiences. They are solved using standard procedures familiar to the problem solver. Learning to solve routine/applied problems is essential to modern living. In daily life everyone is faced with the need to solve mathematical problems. In school routine/applied problems can be problems of daily life faced by children or story problems, which are mathematical questions embedded in descriptions of events or situations.

Routine/nonapplied problems deal with

TABLE 3-1. CATEGORIES OF PROBLEMS FOR ELEMENTARY SCHOOL INSTRUCTION

	Routine	Nonroutine
Applied	Recall procedures to solve *experience-related* problems: real world, science/social studies, textbook, and formula.	Design procedures to solve *experience-related* problems: real world, science/social studies, fanciful, and textbook problems that may be open-ended, value-oriented, or process.
Nonapplied	Recall procedures to solve problems involving *numerical and space relations:* number questions, geometric relations and constructions, formulas, and counting.	Design procedures to solve problems involving *numerical and space relations:* patterns, spatial arrangements, and logic problems that may be open-ended or process.

BOX 3-1. EXAMPLES OF PROBLEMS IN THE FOUR CATEGORIES

Routine/Applied

Class: If each child in our class of 28 needs $1\frac{1}{2}$ pounds of clay to make the candle gifts for his or her parents, how many pounds must be ordered?

Home: Jan helped her Dad bake cookies. She took 2 dozen to Girl Scouts. He took a dozen to his office friends. They gave 6 to Grandmother and had 18 left for their family. How many cookies did they bake?

Science/ Social Studies: If a builder constructs 840 houses on 120 acres, on the average how much land will belong to each home owner? (Is that enough for a play area for children and a house?)

Textbook: Grace is 12; her brother, 18. How much younger is Grace?

Formula: Mr. Jones built a fence for his square garden patch. One side of the fence was 12 feet. How much fencing did he use?

Routine/Nonapplied

Number: What number is 5 less than 8?

Formula: The length of each side of a square is 6 units. What is its area?

Geometry: Construct a right triangle.

Counting: How many triangles are in this design (Figure 3-1)?

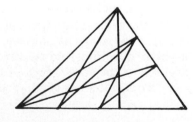

FIGURE 3-1. Puzzle: Find the triangles.

Nonroutine/Applied

Open-
ended: Draw a picture of a frontier town using only geometric shapes.

Value/   Prices at the cafeteria including tax are: Milk, 40¢; Ham sandwich, $1.25;
Open-   Hamburger, 99¢; Soda, 50¢; French fries, 89¢; Apple, 30¢; Banana, 30¢;
ended: Peach, 30¢; Ice cream, 70¢. You can spend up to $2.00, for that is all you
                have. What are you going to eat?

Process: There are 6 children at a Halloween party. Each said "Boo" to every other
                child. How many times was "Boo" heard at the party? (30)

Fanciful: A peculiar kind of beetle invaded my room. This kind produces twins each
                hour. If 2 arrived at 10:00 P.M., how many will be in my room when I awake
                8 hours later?

Nonroutine/Nonapplied

Patterns: 5, 11, 23, 47, ___, ___, ___.

Spatial   Tangrams (Figure 3-2).
Arrange-
ments:

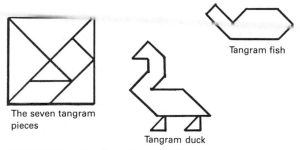

The seven tangram pieces

Tangram fish

Tangram duck

FIGURE 3-2.   Tangram pieces and figures.

Open-   What even numbers less than 50 have the sum of their digits equal to 7?
ended: Use squared paper to make at least 4 figures with an area of 20 square units
                that are not rectangles.

Logic: Tom has bigger feet than Fred. Jim has smaller feet than Fred. Who has the
                biggest feet?

mathematical knowledge rather than life situations. Procedures known to the learner are used to find solutions. These problems include questions related to number operations, but stated in word sentences rather than mathematical equations; geometric constructions not encountered before; and counting situations. These problems enable learners to extend their comprehension of mathematical concepts and generalizations because they deal with familiar ideas and procedures in new settings.

Nonroutine/applied problems deal with real or contrived life situations with such novel dimensions that procedures for their solutions must be devised. These problems can require learners to make value judgments. Some nonroutine/applied problems are fanciful; they involve a little nonsense.

Problems that are **nonroutine/nonapplied** deal with mathematical relations. These problems include pattern searches, arrangements of figures in space, and logic problems.

Both nonroutine/applied and nonroutine/nonapplied problems can be open-ended—that is, involve more than one solution. Both types can also be process problems; these require learners to focus on the process of finding solutions. Usually several approaches to finding solutions to process problems are possible.

INSTRUCTION IN PROBLEM SOLVING

Instruction in problem solving is a major responsibility of teachers. At least one mathematics lesson and two independent study periods a week should be devoted to solving problems. Furthermore, during instructional periods for learning mathematical concepts and generalizations, problems should often be used to illustrate and clarify ideas. Instruction in problem solving involves developing motivation to solve problems, guiding learners to use the problem solving steps, and providing for individual differences in problem solving.

Developing Motivation to Solve Problems

Problem solving is a demanding activity. It requires willingness to expend energy and persevere when, at times, failure seems more likely than success. Educators tend to agree that good problem solvers are motivated to solve problems.

Though *extrinsic motivation* often encourages individuals to find answers to problems, *intrinsic motivation* leads to persistence and self-monitoring in problem solving. Problem solving requires energizing oneself; one must be intrinsically motivated to engage in such behavior. Helping learners become self-motivated involves giving attention to the variables associated with intrinsic motivation discussed in Chapter 1: expectancies, supportive models, interesting content, awareness of the relation between achievement and effort, and peer interaction.

Life involves solving problems. Learners should be helped to *expect to be problem solvers.* Such expectations are based, in part, on an awareness of the importance of problem solving. To guide children to build this awareness, teachers can ask them to find out about the problems their parents solve that have numerical or geometric solutions. Learners can report their findings to the class and also discuss their own experiences solving problems. The teacher can contribute to the discussion by supplying examples of real mathematical problems. A bulletin board, "People Solve Math Problems," can

be used to emphasize problem solving in the lives of children and adults. To enhance learner involvement, the bulletin board can be a class or small-group project.

Motivation for problem solving is also associated with expectations of success. Children must experience success to be motivated to persevere in solving mathematical problems. Success in solving routine problems is related to understanding the concepts and generalizations embedded in the problems. Teachers insure that learners have constructed ideas that are exemplified in these problems. To help learners achieve success in solving nonroutine problems, teachers explain that these problems require inventing solution procedures. Children are encouraged to be creative and flexible in their thinking as they consider solution plans.

Teachers give guidance and support to children as they solve problems. Children know that they have a resource person to help them as they solve problems. Guidance can be in the form of questions and comments that lead learners to discover essential meanings in the problems they are trying to solve. It can be hints about solution procedures. Being told procedure options is helpful to many learners. Teachers can suggest using concrete or graphic materials to aid solving problems.

Motivation for problem solving is related to the content of problems presented. All of us seem to be motivated by experiences relating to ourselves. Therefore, topics of interest to learners can be incorporated into routine type problems—for example, problems about dirt bikes. Children can write problems for others to solve. Children's names can be used in problems written by the teacher or members of the class. Problems written by parents similar to those they solve in their daily lives can be motivating to learners. Novel and nonsense problems can be presented to arouse curiosity. Problems from science and social studies are often challenging to learners.

Teachers help learners relate achievement and effort by comments of commendation to particular children or to the class when they have demonstrated perseverance in solving problems. The need for effort is frequently noted by the teachers. The attitude that success is due to luck is discouraged. Instead, the importance of effort in achievement is stressed.

Many children will exert effort to solve problems if they have control of the time they will devote to solving the problems. For these children, being required to find solutions in one mathematics period is anxiety producing. Problems-of-the-week assignments that they can complete during mathematics or free-time periods will often motivate these children to solve problems. At the end of the week, answers and methods of solution can be discussed.

Cooperative learning usually motivates problem solving. Working with a supportive peer stimulates the expression and evaluation of ideas. Children appear to be helped by sharing the difficulties often involved in problem solving. They encourage each other to persevere.

Motivated children will also use the four problem-solving steps discussed in the next part of this section.

Guiding Learners to Use Problem-Solving Steps

It is widely accepted that problem solving involves four steps as described by George Poyla, a mathematician at Stanford University, in his book *How To Solve It*, first published in 1945. The steps are understanding the problem, devising a plan, carrying out the plan, and looking back. Although problem solvers do not always follow the steps in the order given, it is important that they understand the steps and can use them effectively. This section describes the steps and gives activities to help learners become competent in using them.

Understanding the problem is stating the question to be answered and determining the information given that relates to the question. Good problem solvers can sort out relevant ideas and comprehend the question and structure of the problem; summarizing the meaning of the problem in a phrase or sentence is not difficult for them. Activities to help children carry out this first step successfully guide them to be attentive and use cognitive processes such as translating, classifying, relating, and hypothesizing.

Suggestions for activities to help pupils become skillful in understanding the problem are:

1. Children are helped to become attentive by studying problems with missing information or irrelevant information. After children have examined the problem, they discuss what they have noticed. For example:

John has 3 rabbits. One rabbit had 6 baby rabbits. John showed his friend his rabbits. The friend wanted to buy one or more rabbits. (Selling information and question are missing.)

Jim went to a record-store sale. He saw records at half price. He bought 4. How much did the records cost him? (Information about price is missing.)

Jill and two friends took a bike trip to a town 10 miles away. They biked 2 hours each way. When they got back from their trip, they got ice cream cones. Each cone cost 50¢. What was their average speed? (Irrelevant information is included.)

2. Children draw pictures and diagrams to show the relations in problems. This activity helps them visualize relations. Visualizing or producing images has been shown to help some learners become successful problem solvers.

3. Pupils act out the story given in problems to provide opportunities to translate symbolic statements into action experiences.

4. Children are asked in a teacher-led discussion to tell what they thought after they have read a problem. The objective is to give learners examples of summarizing problems into meaningful verbal statements.

5. Children classify routine textbook problems according to the categories: joining, separating, comparing, and partitioning. This activity stresses problem relations.

6. Children solve process problems to emphasize the relations implied in nonroutine problems. An example of a process problem is: How many different ways could the four children at your table (or row) be arranged for seating?

7. Children read a problem or listen to one given orally and write a second step to the problem to focus attention on two-step problems.

8. Children classify problems as one-step or two-step and discuss with another pupil the reasons for their classifications; this gives them opportunities to compare the characteristics of these types of problems.

9. Children write problems and solve each other's problems.

10. Pupils substitute small numbers for large

or fractional numbers in problems and discuss whether or not the substitution clarified the meaning of the problem.

11. Children are encouraged to use creative, flexible thinking. Activities under (a) and (b) are especially useful for gifted learners.

(a) What Happens If puzzles:
We fold an equilateral triangle, square, or rectangle 1, 2, 3, . . . times?
We double a number once? Two times? . . .
We "halve" a number once? Two times? . . .
We compute the area of a square before and after we double the length of a side?

(b) How Many Ways puzzles:
How many classifications can be made for these numbers? (For example: 11, 5, 3, 6, 12, 15, 9, 7.)
How many ways can these figures be classified? (For example: squares, rectangles, ovals, polygons, circles, triangles, trapezoids, and hexagons.)
Using a map of your state, how many ways can be found to travel to the county seat or the state capital without retracing any portion of the route?
A set of squares connected along their edges is a polyomino (Figure 3-3). How many monominoes, dominoes, triominoes, tetrominoes, pentominoes, and hexominoes can be constructed? Use squared paper to find out. (1, 1, 2, 5, 12, and 35, respectively.)

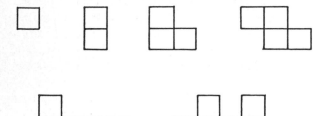

FIGURE 3-3. Polyominoes.

(c) What Can Be Done With activities:
Cans of nuts, bolts, and nails? (Count, classify.)
Certain pentominoes? (Make boxes; Figure 3-4.)
A mirror and geometric figures? (Study symmetry; Chapter 11.)

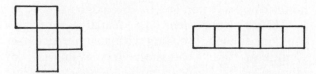

Which will fold into boxes?
(Make other boxes from pentominoes.)

FIGURE 3-4. Pentominoes.

(d) Matching Fun
Parts of figures with figures. (For example: 6 line segments to a hexagon.) Two-dimensional shapes with three-dimensional shapes. (For example: a pattern for a pyramid with a picture of a pyramid.)

(e) Fantasy Fun
Teacher or pupils make up amusing or fantasy questions for each other to think about:
What is the average nose length in this class?
How many pounds of food do you eat a day? week? year?
What is the average Pac Man size?

12. Precise thinking can be encouraged by
(a) Asking learners to draw figures that are, or are not, examples of definitions of geometric figures. Children can share drawings with each other and discuss why the drawings do or do not show examples of definitions. Drawings could be supplied by the teacher.

(b) Difficult concept formation puzzles to solve and make (Figure 3-5).

(c) Attribute monsters (Figure 3-6).

(d) Drawing a picture and making up logic problems that can be derived from the picture. (For example: Tom is taller than . . . . Who is shortest?)

Devising a plan follows understanding the problem. If problems are understood, solutions can be planned with confidence. Problem solvers recall plans they have used previously or consider optional plans, such as using tables or lists. Model problems or examples of types of prob-

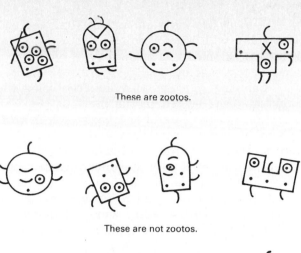

These are zootos.

These are not zootos.

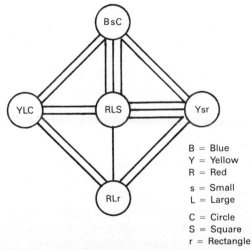

Which are zootos?

FIGURE 3-5.   A concept-formation puzzle.

lems solved by the same solution plan can also be recalled to devise a solution plan.

Routine problems usually require planning to write a mathematical sentence that states the problem relations. Nonroutine problems are often solved using charts, lists, tables, graphs, diagrams, or counting.

Activities to help learners rethink the meaning of the operations, become acquainted with different solution plans, and develop knowledge of model problems include:

B = Blue
Y = Yellow
R = Red

s = Small
L = Large

C = Circle
S = Square
r = Rectangle

FIGURE 3-6.   Attribute monster. Number of lines gives number of attributes different in segments of monster's body. Place attribute piece on circular shape to make monster. (Letters are not in puzzle.)

1.   Assign problems for one assignment that can all be solved using the same standard (for example, division) or nonstandard (for example, tables) solution plan. After the assignment is completed, ask children what they noticed in the solutions. After children report that the solutions were similar, discuss the nature of these similarities. Suggest to the class that if they remember a problem of a certain type, it can be a help in solving similar problems. Have children choose a model for the type of problem in this lesson. Begin a poster that eventually will include many model problems and suggested solutions. Ask learners to write problems that will match the various model types and discuss them with other children to clarify thinking.

2.   Learners classify routine arithmetic textbook problems according to the operation used for solutions; this gives opportunities to compare problems that exemplify the same or different operations. Group discussion further clarifies the comparisons.

3.   Ask children to classify nonroutine problems by solution plans. The children do not need to solve these problems but can do so to verify their thinking. The class later works as a group, discussing the solution plans for a class of problems. Reasons for choices are emphasized in the discussion. Expression of different solution plans (with reasons) is encouraged.

4.   Give a list of problems and a corresponding list of solution plans. Ask children to match the problems and solution plans. Children should work in pairs to give opportunities for expression and clarification of ideas. An all-class discussion should conclude the period.

5.   Review the meanings of the operations, using story problems to illustrate the meanings. A chart stating operation meanings together with illustrative story problems and equations should be constructed and displayed.

6.   Children write problems for basic facts assigned by the teacher. A bulletin board display is made of many different problems for one basic fact. The problems are classified by learners for different interpretations of a basic fact, if possible.

7.   Pupils participate in an "I Remember" discussion. Read a problem and ask learn-

ers to recall a similar problem or make up one. Solution plans can be included in pupils' responses. This discussion must be conducted with a small group to give all learners opportunities to participate. To keep the discussion moving, the problems to be read can be posted prior to the discussion.

8. Pupils study solution plans for two-step problems:

   a. For capable pupils the mathematical sentence employing parentheses is introduced in an inductive lesson. Children are given problems and solution plans to study and use in drawing conclusions. A typical problem is: Jane bought 3 hairbows at 75¢ each. She gave the clerk $5. What was her change? The equation is $5 - (3 \times .75) = N$.

   Children are guided to conclude that the first step is denoted by the expression in the parentheses.

   Further lessons give learners opportunities to identify, devise solution plans for, and write two-step problems.

   b. For learners unable to use the equation form involving parentheses, a two-step solution plan is introduced. For the above problem it is:

   1. $3 \times \$.75 = \text{Cost}$ 2. $\$5 - \text{Cost} = N$

   This plan labels the unknown in the first step to help learners retain the meaning of the problem.

   This plan can also be introduced inductively. Pupils study problems and solution plans presented by the teacher to enable them to form the concept of a two-step solution. Further activities provide opportunities for identification, writing solution plans, and writing two-step problems.

9. In a class discussion review and list the formulas pupils have studied. Ask learners to give examples of problems solved by using a specific formula. A chart displaying model problems for formulas can be made, posted, and reviewed as necessary to promote recall.

As children are taught various plans to use in solving problems, they need to be reminded

that if they do not understand the problem, their plan will usually not lead to the correct solution. A plan is a map only if you know where you are going.

Carrying out the plan involves using the solution plan devised in the previous step. Instruction stresses careful and neat work in writing mathematical sentences and in producing tables, graphs, diagrams, or lists. Children are urged to use labels with numerals whenever possible; labels enable problem solvers to retain problem information and recognize any inconsistencies that surface while work is being done. If the solution calls for computation, estimation is part of carrying out the plan.

Computation procedures must not be a source of difficulty for problem solvers. If children cannot do the computation necessary to solve problems, the problems should be revised so pupils can be successful in this aspect of problem solving. At another time, computation can be taught for mastery. The calculator is a superior computational aid in problem solving and should often be used.

Often while one is carrying out a somewhat tedious procedure, a shorter method comes to mind. Children should be aware of this possibility and the need to decide whether to discard the present method in favor of the shorter one or to continue using the plan and use the shorter method as a check. This decision is contingent on the learner's attitude and the nature of the solution methods.

Looking back is evaluating a solution. The solution must be reasonable. A hypothesized solution, if made, should be recalled and judged. If computation was required, it is checked. Problem solvers often reflect on procedures they used to see if other plans would lead to the same results. They sometimes consider how the procedures followed could be used for solving other problems.

Activities to help children develop habits of looking back are:

1. Provide problems and solutions in an "Is Anything Wrong Here" activity. Some solutions are incorrect. Children study the material and discuss their conclusions. Learners are encouraged to explain their reasoning to others during the discussion.

2. Share unreasonable solutions pupils have given. (No pupil names are used.) The discussion can help those who submitted the

solutions understand how to think about sensible solutions, as well as provide good learning experiences with nonexamples for others.

Learning the four-step plan is stressed at all grades. Children in the primary grades are helped to use the steps intuitively. During small-group discussions, teachers informally guide young children to carry out the problem-solving procedure. Comments made include: We must first understand what's going on in the problem; imagine what is happening; tell us what you thought. Let's act out the problem. Draw a picture of the problem story. Can you find the solution another way? How? Does that answer make sense? Why?

In the postprimary years, teachers help learners to grasp the meaning and significance of the steps and to use them consciously in problem solving. To teach the steps, teachers use an inductive or deductive method. Using an inductive method, teachers ask learners to solve a problem and to remember what they thought as they found the solution. The problem assigned should be readily solved by learners so they can focus on the process. The discussion of how the problem was solved provides the group with examples of the four steps. The teacher can write samples of learners' reports of their thinking processes on the chalkboard. The problem-solving steps are made explicit in an examination of these samples. A statement of the four steps is given. A poster stating the steps is made by the teacher or a child. The poster is displayed in a prominent place and its content referred to frequently.

Using a deductive method, the teacher presents the steps, emphasizes the importance of their use, and guides children to examine their thinking in regard to each step as they solve several problems. Children are encouraged to tell how they thought about the problems to illustrate each step. A poster is made and displayed.

An alternative procedure is for the teacher to model the thinking in each step. Next, several problems are distributed to children. Each child solves one or more problems, making mental or written notes of his or her thoughts while solving the problem. A group discussion enables learners to share their thinking and to examine the steps in problem solving. A poster of the steps is also made, displayed, and referred to frequently.

Instruction for using problem-solving steps, like all instruction, requires attention to individual differences. This has been alluded to earlier. The next section discusses the topic more fully.

PROVIDING FOR INDIVIDUAL DIFFERENCES

Individual differences are very evident as children solve problems. Mathematically gifted learners quickly grasp relations and easily find solutions to assigned problems or those they devise. They like the challenge of problems. Those who learn mathematics slowly often experience frustration when assigned problems to solve and have difficulty keeping "on task."

To provide for individual differences in problem-solving instruction, teachers first assess problem-solving abilities of learners. Teachers then adapt instruction to children's levels of prerequisite understanding and conscientiously use feedback and final evaluation to help children learn problem solving.

Instruction

In *assessing*, it is important to learn children's approaches to problem solving as well as their abilities to obtain correct solutions. Teachers ask children in small groups or individually to think solutions "out loud." They judge children's responses in terms of using the problem-solving steps.

Assessment provides answers to such questions as:

1. What embedded operations give pupils the least difficulty in understanding routine/applied problems?

2. Can children classify routine/applied problems by operations?

3. Are routine/applied problems less difficult for learners than routine/nonapplied problems?

4. What are pupils' responses to nonroutine problems, either applied or nonapplied? Do they accept the challenge of open-ended and process problems?

5. What supplementary aids do children use in solving any type of problem? Do they use aids such as diagrams only when the teacher suggests them or do they use aids spontaneously?

6. Do children have more difficulty understanding the problem or planning a solution?

7. Is computation the source of children's success or failure in problem solving?

8. Do children check their solutions?

When teachers know how children solve problems, they *plan a program* to enable children to improve in their problem-solving abilities. All children should have instruction to enable them to become good problem solvers. Pupils identified as gifted have instructional needs as well as children who learn mathematics slowly. However, instruction for children will differ because of their prior achievement and thinking capabilities.

Gifted learners, especially in the postprimary years, should be told their areas of mastery and the objectives of the next phase of instruction. They can plan a program cooperatively with teachers; they should be given some responsibility for choosing learning activities. Instruction should help these learners be flexible in problem solving, look for alternative solutions to problems, and persevere in solving problems. They should be encouraged to find problems in other subject areas or in nonschool activities.

Children who learn mathematics slowly usually need special help in identifying the mathematical relations embedded in problems. They can be assigned problems that state relations in as straightforward a manner as possible. They often need to develop habits of using concrete and graphic aids to understand problems. The activities described in the previous section that involve aids and pupils' writing problems are especially useful with these children. To help children recognize the relevance of using objects or pictures to solve problems, they can decide whether a solution involving concrete or graphic materials is most meaningful to them. If children have difficulty reading problems, the problems can be read to them or they can be available on a tape prepared by the teacher. The instruction for children who learn mathematics slowly is especially designed to give them success in problem solving. When children can do, they do "do."

As mentioned previously, several periods a week should be given to the problem-solving instructional program for all children. Problems should be incorporated into the instruction frequently to insure that children relate problem solving to the mathematics concepts they are learning.

Feedback is included in the program for learning problem solving so both teachers and children know what progress is being made. Feedback should relate to the specific facets of problem solving that have been emphasized in instruction, so it is possible to determine what has been learned and what needs to be studied further.

Final evaluation at the end of a period of instruction that has emphasized one or more aspects of problem solving will demonstrate that learners have improved if: (1) feedback evaluation has led to reteaching and relearning those aspects of problem solving; and (2) the final evaluation relates to what has been studied. If final evaluation includes more difficult problems or more complex cognitive processes than included in instruction, scores for material related to what has been taught and scores for material at a higher level should be kept separate. Insofar as possible, children should be helped to understand the significance of both types of scores.

Children should also be helped to evaluate their progress in becoming competent problem solvers. Self-evaluation is particularly important because recognizing and acknowledging growth increases motivation. To foster self-evaluation, children can keep a log of the problems they have solved correctly. Comments can be included in the log about the progress made—for example, in regard to each of the four steps. Children should be encouraged to write comments such as: I believe I can see problems in my mind better than I did a month ago. I am remembering to check the sense of my solutions more often than when school started. Now I never forget to check the sense of my solutions!

SUMMARY

The key idea in this chapter is that the learning of problem solving cannot be left to chance. A program must be designed and implemented to insure that learners are motivated to solve problems, become knowledgeable about the steps in problem solving in order to use them confidently and competently, and are helped to improve in problem-solving abilities for different types of problems in terms of their individual learning needs. In learning problem solving, as well as other topics, what teachers do makes a difference in the children's learning.

STUDY QUESTIONS

1. Begin a file of problems for use by elementary school pupils. Include problems in each of the four categories and for every grade level. Use 3-by-5 cards. Color- and letter-code the cards for filing and retrieving. If possible, work cooperatively with one or more other students to build a larger file than you could create alone. (Ideas for problems can be found in sources listed in References.)

2. Ask pupils in the primary and the upper grades what they think about word problems. Compare their responses. If you can, include gifted children and those who learn mathematics slowly and compare their responses. What hypotheses do you have that explain pupils' responses and the results of your comparisons?

3. Use word problems for a particular grade. Solve the problems yourself, making notes of your thinking. Ask children at the proper grade level to solve the problems and explain their thinking to you. How does your thinking and that of the children compare? Why is it alike or different?

4. Write an assessment activity for children in the late primary or upper grades. What objectives will you use to construct your assessment instrument? Use it with children. What does it reveal? If you were responsible for teaching the children, what would have highest priority in your program? Lowest? Why?

5. Write problems in each of the four categories for children at a certain grade level. Ask children to rank the problems in terms of their interest in them or to choose the least and most interesting. What are the implications of their responses for your teaching?

REFERENCES

Brannan, Richard, and Oscar Schaaf, "An Instructional Approach to Problem Solving," in *The Agenda In Action*, 1983 Yearbook of the National Council of Teachers of Mathematics, eds. Gwen Shufelt and James R. Smart. Reston, VA: The National Council of Teachers of Mathematics, Inc., 1983.

Bruni, James V., "Problem Solving for the Primary Grades," *Arithmetic Teacher*, 29, no. 6 (February 1982), 10-15.

Burns, Marilyn, "How to Teach Problem Solving," *Arithmetic Teacher*, 29, no. 6 (February 1982), 46-49.

Burton, Grace M., "Problem Solving: It's Never Too Early to Start," in *The Agenda In Action*, 1983 Yearbook of the National Council of Teachers of Mathematics, eds. Gwen Shufelt and James R. Smart. Reston, VA: The National Council of Teachers of Mathematics, Inc., 1983.

Carpenter, Thomas P., and others, "Solving Verbal Problems: Results and Implications from National Assessment," *Arithmetic Teacher*, 28, no. 1 (September 1980), 8-12.

Charles, Randall I., "Evaluation and Problem Solving," *Arithmetic Teacher*, 30, no. 5 (January 1983), 6-7, 54.

_____, Robert P. Mason, and Catherine A. White, "Problem Solving for All Students," in *Mathematics for the Middle Grades (5-9)*, 1982 Yearbook of the National Council of Teachers of Mathematics, eds. Linda Silvey and James R. Smart. Reston, VA: The National Council of Teachers of Mathematics, Inc., 1982.

Fennell, Francis (Skip), "Focusing on Problem Solving in the Primary Grades," in *The Agenda In Action*, 1983 Yearbook of the National Council of Teachers of Mathematics, eds. Gwen Shufelt and James R. Smart. Reston, VA: The National Council of Teachers of Mathematics, Inc., 1983.

Grossnickle, Foster E., and others, *Discovering Meanings in Elementary School Mathematics* (7th ed.), chap. 10. New York: Holt, Rinehart and Winston, 1983.

House, Peggy A., Martha L. Wallace, and Mary A. Johnson, "Problem Solving as a Focus: How? When? Whose Responsibility?" in *The Agenda In Action*, 1983 Yearbook of the National Council of Teachers of Mathematics, eds. Gwen Shufelt and James R. Smart. Reston, VA: The National Council of Teachers of Mathematics, Inc., 1983.

Jones, Billie M., "Put Your Students in the Picture for Better Problem Solving," *Arithmetic Teacher*, 30, no. 8 (April 1983), 30-33.

LeBlanc, John F., Linda Proudfit, and Ian J. Putt, "Teaching Problem Solving in the Elementary School," in *Problem Solving in School Mathematics*, 1980 Yearbook of the National Council of Teachers of Mathematics, eds. Stephen Krulik and Robert E. Reys. Reston, VA: The National Council of Teachers of Mathematics, Inc., 1980.

Lee, Kil S., "Guiding Young Children in Successful Problem Solving," *Arithmetic Teacher*, 29, no. 5 (January 1982), 15-17.

Moser, James M., and Thomas P. Carpenter, "Young Children Are Good Problem Solvers," *Arithmetic Teacher*, 30, no. 3 (November 1982), 24-26.

Moses, Barbara, "Individual Differences in Problem Solving," *Arithmetic Teacher*, 30, no. 4 (December 1982), 10-14.

Muller, Adelyn C., and Ray Kurtz, "Students Like Personalized Word Problems," *Arithmetic Teacher*, 28, no. 9 (May 1981), 13-14.

National Council of Teachers of Mathematics, Inc., *An Agenda for Action: Recommendations for School Mathematics of the 1980s*. Reston, VA: The National Council of Teachers of Mathematics, Inc., 1980.

Polya, G., *How To Solve It*, 2d ed. Garden City, NY: Doubleday & Company, Inc., 1957.

Spencer, Patricia J., and Frank K. Lester, "Second Graders Can Be Problem Solvers!," *Arithmetic Teacher*, 29, no. 1 (September 1981), 15-17.

Suydam, Marilyn N., "Untangling Clues from Research on Problem Solving," in *Problem Solving in School Mathematics*, 1980 Yearbook of the National Council of Teachers of Mathematics, eds. Stephen Krulik and Robert E. Reys. Reston, VA: The National Council of Teachers of Mathematics, Inc., 1980.

Wirtz, Robert W., and Emily Kahn, "Another Look at Applications in Elementary School Mathematics," *Arithmetic Teacher*, 30, no. 1 (September 1982), 21-25.

Worth, Joan, "Problem Solving in the Intermediate Grades: Helping Your Students Learn to Solve Problems," *Arithmetic Teacher*, 20, no. 6 (February 1982), 16-19.

4 GUIDING YOUNG CHILDREN TO LEARN MATHEMATICS

The cognitive processes and mathematical knowledge that develop during the beginning school years are crucial to future progress in the study of mathematics. Early learning enables children to comprehend complex concepts in later years. Therefore, young children are helped to develop cognitive processes necessary for learning and to construct fundamental concepts of number, space, and measurement. The aims of instruction relate to both process and content. To attain these goals, teachers provide learners with time for investigation and exploration together with opportunities for discussion and problem solving. Instruction emphasizes concrete experience to enable young learners to abstract thinking processes and mathematical concepts from their actions.

This chapter describes learning mathematics in kindergarten and the early primary grades. The first three sections discuss learning number concepts, developing intuitive ideas of geometry, and forming prerequisite understanding for the study of measurement. The Cognitive Model as a guide for teaching young children is examined in the last section. Both instructional and managerial procedures are discussed.

LEARNING NUMBER CONCEPTS

Number concepts are constructed by children as they examine and think about sets of concrete materials. A set is a group or collection of objects that is accurately defined; the objects are called **elements** or **members. Number,** a property of sets, is an intricate concept. According to

Piaget, a synthesis of classifying and ordering is necessary to construct the concept of number. Therefore, classifying and ordering are emphasized in mathematics instruction. All phases of the learning-teaching sequence provide opportunities for children to employ these cognitive processes.

This section discusses learning and teaching number concepts in terms of the three phases of the learning-teaching sequence: guiding the development of prerequisite understanding, (2) helping children construct number concepts, and (3) providing learning experiences for extending and consolidating conceptual knowledge. Suggestions for evaluating children's progress are included in the discussions pertaining to instructional areas.

Developing Prerequisite Understanding

Number concepts are derived from thinking about relations among sets. Therefore, prerequisite understanding begins with a study of set members and sets. Experiences to develop prerequisite understanding enable learners to describe, compare, sort, seriate, and make patterns with objects, construct the set concept, match the elements of two sets one-to-one and learn the concept of same number, classify and order sets, and count. Instruction related to each topic will be discussed in terms of introducing ideas and providing learning activities.

Children begin their study of mathematics soon after they enter kindergarten. Their first lessons involve *examining and describing the objects* they will use to represent concepts of

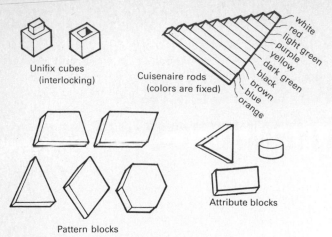

Unifix cubes
(interlocking)

Cuisenaire rods
(colors are fixed)

white
red
light green
purple
yellow
dark green
black
brown
blue
orange

Attribute blocks

Pattern blocks

FIGURE 4-1. Commercially produced objects for children to examine and describe.

counting numbers (1, 2, 3, . . . , N) and whole numbers (0, 1, 2, 3, . . . , N). Objects include screws, nuts and bolts, tiles, beans, beads, buttons, bottle caps, poker chips, and commercially produced materials such as Unifix cubes, Cuisenaire rods, pattern blocks, and attribute blocks (Figure 4-1). Children are asked to look at the objects, handle them, and tell about them. Children observe color, size, shape, and other special characteristics (called **attributes**), such as the holes in buttons.

To guide children to attend to the attributes of the elements of sets, teachers often ask the open question, "What do you notice about these objects?" Children are given time to make their observations before they discuss what they have noticed. Sometimes teachers ask direct questions, such as: Find a block that is green. Find a button that is black and big. Children are encouraged to ask each other questions. Asking questions is as important as answering them, because to ask a question requires manipulating ideas.

If children cannot name attributes of objects, teachers plan lessons for attribute learning. Children are helped to examine different objects with one like attribute, such as blue color. Teachers tell children the words to describe the attribute. Children work with examples and nonexamples until they can identify at least color, shape, and size attributes.

When children can describe objects, the teacher introduces *comparing*. The ideas taught as children study comparison include:

longer than	darker than
shorter than	lighter than
smaller than	same color as
taller than	not the same color as

To introduce any of these concepts, the teacher chooses several examples of two objects that are easily compared and says, "What do you notice about these . . . ?" As children respond, the teacher emphasizes appropriate vocabulary. The new words are used in asking children to make comparisons of other objects.

Another procedure is teacher modeling: The teacher selects two objects and thinks out loud how they compare. Children observe and then tell what they have noticed. They compare other objects. The teacher continues to guide the formation of ideas by requests such as: Please explain what you are thinking. Tell us why you think that.

Play activities involving walking, hopping, or jumping provide opportunities for comparing. Children can be asked to take a step, hop, or jump and follow it with a longer or shorter step, hop, or jump. The teacher or a child can be the leader and give directions for longer, shorter, or same distance to move after the first step, hop, or jump.

Children can compare heights, hand spans, distances to travel to school, and weights of filled cans or boxes. Attribute blocks are especially versatile materials for teaching comparing. Many activities or games can be devised using the attribute blocks. One such activity is MAKE A SNAKE (Figure 4-2). The snake has a head and body of attribute pieces. Each part of the body is one or two attributes different from (or same as) the preceding part of the body. Attribute rules are given as appropriate for the players' abilities. Children are encouraged to discuss their thinking as they play or work together.

B = blue
Y = yellow

FIGURE 4-2. An attribute snake with each segment one attribute different from the preceding segment.

A game enjoyed by many children is COMPARE. Two children play as a team. Each chooses a ribbon from a set of ribbons to place in front of him or herself. A dial on a spinner card that has sections showing long or short (dark or light, and so on) ribbons is flipped by a player. The child who has the same type of object as shown by the spinner dial (for example, a long ribbon) is the winner and can flip the dial the next time.

Children are usually taught to play a game

under the direction of the teacher. When they can remember the rules, they play independently.

When children show they can compare objects, teachers introduce *sorting*—that is, classifying by perceivable characteristics of objects. One way to begin instruction is to give each child some blocks of one color and some of another color. (Size or shape can be used instead of color.) The teacher says: "Please put the blocks together that are the same in some way." After children complete the task and, as a class, produce many examples, they discuss what they have done. The word *sort* is introduced.

If children cannot sort, the teacher models a sorting task. Pupils are directed to observe the teacher's performance and are asked what they noticed. They imitate the teacher's performance and sort other objects. Time is given to discussion, so learners have opportunities to examine their actions and the meanings they attach to them. As children become more mature, they sort a set of objects in more than one way—for example, first by color, next by shape, and lastly by size of objects.

Seriation is arranging objects in a series in terms of an increasing or decreasing attribute (Figure 4-3). Seriation requires making comparisons. Objects are arranged in order using different sizes, shades of color, or other varying attribute.

FIGURE 4-3.   Objects ordered by size.

Objects to seriate are found everywhere. They include sticks, Cuisenaire rods, pencils, ribbons, jars, lids, bottles filled with water, soft to hard items, fine to coarse sandpaper, and tone bells. Creative teachers will find other objects that motivate seriating activities.

Procedures to teach seriating often follow an inductive questioning method. Examples are displayed; learners observe and discuss the ex-

amples. Children can copy or complete examples immediately or in later lessons. They should also produce their own examples of objects in ordered arrangements in teacher-directed or independent study lessons.

Learning mathematics involves the study of patterns and sequences. Children begin this study by working with *patterns* made with objects. Beginning experiences in patterning are observing, copying, continuing, and creating patterns, together with expressing ideas about work in progress or completed.

Background activities for patterning include rhythmic clapping (clap, clap, snap); rhythmic clapping and motions (clap, turn); rhythmic clapping with space directions (clap over your head, clap over your head, clap in front of you); and numerous other variations. The teacher can begin these lessons by asking children to observe his or her performance and imitate the pattern exhibited. The patterns gradually become more complex; sometimes a child can serve as leader, with the teacher and class playing a FOLLOW THE LEADER game.

Attribute blocks, pattern blocks, beads, paper clips (large and small), buttons, and other common objects can be used in making patterns. Making dot, line, and curve patterns is interesting to some children (Figure 4-4).

Teachers begin lessons in making patterns by calling attention to designs made by children or occurring in the environment (for example, in clothing decoration) or by making patterns for children to observe. Children discuss their observations of patterns and possibly copy one or more patterns. They talk about what "a pattern" means to them. In the course of instruction, children are given many opportunities to complete and create patterns and to explain what they have done. Later children are asked to reverse a pattern; this requires a higher level of cognitive development than completing a pattern.

Children are helped to construct the *concept of a set* when they can sort objects. They are asked to put together objects that are *alike* in some way, such as having the attribute red color. They sort several times, using objects

FIGURE 4-4.   Patterns made with dots, lines, and curves.

with different attributes. Each time, the teacher tells the children that each pile (group, collection) of objects is called a *set* of . . . . The children discuss what "a set" is in their own words. They are asked to form and describe other sets to enable them to construct the concept of set. It is important for both the teacher and the pupils to use the word *set* when discussing collections of objects.

Children should also have experiences examining and thinking about the **subsets** of a set. Children are guided to notice and describe subsets—for example, white beads in a set of white and red beads.

The idea of *class inclusion* is introduced and extended as learners compare a set and a subset (a set of red plastic beads and blue plastic beads is greater than the subset of blue plastic beads). Children are given opportunities to develop this understanding by examining objects and responding to questions in the form: Are there more objects in the set or the subset? For example, a child playing with plastic toy cars that are passenger cars and racer cars can be asked: Do you have more plastic toy cars or more racer cars?

Matching the elements of two sets one-to-one is called **one-to-one correspondence**. One-to-one correspondence is the basis for comprehending number ideas. Sets whose elements are in one-to-one correspondence are **equivalent** sets and have the same number (Figure 4-5).

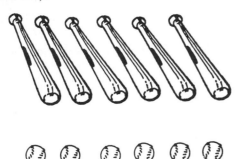

FIGURE 4-5. Objects in a one-to-one correspondence.

Familiar experiences brought to their attention help learners intuitively to understand sets in one-to-one correspondence. Experiences include matching children and pencils, children and chairs, boots and feet, and crackers and children. To guide pupils to think about matching, teachers ask questions such as: How can we find out if we have enough boxes of crayons for each child in this group? Do we have more boys or more girls in this group? How do we know?

A lesson to introduce one-to-one correspondence stresses pupil examination of examples of equivalent sets. All children in a group are given equivalent sets, such as red beads and black beads. The teacher asks: What do you notice about the red beads and the black beads? What goes together? Why? After answering the questions, children match other sets one-to-one. They also select sets that are equivalent.

When children can make a one-to-one correspondence between the elements of two sets, the teacher explains: "Sets that match one-to-one have the same number." Children are encouraged to think and talk about sets with the same number. They are also guided to notice sets that cannot be matched one-to-one. They learn that if the elements of two sets cannot be matched one-to-one, the sets do not have the same number (Figure 4-6).

Set A

Set B

FIGURE 4-6. Set A is greater than Set B.

Experiences to enable learners to form concepts of one-to-one correspondence and same number (or not the same number) are planned to be motivating and thought-provoking. Activities are designed to require production of equivalent sets. Paper-and-pencil exercises that direct pupils to draw lines between elements of sets constructed by the teacher or workbook authors are rarely used.

Since children enjoy bodily movements and learn as they engage in physical activities, many experiences are planned to include bodily motion. For example, children are shown a set of objects or pictures and directed to make the same number of movements (for example, jumps) or to produce the same number of sounds (for example, claps) as shown in the set. Children are asked how they knew what to do.

Another activity is IMAGINE. "It" (the teacher or a child) says to a group: "Imagine a set of flowers that has the same number as the eyes on my face." "It" then asks one child to tell about his or her mental picture. A child could say: "I thought as many big flowers as the eyes on your face." All children then draw in the air what they imagined.

Children build ideas of one-to-one correspondence and same number as they play the games described in Box 4-1. Activities involving matching can be introduced as puzzles; children find pictures of sets that match one-to-one. Children can use objects or make pictures of sets

having the same numbers as sets shown on cards or on the chalkboard. An independent study activity is for a pupil to reach, with eyes closed, into a box filled with cards showing pictures of objects (set cards) and to take a card. He or she looks at the card and makes a set with the same number as the set shown on the card. Yarn is used to check the one-to-one correspondence.

A team activity for children as they study one-to-one correspondence is SHOW. Materials

---

BOX 4-1. *RULES FOR FISH, RUMMY, AND SMILING FACE GAMES*

Fish

Objective: To make a set (or book) of two or more cards that are alike, different, or are ordered.

Rules:
1.   The dealer is chosen by a chance procedure, such as the person who draws the highest card from the stack.

2.   The number of cards given each player by the dealer depends on the age of the players. It may vary from three to seven. The remaining cards are laid face down to make a "fish pond."

3.   The dealer begins and players take turns by going to the left of the dealer.

4.   A player takes his turn by "fishing" or asking one other player for a card of a certain type. (The player may show the card needed or say while displaying a card, "One more than this.") The request must be granted, if possible.

5.   If a request cannot be granted, the player is out of luck. He or she couldn't catch a fish. When no player can catch a fish, each takes a card from the pond.

6.   When one player has no more cards, the game is over.

7.   The winner of the game is the player with the most books.

Rummy

Objective: Same as for FISH.

Rules: Same as for FISH except that, when given a turn, a player does not fish for cards but takes a card from the top of the stack of cards left over after the deal.

Smiling Face

Objective: Same as for FISH.

Rules: Same as for FISH except that cards contain one card which is fun to obtain (the Smiling Face card). When it is a player's turn, he or she draws a card from the player to the left. When a player has no more cards, the game ends. The player holding the "Smiling Face" gives a big smile. The player with the most books wins.

needed are about 20 set cards and a box of small toys. One child picks a card from a stack of face-down cards and says: "Show a set of toys the same number as the set on my card." The other child makes the set. They check the one-to-one correspondence using string between the elements of the two sets. The children continue by trading roles—the child who made the set now taking a card, and so on.

When children can make a one-to-one correspondence between two sets and understand that the sets have the same number, the teacher determines if the idea of "same number" is **conserved**—that is, remains invariant even though the members of one set are rearranged. (The Piagetian task used to assess conservation of number is given in Appendix I.) When administering the task, the teacher asks a child to decide if Set B (which the child placed in one-to-one correspondence with and verified was equal in number to Set A) has the same number as Set A after the members of Set B are rearranged. A child's explanation of his or her answer is an important part of the task procedure.

If children cannot conserve number, they work with equivalent sets, matching the elements, rearranging, and discussing what they are doing. The games described in Box 4-1 are also played. Teachers can occasionally pair conservers with nonconservers. Conservers challenge nonconservers by their comments and help nonconservers grasp the idea of invariance.

Before introducing classifying sets, teachers assess children's progress. They determine if children can conserve number and if they understand the concepts *same number* and *not the same number*. Children demonstrate understanding of these concepts by making two sets with the same number and choosing two equivalent sets in a group of three sets. They also correctly use the phrases "same number" and "not the same number."

Children who grasp the concept of same number are introduced to **classifying sets**. This involves arranging a collection of sets into groups of equivalent sets. Classifying sets gives experiences necessary to create number concepts.

Beginning classifying activities include sets with from 1 to 5 objects (Figure 4-7). Children are asked to "put the sets together that are alike in some way." If further guidance is needed, the teacher says: Put the sets with the same number together. After children complete the activity,

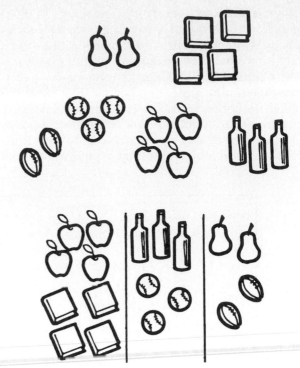

FIGURE 4-7. Sets classified by number of elements in a set.

they explain how they grouped the sets and why they decided on a particular classification.

Independent activities with classifying sets can make use of cards with pictures in various arrangements. Children can work alone or with a partner to classify the picture cards so that all in a grouping have the same number.

A collection of paper cups containing tinted pieces of macaroni provides another type of material for children to use in classifying sets. Children separate the cups into equivalent sets by placing cups on paper mats; all the cups on a mat have the same number of macaroni pieces.

To give classifying experience, the games FISH, RUMMY, and SMILING FACE are now played with new rules. The new rules state that a book will have at least three picture cards that show the same number.

If children have difficulty classifying sets, they can be given a preliminary task in which equivalent sets are displayed in the same color on picture cards or with macaroni pieces. After children classify by color, the teacher directs them to make other observations about the sets grouped together by color. Probing questions lead children to observe that they can place the sets with the same colored objects in one-to-one correspondence. This discovery is discussed, and the children are given opportunities to classify equivalent sets with objects of varying colors. The preliminary activity may need to be used more than once to help children learn to disregard the colors of objects and focus on the numbers of sets.

Children who need special help in classifying sets can also watch the teacher perform the task and discuss what he or she has done before attempting the activity. Teachers sometimes start the activity and let children finish the classification of sets to help pupils grasp the concept.

Ordering is introduced about the same time as classifying sets. Initially children can be requested to place in order sets with 1 to 5 objects (Figure 4-8). They discuss what they have done. An alternative approach is for the teacher to model ordering sets and ask children to observe and explain what he or she is doing.

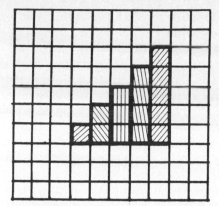

FIGURE 4-9. Squared-paper diagram showing order of numbers 1 through 5.

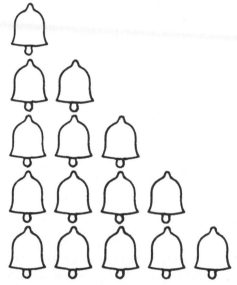

FIGURE 4-8. Sets ordered by number of elements in a set.

In activities for ordering sets, the "one more" concept is emphasized. Teachers ask questions to encourage children to explain why the sets are "in order." Questions often used are: Why are the sets in order? What do you notice about the sets?

Children order Cuisenaire rods and Unifix cubes. They cut pieces from squared paper showing 1, 2, . . . , 5 square regions and place the pieces in order. They color squared paper sections to show the order of numbers 1 to 5 (Figure 4-9). Teachers can make cardboard strips of 1, 2, . . . , 5 square regions for children to use in ordering. Questions teachers use with these

materials are similar to those used with ordering sets.

As children study ordering, they are introduced to the phrases "greater than" and "less than." They use materials to show the meaning of these words. Numbers differing by 1, 2, or 3 are illustrated with materials as children use the phrases "greater than" and "less than."

When children can classify and order sets with numbers to 5, teachers conclude that they have formed intuitive ideas related to number concepts. Children are therefore ready to construct concepts of numbers to 5.

Classifying and ordering sets with numbers greater than 5 is still an educational objective. Children engage in classifying and ordering activities using materials representing numbers 6 to 10 prior to learning the numbers 6 through 10. The activities are patterned after those described for classifying and ordering with materials showing numbers to 5.

Lessons to help children learn counting are planned to parallel instruction in classifying and ordering. **Counting** is the process of making a one-to-one correspondence between the members of a set and the set of number names. Many children know how to count by rote when they come to school. A few know that the purpose of counting is to find "how many." Children who do not know how to count learn the counting words and their order as they engage in learning activities such as finger plays and songs that use the number words in order.

Real class *problems solved by counting* are used to emphasize the purpose of counting. Examples are: Finding the number present, determining how many will eat in the cafeteria, reporting how many children will ride the school bus. Solving problems such as these contributes to the development of the notion that counting tells "how many."

Contrived problems are also used to give counting experiences. Contrived problems are similar to: How many days is it until Halloween? How many children have birthdays this month? How many books do we have in this room? Altogether, how many sisters, brothers, or both do we have? How many trees are growing in our school grounds? How many swings do we have?

Problems solved by counting help children understand the usefulness of counting, as well as rehearse number words and their order. Counting becomes a meaningful process, important to learn because it gives valuable information.

Helping Children Construct Number Concepts

Classifying and ordering give children the prerequisite knowledge to use in constructing number concepts. They know that sets in one-to-one correspondence have the same number. They understand that materials representing numbers can be arranged in order if they differ in number by 1. Children fuse these ideas to *create number concepts*.

Numbers 1 through 5 are learned when children can classify and order sets showing these numbers. Instruction helps children give the number of 1 to 5 objects without counting—that is, by sight.

After children have learned numbers to 5 and can classify and order sets representing numbers to 10, they are taught the numbers 6 to 10. To name the numbers of sets with more than 5 objects, children usually use counting. After pupils study various groupings of more than 5 objects (for example, 4 toys and 4 toys are 8 toys), they are guided to recognize the numbers of these sets by sight. Sight recognition of the numbers of sets is encouraged to give children readiness for studying the basic facts. Counting to determine sums, differences, products, and quotients is an immature procedure. This is discussed further in Chapter 6.

An understanding of the *number 1* develops as children match and order materials. (The word *one* is often used in ordering.) Children generally need little direct instruction to name the number of a set with 1 element. However, teachers should review with pupils what they have learned by displaying 1 object and asking the children the number shown.

Box 4-2 gives a sample lesson to introduce the number 2. This lesson can be used with any number to 5. The sequence is easily adapted to teaching numbers greater than 5 by including questions and comments that guide pupils to count when the number of a set is not known by sight. If any child is observed using grouping and sight recognition for determining the number of a set of more than 5 objects, he or she is asked to explain the method. Other children are encouraged to adopt the grouping method for sight recognition of numbers of sets 6 to 10.

Zero, the number of the empty set (the empty set has no members), is usually learned after the numbers 1 to 5 are introduced. The notion of the empty set is difficult for children to grasp because of its abstractness. Piaget claims that the idea of the empty set is not fully comprehended until children near the end of the concrete operational period of development. However, children do understand the notion "not any" or "none." Teachers help learners examine sets with no objects and use language that reflects their level of understanding. Silly questions are often used to develop an awareness of the idea of the empty set. For example, the teacher may say, "How many blue poodles are in this room?" An acceptable answer is, "Not any." Teachers can introduce the word "zero" by stating: "We can say 'not any' or we can say 'zero.' Zero is the number that means not any."

Learning to give the *number words* for sets representing numbers precedes work with numerals. Children must often employ the number words before learning to read and write numerals. To insure understanding and memory of number words, teachers plan a variety of activities for children. Learners play the games in Box 4-1 using number words. They are asked to notice the numbers of sets they see every day and to draw pictures of these sets. Examples include: the goldfish in my fishbowl (3); my family (4); the streets I cross coming to school (4); and the cookies I had for lunch (3). When the pictures children draw are displayed, the teacher writes number words (for example, four) in the display or uses numerals in order to foster awareness of written symbols.

Activities for studying numbers to 5 and later to 10 include comparing numbers. Examples of activities are:

1. Each child is given a set of picture cards. A child ("It") is chosen to begin the activity. "It" chooses a card and says: "Look

BOX 4-2.   SAMPLE LESSON: INTRODUCING THE NUMBER TWO (GRADE K)

1. Boys and girls, you can play our number games very well. It will be easier to play the games if you know the names of the numbers. Today we will begin learning the number names.

2. I have some sets for you to look at. What do you notice about these sets? (They have the same number. They match one-to-one.)

3. Yes, they have the same number. What is the number? (If no child responds, the teacher tells the number name.) Yes, the number of things in each set is two. You can count, one, two, to figure out the number, but I know you can remember the number without counting. You don't need to count. Look at the set and think the number two.

4. As I point to a set, you say the number of things. Remember each set shows two things. (Teacher points to each set and children say the number of elements in the set.)

5. Good. Let's make a set in the air of two things. Let's make two flowers. . . . Let's make two raindrops.

6. Two is how many greater than one? . . . (Yes, one greater.)

7. I have paper for you to use to draw a set of two things. If you have time, draw another set of two things. You can draw boats, like this

    You can draw trees or anything you like. . . . Ken, tell us what you have drawn. (Children take turns explaining what they have drawn and the number of objects drawn.)

8. Very good. Later I will hang your pictures on this bulletin board. It will show pictures of two things.

9. What is true about all the sets of two pictures that you have drawn? (They all match. They all have the same number.) I have some cord. I will give pieces to some children. They can use the cord to match their pictures with a neighbor's. Then the neighbor can have a turn. . . . What do you notice? (The cord matches every picture with another picture. All the sets have two things.)

10. After lunch, you can take a magazine from the magazine box and cut out pictures that show two things. We will also hang these pictures on the bulletin board.

at my set. What number is 1 (2) greater (less) than the number of my set?" "It" calls on a member of the group to answer the question. If that child correctly answers the question, he or she becomes "It." If not, "It" has another turn.

2. Each child in a group writes his or her name on a strip of squared paper, using a square for each letter. Children can compare the number of letters in their names, find names with the same number of letters, and place their names in order by number of letters. A bulletin board can be prepared using the strips to show the various relations.

3. Children use Cuisenaire rods in a game for 2 to 4 players which we call FIND. A child is designated "It" and children are "It" in turn. "It" chooses a rod, saying: Find a rod 1 (or 2) greater (less) than my rod. The children use rods to carry out "It's" direction. "It" replies: Yes, . . . is 1 greater than . . . . The next "It" continues, giving a direction and responding in the same manner.

Instruction in learning the number names is followed by teaching pupils to read and write the *numerals* for numbers and associate sets of given numbers with the correct numerals. To teach writing numerals, the teacher demonstrates the correct form. Children are usually taught the numerals to 5 after they have learned the number names of sets to 5. The numeral 0 is taught after the numeral 5. The numerals 6 to 10 are taught after children learn the number names for sets of 6 to 10 objects.

Directions for making numerals are given in Figure 4-10. Many practice periods are needed by most pupils to learn writing numerals. Whenever possible, exercises are related to ongoing class activities, such as recording an inventory of one's desk or of the book corner. However, re-

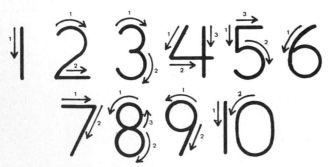

FIGURE 4-10. Numerals with directions for writing.

hearsal activities such as drawing sets of pictures and labeling the sets with the correct numeral are often assigned for independent study. A variation is for one child to draw pictures and ask another child to write the numeral showing the number of the set.

A culminating activity is for each child to make a book using pictures and colored squares to show the meaning of each number to 10 and to write numerals for the numbers illustrated. The last page in the book can give a summary of what was learned by showing ordered sets and their corresponding numerals (Figure 4-11).

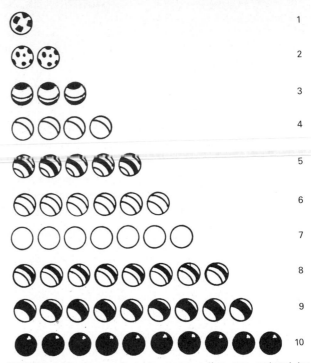

FIGURE 4-11. Numerals and corresponding sets ordered by number of elements.

Teachers use the books prepared by pupils to evaluate whether or not the children should begin to extend and consolidate understanding of number concepts. Children who are successful in making books illustrating numbers to 10 and writing numerals for the numbers represented are ready for the next phase of instruction. Children who are not yet successful continue with activities to enable them to construct number concepts.

An exercise, as in Figure 4-12, can also be used to evaluate children's abilities to write numerals for the numbers of sets. A companion activity directing children to draw pictures to illustrate the meaning of a numeral should also be used in evaluating.

FIGURE 4-12. An evaluation activity: Write the numeral for the number of each set.

Extending and Consolidating Knowledge of Number Concepts

During this phase of instruction children are helped to: (1) represent a number in more than one way; (2) use numerals to stand for number concepts; and (3) explore number ideas through counting.

Representing a number in more than one way develops readiness for learning the operations. Both additive and multiplicative structures are illustrated. Young children study the additive structure of the numbers 2 through 10 and the multiplicative structure for the numbers 4, 6, 8, 9, and 10 (Figure 4-13). To show the additive structure of a number, children use objects or pictures to represent the number so that two subsets are recognizable. They represent a number so that two or more subsets have the same number to show the multiplicative structure of the number.

To introduce the idea of showing a number in more than one way, a teacher gives each child in a group counters, some of one color and the remainder of another color. The pupils are asked to show a number, using objects of both colors. After completing the task, each child tells the group or a partner what he or she has done. For example, a child may say, "Three red beads and 4 blue beads make 7 beads." Children are helped to conclude that one way to show a number is to use objects of two colors.

Other individual and group activities to develop the concept are:

1. Children make books of the ways each number from 1 to 10 can be represented by two groups of pictures (1 is an exception). The pictures in the number book can be drawn by the children or cut from magazines. Sentences are used with the pictures, such as: 5 dogs and 1 dog are 6 dogs.

2. Children color the squares in squared paper using crayons of two colors to represent numbers in various ways.

3. Children use rods, cubes, or strips to represent a number more than one way. Two rods (connected cubes or teacher-made strips) are placed against a third rod to show that a number can be represented in

4 cones are
1 cone and 3 cones

4 cones are
3 cones and 1 cone

4 cones are
2 cones and 2 cones

FIGURE 4-13. The additive and multiplicative structures of the number 4.

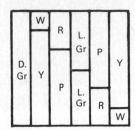

FIGURE 4-14. Placing rods to show representations of the number 6.

various ways. This is done several different ways (Figure 4-14).

4. Children toss beans painted on one side making a set with two subsets (Figure 4-15) to show a number in more than one way. This can be a team activity in which a child tosses and the partner tells about what is seen. Children can color in outlines of beans on study sheets to keep a record of what they did individually or together.

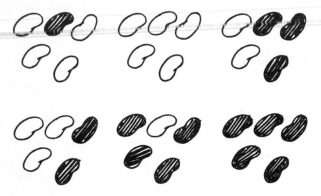

FIGURE 4-15. Using beans painted on one side to represent the number 5 many different ways.

5. Children can play a SCREEN GAME in teams of two. One child makes a set to represent a number and places a cardboard screen across his or her display to show two subsets of the set. The other child explains what was done.

6. Children show numbers using two or more sets of equal size to give intuitive experiences in multiplication. They can represent 2, 3, 4, 6, 8, 9, or 10 using only sets of 2, 3, or 4. Some learners can guess how many numbers, 10 or less, can be shown with only sets of 2 or 3 objects, before carrying out the assignment. This provides an opportunity to predict and make a record to check a prediction. Rods can also be used in this activity.

Using numerals to represent numbers in comparing and ordering experiences helps children extend and consolidate number concepts. Activities include:

1. A game, WAR. Twenty cards, each showing a numeral from 1 to 10, are used. The game is played for "greater than" or "less than" to be the winning card. Two children play, each choosing a numeral card from the stack of 20 cards. The child picking the card with the greater (lesser) number shown takes both cards. If the children choose cards with the same numerals, there is a WAR. They choose cards until a winning card emerges. The child with this card gets all the cards chosen since the WAR began. When the card stack is depleted, the child with the most cards is the winner of the game.

2. Activities that ask children to write a series of numerals in the order of the counting numbers. For example: Write in order: 6, 4, 8, 2, 1, 3. These activities can be adapted to a group. Numeral cards can be placed for the group to see. Children in turn put the cards in the order of the counting numbers.

3. A group activity, SHOW US. Each child is given 4 or 5 numeral cards. The teacher or a child designated as "It" picks a card from a stack and says: Show us . . . [reads from the card the words "what is before (or after)" and a numeral]. Children show numeral cards and say the correct number word.

4. Children can work together to complete exercises, as in Figure 4-16. The children should take turns reading the items in the list after the exercise is completed.

Write the numeral that belongs on the line. Think how the numbers go before you write a numeral.

```
_____   9
_____   4
    5      _____
    1      _____
    3      _____
_____   7
_____   6
    8      _____
```

FIGURE 4-16. An exercise with numerals.

5. The games FISH, RUMMY, and SMILING FACE can be played with numeral cards. A book should show numerals representing numbers with a difference of 1 or 2. For example, cards in a book could show numerals 1 and 2 or 5 and 3. The game can be called UPSY-DOWNSY.

Counting activities extend and consolidate number concepts. For example, backward counting gives intuitive ideas of the inverse nature of addition and subtraction. Children enjoy counting forward and backward as they stand up and sit down.

Gifted children can predict how many numbers will be named as they count from one number to another between 1 and 10. For example, to count from 3 to 7, four numbers are named (4, 5, 6, and 7).

Skip counting or counting by multiples of a number (for example, 2, 4, 6, 8, 10) provides prerequisite experience for the study of multiplication. Rhythmic clapping (soft clap, hard clap, soft clap, hard clap, . . .) with counting is useful in grasping the notion of skip counting.

Children can count with jumping, hopping, or stepping. Stairs can be drawn on the playground and used for movement and counting forward, backward, or by 2s. It is important for children to count jumping to the first step as 1 jump.

Counting experiences should not be limited to numbers to 10 but include numbers greater than 10. The ability of the group determines how far counting should continue in activities such as skip counting. Problem solving, of course, continues to involve counting beyond 10, as discussed previously.

Counting is used in an **ordinal** sense to give position. For example, counting the children at a table—one, two, three—tells who is number three or third. Children seem to have little difficulty with the ordinal idea. They recognize that counting tells how many and which one. Pupils often need help, however, with the ordinal words: first, second, third, ... The teacher may use everyday experiences, such as waiting in line, to teach the ordinal words and extend ordinal ideas. For example, as children are waiting in line, the teacher can say: "Who is number six?" "The fourth and fifth children please shake hands." "The second child may take the first place in line." A classroom activity is: Children gather in small groups and count off using ordinal words. The teacher gives the class novel directions, such as: The fourth child may cough; the second child may laugh.

Teachers determine children's progress in extending and consolidating number concepts by *evaluating* pupils' written and oral work. Teachers also assign evaluation exercises to assess progress. Evaluation exercises ask children to show numbers, each more than one way, by using sets of objects or making drawings. Exercises require children to write numerals in order or to ring a numeral in a set of two to show the greater number. To evaluate counting, teachers ask children to count forward and backward. They often ask children to begin with a number other than 1 (or 10 in backward counting). Children who are successful in evaluation exercises demonstrate progress in developing number concepts and are ready to begin the study of addition and subtraction. Learning the operations is discussed in Chapter 6.

This section has emphasized that young children should have many opportunities to attend, translate, compare, and classify as they work with materials, numbers, and numerals. As children use concrete objects and draw or study pictures, they are guided mentally to manipulate their experiences. They learn words and, gradually, written symbols to represent their ideas. Many activities have been described for each phase of the teaching-learning sequence. Suggestions for evaluating progress have also been given.

PREREQUISITE UNDERSTANDING FOR THE STUDY OF SPACE

As young children learn about space, they are developing prerequisite understanding for the study of geometry in the late primary and upper grades. Intuitive ideas are formed as children explore their physical environment. Their experiences are with examples of both topological and Euclidian concepts. **Topology** involves the study of location or position. **Euclidian geometry** deals with points, lines, and rigid figures.

Piaget's research suggests that children's first space concepts are *topological*. In topological space, a figure's shape may be changed by stretching or squeezing, but its basic property of being open or closed does not change. Preschool children can distinguish open and closed

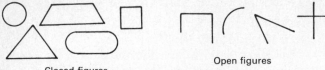

Closed figures   Open figures

FIGURE 4-17. Examples of open and closed figures.

figures but generally have difficulty differentiating, for example, squares and rectangles (Figure 4-17).

Instruction in the first years of school stresses four topological relations:

1. *Separation:* "A part of" or "not a part of."
2. *Proximity:* "Close to" or "not close to" ("far from").
3. *Order (patterned arrangement):* "Before" or "after."
4. *Enclosure:* "Inside of" or "not inside of" ("outside of").

Very young children first learn about these relations through exploration and play as they adapt to their surroundings. Hands are separate from feet; toys are near or far; washing hands comes before eating; cookies are inside of boxes. In kindergarten and grade one, an understanding of space concepts is enriched and extended. Play activities with blocks and toys give experience with topological relations. Activities such as those listed below also give learners opportunities to construct new meanings by acting and inferring from their actions. Language is used, whenever possible, as a natural part of the activity.

Though some activities involve more than one relation, they are listed according to the main relation involved to give readers examples of activities for each area.

Separation

1. SHOW HOW IT GOES is an activity that involves placing play objects in correct position to show connection or separation. Some examples are:

    Placing doll furniture in the rooms of a doll house. (Does the child separate and place the furniture as in a real house or does he or she push it all together? Is the lamp on the table? Is the chair on the bed?) Children may be asked to explain what they did. A

follow-up discussion can emphasize placement of furniture in rooms in the children's homes.

Placing wheels on pictures of cars. (Are the wheels separate or together?)

2. MAKE THE FACE is a teacher-made activity (Figure 4-18). The materials, made of cardboard, include a face shape, nose, mouth, eyes, ears, and hair. Ask children to make the face; observe if the proper arrangements and separations are exhibited. Make a face with incorrect placements and say: What do you notice? . . . Please make it right.

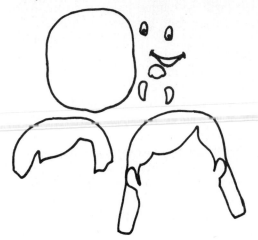

FIGURE 4-18. Pieces for Make the Face activity.

3. Wooden picture puzzles are used extensively with young children. In selecting pieces that fit, the child is learning, among other things, that the pieces fit together or do not fit together.

Proximity

1. WHERE AM I? Two children are chosen to begin a game. One closes his or her eyes. The other moves (the "Mover") close or not close to the first child (the "Caller"). The Caller says: You are close to (far from) me. All the group answers, Yes (No) . . . is close to (far from) you. If the Caller was correct, he or she chooses the next Caller and Mover. Otherwise the Mover chooses both. ("Close" is 3 steps away.)

2. TREASURE. A "Placer" and "It" are named to begin the game. "It" closes his or her eyes or is blindfolded. The Placer lays a treasure (box wrapped with fancy

paper) someplace on the playing area. The other children scatter while the treasure is being placed. "It" has 5 moves. After each move, the children say: Closer to (Farther from) the treasure. After the fifth move, "It" uncovers his or her eyes and takes no more than 5 steps to get to the treasure. If "It" reaches the treasure, he or she becomes the Placer. If not, the former Placer gets another turn.

3. THAT'S MY POSITION. Each child in the group moves until the teacher says: That's your position. The children relax and "freeze." The individual designated to begin asks a question, such as: Who has a position far from (close to) me (Fred, the teacher, the door, etc.)? The child in that position says: That's my position. He or she then asks the next question.

4. Discuss what is close to (far from) home (school).

Order

Activities discussed earlier to teach making patterns with objects can be used to teach order. An additional team activity follows.

1. TELL ABOUT THE ORDER. Children work in teams of 2. Each makes a pattern. The children then each have a turn saying to the partner: Tell about the order. What comes before (after) . . . ? A variation of the remark is: I can tell about your order. . . . comes before (after) . . . . The 2 children resolve any disagreement by discussion and reference to the pattern.

Enclosure

1. Play circle games, such as DROP THE HANDKERCHIEF. Sometimes have "It" run inside the circle, sometimes outside the circle. Have the children chant while "It" is running: (Name of child) is running inside (outside) the circle. Where will the handkerchief fall inside (outside) the circle?

2. STEPO. Make free-form closed figures using chalk on the blacktop. Have children play in groups of 2. One child is given two markers. He or she places the markers inside or outside the figure, then directs the partner to go from one marker to the other by not crossing the boundary or crossing 1 . . . 4 times. The partner carries out the directions. If it is impossible, he or she says "Stepo" and changes the given directions. After carrying out the directions, the partner places the markers and gives directions to the other child.

3. SIMON SAYS. Give each child a piece of yarn to make a free-form closed figure on his or her desk. Play a variation of SIMON SAYS: Simon says hand inside (outside) the figure.

4. During free-play activities, ask children questions about their play which involve thinking about enclosure. Examples are: Where is the doll? (Inside the doll buggy.) Where is the truck? (Outside the garage or on the highway.)

The activities described can be varied in many ways by teachers. The activities and their variations will provide opportunities for learners to "act out" and discuss examples of space ideas to form topological concepts. Team games and activities give opportunities for children to teach each other by providing questions, models, and explanations at learners' levels of understanding.

In *Euclidian geometry* figures are rigid; they do not change shape. Children in the first years of school develop an awareness of common geometric figures and their properties. They learn to identify objects and produce drawings that show square, triangular, and rectangular figures. They begin to identify objects representing cubes, spheres, and perhaps prisms and pyramids. Some children learn to classify objects having these shapes.

Activities for learning about geometric figures emphasize manipulation of objects by learners because young children need action experiences to internalize ideas:

1. *Feel It.* A box with a sock securely attached to an open side is filled with objects. The objects may be cardboard or wooden figures that are open or closed (Figure 4-19), common objects such as spoons, or Euclidian figures. A child puts a hand through the sock, finds an object, and carefully feels it with his or her hand so that it can be identified. To indicate that

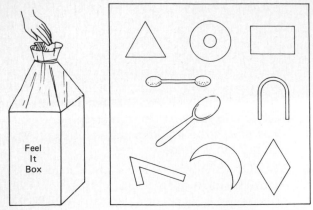

FIGURE 4-19. Feel It Box and a display of the objects in the box.

FIGURE 4-21. Pictures made from geometric shapes.

he or she has the shape in mind, the child points to a picture of the object or to the object in a display of the objects. The child may also name the object and draw it to show he or she can identify it. The child should take the object out after it is identified to check the identification.

2. *Attribute blocks.* When children work with objects, attribute blocks are often used, as discussed earlier in this chapter. Comparing and classifying are frequent experiences with attribute blocks. As children engage in these activities, the names of the figures are given, and children are encouraged to use the names. Properties can be identified by learners.

3. *Pattern blocks.* Pattern blocks are used by learners in copying and creating designs (Figure 4-20). As children handle the pieces, they are developing an intuitive understanding of geometric figures as well as arrangement.

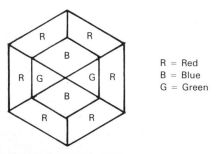

R = Red
B = Blue
G = Green

FIGURE 4-20. Pattern-block design.

4. *Pictures.* Geometric figures can be made into pictures (Figure 4-21). Children can copy pictures made by others or make their own pictures. They should be encouraged to tell the teacher, aide, or another child the names of the figures they used, as well as describe the picture.

5. *Covering.* Covering or tiling an area with a particular figure is known as **tessellating** (Figure 4-22). Children often enjoy discovering that a region can be completely covered by only certain shapes, for example, triangles or squares.

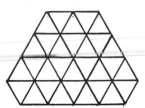

FIGURE 4-22. Tessellation.

6. *Geoboard shapes.* Geoboards are wooden or plastic square-shaped boards with pegs or nails in square arrays and, in some cases, a circular arrangement. Rubber bands are stretched across the pegs to represent figures (Figure 4-23). Children first explore geoboards by making shapes to represent familiar objects, such as a house. Next independent study activities direct children to display geometric figures on the geo-

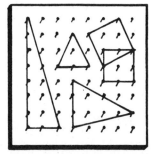

FIGURE 4-23. Geometric figures shown on a geoboard.

board. These assignments are followed by group discussions of children's observations of the properties of figures.

7. *Building blocks.* Children in kindergarten and first grade should play with large

blocks. They make towers, walls, and houses. Teachers encourage children to attend to the shapes of the blocks and compare them whenever possible. Occasionally children can be asked to sort the blocks by shape. The teacher tells children common names, such as cube or sphere.

8. *Shape books.* Children can make shape books. On each page they paste pictures cut from magazines. The pictures show objects that represent the same geometric figure. For example, a page can show objects that represent circular regions such as plates, tables, and frisbees.

9. *Bulletin board displays.* A bulletin board display can be made instead of shape books. Children contribute pictures cut from magazines to the bulletin board and explain their pictures during a class discussion. This activity and the book-making activity involve either two- or three-dimensional objects. Both are emphasized in the course of instruction.

Teachers help children realize that each two-dimensional figure has many sizes, but each type of figure has the same number of corners and sides. Discussions of three-dimensional objects help children notice corners, edges, and the figures that bound the faces of the object.

Activities that give learners intuitive understanding of geometric shapes are usually action experiences. Children need to feel corners, sides, edges, and surfaces to construct geometric ideas. After handling objects representing geometric figures, children discuss what they have done and observed. Many activities, often in the form of play, are planned so learners can build intuitive notions of geometric shapes.

As children investigate objects representing geometric shapes, their progress is evaluated informally. Teachers ask children to identify figures represented by objects or draw pictures showing figures. Before teachers begin lessons to help children construct certain geometric concepts, they conduct more formal evaluation. This is discussed in Chapter 11.

DEVELOPING PREREQUISITE UNDERSTANDING FOR STUDYING MEASUREMENT

This section discusses guiding children to develop prerequisite understanding for the study of measurement. Prerequisite understanding can be considered from several perspectives. It can be thought of as an intuitive awareness of a measurable property of objects or phenomena. It can refer to developmental readiness—that is, a cognitive outlook that enables the learner to grasp new ideas. It can also be knowledge that is the basis for new learning. A cognitive approach to learning and teaching measurement concepts and skills takes into account these several perspectives.

Intuitive Awareness

An understanding of measurement begins when children become aware of measurable properties by being attentive to what others say and do. Mother says that Sally is taller than her cousin, and Sally thinks about what that means. The teacher writes the month, day, and year on the chalkboard each morning, and Sally gets some notion of calendar time. Life experiences rich in references to measurement help children develop intuitive understandings of properties to be measured. Therefore, teachers refer to measurement whenever possible. Ongoing class activities or out-of-school experiences provide opportunities to communicate about measurement. Teachers guide children to be attentive to measurable properties by frequently commenting and questioning to highlight what is to be observed.

The specific instructional suggestions given below are samples of what can be done. Teachers of children in kindergarten and grade one will find many other opportunities to refer to the measurement aspects of classroom or home events.

1. When children are measured and weighed by the teacher or school nurse to provide information for school records, discuss the significance of the activity with learners. Say, for example: When we measure your height, we find out how tall you are. The next time you are measured, you will be taller. Why?

2. After the children's desks have been readied for a new school year, ask children to observe what was done. Say: Our desks were cleaned and waxed over the summer. Look at the shiny surface on your desk. Move your hand over the smooth surface. Close your eyes and make a picture of your desk top.

3. Ask: Who would like to erase the writing from the surface of the chalkboard?

4. Ask children to look at the wall clock when the two hands are at 9 (12, 3, . . .). Say: That means it is time for school to begin (lunch, go home, . . .). Close your eyes and "see" the clock when school begins (lunch, go home, . . .).

5. Discuss the divisions of the day: morning, afternoon, evening, and night. Ask: What do you do in the morning at school? At home on Saturday? In the afternoon? Evening? At night?

6. Mark off each day on the calendar. Give special attention to birthdays and holidays.

7. Ask if children help in the kitchen with cooking. If so, inquire about what they do. Guide children to discuss measuring experiences with cooking. Ask: Did you measure milk (flour, salt)? Tell what you did. Close your eyes and picture a cup (teaspoon, etc.).

8. Cook at school and give special attention to the measuring involved in cooking.

9. Talk about the weather. Ask: Is it hot today? Is it cold? How do you know?

10. Discuss distances from home to school. Ask: Is your home near or far from school?

11. Have children make a book of the tallest things in the world and the shortest things in the world.

Developmental Readiness

Developmental readiness refers to the level of cognitive functioning a child demonstrates in responding to experience. For measurement concepts to be meaningful, children must have attained concrete operational thought. According to Piaget, two attainments in this period are of special importance. The first is conservation; the second, understanding of comparison in a measurement situation.

Over time children become conservers of various properties: amount, length, area, volume, and time. The table in Appendix I gives descriptions of tasks patterned after Piaget to determine conservation abilities of children.

Conservation of amount, or continuous quantity (of water, sand, rice, and the like), is attained when a child understands that two equal amounts in two similarly shaped containers remain equal if one amount is poured into a container of a different shape. A conserver of *length* knows that if two objects have the same length, a change of position of one object does not change its length, which remains equal to the length of the other object. The child who conserves *area* grasps the idea that if two areas are equal, they continue to be equal if one is separated into parts and repositioned or if an equal area is added or subtracted from both areas. Those who conserve *volume* can predict how to reconstruct an object made from small cubes so that the new object has the same volume as before but a different shape. *Time* is conserved by children who understand that their rate of motion—fast or slow—does not affect the passage of time; they also know that the type of clock—grandfather, wristwatch, sandglass, or stopwatch—does not influence the time measured.

To summarize, conservation of measurable properties involves knowing that attributes of objects or phenomena are invariant under certain transformations. For example, if two crayons are equal in length, after one crayon is moved (a transformation) the crayons remain equal in length; a crayon can be broken (a transformation) but the length of the pieces taken together remains the same. Children develop conservation concepts over several years. The following listing is a general guide to the age at which children become conservers of various properties:

Amount:	7 years
Length:	8 years
Area:	8 years
Time:	9 years
Volume:	11 years

Most classes are not provided with support personnel so that the teacher can *assess* each child for conservation of amount, length, area, time, and volume. To gain an idea of the developmental readiness of learners, however, teachers can present a conservation task as a problem to be solved by a small group. The ensuing discussion will give the teacher insights regarding the level of cognitive development of different children. An alternative approach is to present the problem and give a solution supposedly given by a child; the group is asked why they agree or disagree with the child's solution.

Most children will not demonstrate conservation of length and area or abilities to use units to compare lengths or areas until grade two. Conservation of volume develops about grade five. Until children show these abilities, instruction emphasizes background learning experiences.

Experiences to help children develop ideas of invariance of amount (continuous quantity), length, area, and time provide opportunities for children to study the equality of measurable properties of objects or phenomena after transformations, such as change of position or division. Examples of these activities are given in the following list. A skillful teacher will use incidents that arise in the daily life of the class as well as planned activities to bring the notion of invariance of measurable properties to children's attention.

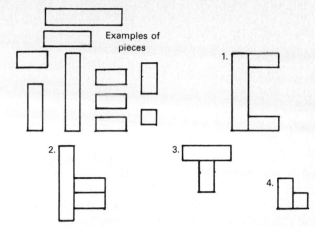

FIGURE 4-24. Shapes-to-Make puzzle: Using the various pieces, make shapes 1, 2, 3, and 4. Make other shapes.

1. Ask children to tell about the distance they come to school and home again. Inquire: Is the distance the same to school and home again? Why?

2. Have children trace around their shoes and cut out the resulting patterns. Each child uses his or her pattern to make other shoe pictures. Direct the children to place their cutouts side by side; inquire about the length of the shoes (steps). Have children move one cutout and ask: Are the shoes (steps) the same length now, or is one longer or shorter?

3. Point to an article of clothing draped on a hook and say: Will the coat be the same length when you put it on? Why?

4. As children play with tangrams (see Chapter 3), ask: What is different in these two figures? What is the same? Why?

5. Distribute Shapes-to-Make Puzzle (Figure 4-24) to a group. The puzzle objective is to make as many shapes as possible from the pieces a child chooses. Ask children to tell group members which shapes cover the same space and why. (Pattern blocks may be used.)

6. After moving a table to another position in the room to carry out an art project or a game, say: Is the top of the table the same size as before? Why?

7. Plan to have different sizes of glasses for juice snacks. Say: Everyone will get a cup of juice. I will pour it to this mark on the measuring cup. After all have been served, say: Do you all have the same amount of juice? Why or why not?

8. Have children make different-shaped roads using 4 sticks. Ask: What is the same about the roads? What is different?

9. If children wear different makes of watches to school, say: Do your watches tell the same time? Why or why not? Compare "time" on a watch and the room clock. Have them predict the time in another room or at home.

10. Arrange for children to play at a sand box or table. (Vermiculite, used in gardening, is more easily cleaned up than sand.) Different-sized boxes or containers should be provided for children's play and investigation. As they play, say: I saw you pour the sand from the small cup into the big cup. Is there more, less, or the same sand in the big cup as you had in the small cup? Why? If you pour the sand from that bottle into these two cups, will you have more sand? Why?

11. Play a sharing game. Use pictures of bread or crackers. Have children fold and cut the pictures in half and give a half to another child. Say: If we put the bread (cracker) together, would it be the same amount as before, or not the same amount? Why? Have children continue to share pieces and then repeat the question. Have children end the game by observing the equivalency of the pieces and the whole by putting the parts together.

The second aspect of developmental readiness involves ability to *compare the measurable properties* of objects or phenomena. To do this, the learner first is aware: (1) that a property can be divided into parts of equal size (units); and (2) that an object (the measuring instrument) also possessing the property can be used repeatedly to determine the number of parts (units) that are to be assigned to the object being measured. A ratio comparison of the number of units of the property of the measured object to that of the measuring object is made. (My room is 3 yards long—3 yards to 1 yard.)

Teachers assess to determine if learners have developed the comparison idea inherent in measurement. Length measurement is usually used in this assessment. Teachers ask pupils to compare the length of an object with the length of another object in a situation in which a direct comparison (matching) cannot be made. Depending on their level of development, children will use parts of their bodies or sticks that are shorter or longer than the given object to answer the question. Children who measure by using an object shorter than the given object and repeatedly change their "instrument's" position (Figure 4-25) demonstrate that they grasp the concept of comparison. Children who use parts of their bodies (Figure 4-26) to make a crude comparison or who can only use an object longer than the given object to compare the measurements of two objects (Figure 4-27) have not yet grasped the notion of using units for comparison in measurement.

When it is not possible to assess each child individually, teachers work with small groups of children to assess their abilities to compare lengths of objects. As children solve comparison problems together, they express ideas which reveal their understanding of ways to compare lengths.

Three types of comparing experiences guide children to develop abilities to compare measurable properties: (A) objects are compared directly by positioning side by side or superimposing; (B) a third object is used to compare objects; and (C) nonstandard units are used in comparing. Children should be able to use nonstandard units in their measuring before they work with standard units. Nonstandard units are chosen so they are meaningful to learners (hand width, foot length, and so on). Their use is an important aspect of instruction.

The activities listed below include activities for length, area, weight (mass), amount, and

FIGURE 4-25. A child measuring a table using an object shorter than the table.

FIGURE 4-26. A child measuring a block tower with part of her body.

FIGURE 4-27. A child measuring a table with a stick longer than the table.

time. Experiences for the three types of comparison are described. Generally types A and B are used before type C, which requires more advanced understanding. An activity can be used by children for independent study, it can be supervised by an aide, or it can be structured by the teacher as a group lesson. Other learning experiences will arise in the classroom that provide opportunities for comparisons that are personally meaningful to learners.

A. Comparing objects directly (pupil activities)
   1. Compare your height with that of a friend by standing back to back. Use a hand to feel the top of the heads to decide who is taller.
   2. Put your hand against that of another. Decide whose hand is larger or smaller.
   3. Find the largest (smallest) book in the classroom. How will you do this? Close your eyes and picture what you will do.
   4. Find the shortest crayon in your crayon box.
   5. Are all the balls in the ball box the same size? Why or why not?
   6. Who has the longest pencil at your table (in your row)?
   7. Find a friend to work with on the playground. Decide who can take the biggest step (jump, hop). How will you do this?
   8. Ask the teacher to bring an extra shoe to school. Take off your shoe. Hold one in each hand. Which is heavier? How do you know?
   9. Find things at home (school) that are taller than (shorter than, the same size as) you.
   10. Close your eyes. Picture two things taller (shorter) than your desk or table. Open your eyes and check yourself.
B. Comparing using a third object (pupil activities)
   1. Find out if the chairs in your room are the same size as the chairs in the other kindergarten (first grade). How can you do this without moving the chairs?
   2. Find out which is higher—the ladder to the jungle gym or the ladder to the slide? How will you do this?
   3. Sue says the chair in her classroom is comfortable, but the lunch bench is not comfortable. How can you find out if the lunch bench is too high or too low for her?
   4. Bring a string to school to show how tall your mother (father) is. Is she (he) taller or shorter than your teacher? Who else is taller (shorter) than your teacher?
   5. Which tree in your schoolyard has the fattest trunk? (Use string around each trunk at your waist height to check your idea.) Which is the next fattest? The skinniest?
   6. Which is the tallest bush in your schoolyard?
   7. Ask a friend to build a tower with blocks in one corner of your classroom. You build a tower the same height in another corner of the classroom. How can you do this without moving his or her tower?
   8. Solve the Shapes Puzzle (Figure 4-28). Find out which shapes have the same surface. (Use the shapes in the envelope to solve the puzzle.)

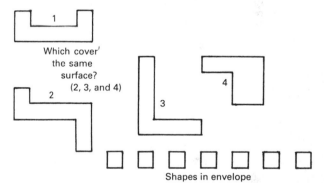

FIGURE 4-28. Shapes puzzle.

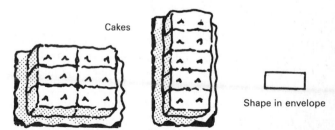

FIGURE 4-29. Comparing puzzle.

   9. Help Jake with his problem. Jake wants the biggest cake (Figure 4-29). How will you help him? Look in the envelope for a hint.
   10. Choose a partner. Use string to find out who has the longer (shorter) waist, nose, ankle, knee, or other part

of your body. Make a list of what you find out.

C. Using nonstandard units in comparison enables children to use units meaningful to them. Nonstandard units can be more directly related to the child's environment than standard units. Nonstandard units are chosen by the learner whenever possible. Activities for independent or group work stated as pupil activities include:

1. Choose a partner to work with. Everyone in the class will get a long piece of wrapping paper from the teacher. You will lie down on the paper and your partner will trace around you so that your hair, clothing (jeans), shoes, and fingers are showing on the picture of you. Then your partner lies down and you trace him or her. Each of you cuts out your picture. Finish it by drawing in your face and clothes. Then use your picture to find out how many "hands" tall you are. To do this, put one hand next to the other along your body. Count the times you put down a hand to find out how many "hands" tall you are. What other objects can you think of to find out about yourself using your large picture? Make a record of what you have learned. You may want to make a graph to show the "hand" heights of some friends.

2. The height of horses is really measured in "hands." If you have a pet, measure his or her height in hands. Measure the height of your bicycle in hands.

3. How many objects in your room can be measured with unsharpened pencils? Work with a partner to measure as many as you can. What problems do you sometimes have? (Pencil not long enough or a little too long.) How do you and your partner solve your problems? Ask your teacher to have a discussion about these problems to find out how other members of your class solve them.

(The use of non-standard units will involve approximation. Usually it is apparent that a whole number of units is not the measurement. Children are guided to use the whole number of units that is the best approximation. Teachers discuss this with children, model the thinking process, and ask several children to model how they thought about what they were doing for others in the class to observe. This is children's introduction to the notion that measurement is always approximate.)

4. Decide on a weight, such as 25 nails. Put them in a plastic bag. Use the pan balance. Find as many objects as you can that weigh 25 nails. Decide on other weights. You can use bolts, candy, or other things. Find out what weighs the same as the weight you have chosen.

5. Trace your foot to make a pattern. On a strip of paper (cash register tape) make a 5-feet ruler using your pattern 5 times. Ask a friend to make his or her own 5-feet tape the same way. Choose 6 objects in the room. Use your 5 feet tape to measure them. Ask your friend to use his or her tape to measure the same objects. Keep a record of what you and your partner have done. What do you notice?

6. Your teacher will give you squared paper. (Use different-size squares for different children.) Use it to trace your hand. About how many squares is your hand? Use the paper to trace your foot. Does your foot measure more squares than your hand? Do other members of your class give the same answer to that question? Ask your teacher to put up a chart showing the size of everyone's hand and foot. Do you notice anything interesting about the numbers in this chart? Why? What do you think this means? Ask your teacher to have a class discussion about this.

(The last activity should be carried out by all members of the class after many experiences with nonstandard units. The discussion following this activity should lead to the conclusion that we all should use the same units—standard units—to measure.)

7. Observe how many sheets of newspaper are needed to cover a table for an art project.

8. Estimate how many sheets of orange construction paper are needed to cover the Halloween bulletin board the second-grade class is putting in the school office. After the bulletin board committee covers the bulletin board with the orange paper, compare the estimate and the needed number of sheets.

9. Solve a class problem: The teacher said: "The shelves of that bookcase would look more attractive if we covered them with tiles. I have some tiles at home. They look like this. How many are needed to cover this bookcase top?" Use the tile to determine the number needed to cover the bookcase. (*Note to the teacher:* Do not fasten the tiles securely so they can be removed and used again next year.)

10. Solve the quilt problem: Janet found out that there was a quilt guessing contest at the County Fair. A quilt to cover a single bed is to be given to the person who guesses the correct number of squares in the quilt. Janet talked to the person in charge. She thinks the quilt squares are about the size of a double light-switch fixture. (She is right.) How many quilt squares should she guess to win the quilt? How will you decide?

11. How many capfuls of water is the right amount for you to drink? Make an investigation to find out.

12. Estimate how many cups of water will fill the room sink (or a bowl, or the like). Then find out. Decide why your estimate was close or not close.

13. Have fun with the length puzzle. Decide which of the rock paths on the sheet (Figure 4-30) in the blue envelope are the same length. Use the red stick in the red envelope to help you. Then use the green stick in the green envelope to help you. Explain to a teacher or to a classmate what you have done. Tell what is different about using the red stick and the green stick. Tell what is the same. (*Note to the teacher:* The red stick is 2 cm. The green stick is 10 cm. Other paths may be used.)

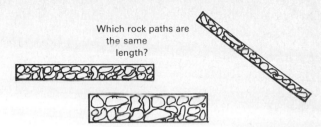

Which rock paths are the same length?

FIGURE 4-30. Length puzzle.

14. Ask your teacher for a sand-glass egg timer. What can you do that takes the same time as the sand spilling from the top to the bottom of the timer? What takes two, three, . . . times as long?

15. Have a Cover-It bulletin board. Children make posters or reports to place on the bulletin board that show or tell how they figured out the number of small surfaces needed to cover a large surface. (Examples to use in introducing the project are: tiles on your kitchen counter, erasers on your desk, or boards on the school floor. This project can generate many creative ideas.)

16. How many boxes of your favorite cereal fit into the shipping carton? How could you find the answer to this question?

17. Ask your teacher for a small cracker box. How many caramel candy cubes do you think will fit into the box? Fill the cracker box with candy caramel cubes to find out. Think how close an estimate you made.

18. Ask your teacher for a box of sugar cubes. How many do you think are in the box? Take them out and find out how close you were. Then put the cubes back in the box for the next child to use. What is the best way to put them in to make sure they fit the way they did when you got the box?

Knowledge

Many measurement ideas and skills require prior learning to be meaningful. Prerequisite knowledge usually involves content attainments in areas of arithmetic and geometry. For example, children must be able to count and read and write numerals before using nonstandard units and keeping records of their work. These learnings must be assessed before many activities in comparing measurements are carried out.

Determining knowledge that should have been acquired by learners prior to the introduction of measurement concepts or skills is an important instructional task. It is discussed further in Chapter 12, "Learning and Teaching Measurement."

THE COGNITIVE MODEL AS A GUIDE IN TEACHING YOUNG CHILDREN

The Cognitive Model provides a framework for instructing and managing programs for young children as well as for more mature learners. Teachers in kindergarten or early primary grades see teaching from the viewpoint of the model and focus on each of its principles. This section summarizes the use of the Cognitive Model as a guide in teaching young children.

Using Model Principles

Teachers *encourage cognitive processes* by insuring that the games children play and the tasks they carry out require cognitive processes, such as translating, comparing, classifying, and ordering. As learners engage in motivating activities that require the use of various cognitive processes, they are taking the first steps in acquiring the abilities essential to learning mathematics. The structures of thought become more complex as the years of learning accumulate. The beginnings, however, are in the activities that promote thinking outlined in this chapter.

All teachers of mathematics *stress concepts and generalizations* in their instruction. This chapter discussed beginning understandings of number, space, and measurement concepts. To guide the learning of young children in these areas, teachers often use inductive questioning methods. The question "What do you notice" is asked frequently by teachers in lessons in which children investigate concept examples. Modeling is also used to help young learners. For example, a teacher may group triangular shapes in one box and rectangular shapes in another while thinking out loud about the task to help children differentiate between the shapes. Children discuss, imitate the teacher's actions, and classify shapes on their own.

Many of the activities presented in this chapter can be adapted to promote children's understanding. Other activities can be designed by teachers to meet the objective of providing learners with opportunities to explore ideas in a variety of settings and solve problems.

Teachers *emphasize intrinsic motivation* by enlisting children's natural curiosity and interest in exploration and investigation. Learning is fun. Tasks can be mastered. Teachers also provide an environment in which trying and thinking are encouraged rather than discouraged. They show pleasure in children's accomplishments and praise their efforts. Teachers' attitudes help learners begin to establish expectations for themselves. They start to view themselves as learners.

Extrinsic motivation is often used with young children because they are just developing internal sources of drive and effort. External events such as receiving gold stars for good work serve as reinforcers and generally insure that learners will behave in certain ways. However, reinforcers are often not directly related to the learning task. The recipient of a reinforcer probably receives satisfaction from the "prize" rather than the learning. Therefore, while teachers of young children use extrinsic motivation, they strive to help learners experience joy in learning. Teachers also help learners associate feelings of satisfaction with effort and accomplishment by remarks such as: "You must feel happy about the good work you did today."

To *attend to individual differences*, teachers group children for instructional activities after assessing their progress. Sometimes preoperational children are grouped with concrete operational children so that they can learn from each other, but teachers frequently plan directed lessons for children at similar levels of cognitive development. Conservers, for example, can be expected to study number names sooner than nonconservers. Therefore, different lessons are often planned for conservers and nonconservers.

Organizing

Successfully carrying out an instructional program for young children involves good organization. Three facets of effective organization are taken into consideration by teachers of young children.

First, children must be taught to *work independently*, often in special areas, while the teacher instructs other children. To encourage independent work, children are provided with interesting, colorful material and are given explicit directions for simple tasks to be pursued alone. Games are taught to the whole class before children play independently. Role playing may help children understand the idea of independent work.

Second, children must learn to *perform certain housekeeping chores* to facilitate the retrieval and storage of materials. Early in the school year, the teacher demonstrates how to use storage boxes or bins. The children are helped to associate special markings on the storage facilities—colors, pictures, or symbols—with the materials. Children are given opportunities to role-play the procedures demonstrated by the teacher. Ample time is given to practice to insure that children are capable of carrying out the routines. Whenever children are asked to gather materials for group work or to return them to storage, each member of the class must know his or her responsibility to insure an orderly transition from one activity to another. For some children, the task is to remain seated, waiting quietly until all are ready to begin the next activity. Other children will be doing the housekeeping chores. Children's responsibilities change daily or weekly to give all a chance to engage in the housekeeping tasks.

Third, there are special *work areas*, and children must be helped to find their work areas easily. Special designations, such as colors, are used to mark learning stations. Some teachers give children tags to hang around their necks displaying the same designation shown in the work area. Until children can remember their assigned areas, the tags children wear are helpful in keeping them properly grouped.

Children in different areas usually pursue different kinds of tasks. At the beginning of a school year, however, to acquaint young children with procedures, they often are all engaged in similar activities but in different areas. Gradually children in different areas are assigned different tasks. Frequently children rotate through two areas during a class period.

Helping young children to be independent workers takes time. It is well to remember that children are learning independence throughout the elementary school years.

SUMMARY

This chapter has discussed guiding the learning of beginning mathematics concepts. Initial experiences are with concrete materials. Later experiences are with pictures and written symbols. A number of learning experiences were described. Evaluation activities were also suggested. The final section of the chapter discussed guidelines for using the Cognitive Model to teach beginning concepts.

STUDY QUESTIONS

1. Review with other students how children learn number concepts.

2. Write a deductive lesson to teach ordering objects from large to small.

3. Why would a teacher pair conservers and nonconservers for some all-group work? What cognitive challenge is provided for each ability level?

4. List counting experiences that could arise in the course of a week. Compare your list with that of another student.

5. Write five questions about class-inclusion concepts to ask children as they are playing in the doll house, garage area, or on the playground.

6. Prepare an activity to give learners action experiences with enclosure.

7. Make a game to teach invariance of area.

8. List objects in a school that could be compared directly with a third object.

9. Visit at least two kindergarten classes during the time devoted to mathematics instruction. Observe the experiences children are having. In what ways have the teachers used the cognitive model in carrying out their teaching responsibilities?

REFERENCES

Baratta-Lorton, Mary, *Mathematics Their Way*. Menlo Park, CA: Addison-Wesley Publishing Company, 1976.

Copeland, Richard W., *How Children Learn Mathematics: Teaching Implications of Piaget's Research*, 3d ed., chaps. 15–19. New York: Macmillan Publishing Co., Inc., 1979.

Cruikshank, Douglas E., David L. Fitzgerald, and Linda R. Jensen, *Young Children Learning Mathematics.* Boston: Allyn and Bacon, Inc., 1980.

Nuffield Foundation, *Beginnings.* New York: John Wiley & Sons, Inc., 1967.

————, *Pictorial Representation.* New York: John Wiley & Sons, Inc., 1967.

Payne, Joseph N., ed., *Mathematics Learning in Early Childhood.* Thirty-seventh Yearbook of the National Council of Teachers of Mathematics. Reston, VA: The National Council of Teachers of Mathematics, Inc., 1975.

Piaget, Jean, *The Child's Conception of Number*, trans. C. Gattegno and F. M. Hodgson. New York: Humanities Press, 1952.

————, Barbel Inhelder, and Alina Szeminska, trans. E. A. Lunzer, *The Child's Conception of Geometry.* New York: Basic Books, 1960.

Schminke, C. W., Norbert Maertens, and William Arnold, *Teaching the Child Mathematics*, 2d ed., pp. 262-70. New York: Holt, Rinehart and Winston, 1978.

Silverman, Helene, "Geometry in the Primary Grades: Exploring Geometric Ideas in the Primary Grades," *Arithmetic Teacher*, 26, no. 6 (February 1979), 15-16.

Steffe, Leslie P., and James J. Hirstein, "Children's Thinking in Measurement Situations," in *Measurement in School Mathematics*, 1976 Yearbook of the National Council of Teachers of Mathematics, eds. Doyal Nelson and Robert E. Reys. Reston, VA: The National Council of Teachers of Mathematics, Inc., 1976.

5 LEARNING AND TEACHING BASE VALUE AND PLACE VALUE

In daily life items must often be counted. Supplies are inventoried; money, spent or saved, is accounted for. Since counting matches a set of number names with the objects being counted, it involves the use of many number names. Such counting could be very burdensome, requiring the remembering of many, many number words. However, a remarkable scheme was invented in ancient times: Use the same words over and over in a system that employs the concept of *grouping*. The grouping number (**base value**) in our system is 10. At 10 we begin to think in terms of tens and ones. In counting many objects, we proceed as follows:

1, 2, 3, 4, 5, 6, 7, 8, 9, 10

10 and 1, 10 and 2, . . . , 10 and 10 (that is, 2 10s)

2 10s and 1, 2 10s and 2, . . . , 2 10s and 10 (that is, 3 10s)

3 10s and 1, . . .

. . .

9 10s and 1, 9 10s and 2, . . . , 9 10s and 10 (that is, 10 10s)

. . . , N

Special names have been given to numbers in the counting system: 11 and 12; the teen numbers (13, . . . 19); the 10s numbers (20, 30, . . . , 90); 10 10s (100); and so on.

While this extraordinary system relieves learners of committing to memory a vast number of counting words, it is not necessarily easy to learn. It involves both multiplicative and ad-

ditive ideas [for example, $56 = (5 \times 10) + 6$]. Children must participate in carefully designed learning experiences to understand the base-10 enumeration system.

Learning the meaning of base-10 counting is but a first step, however. Children must learn another splendid system: the place-value system of notation. Only 10 symbols (0, 1, 2, . . . , 9) are used to communicate any number, no matter how large! The fundamental concept in the base-10 notational system is **place value**: the meaning of a numeral changes with its position. Every numeral represents two number meanings: the place value, or power-of-10 value ($10^0 = 1$; $10^1 = 10$; $10^2 = 10 \times 10$, . . .), and the face value, or value in 1s. Thus, 11,111 means: $(1 \times 10^4) + (1 \times 10^3) + (1 \times 10^2) + (1 \times 10^1) + (1 \times 10^0)$ or $(1 \times 10 \times 10 \times 10 \times 10) + (1 \times 10 \times 10 \times 10) + (1 \times 10 \times 10) + (1 \times 10) + 1$. (The small raised numeral is called an **exponent**. It shows how many times the number to which it is assigned is used as a factor.)

To learn mathematics, children must understand both the base-10 enumeration system and the base-10 place-value notational system. Of course, other base and notational systems could be used—for example, the Mayan culture used base 20, and in some situations we use Roman numerals (a non–place-value system).

This chapter deals with learning and teaching base-10 counting and place-value notation. These learnings begin in kindergarten and continue throughout the elementary school years. The chapter also discusses helping learners in the middle and upper grades apply base-10 ideas to mental calculation. Instruction continues to guide learners to relate prior learnings in creating new concepts. The chapter discusses developing prerequisite understanding, constructing concepts of decimal numerals for whole numbers, extending and consolidating knowledge, and mental computation.

DEVELOPING PREREQUISITE UNDERSTANDING

Concepts of base value and place value develop slowly. A first awareness of the use of a base number is formed by young children as they learn counting. Later, children deepen their understanding of base value as they group and count objects. An intuitive understanding of the relation of base value to place-value notation develops as children use materials in which the position of an object gives information about the meaning of the number represented. This section discusses the development of prerequisite understanding in two subsections: (1) assessment and (2) materials and experiences.

Assessment

Before beginning instruction in base value and place value, teachers assess children's developmental readiness. Two abilities, reversibility and decentering, are related to comprehending base- and place-value ideas. These abilities are evaluated in part by using Piagetian tasks to assess knowledge of conservation involving groups.

1. $N(1) = 1(N)$
   Equality task using singles and a package of singles (Appendix I)
2. $(N)S = S(N)$
   Task of multiequivalence (Appendix I)

Children who are successful with the assessment tasks show readiness to represent numbers in base 10 and other bases. Children who are not successful continue to work with sets, represent numbers 10 and less with objects and numerals, and count sets of objects with numbers greater than 10. They can play games involving grouping ideas, but the activities will be less meaningful to them than to other children.

Materials and Experiences

Proportional and nonproportional materials are used to help children develop intuitive ideas of base values. **Proportional materials** show multiplicative relations in base-value systems by means of size (Figure 5-1). The materials represent 1s, the base (for example, four or 10), the base to the second power (four times four; $10^2 = 10 \times 10$), and the base to the third power (four times four times four; $10^3 = 10 \times 10 \times 10$).

Nonproportional materials do not represent the multiplicative relations of base systems directly but use color or position to stand for

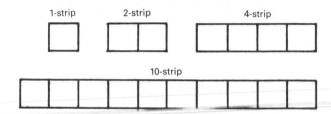

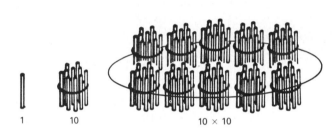

Sticks grouped by 10 and 100

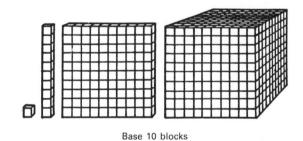

Base 10 blocks

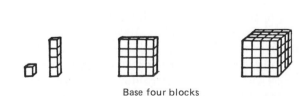

Base four blocks

FIGURE 5-1. Examples of proportional material.

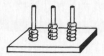

FIGURE 5-2. An abacus showing 345.

them. An abacus (Figure 5-2) and colored chips are examples of nonproportional materials.

Play experiences with blocks designed to show powers of a base are appropriate for young children. Using units, they copy models representing the base, the base times the base, and the base to the third power. They also show that models for the base can be used to construct the base times the base, and that these models, in turn, can be used to construct a model of the base to the third power. In working with these materials, descriptive words should be used, such as singles, towers, squares, and blocks. The Dienes multibase arithmetic blocks use the labels units, longs, flats, and cubes.

Games with proportional and nonproportional materials are frequently used in instruction. The game FOUR FOURS is easily adapted to other bases.

> FOUR FOURS. Two to five children use a sponge die showing 1, 2, 3, or 4 dots on different faces and cards representing powers of 4. The children take turns tossing the die and collecting as many one-cards as shown by dots on the die. Having collected four one-cards, a player exchanges them for a four-card (a 4-strip). A player who has four of these cards exchanges them for a four-fours card (a 4 × 4 square) and wins the game.

The game GO FOR RED helps children develop an understanding of the concept of grouping through the use of nonproportional material. It can be adapted to bases other than 10.

> GO FOR RED. The materials for the game are 2 dice, 1 red paper rectangle, 25 blue paper rectangles, and 50 white paper rectangles. Two to six players toss the dice, sum the numbers shown, and take that number of white rectangles. When 10 white rectangles are collected, they are exchanged for a blue rectangle; 10 blue rectangles are exchanged for the red rectangle. The first player to obtain the red rectangle wins. (Chips can be used instead of paper rectangles.)

Over a period of time, primary grade children are helped to count sets of objects with numbers to 100. Objects to count include: seeds from pumpkins, squashes, or melons, jelly beans, straws, sticks, toothpicks, pennies, nails, screws, and macaroni. (If seeds number more than 100, count each 100.) The "when you get to 10, start all over again" pattern is observed and emphasized as children count. Counting is motivated by having pupils estimate the number of objects in a jar or plastic sack and count to find the number in the container.

Grouping objects for counting is introduced by teachers as children develop skill in counting 10 to 100 objects. To develop intuitive ideas of grouping, children gather straws, sticks, or toothpicks into packages of 10 and use small rubber bands to form 10-bundles. Objects such as jelly beans or screws are put in small plastic sacks. Bases other than 10 are sometimes used in grouping. When children group and count objects in bases other than 10, they use the name of the base or invent new names for the base and powers of the base.

After children have grouped objects, they have many opportunities to *give the number* of a set of objects shown with proportional materials. They also use proportional materials to show numbers named orally by teachers. Some children profit from using a nail-and-spool board (Figure 5-3). Children can work in pairs, naming numbers for each other to represent. They can play the old games, with a book being two representations of a number (for example, one card with a picture of strips showing 26 and another card showing 26 with 10-bundles and singles). Each child can make a poster of 100 things grouped by 10s. In discussing their work, children are often asked to use both the standard name and the expanded-form name for a number (for example, twenty and two tens).

The *numbers 10 to 19* are emphasized as children play games and engage in activities to develop intuitive awareness of the meaning of

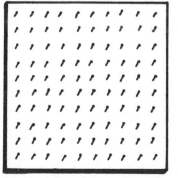

FIGURE 5-3. A nail board with spools.

numbers. Children show the numbers 10–14 and then 15–19 using grouped objects and singles. Games to play include:

TEN AND MORE. The materials for this game are straws packaged into bundles of 10, each bundle bound with a small rubber band. Three to six players each take 10 straw packages to begin the game. The players in turn spin a spinner with the numerals to 9 and select as many single straws as shown on the spinner. The singles are arranged beside the straw packages to show the numbers 10 to 19 in order. The first player who completes the sequence is the winner.

FISH A DECADE. Each of three to six players receives 7 cards. A pile of cards is also face down in the center of the playing area. Each card represents a number from 10 to 19 by means of a 10-strip and a strip 1 to 9 squares in length. The objective of the game is to make a sequence with the cards that shows the numbers 10 to 19. Players in turn ask the player to their right for a card showing a certain number. If the request cannot be granted, the asking player takes a card from the pile in the middle. When one player is out of cards or no cards remain in the center of the table, the player with the most complete sequence is the winner.

Counting by 10s is encouraged as children develop concepts of base values in counting. Children count 1 10, 2 10s, . . . , 10 10s, as well as use the standard names, ten, twenty, . . . , one hundred. Experiences to help learners count by 10s and work with representations of 10s numbers include:

COUNTING TEN-STRIPS. This is an activity using 10-strips cut from squared paper and glued on cardboard (shown in Figure 5-1). The strips are put in envelopes. Each child in a group gets an envelope. They count their strips by 10s. A pile of 10-strips is in the center of the table. After each child counts his or her strips, all take strips so that they have the same number. This activity involves counting 10-strips several times. The activity can be adapted to other bases.

THE MOST (LEAST) TENS. Each child in the group gets 3 cards, each of which shows 1 to 3 10-strips. Each child counts the 10s displayed on his or her cards. The child with the most 10s gets a chip, collects the other children's cards, shuffles them, and passes out 3 to each child in the group. After 5 chips have been distributed, the child with the most chips is the winner. The game can be played for the least number of 10s or adapted to other bases.

As children develop ideas of base 10 in counting and representing numbers, materials

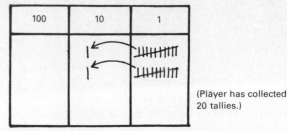

(Player has collected 20 tallies.)

FIGURE 5-4.   Place-value tally frame used in Tally-Ho game.

to develop intuitive understanding of *place-value concepts* are introduced. The place-value frame and abacus are first presented as materials to use in playing games. Two such games are:

TALLY-HO. The materials are a place-value tally frame for each player and dice (Figure 5-4). Two to four players in turn make tallies on their tally frames in the 1s column to indicate the sum of the dots on the dice. When the 1s area has 10 tallies, 1 tally is made in the 10s column. The 1s tallies are crossed out. Ten tallies in the 10s column give 1 tally in the 100s column. The winner is the first player to cross out 10 tallies in the 10s column and place a tally in the 100s column. (Beans or toothpicks can be used instead of tallies.)

ABACUS GAME. This game is played like TALLY-HO, except that players put rings on the posts of an abacus to indicate the sum of the dots on the dice. Ten rings on the 1s post give a ring on the 10s post. The winner is the first player to get a ring on the 100s post. (A paper-and-pencil abacus and toothpicks or beans can be used.)

Teachers *evaluate* children's readiness to work with numerals 11–19 by asking pupils to show a number from 11–19 with proportional materials or to name a number 11–19 shown with proportional materials. Representing numbers to 100 with proportional materials and counting to 100 is evaluated prior to the introduction of numerals 20–100. Nonproportional materials are used in evaluation, but to a lesser extent than proportional materials.

CONSTRUCTING CONCEPTS OF DECIMAL NUMERALS FOR WHOLE NUMBERS

Children are ready to construct concepts of decimal (standard) numerals for whole numbers when they have developed ideas of using base 10 in naming and representing numbers of sets of objects to 100. When children are successful in using proportional and nonproportional materials in their work with numbers greater than 10, they study: reading and writing numerals to 100; the two meanings of each digit in a decimal numeral—face value and place value; the base-value relations implicit in place-value notation; and expanded notation. They study first the numerals for numbers 10–19, then the multiples of 10 (20, 30, . . . , 90) and the remaining numerals for numbers to 100.

Numerals for Numbers 10-19

An *instructional plan* for guiding the learning of numerals for the numbers 10–19 is:

1. Ask pupils to use number strips to show 10 and 11. (With some groups, more than two numbers and numerals can be examined.) Tell pupils to place their strips on a piece of writing paper. Make a display yourself so all in the group can see it. (For example, tape strips to the chalkboard or tack strips to a small bulletin board placed in the chalkledge.)

2. Write the numerals 10 and 11 beside the corresponding strip displays.

3. Have children read the numerals with you and alone.

4. Ask pupils to write the numerals on their paper beside their strip displays and to think how the numerals tell about the number shown with strips.

5. Discuss with pupils how these numerals tell about the numbers they represent. Stress the idea of the 10s and 1s places in the numerals and the times-10 relation implicit in the place-value scheme.

6. Have children write the numerals several times and underline or circle different places.

7. In subsequent lessons, introduce 12, 13, . . . , 19 in sequence, two or more in the same lesson. Follow the same procedure as for numerals 10 and 11, except that when pupils can infer the numerals to be written beside the strip display, they should do so.

8. Rehearse reading and writing numerals introduced. Provide opportunities to review the meaning of numerals and to use proportional material and the abacus to represent numbers given by the numerals 10–19. In using the abacus, pupils often show grouping 1s as 10 and 1s.

9. Later introduce expanded form by saying: We know how to show numbers with materials. We know 16 is 10 and 6. We can write that this way, $16 = 10 + 6$. Some other examples are . . . . Let's read these sentences and talk about what they tell us. Write a sentence for 19, 14, ... Make up some sentences like these to read to the group.

10. As children learn to read and write numerals to 19, have them play the old games with new labels. (For example, FISH could be called GIVE AND TAKE; RUMMY could be called TEN PLUS.) The cards give numerals or numbers represented by pictures of proportional materials or the abacus.

Numerals for Numbers to 100

After learning numerals for numbers to 19, children are introduced to numerals for numbers 20, 30, . . . , 90. They learn these numerals before numerals for the numbers that are sums of multiples of 10 plus 1s (for example, 26) to provide many examples of the meaning of the 10s place in numerals. The sequence to follow is the same as that for numerals 10–19.

Next children study numerals for numbers to 100 that have not yet been introduced. Many children can infer the form of these numerals by using prior knowledge. The teacher can encourage this kind of thinking by saying, "You know how to write 20. How do you think you would write 21? 22? 23?" If pupils cannot infer the form, the teacher can show several numerals, read them, and ask pupils to read them and explain their meaning. Later, pupils infer how to write other numerals. Many pupils will be able to write numerals because the teacher has often written numerals for the days of the month, number of pupils present, and the like; pupils have read these numerals frequently.

Children write numerals to 100 in one or more lessons. They observe patterns in the numerals given in a 100-chart:

1	2	3	4	5	6	7	8	9	10
11	12	13	14	15	16	17	18	19	20
21	22	23	24	25	26	27	28	29	30
. . .									
91	92	93	94	95	96	97	98	99	100

They can also use numeral tags on a nail-and-spool board to study patterns. Children can use the 100-chart and the nail board with tags to examine differences in numbers and to order 3 to 5 numbers using numerals.

As children know how to write the expanded form for numerals to 19, many will be able to infer how to write the expanded form for numerals such as 26 (26 = 20 + 6). If they cannot infer the expanded form for numerals to 100, teachers give examples and ask pupils to determine a rule for expanded form. They use their rule to write examples.

To insure understanding of the meaning of numerals to 100, pupils occasionally work in pairs or small groups, using proportional materials or the abacus to show the meaning of numerals. They write numerals from dictation. The meaning and relationship of the places in numerals is often discussed.

Children also play the old games, using numeral, expanded form, or picture cards (Figure 5-5). BINGO is adapted to give learners opportunities to relate oral and written forms: Each player has a 5-by-5 section of a 100 chart. Chips are placed on numerals called by the caller. Five chips in a row, column, or diagonal is the game objective. The lucky player can say, "Numeral!" (Bingo!)

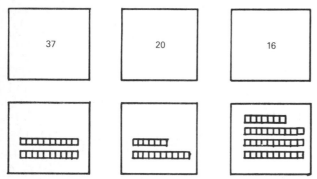

FIGURE 5-5.   Examples of cards for matching games.

Children can make books illustrating numbers to 100. Each child can choose several numbers in each decade to represent with squared-paper diagrams or paper-and-pencil abacuses. The numerals for the numbers are given in standard and expanded forms. An alternate way to organize the book is to begin with a number less than 10 and represent numbers determined by repeatedly adding 10, such as 3, 13, 23, 33, 43, . . . , 93.

Usually numbers and numerals to 100 are learned in grades one and two. Numbers and numerals to 1000 are learned in grade three.

Learning numbers greater than 100 is discussed in the next section.

EXTENDING AND CONSOLIDATING KNOWLEDGE

When children have attained an understanding of the meaning of numbers to 100 and the sense of place-value notation, they extend their understanding to numbers greater than 100 and the use of place-value ideas in the numerals for large numbers. In this section numbers and numerals to 1000 and then beyond 1000 are considered.

Numbers and Numerals to 1000

The initial lesson in numbers and numerals to 1000 involves numbers that are multiples of 100. Some possible comments and questions are: Let's talk about 100. What do you know about 100? . . . Yes: It is many 1s. It is 100 1s. It is 10 10s. We can show 100 by writing "100." I know you can count by 1s and by 10s. Let's count together by 100s. . . . Great! How did you know what to do? . . . We can show 100s with materials. There are toothpicks, strips, and square pieces (10 × 10) in the boxes on your table. Each person please show 100s numbers. Show the numbers you wish, or begin with 100, 200, and go on for the time you have. . . . What pieces did you use to show 100s numbers? . . . Yes, squares or lots of 10s.

Children are helped to infer how to write numerals for multiples of 100 from their knowledge of how to write 100. The teacher explains, if necessary, how to write the numeral 1000 (10 100s).

In follow-up study, children work in small groups or in teams of two, using materials to show the meaning of multiples of 100. They use the abacus and 100 squares. Children make 1000-strips by taping together 10 100-squares. They play the game THE MOST (LEAST) TENS adapted for 100s (100 squares cut from squared paper and glued on game cards).

Soon thereafter, children are asked to use their knowledge to explain the meaning of numerals such as 321, 542, and 745. The teacher opens the lesson by saying, "Think about the meaning of these numerals. What do you know that will help you show the meaning of each digit using the 1s, 10s, and 100s materials? Using the abacus?" If children have difficulty with the question, the teacher says, "I will show some examples using materials. That will help us think about the meaning of a 100s number." Pupils discuss what the teacher does. In the same and following lessons, pupils represent the meanings of numerals for numbers to 1000 using proportional and nonproportional materials. They discuss relations among places and compare numbers.

In subsequent lessons and activities two objectives are emphasized:

1. Using both standard and expanded notation for numerals. Children complete assignments such as: Write the expanded (standard) form for 784 [(7 × 100) + (8 × 10) + (4 × 1)]. They write exercises for each other and together evaluate work completed.

2. Renaming 100s numbers greater than 100 in terms of 10s, and 10s numbers in terms of 100s + 10s—for example, 340 = 34 10s; 56 10s = 560; or 340 = 34 × 10; 56 × 10 = 560. Children use prior knowledge and materials (especially the abacus) to develop the idea of renaming numbers greater than 100 in terms of 10s and vice versa.

Activities to further learning include:

A bulletin-board project that includes newspaper clippings with illustrations of the numbers used in the news report.

A class book in which pupils select numbers to 1000 to illustrate using squared paper, place-value frame, or paper-and-pencil abacus. Ordering is stressed.

Extension of games such as FISH, RUMMY, and BINGO to include numbers greater than 100. Both standard and expanded form are used.

Counting experiences are used frequently to extend pupils' understanding of numbers and numerals. Children are asked to count forward and backward by 10 or 100, beginning with a number that is not a multiple of a power of 10. Occasionally they write the numerals for a counting sequence. Materials such as blocks or squared paper (Figure 5-6) give learners opportunities to represent counting that begins with a number not a multiple of 10. The number line can be used (Figure 5-7). Children also count by

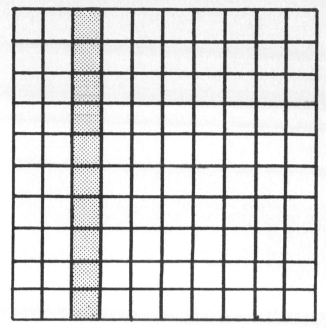

FIGURE 5-6. Diagram to show counting by 10 beginning with 3.

numbers that are multiples of a power of 10—for example, count by 20 beginning with 20; count backward by 20 beginning with 200; count backward by 20 beginning with 440. These activities are good "fillers." (You have the class ready to leave the room for lunch but the lunch bell has not rung. You need a "filler"!) Children can also team up with a partner to practice this kind of counting. If they need assistance, they use a chart showing numerals to 100 or the nail board and tags to visualize part of a counting pattern. Counting by powers of 10 and multiples of powers of 10, forward and backward, gives intuitive understanding for mental computation (discussed later in this chapter).

FIGURE 5-7. Diagram to show counting by 10 beginning with 5.

Numbers and Numerals Beyond 1000

Instruction for numbers greater than 1000 and the meaning of the numerals representing these numbers continues during the upper grades. Numbers and numerals to 10,000 are learned first and 1,000,000s and 1,000,000,000s introduced later, often in grade six. Children are helped to extend their ideas of base value and place value in the decimal system as they study very large numbers. A chart such as shown in Figure 5-8 is constructed by children (to the powers of 10 being studied) and used in learning about very large numbers.

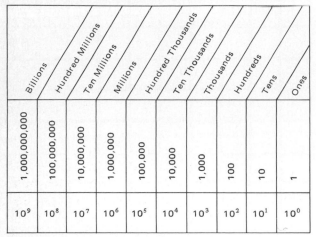

FIGURE 5-8.   Place-value chart for base 10.

Children can collect references to very large numbers in newspaper and magazine articles and in books. They share their findings and demonstrate how the numbers can be represented using such nonproportional materials as an abacus or a place-value tally frame. Children can discuss how they would represent very large numbers with proportional materials to deepen their understanding of these numbers. For example, they discuss how many 1000-strips would be needed to make 1,000,000. They talk about hanging these like flags in the classroom or outside, and they consider the space needed to display the strips.

Children write both expanded and standard forms in some activities. They compare and order very large numbers using numerals. Teachers also plan activities to help children learn renaming of very large numbers. The ability to think of 1000s in terms of 100s in mental division [for example, $7200 \div 9 = 72(100) \div 9$] is but one example of the need to learn renaming.

MENTAL COMPUTATION

In the contemporary world of calculators and computers, mental computation is an important skill. While exact answers in computation can be speedily and accurately found with machines, work must be evaluated. Mental computation, particularly estimation, is often an aspect of processing numbers using machines. Furthermore, relational thinking about personal and public problems requires mental manipulation of quantitative ideas. For example, while talking to a car salesman about a new car, I learn that I need a down payment of $2500. What must I save each month to have a down payment of $2500 for a car in about a year? Mental calculation leads to a figure of about $200 a month, and I think, "There goes my vacation to Hawaii next winter!"

Mental computation with multiples of powers of 10 is taught before paper-and-pencil computation. This sequence enables children to estimate answers in paper-and-pencil calculation and gives meaning to their work. It also enables children to deal with quantitative relations in other subject areas and in life. This section examines the teaching of mental computation for the four operations. The subsections are: addition and subtraction mental computation with multiples of powers of 10, multiplication and division mental computation with multiples of powers of 10, rounding, and estimating.

Addition and Subtraction Mental Computation: Multiples of Powers of 10

Mentally adding and subtracting multiples of powers of 10 involves the use of addition and subtraction basic facts with powers of 10:

$$
\begin{aligned}
30 + 20 &= 3 \times 10 + 2 \times 10 \\
&= (3 + 2) \times 10 \\
&= 5 \times 10 \\
&= 50
\end{aligned}
$$

In this work, the distributive property of multiplication over addition [ab + cb = (a + c)b] is used primarily as the basis for the computation. Children at grade two or three, however, state the rule in a way similar to: Add (or subtract) 10s like 1s; remember the answer is 10s (100s, and so on), and give it a 10s (100s, . . .) name.

To teach mental calculation with 10s, teachers create a need-to-learn situation for children by inserting cards requiring this type of computation in children's games (FISH, RUMMY, WAR). After explaining what has been done, the teacher says, "Let's figure out a rule to do this kind of mental addition. The cards show: 30 + 40, 20 + 20, 10 + 50, and so on. Let's read these statements. Next I'll pass paper with pictures of abacuses to each of you. Please use the abacuses to get the sums. I'll write what you decide on the board.

$$30 + 40 = 70$$
$$20 + 20 = 40$$
$$10 + 50 = 60$$

Look at the addends and the sum. What do you notice? What goes together? What can you think to get 7? 4? 6? Why is each sum 10s?"

Pupils make observations, answer these questions, and state the rule: Add 10s like 1s, but call the sum 10s. At this time or during another lesson, the teacher helps children reexamine the meaning of their rule by using strips, squared paper, or counting by 10s. Pupils apply the rule frequently in playing games and engaging in oral practice with a partner, using materials prepared by the teacher. These materials are lists of examples with answers or cards that give answers on the back for checking.

Soon the sums used in games and practice involve renaming, such as $40 + 80 = 12 \times 10 = 120$. Lessons to introduce or review renaming use materials to clarify concepts. The abacus is especially helpful in showing the renaming of 10s as 100s + 10s.

Subtraction of 10s is introduced and mastered in a sequence of lessons and activities similar to those for addition.

Multiplication and Division Mental Computation: Multiples of Powers of 10

Mental multiplication and division of powers of 10 involves applying knowledge of the decimal base-value system ($1 \times 10 = 10$; $10 \times 10 = 100$; $10 \times 100 = 1000$, . . .) and basic facts: for example, $2 \times 40 = 2 \times 4 \times 10 = 8 \times 10 = 80$.

Inductive or deductive procedures are used to help children construct the rules (see lesson plans in Chapter 2):

1. Ten times 1s equals 10s.
2. Tens times 10s equals 100s.
3. Tens times 100s equals 1000s.

Children have opportunities to verify the rules using the abacus and squared-paper arrays. They can use 10 bundles or 10 strips to show the meaning of the rules. Some children will begin with materials, counting, or repeated addition to form the rules.

Games or practice with a partner using examples prepared by the teacher are helpful to children in developing skill. Special attention may need to be given to renaming 10s as 100s + 10s or 100s as 1000s—$9 \times 40 = 36 \times 10 = 360$, $50 \times 80 = 40 \times 100 = 4000$.

Children begin mental computation of products in grade three. In grade five or six, many pupils learn the shortcut: annex to the basic fact the sum of the zeros in the factors.

After children show skill in mental multiplication with powers of 10, teachers introduce mental division. The rules children form are similar to: Think the basic division fact times 1 or 10; remember 10 divided by 1 equals 10; 10 divided by 10 equals 1; 100 divided by 100 equals 1; 100 divided by 10 equals 10. Children construct each rule by examining the related multiplication rule, using materials, or counting backward. In working with materials, an example such as $60 \div 20 = 3$ is best interpreted as a measurement situation. (How many 20s = 60?) The partitive interpretation is used in an example such as $60 \div 3 = 20$. (What is 60 divided into 3 equal-size groups?) These interpretations are discussed in Chapter 6. As with multiplication mental computation, activities for practice are usually necessary.

Rounding

Children are helped to understand that the purpose of rounding is to enable them to work mentally with numbers and to judge the sense of calculations. They should be told that skill in rounding makes it possible for them to be intelligent users of calculators and computers.

Certain understandings are prerequisite for developing skill in rounding: (1) use of the 1, . . . , 9 sequence in counting multiples of any power of 10; (2) use of addition (subtraction) facts for 10 with 10s, 100s, . . . ($30 + 70 = 100$; $100 - 30 = 70$); and (3) knowledge of relations between ideas expressed by names given to powers of 10.

The concept of rounding is introduced when children demonstrate these prerequisite understandings. The teacher explains the purpose of rounding and gives examples:

53 is rounded to 50;	56 is rounded to 60
42 is rounded to 40;	48 is rounded to 50
33 is rounded to 30;	35 is rounded to 40

The children discuss the examples, describe the meaning of rounding, and develop the rounding rules (round *down* to the 10s given in the number if the 1s number is less than 5; round *up* to the next 10 if the 1s number is 5 or greater than 5). They also give their own examples. At a later time, the rule is extended to numbers greater than 100.

Activities can help children develop prerequisite understanding, conceptualize rounding, and practice with different examples. Some examples of activities are:

1. Have children use a 100-chart to find a given number and locate the nearest multiple of 10. They explain how they decided which 10-number to choose as the "nearest" to the number given. The 1000-strip can be used in a like manner to illustrate rounding 100-numbers.

2. Use number lines labeled by 10s from 0 to 100 (later by 100s from 0 to 1000) and carry out an activity similar to activity 1.

3. Have pupils count forward and backward by 10s from 100 to 200, 200 to 300, ... When studying rounding 100s, ask pupils to count forward and backward by 100s from 1000 to 2000, 2000 to 3000, ... Occasionally signal pupils to stop at a number and discuss which 100 or 1000 is "nearest" or "farthest."

4. Present counting puzzles such as: Jim counts backward from 43 to 40; Tad counts forward from 43 to 50. Who says more numbers? Why?

5. Have children write counting puzzles as in activity 4 to share with other pupils.

6. Have pupils write numerals to show counting by 10s, 100s, and 1000s, forward and backward.

7. Ask pupils to review equations with missing addends such as:

$$40 + \underline{\quad} = 100 \qquad 70 + \underline{\quad} = 100$$

8. Introduce four games to develop ideas of rounding and to give rehearsal experience:

OVER 150 (or UNDER 150). This is a game for two players. Materials needed are: a number line about 40 centimeters in length showing 0, 100, 150, and 200; toothpicks of two colors; and about 30 numeral cards, half for numbers less than 150 and half for numbers greater than 150. To begin the game, the cards are shuffled and pupils decide who will begin and select the color of toothpicks for each player. The first player chooses a card and places one of his or her toothpicks on the number line to indicate the number represented on the numeral card. The players take turns until each has 8 toothpicks on the number line. The player with the most toothpicks indicating numbers OVER 150 wins.

ROUND DOWN–ROUND UP. The game is for two players, who toss a die to determine who will use the round-down idea and who will use the round-up idea. (The lower number on the die is "round down.") The materials for the game are 30 numeral cards representing numbers in the 10s (100s, 1000s). There are the same number of cards less than and greater than 50 (150, 1500). The cards are shuffled, and players take turns drawing cards face-down from the stack. If the card gives a number less than 50 (150, 1500), the ROUND DOWN player claims it; if a card gives a number greater than 50 (150, 1500), the ROUND UP player claims it. After each has had 5 turns, the player with the most cards gets a token. The cards are returned to the stack, shuffled, and the players play another round by each drawing in turn 5 cards. A game is 3 rounds. The player with the most tokens after 3 rounds wins.

500. This is a board-and-die game (Figure 5-9). Players take turns tossing a die. A player notes the numeral on which the die lands, rounds the number represented to obtain his or her score, and writes the score on a tally sheet. The first player to get a score of 500 or greater wins.

BINGO. The playing boards give multiples of 10 and 100. Pupils round numbers the caller reads to decide where to place a token on their playing cards.

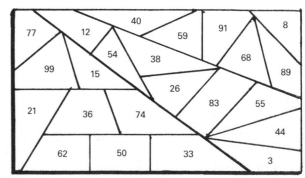

FIGURE 5-9. Board for the 500 game.

9. Have pupils discuss which is the number to round and which is the number that "flags" how to round (up or down). Ask pupils to discuss the reasons for their responses. Examples of numerals to use in the discussion are:

83 67 29 92 439 325 691

Children who can round are ready for estimating. Children cannot learn estimating if they have not developed skill in rounding.

Estimating

Estimating is a very important learning. Estimated sums, differences, products, and quotients are used to evaluate computation performed with paper and pencil or with calculators. Estimated solutions to problems are used to check the reasonableness of calculated solutions. Skill in estimation ranks in importance with immediate recall of the basic facts.

If children can round and perform mental computation with 10s, they are introduced to estimating. Estimating requires holding several ideas in mind for processing. To estimate, children must round, remember the rounded numbers, and mentally obtain a sum, difference, product, or quotient. Ability to estimate requires not only attainment of prerequisites, but also cognitive maturity, effort, and practice.

Estimation is introduced with the comment that it is another step in learning to think mathematics and become ready to compute and to use calculators. An inductive questioning lesson can be used to present the concept of estimating. Examples to use for addition are:

33 + 24 rounds to 30 + 20, which equals 50

48 + 24 rounds to 50 + 20, which equals 70

14 + 81 rounds to 10 + 80, which equals 90

27 + 39 rounds to 30 + 40, which equals 70

Children examine the examples, discuss their meaning, and describe in their own words what estimating means. They write examples and share them with each other. With many chil-

dren, only "round-down" examples are included in the first lessons.

Learning experiences to help learners extend and consolidate knowledge include individual and partner practice using examples prepared by a teacher or pupil. (Answers are provided if needed.) Children play the old card games with a book including a sum (difference, product, or quotient) question and the estimated answer. Estimations of numbers in newspaper articles or other content areas are brought to their attention by the teacher.

Skill in estimation is developed before paper-and-pencil algorithms for an operation are introduced. If children cannot estimate, they have no way to evaluate the sense of what they are doing. Furthermore, in the modern world machines do the onerous tasks, but people must use machines intelligently and make decisions about the output of machines. Children must learn to estimate!

SUMMARY

The focus of this chapter was on helping children learn base- and place-value concepts by (1) forming concepts of base-10 relations working with materials that illustrate these ideas, and (2) learning to write decimal numerals for whole numbers and constructing the meaning of the place-value system of numeration. Mental computation, rounding, and estimation were discussed as related to knowledge of base-10 and place-value concepts.

STUDY QUESTIONS

1. Work with a partner to count and write numerals in another base. The form is usually, for example, in base five: 1; 2; 3; 4; 1 five; 1 five, 1; 1 five, 2; 1 five, 3; 1 five, 4; 2 fives; . . . ; five fives; five fives, 1; . . . . To write numerals in base five, a subscript is used: 10_{five} means 1 five. It can be read "1 zero, base five." If you work with children, they can say "1; 2; . . . ; 1 group of five; 1 group of five and 1 more . . . ." Discuss with your partner the benefits of using other bases for yourself and children.

2. Assess a few young children for readiness

to study base- and place-value concepts. Use the Piagetian-type tasks of multiequivalence and the equality test given in Appendix I. What do the results of this assessment tell you about the abilities of these children to decenter? Why is decentered thought necessary for studying the material discussed in this chapter?

3. Write a lesson plan to teach the use of exponents to capable fourth- or fifth-grade pupils. At some point in the plan use the deductive questioning method. Compare your plan with that of another student. How are they alike and different?

4. Learning base- and place-value concepts involves learning counting, representing number-concept examples with materials, reading and writing numerals, and expressing the meaning of numerals using concrete, graphic, and symbolic materials. Write an outline for several weeks of instruction to teach concepts of 10s, 100s, 1000s, or 10,000s that includes these learning-teaching objectives. Insure that pupils have opportunities to use cognitive processes such as classifying, ordering, relating, translating, and problem solving.

5. Assess five children's ability to count by powers of 10 and multiples of powers of

10. Work with upper-grade children. Ask the children to rename when appropriate (for example, 15 10s = 150). Summarize your findings and give your reactions to their levels of abilities to count. How would these findings help you in planning instruction if you were these children's teacher?

REFERENCES

Brumbaugh, Frederick L., "Big Numbers in a Classroom Model," *Arithmetic Teacher*, 29, no. 3 (November 1981), 18-19.

Burnett, Peg Hampton, "A Million! How Much Is That?" *Arithmetic Teacher*, 29, no. 1 (September 1981), 49-50.

Gundlach, Bernard H., "The History of Numbers and Numerals," in *Historical Topics for the Mathematics Classroom*, Thirty-first Yearbook of the National Council of Teachers of Mathematics. Washington, D.C.: The National Council of Teachers of Mathematics, Inc., 1969.

Holmes, Emma E., "Teach Estimation! Of Course!" *Arithmetic Teacher*, 22, no. 5 (May 1975), 367-69.

Underhill, Bob, *Teaching Elementary School Mathematics*, 3d ed., chap. 7. Columbus, OH: Charles E. Merrill Publishing Company, 1981.

6 LEARNING AND TEACHING THE OPERATIONS FOR WHOLE NUMBERS

If children are to complete the study of elementary school mathematics satisfactorily and continue to learn mathematics beyond the elementary grades, they must understand addition, subtraction, multiplication, and division. They must also have immediate recall of the basic facts for the operations. Knowledge of the four number operations is fundamental to learning mathematics at all levels. Furthermore, such knowledge contributes to understanding ideas in other subject areas, such as science and social studies.

Number operations are defined as a pairing of two numbers with a third number. From the point of view of learning, number operations are concepts. Using whole numbers, concept ex-

amples called **basic facts** can be generated for each number operation. With the numbers 0–9, 100 basic facts are generated for addition and for multiplication (Figures 6-1a and 6-1b). The inverse of the 100 basic addition facts are the 100 basic subtraction facts. The inverse of the basic multiplication facts, deleting division by 0, are the 90 basic division facts.

The three-phase learning-teaching sequence is used to enable children to master the four operations. The first section of this chapter gives an overview of the use of the sequence in teaching any of the number operations. The remaining sections deal with specific instructional procedures and activities to promote the learning of each operation.

+	0	1	2	3	4	5	6	7	8	9
0	0	1	2	3	4	5	6	7	8	9
1	1	2	3	4	5	6	7	8	9	10
2	2	3	4	5	6	7	8	9	10	11
3	3	4	5	6	7	8	9	10	11	12
4	4	5	6	7	8	9	10	11	12	13
5	5	6	7	8	9	10	11	12	13	14
6	6	7	8	9	10	11	12	13	14	15
7	7	8	9	10	11	12	13	14	15	16
8	8	9	10	11	12	13	14	15	16	17
9	9	10	11	12	13	14	15	16	17	18

FIGURE 6-1a. Table showing addition and subtraction facts.

X	0	1	2	3	4	5	6	7	8	9
0	0	0	0	0	0	0	0	0	0	0
1	0	1	2	3	4	5	6	7	8	9
2	0	2	4	6	8	10	12	14	16	18
3	0	3	6	9	12	15	18	21	24	27
4	0	4	8	12	16	20	24	28	32	36
5	0	5	10	15	20	25	30	35	40	45
6	0	6	12	18	24	30	36	42	48	54
7	0	7	14	21	28	35	42	49	56	63
8	0	8	16	24	32	40	48	56	64	72
9	0	9	18	27	36	45	54	63	72	81

FIGURE 6-1b. Table showing multiplication and division facts.

OVERVIEW

Instruction to foster the learning of the four number operations includes: (1) developing prerequisite understanding; (2) guiding learners to construct a concept of the operation; and (3) helping learners extend and consolidate conceptual knowledge. This section discusses the phases in terms of guidelines applicable to learning and teaching any number operation. Evaluation is also examined briefly.

Developing Prerequisite Understanding

An intuitive understanding of a number operation is a necessary first step in constructing the concept. To gain an intuitive understanding, children join and separate objects and work with graphic materials. They have many opportunities to discuss the meaning of what they have done.

Chapter 4 gave activities that require children to use sets of objects and pictures to represent a number as a sum and product. Young children frequently use materials to show that a number has many names. Working with sets in different arrangements to represent numbers gives an immediate awareness of the meaning of an operation.

If an assessment of prerequisite understanding shows children have not developed an intuitive understanding of an operation during their first years of school, teachers in later grades plan activities with concrete and graphic materials to help learners develop prerequisite understanding prior to formal introduction to an operation. A child's initial comprehension of a number operation is derived, not from the manipulation of symbols, but rather from the manipulation of objects and the study of graphics. Learning in the enactive and iconic modes is of great importance to further progress.

The activities designed to help learners develop intuitive understanding provide numerous opportunities for encouraging cognitive processes. To foster thinking, teachers ask questions such as: What do you notice? What is your "mind picture" of what you noticed? How are these pictures (arrangements) alike? Different? What goes together? How would you put them in order? Individual learners are often asked these questions as teachers discuss children's work with them.

Guiding Learners to Construct the Concept of a Number Operation

When children can make object arrangements or pictures that illustrate a number operation and can discuss what they have done using number words together with object words (for example, 3 blocks and 3 blocks are 6 blocks), they are ready to be introduced to the operation. In lessons to introduce the operation, teachers guide learners to produce and examine set arrangements showing basic facts, describe similarities in the set arrangements, construct the meaning of the number operation, and use correct words and symbols in discussing an operation and in working with the basic facts. The procedures used to teach a number operation are generally inductive but for some groups of learners can be deductive.

Work with concrete and graphic examples accompanies the use of symbols until learners can (1) represent a basic fact when given a mathematical sentence orally or in writing and (2) produce a basic fact to describe a set arrangement that represents a fact. Understanding an operation involves manipulating numbers. Having created the concept of a number operation, the child is not dependent on materials. Number ideas have been freed from their concrete representation. However, a child still uses materials to demonstrate and extend understanding.

During this phase no attempt is made to represent facts from fact tables in an ordered way. Rather the facts are drawn from tables in a random manner to help learners abstract the number operation concept from concrete examples that do not show the patterns that tables show. Furthermore, memorization of facts is not emphasized until toward the end of the next instructional phase.

Helping Learners Extend and Consolidate Conceptual Knowledge

During this phase children engage in activities that enable them to create examples and related concepts and consolidate ideas. They are given opportunities to produce basic facts, construct generalizations for an operation [for example, commutative property of addition $(a + b = b + a)$], explore relations among facts, examine new interpretations, solve problems, and memorize basic facts. A period of several years is usually necessary to attain these learnings. This section gives general suggestions to guide learners to extend and consolidate understanding. Instructional procedures and activities designed to attain the objectives for each operation are described fully in later sections of this chapter and in Chapter 3 on problem solving.

When learners construct the concept of a number operation, they can *generate the basic facts*. If children know the meaning of an operation, they can use materials to produce the facts. They should not be given the facts and denied the fulfilling experience of producing knowledge.

The process of generating facts is adapted to the individual needs of learners. Some need their teacher's guidance to represent and to write a set of facts—for example, basic facts with the sum of 8. Gifted children can usually work independently with minimal direction to make their fact records. Drawings and facts produced by learners are often made into books, possibly both a class book and individual books. It has been reported by my students that children take great pride in these books.

The easy facts (with no number greater than 5 as an addend or factor) are usually generated by learners and studied for extended understanding and retention before the introduction of the so-called hard facts (those with numbers 6–9 as addends or factors).

As children are generating the basic facts, opportunities arise to learn *generalizations* for the operation. Often children discover them through an examination of their basic-fact illustrations. If not, they are introduced by the teacher. When generalizations are known, they are used in producing new facts. Children are also helped to find relations in fact tables, such as multiplication facts that include the factor 5 have products ending in 5 or 0. Sensing relations aids in the retention of basic facts.

Children learn to interpret all the operations except addition in several ways. *Various meanings* of the operations can be constructed by using sets. For example, subtraction gives a remainder (take-away situation) or a difference (comparison situation). During the phase of extending knowledge, children are introduced to the different interpretations possible for subtraction, multiplication, and division.

Problem solving is an important aspect of extending and consolidating knowledge. Learners write problems, classify them, and discuss how they think as they solve problems. Lessons help children sort out and comprehend relations involved in different problem situations. Instruction in problem solving is of such importance that Chapter 3 discussed only the teaching and learning of problem solving.

Immediate recall of facts is also an objective of this instructional phase. Children must master the basic facts. They are penalized in their study of mathematics if they must count to give answers or if they give wrong responses. Many children gain immediate recall of the facts as they engage in activities to further comprehension of an operation. Other children need guidance in studying the facts for immediate recall.

A *test-study-retest* procedure helps many children master the facts. Teachers help learners use the procedure after children have generated a group of 10–25 facts and have had many experiences to foster understanding. Most children will not use the procedure for memorizing addition facts until grade two. They use the test-study-retest procedure for each of the other operations after they have grasped the meaning of the operation and have had many experiences with specific facts.

To begin the procedure, children take a *test* of the facts that have been the focus of instruction in recent lessons. They are told the purpose of the assessment activity. The test gives a record of basic facts correctly recalled in a given period of time. Satisfactory progress is 22 of 25 correctly written answers in 60 seconds. (Mastery, a goal of learning by the end of grade four for most children for all the operations, is 30 of 33 correctly written answers in 60 seconds. Mastery is attained gradually.)

The procedure next involves *studying facts*. Pupils work to memorize facts they cannot recall and also review facts answered correctly on the test. The teacher and the pupil first examine the child's test to determine which facts need to be memorized. The *study plan* for these facts involves the use of flash cards (Figure 6-2). The steps children learn are:

1. Find the side of the card that gives the fact question with the answer.

2. Read the fact to yourself and think about remembering it.

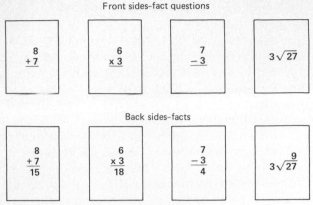

FIGURE 6-2.   Examples of flash cards.

3.   Close your eyes and picture the fact. Without looking, say the fact. Look at the fact to check yourself.

4.   Look at the fact question, say the fact, and check yourself.

5.   Look at the fact question, write the fact, and check yourself.

The teacher can guide a small group as they use these steps to study facts, or children can use a posted list of the steps for independent study after they have been introduced to the procedure. Children are encouraged to rehearse facts conscientiously. It is important to tell children that counting silently or with the help of fingers is a handicapping approach and will interfere with their study in later years.

To help learners memorize and review facts, activities and games are also used during the study aspect of the test-study-retest procedure. Activities and games described in Chapter 4 can be adapted to learning basic facts. Games should be played by two to six children to insure that all have rehearsal opportunities. A variety of other rehearsal activities can be devised. Many of these are described later in this chapter.

In memorizing facts, pupils should feel successful in their efforts. Making a record of facts a learner believes have been mastered is a good way to demonstrate accomplishment. Acknowledging achievement generates motivation to master other facts.

Teachers compliment children on their progress. Efforts should be made to avoid comparing children's achievements and to focus instead on the progress a learner has made by taking responsibility for his or her own learning.

When learners decide they are ready for the retest or when the teacher believes children can demonstrate learning, a second test (retest) is taken. This test should show achievement in learning facts if (1) the study plan and games or activities to aid recall and review have been conscientiously carried out and (2) teachers have taken individual differences in learning into account in working with children to set objectives. If children cannot demonstrate satisfactory progress, the teacher gives serious consideration to possible reasons for the failure to meet expectations. For example, if anxiety seems to be the reason for lack of progress, the teacher makes observations of the child in situations other than test-taking to determine his or her level of attainment.

The goal of mathematical learning is demonstrated progress. One responsibility of teachers is to help learners set goals, so that with reasonable effort they can demonstrate construction of mathematical concepts and memory of facts.

Evaluation

As children learn addition, subtraction, multiplication, and division, teachers evaluate progress at each instructional phase to insure that they are ready to engage in learning at a higher level or to begin a new area of learning. Evaluation includes assessment of prerequisite understanding, feedback evaluation during the phases when pupils construct, extend, and consolidate concepts, and final evaluation at the end of a topic. When children are mature enough to comprehend the significance of evaluation, they are told which activities are used to assess readiness, which promote learning and serve as feedback to learner and teacher, and which are tests for purpose of final evaluation.

Teachers keep records of pupils' progress to give direction in planning instruction. Children also keep records of their attainments as soon as they are old enough to do so. These records help learners relate achievements to expectations. Records give evidence of achievement in a cognitively oriented approach to instruction. They communicate success and failure in attaining objectives. Pupils' own records also encourage them to be responsible for their own learning. Teachers communicate to learners and their parents scores on final evaluation activities at the end of one or more topics of instruction. As indicated in Chapter 2, final evaluation scores will indicate satisfactory progress if feedback evaluation has been used in designing subsequent learning experiences appropriate for learners with different needs.

The next four sections of this chapter discuss teaching and learning the four operations. Each section discusses the meaning of the operation, prerequisite understanding, constructing the concept of the operation, and extending and consolidating conceptual knowledge. A final section discusses reintroducing the operations.

LEARNING AND TEACHING ADDITION

Meaning of Addition

Addition is an operation on two numbers, the **addends**, to obtain a third number, the **sum**:

$$4 \quad + \quad 3 \quad = \quad 7$$

addend + addend = sum

Addition is related to the union of disjoint sets (no common elements). Children develop the idea of addition by joining sets and slowly abstracting the operation meaning from their actions.

Prerequisite Understanding for Addition

Children use knowledge of sets and numbers to create concepts of addition. Prerequisite knowledge and examples of questions and observations used to assess prerequisite understanding are listed below.

If children do not show that they have developed prerequisite understanding, teachers continue with the activities and games given in Chapter 4 to develop and extend number concepts. Additional activities are:

CLAP GAME. "It" claps up to five times and children in group show number of claps with objects. "It" raises hands over his or her head and claps again. Children join objects to first set to match new number of claps. Children take turns telling total number of objects (claps).

SHOW A NUMBER IN TWO HEAPS. Two children take turns calling a number from 1 to 10. When a number is called, each child shows the number in two heaps of counters, without watching the other child. They discuss whether their heaps show the same or different arrangements.

CONNECT. A diagram such as one of those shown in Figure 6-3 is distributed to a group or a team or shown on the chalkboard. The children decide

Knowledge	*Assessment Example*
1. Knows that a set is a group.	We say, "This is a _____ of red beads. What word did I leave out?" Does the child use the word "set" in discussing work?
2. Knows that changing the arrangement of the elements of a set does not change the number of a set. (Conservation.)	Piagetian conservation of number tasks given in Appendix I.
3. Knows that a set can be thought of in terms of different pairs of subsets.	Observe child's book made to show representing a number with a set of two observable subsets. Note how child plays a game such as SCREEN GAME.
4. Knows the number names of sets to 20.	Ask the child to count sets of various sizes.
5. Writes numerals for numbers of sets to 10.	Ask child to write numerals for sets with numbers to 10.
6. Gives the number of sets to 5 without counting.	Can the child instantly recognize sets with numbers to 5? Any hesitation can indicate child is counting silently.
7. Knows that two sets can be joined to form a third set.	Observe how child explains activity of joining sets.

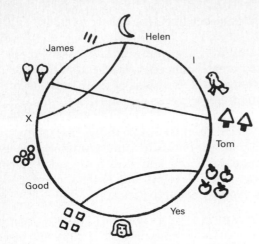

FIGURE 6-3. Example of Connect game.

where to make the connections, using the relation exhibited by the given "connections."

Variations of FISH, RUMMY, and SMILING FACE. A book is made with two different arrangements of sets displaying the same number. In another version of these games, the rule is: Book is 3 cards, 2 red and 1 blue. The red cards must be joined to show the set displayed on the blue card. (Game can be called JOIN-O or JELL.)

Children do not work with symbols as discussed in the next subsection until they have had many prerequisite experiences joining sets of objects, working with Cuisenaire rods, and drawing pictures. The reader is referred to Chapter 4, particularly the section on "Extending and Consolidating Knowledge of Number Concepts," for a discussion of instruction for prerequisite understanding.

Constructing the Concept of Addition

To help learners construct the meaning of the number operation of addition, teachers provide learning experiences which (1) enable children to review joining sets, (2) guide learners to study "word" records of joining sets, (3) help learners by means of an inductive questioning method to create the idea that "adding matches two numbers with an equal number, the sum," and (4) insure learners think and write facts as they study sets. Box 6-1 gives steps in an inductive procedure to introduce addition.

Soon after the equals sign is introduced, concepts of "greater than" and "less than" are reviewed. The symbols representing these ideas are explained to learners during this review period: > (greater than) and < (less than). The

"greater than" and "less than" concepts can be related to addition facts—for example, $5 + 1 > 4 + 1$.

Number lines can be introduced at this time (Figure 6-4). Walk-on number lines give children opportunities to act out number facts. A line can be used by pairs of children, one giving a fact question and the other "walking" the sum. Paper-and-pencil number lines are introduced after children have become familiar with the walk-on number line. Children show facts on number lines to further their comprehension of addition.

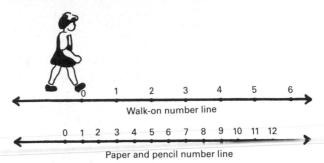

Walk-on number line

Paper and pencil number line

FIGURE 6-4. Number lines.

Measurement ideas are implicit in number lines. If children cannot conserve length, the use of number lines is probably not entirely meaningful to them.

Activities for developing the concept of addition continue until learners can produce basic facts to correspond to displays of joining sets or can show sets or draw pictures to represent basic facts. Games in which they match set diagrams and basic facts are one type of activity to help learners create the concept of addition. When teachers ascertain that learners can interpret pictures representing facts and can show objects or pictures to demonstrate their understanding, they introduce activities at the next phase of instruction.

Extending and Consolidating Knowledge of the Addition Concept

The first activity teachers plan after learners demonstrate that they have constructed the concept of addition is the *generation of facts*. Pupils work with groups of facts. First, they produce facts to sums of 5 and work to extend and consolidate these facts. Next they produce and study sums to 10. Later, perhaps the following semester or year, facts to sums of 18 are gen-

BOX 6-1. SAMPLE LESSON: INTRODUCING ADDITION (GRADE 1)

1. Boys and girls, today we are going to learn something about numbers. We are going to learn about addition. You will feel special when you know addition.

2. Let's begin by remembering that we have talked about putting sets together and getting a new set. Remember yesterday we put red books with blue books and took them to the other first grade.

3. I have some sentences on the board about different combinations of books. Let's read them. Take your counters. Show what it says in the sentences.

> 3 books and 2 books make 5 books.
> 2 books and 2 books make 4 books.
> 4 books and 2 books make 6 books.
> 3 books and 1 book make 4 books.

What did you do with your counters to show what each sentence means? (Put them together to get a stack.)

4. Watch what I am writing. (Place beside the above sentences.)

> 3 and 2 are 5.
> 2 and 2 are 4.
> 4 and 2 are 6.
> 3 and 1 are 4.

What do you notice? (You wrote only the numbers.) Are the sentences true? Why? (The two numbers together make the last number.)

5. Thinking about numbers in this way is thinking addition. In addition we use special words and marks: $3 + 2 = 5$. We read this: three plus two equals five. It is an addition fact. It says $3 + 2$ and 5 are the same number.

6. Let's make the other sentences addition facts and read them.

> $2 + 2 = 4$
>
> (and so on)

What do you know about the numbers in these sentences? (The two numbers together are the same number as the one number.)

7. Now I'll write some more sentences.

> $3 + 3 = 6$
> $2 + 1 = 3$
> $4 + 4 = 7$

What do you notice about these? (One is not true or not an addition fact.) Let's make it an addition fact.

8. Now you make some addition facts. If you want, you can use the counters on your desk to make addition facts. (Write some of the facts pupils generate on the board; read and discuss.)

9. Let's review what we learned. Find an addition fact on the board. Read it. What is addition? Think an addition fact. Whisper it to your neighbor (and so on).

10. Very good! How do you feel about learning addition facts? (Grown-up.)

erated and studied. The zero facts are studied as a group, after the facts with sums to 10 are generated and their meaning enriched through many different learning experiences.

To help learners produce facts, teachers can distribute a given number of counters to each child in a group. Pupils use the counters to generate facts with sums corresponding to the number of the set of counters distributed. This procedure minimizes counting. Some teachers distribute paper plates with a line across the middle, or two sections of egg cartons, to aid learners in their work. After a fact is shown, a fact sentence is written.

With some groups of learners, teachers can suggest that children generate fact tables after they have generated the first few facts in a table. Often learners can use inference to generate a fact table—for example, $3 + 1 = 4, 3 + 2 = 5, 3 + 3 = 6, 3 + 4 = 7, 3 + 5 = 8, \ldots, 3 + 9 = 12$.

Pupils make and keep records of their work. The records show set pictures of addition and the basic facts "discovered" in equation and vertical form. (Set pictures are made using pictures of objects, rod diagrams drawn on squared paper, number lines, or tallies.) The records are usually made into books. A class book or bulletin board display can be planned as a cooperative project.

As learners produce facts and make their records of work accomplished, they are encouraged to remember the facts. Teachers sometimes ask learners to work in pairs, rehearsing what they did that day. They can read their addition facts to each other. Children can take their book pages home to be read to parents, siblings, or friends.

As pupils generate addition facts, they study generalizations. The following is a list of examples and generalizations introduced while pupils are learning addition.

As noted earlier, the zero rule is learned soon after children know the facts to sums of 10. It is an especially useful rule, for it saves the child from memorizing 19 zero facts. The commutative property is also useful, for it aids the generation and memory of facts. Children learn this generalization soon after they have studied the facts with sums to 6. Children can refer to it as the *order rule* to aid comprehension of the generalization. A lesson example to teach the commutative property of addition is given in Chapter 1.

Children develop an intuitive understanding of the other generalizations as they use materials to generate the facts and extend meaning. For example, solving and checking an addition example with three or more addends gives an intuitive understanding of the associative property of addition. Learners can be assigned activities that foster an intuitive awareness of generalizations. Examples of exercises that enable learners to work with relations and patterns in sets of addition facts are given in Box 6-2. The WHAT'S MY RULE games described later also provide opportunities for learners to study relations among facts.

Understanding can be enhanced and retention aided by games children play during some of their study periods. If they do not know the facts, children often find it awkward to play games and are therefore motivated to remember the facts. A list of games follows.

FISH, RUMMY, SMILING FACE, and WAR are now played with basic facts. Cards give addition questions or sums. The games may be given new names, sometimes by the children.

DOMINOES. A set of dominoes (36-48) is made with one side a basic fact question and the other a sum (Figure 6-5a). No more than four children should play. The dominoes are turned upside down and rearranged. Each child picks seven. The

	Example	*Generalization*
a.	$5 + 4 = 4 + 5$	Commutative property (Order rule)
b.	$(2 + 1) + 3 = 2 + (1 + 3)$	Associative property (Grouping rule)
c.	$4 + 4 = 8$	Compensation rule
	$4 + 4 + 1 = 8 + 1$	
d.	$6 + 0 = 6$	Zero rule for addition
e.	$4 + 4 = 8$ or	Symmetry property
	$8 = 4 + 4$	
f.	$9 + 7 = 9 + (1 + 6) = 10 + 6$	Making-ten rule

BOX 6-2. *EXERCISES EMPHASIZING RELATIONSHIPS,
            PROPERTIES, AND RULES*

1.   Match the facts that have the same sum. Think why this is easy.

$$4 + 2 \quad 3 + 9$$
$$6 + 7 \quad 5 + 2$$
$$9 + 3 \quad 7 + 6$$
$$2 + 5 \quad 2 + 4$$

2.   Place the correct sign, equality or inequality, on each line. Is it easy? Why?

$$6 + 2 \underline{\quad} 5 + 3$$
$$8 + 2 \underline{\quad} 9 + 2$$
$$6 + 4 \underline{\quad} 5 + 5$$
$$7 + 2 \underline{\quad} 8 + 1$$

3.   Think what is happening here. Then finish this exercise by writing numerals in the blanks.

$$8 + 7 = 9 + \underline{\quad}$$
$$4 + 7 = \underline{\quad} + 6$$
$$\underline{\quad} + 6 = 5 + 7$$
$$\underline{\quad} + 3 = \underline{\quad} + 2$$

4.   Write a related fact beside the fact given by using the order rule. The first one is done for you.

$$3 + 6 = 9 \quad 6 + 3 = 9$$
$$5 + 2 = 7$$
$$6 + 4 = 10$$
$$3 + 8 = 11$$
$$5 + 4 = 9$$

5.   Write 3 facts that you can think of if you know:

$$3 + 3 = 6 \quad 1.$$
$$2.$$
$$3.$$
$$4 + 4 = 8 \quad 1.$$
$$2.$$
$$3.$$

6. Think which additions belong together in some way. Make sets by drawing a line of the same color around additions that go together.

$$
\begin{array}{ll}
2 + 2 & 3 + 4 \\
3 + 3 & 5 + 6 \\
5 + 5 & 4 + 5 \\
4 + 4 & 2 + 3
\end{array}
$$

7. Children are given a set of shuffled flash cards for a table of facts—for example, the 2 table, $2 + 1, 2 + 2, 2 + 3, \ldots, 2 + 9$. The task is to put them in order. Good questions to ask are: What do you notice about the addends when the sums are in order? What do you notice about the sums? Children can engage in this activity independently or in teams.

$$
\begin{array}{|c|c|c|c|}
\hline
\begin{array}{r}2\\+7\end{array} & \begin{array}{r}5\\+2\end{array} & \begin{array}{r}8\\+1\end{array} & \begin{array}{r}6\\+3\end{array} \\
\hline
4 & 2 & 7 & 6 \\
\hline
\end{array}
$$

$$
\begin{array}{|c|c|c|c|}
\hline
\begin{array}{r}3\\+2\end{array} & \begin{array}{r}4\\+2\end{array} & \begin{array}{r}3\\+4\end{array} & \begin{array}{r}5\\+1\end{array} \\
\hline
9 & 8 & 4 & 3 \\
\hline
\end{array}
$$

FIGURE 6-5a. Domino cards.

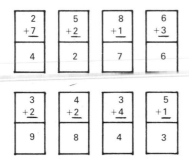

FIGURE 6-5b. Using domino cards to play the game.

others are left to form a pile. The child with the largest sum on his or her domino begins. The children take turns completing facts (Figure 6-5b). If a child cannot play, he or she draws a domino from the pile. The first player out of dominoes wins.

MAGIC SQUARES. See Figure 6-6 for an example of a magic square puzzle. Numerals are written in the blank spaces so that the total of each column, row, and diagonal is the same sum. Magic squares

$$
\begin{array}{|c|c|c|}
\hline
7 & 0 & 5 \\
\hline
2 & 4 & 6 \\
\hline
3 & 8 & 1 \\
\hline
\end{array}
$$

FIGURE 6-6. Example of a Magic Square.

for beginners are 3×3 arrays. The numbers 0–8 are arranged so that the sum of each column, row, and diagonal is 12. The magic square can easily be constructed by making the center number 4. (This game introduces column addition, discussed in Chapter 7.)

BOARD-AND-DICE (SPINNER) GAMES. These games use a board with squares, rectangles, or free forms in which the numerals 2–12 are written. Players have markers of different colors to cover the numerals, if possible, when they have a turn. To begin the game, each child throws a die or spins a spinner. The player with the largest number begins. The children take turns throwing 2 dice or spinning a spinner twice. If they can give the sum of the numbers represented on the dice (spinner), they place a marker on that numeral. If the sum of a throw has been covered, the player must pass. When all the numerals are covered, the child with the most markers on the board wins. Other board-and-dice (spinner) games are designed so that the players travel along a path with a marker. They move as many spaces as the sum of their throws or spins (Figure 6-7). Some spaces have directions which add interest to the game, such as: You are lost; go back 2 spaces. This is a hot place; move ahead 3 spaces.

WHAT'S MY RULE GAMES. A variety of games or activities can be devised to help learners find relationships or patterns in pairs or sequences of numbers. Two versions are given below.

"It" says to the group, "Tell me a number and I'll give you another using my rule." A child says a number and "It" uses a rule, such as "Add 2." The exchange continues until a child figures out the rule and gives two numbers using the rule. He or she then becomes "It."

A NUMBER CHANGER MACHINE is used (Figure 6-8). In later grades it can be labeled a FUNCTION MACHINE. A list of numbers going in the

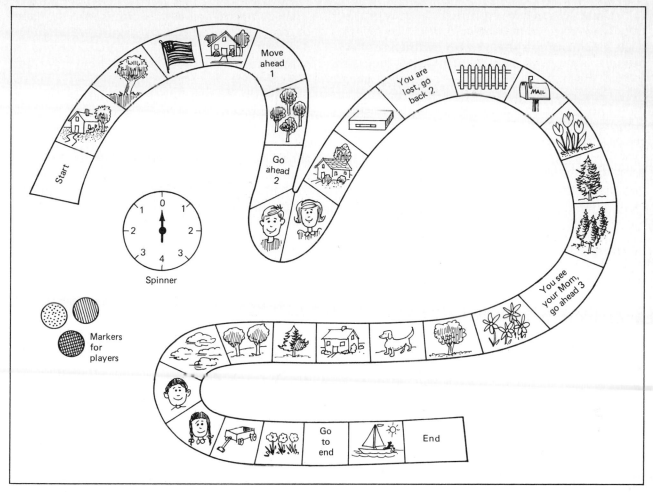

FIGURE 6-7. Example of a board game.

machine is given; a few numbers coming out of the machine are presented. Children complete the "Numbers Out" list by inferring the rule.

While children are extending understanding of basic addition facts, many problem-solving opportunities arise or are created by teachers. Teachers help learners act out verbal problem situations and learn that a problem described in words can be restated in mathematical language. Children also make up problems to ask each other and discuss how they knew the number answer to a problem.

Experiences designed to extend understanding and further retention help learners *memorize facts*. When teachers observe that learners have immediate recall of some facts (for example, as children play games), the test-study-retest procedure discussed earlier is implemented for a group of facts—for example, to sums of 10.

IN	OUT
3	12
6	15
2	11
4	•
7	•

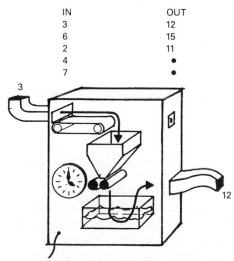

FIGURE 6-8. Example of a number changer machine.

Children are given progress evaluations as they work to memorize the addition facts. Feedback information is shared with children so they become aware of improvement and progress toward mastery. As soon as possible, they keep their own records.

The games and activities presented in this section have stressed a variety of cognitive processes. The reader can easily determine, for example, which activities emphasize comparing. Analyzing several activities for the cognitive processes involved would be a valuable exercise for readers.

LEARNING AND TEACHING SUBTRACTION

Meaning of Subtraction

Subtraction is the inverse of addition. If $a + b = c$, then $c - a = b$ and $c - b = a$. In a subtraction sentence, the names for the numbers are:

$$9 \quad - \quad 4 \quad = \quad 5$$

minuend − subtrahend = remainder or difference

(sum) − (addend) = (missing addend)

For many children learning subtraction seems more difficult than learning addition. This could be because subtraction has several interpretations related to real-life situations: take away, comparison, and how many more. These will be discussed in turn.

In the **take-away interpretation** $9 - 6 = 3$ means: If 6 objects are removed from a set of 9, 3 remain. The answer, 3, is called the remainder. To learn the take-away concept, children study examples that involve removal or separation of a subset from a set. Concrete materials demonstrate this interpretation of subtraction more effectively than graphic materials, but diagrams are used, as shown in Figure 6-9. Story problems in which a subset is removed, lost, eaten, or the like are useful in helping children understand this concept: Tom had 8 crayons. He gave 3 to Jim. How many did Tom have left? ($8 - 3 = N$.)

In the **comparison interpretation** two sets are compared: How many greater is 5 books than 3 books? ($5 - 3 = 2$.) The answer in this interpretation of subtraction is called a difference and tells how many greater (or less) one number is than another. To teach the comparison situation, teachers guide children in the study of examples in which two sets are compared (Figure 6-10). Story problems are useful in helping learners clarify this meaning of subtraction, but cognitive abilities, such as reversibility, seem necessary for understanding the concept.

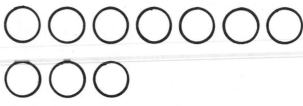

$7 - 3 = 4$

FIGURE 6-10.   The comparison interpretation of subtraction.

In the **how-many-more interpretation** the numbers of two sets (usually nonequivalent sets) are given. The question is: What is the number of the set to join to the smaller set to obtain the larger set? An example is: Jane has $6. She wants $8 to buy a new game. How many more dollars does she need? $6 + N = 8$. In this equation an addend is missing. The problem is to determine the missing addend (Figure 6-11). Reasoning leads to the understanding that since addition and subtraction are *inverse* operations, a missing-addend equation can be solved by subtraction: $8 - 6 = N$. If a child's thought is reversible, he or she grasps the concept of inverse operations and can deal with a missing-addend type equation.

Prerequisite Understanding for Subtraction

If teachers are to help children learn subtraction, they must know what knowledge children have to relate to the new learning. Before introducing subtraction, teachers assess for pupils' comprehension of the following understandings and skills.

Six oranges less two that have been eaten gives four oranges: $6 - 2 = 4$

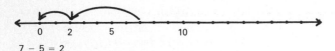

$7 - 5 = 2$

FIGURE 6-9.   The take-away interpretation of subtraction.

Knowledge	*Assessment Example*
1. A set includes subsets, which may be removed from the set.	Here is a set of red and blue beads. If you give me the blue beads, what are left?
2. A set may be compared to one of its subsets. (Concept of inclusion relation.)	Piagetian task of inclusion relation in Appendix I.
3. Two sets may be compared.	Display two sets of unequal size. Ask: Which set is greater? How do you know? How many greater?
4. The addition of numbers relates to the joining of sets.	Ask the child to show the meaning of 3–4 basic facts, using counters or pictures.
5. Satisfactory progress in retaining basic facts for addition related to those being introduced for subtraction.	In 1 minute a child can write 22 of 25 sums correctly on paper-and-pencil test.

If children do not have a grasp of the concepts and skills discussed in the above list, teachers continue to emphasize prerequisite concepts. Activities used to develop addition prerequisite understanding are revised to incorporate subtraction ideas. Children do not work with symbols until they demonstrate understanding of the "take-away" concept and set comparison.

Constructing the Concept of Subtraction

Construction of the subtraction concept is attained as children use numbers to deal with a take-away situation. Initially children develop the meaning of the number operation of subtraction by abstracting the number concept from separating a subset from a set. An instructional plan to use in introducing subtraction is given in Box 6-3. Other lessons provide additional opportunities for children to separate sets and write the indicated subtraction fact. Games discussed previously can be used if they are adapted to provide for a demonstration or picture of set separation and naming of the fact.

Two new games are:

PART WITH YOUR TREASURES. The game is played by 2 children. One child has a sponge die that displays the numerals 4, 5, or 6. The other child has a sponge die that displays the numerals 1, 2, 3, or 4. Child One tosses his or her die and picks up the number of counters (treasures) shown on the die. The other child tosses his or her die, notes the number shown, and says, "Part with . . . of your treasures." He or she receives that amount from Child One. Child One keeps the remainder, moving them to a separate container (treasure box). Child Two reads and circles the related subtraction equation on a game sheet and puts the treasure received in his or her treasure box. The game continues for 5 throws for each child (a round). (Child One keeps a tally record.) At the end of 4 rounds, the children count their treasures. The child who has the most treasures wins. A follow-up activity is for the team members to share drawing dot pictures for the circled equations on the game sheet and to display their sheets on a bulletin board.

PARTNER SPIN. Children take turns spinning a spinner. The spinner card has sections giving subtraction equations. The child who spins the spin-

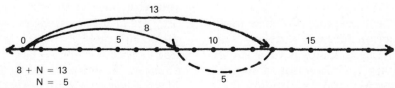

$$8 + N = 13$$
$$N = 5$$

FIGURE 6-11. The missing-addend interpretation of subtraction.

BOX 6-3.   SAMPLE LESSON: INTRODUCING SUBTRACTION (GRADE 1)

1.   Boys and girls, today we are going to learn something new about numbers. It is subtraction.

2.   I have written some sentences on the board. They tell about giving to a friend. Let's read them. Please take out your box of counters and show each sentence with the counters. (Shown on the chalkboard are:

6 cookies take away 4 are 2 cookies.

5 candies take away 1 are 4 candies.

4 pennies take away 2 are 2 pennies.

3 M&Ms take away 1 are 2 M&Ms.)

Tell about what you did. (Made a set and took some away.)

3.   I will write number sentences beside the English sentences. They are called subtraction facts. Think about what you did. That's what subtract sentences mean. (Write beside the above sentences these subtraction facts.

$$6 - 4 = 2$$
$$5 - 1 = 4$$
$$4 - 2 = 2$$
$$3 - 1 = 2 \,)$$

What do subtraction facts tell us? What do they mean? (We took some away.)

4.   Yes, subtraction facts are number facts that tell us about take away. We read a subtraction fact this way: 6 minus 4 equals 2. Let's read the other subtraction facts together. . . .

5.   Please make up a take-away story, show it with counters, and be ready to tell us the subtraction fact. (The group should be small enough for all to respond.) . . . I will write your subtraction facts on the board. We will all show them with our counters and read them. . . .

6.   What have we learned today? What does subtraction tell us? How do we read a fact? . . . Good thinking!

ner shows the partner the meaning of the equation indicated by the spin using counters. The number of counters removed by the child are accumulated and counted at the end of 10 spins. The child with the most counters wins (Figure 6-12).

When children can explain the take-away meaning of a subtraction fact in words and with materials and can explain removal of a subset from a set by writing a subtraction equation, they are ready to extend and consolidate their understanding.

Extending and Consolidating Knowledge of the Subtraction Concept

This instructional phase begins with learner *generation of subtraction facts.* Children first generate facts with minuends of 5, next 6–10, and at a later time with minuends to 18. Children are given counters and asked to use them to show subtraction facts (take-away interpretation). Number lines can be used instead of counters to illustrate facts. Pupils make records of their work as they write the basic subtraction facts. Pupils' records are collected; when several

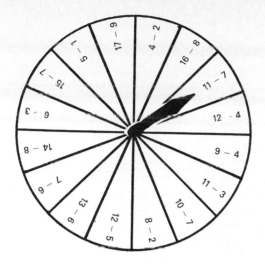

FIGURE 6-12. A spinner for the Partner Spin game.

lists of facts have been completed, subtraction books are made. During the weeks children work on their books, periods are set aside for (1) exploring relations and rules, (2) completing exercises and playing games incorporating subtraction facts, (3) studying interpretations of subtraction other than take-away, (4) solving subtraction verbal problems, and (5) memorizing the facts after many experiences to develop meaning.

Soon after learners begin to generate subtraction facts, teachers introduce the idea that addition and subtraction are *inverse operations*. (Box 6-4 gives a sample lesson.) The generation of subtraction facts is greatly simplified if this concept can be used. If children understand the concept of inverse operations, they can, for ex-

---

BOX 6-4. SAMPLE LESSON: INTRODUCTION TO ADDITION
AND SUBTRACTION AS INVERSE OPERATIONS
(GRADE 1 OR 2)

1. Boys and girls, we are going to make a great discovery today about addition and subtraction.

2. Look at what I have written on the board. Read the equation to yourself and show its meaning with counters.

$$4 + 5 = 9$$

Use the 9 counters to show this equation.

$$9 - 5 = 4$$

What do you notice? Or what number did we begin with and end with? (We started with 4 and ended with 4.)

3. The teacher follows the same procedure with 3 more pairs of equations.

4. Boys and girls, what is going on here? What happens every time? (We begin and end with the same number.)

5. Can you think of words to tell what is going on? (They are opposite. They go together. They can turn into the other. Addition and subtraction are backwards.)

6. This is quite a discovery. If you know an addition fact, what else do you know? (Subtraction fact.) Let's try out our discovery. Think an addition fact you know and its related subtraction fact. . . . Share with us what you were thinking. (Pupils share related addition and subtraction facts. Some may be written on the board and read.)

7. Can this discovery help us in making our books? How? (We can use our addition books to make subtraction books.)

8. Wonderful idea. That will save us some work!

9. Let's review the great discovery we made today. . . .

---

*BOX 6-5. SAMPLE LESSON: TEACHING THAT SUBTRACTION
IS NOT COMMUTATIVE (GRADE 2)*

1. Boys and girls, we know that there is an order rule for addition. Let's recall some examples of that rule.

$$(3 + 5 = 8; 5 + 3 = 8, \text{ and so on})$$

2. Good, we have four examples of the rule on the chalkboard. What does the order rule mean? Look at the examples to help remember. (The order of numbers in addition can be changed without changing the answer.)

3. Let's try that rule with subtraction. Can we change the order of the numbers in subtraction facts and get the same answer? Use your counters and these subtraction facts to find out. First, what should I write to change the order?

$$(5 - 2 = N \qquad 2 - 5 = N$$
$$4 - 1 = N \qquad 1 - 4 = N$$
$$6 - 2 = N \qquad 2 - 6 = N$$
$$3 - 2 = N \qquad 2 - 3 = N)$$

4. What is happening? How are you doing showing the facts with the order of the numbers changed? (It won't work. It's silly. You can't take a big set from a small set. There aren't enough counters.)

5. What have we found out? (There is not an order rule for subtraction.)

6. Good thinking! Knowing that there is not an order rule for subtraction will help us learn other things.

---

ample, use $6 + 4 = 10$ to think $10 - 4 = 6$ and $10 - 6 = 4$.

Fact families are used in activities to emphasize that addition and subtraction are inverse operations. (A fact family includes an addition fact, its commuted form, and the two related subtraction facts. For example, a fact family is: $5 + 6 = 11, 6 + 5 = 11, 11 - 6 = 5, 11 - 5 = 6$.) Learners classify facts by families using flash cards. When given one of the four facts comprising a fact family, they write related facts. The old games can be revised, with rules now requiring a book to be a fact family.

When studying rules and subtraction, children learn that subtraction is not commutative. A lesson plan to teach this idea is given in Box 6-5.

Valid generalizations are:

	Example	*Generalization*
a.	$9 - 3 = 9 - 3 + (1 - 1)$ $= (9 + 1) - (3 + 1)$ $= 10 - 4$	Compensation rule
b.	$9 - 9 = 0$ $9 - 0 = 9$	Zero rules for subtraction
c.	$17 - 9 = 17 - 7 - 2$ $= 10 - 2$ $= 8$	Making-ten rule
d.	$8 - 4 = 4$ $4 = 8 - 4$	Symmetry property

Learning and using the zero rules aid recall of the zero subtraction facts. They are therefore learned after children know facts with minuends to 10. The other generalizations are understood intuitively by many children as they generate the subtraction facts. Discussions of these generalizations occur when appropriate. Children who are capable learners of mathematics can profit from discussions of the rules and opportunities to give examples of them in group or individual activities.

To help learners work with relations and rules when learning subtraction facts, activities are patterned after those for addition given in Box 6-2 (numbers 2, 3, 5, 6, and 7). For example, an activity could ask learners to classify and write in boxes or lists the following facts: $9 - 5 = 4$, $7 - 2 = 5$, $6 - 5 = 1$, $7 - 5 = 2$, $6 - 1 = 5$, $9 - 4 = 5$. The question and answer are both given to help learners recognize that, in these facts, the subtrahend and remainder are reversed. By writing the facts, learners have opportunity to study for recall.

Other assignments are:

1. Classify facts having remainders greater than 5 or less than 5 before giving remainders and discuss how they thought about the task.

2. Investigate how many subtraction facts have minuends 1, 2, 3, . . . , 6 (later to 18) by listing them. Patterns in the list can be observed and discussed.

3. Play the old games with subtraction facts.

4. Work independently or with a partner using the Missing Addend Cards (Figure 6-13). The objective is to collect as many cards as possible.

Other interpretations of subtraction than take-away are introduced while learners are extending understanding, usually early in grade three. Children learn that subtraction is used to answer questions in comparison and how-many-more situations. The lessons enable learners to study the situations by representing them with objects, rods, or pictures and infer that subtraction is the appropriate operation to use to solve the problem. Story problems soon incorporate all interpretations.

When a learner has learned a group of facts by working with them in a variety of activities, he or she takes a test to determine which facts need further study. The subtraction facts that need rehearsal are practiced using the flash-card procedure discussed earlier or other methods (perhaps by writing repeatedly) decided on by a learner.

Subtraction basic facts are usually mastered in late second grade or early third grade. Children are not introduced to multiplication facts until they understand subtraction and have immediate recall of most facts. However, learners can be developing intuitive understanding of multiplication while studying subtraction facts.

LEARNING AND TEACHING MULTIPLICATION

Meaning of Multiplication

Multiplication is an operation on two numbers, the **factors**, to obtain a third number, the **product**:

$$2 \ \times \ 6 \ = \ 12$$

factor $\times$ factor $=$ product

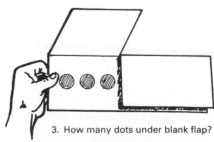

3. How many dots under blank flap?

4. Pick up blank flap to check.

1. Think number of dots on card.

2. Cover with two flaps.

FIGURE 6-13.   Missing-addend card.

When the factors are nonzero whole numbers, the product is said to be a multiple of either factor; for example, 12 is a multiple of 2 and of 6. In discussing learning and teaching multiplication, the topics are the same as those in previous sections: the meaning of multiplication, prerequisite understanding for multiplication, constructing the concept of multiplication, and extending and consolidating conceptual knowledge.

Multiplication is interpreted four ways: (1) as the union of equivalent sets; (2) as repeated addition; (3) as a Cartesian product; and (4) as a ratio (Figure 6-14). The first two interpretations are stressed in the elementary school. The Cartesian-product concept is taught later. The ratio interpretation is introduced in the elementary years but emphasized in junior high school. It will be discussed in Chapter 8.

Prerequisite Understanding for Multiplication

Understanding addition is prerequisite to the study of multiplication. Pupils must also know that $1(n) = n(1)$; for example, a set of 3 objects can be thought of as 1 set of 3 or 3 sets of 1. A child should understand that $5 + 5 + 5 = 3(5)$. Skip-counting by 2s, 3s, and 5s is important to learn before children are formally

Union of equivalent sets

XXXX   XXXX   XXXX

$3 \times 4 = 12$

Cartesian product

Boys (3)	Girls (4)			
	Sally	Kay	Pam	Joan
Dave	D–S	D–K	D–P	D–J
Bill	B–S	B–K	B–P	B–J
Mark	M–S	M–K	M–P	M–J

Repeated addition

$4 + 4 + 4 = 3 \times 4 = 12$

Ratio

x x x   xxxx   xxxx   xxxx

x   xxxx

$$\frac{3}{1} = \frac{12}{4}$$

FIGURE 6-14.   The four interpretations of multiplication.

introduced to multiplication. These prerequisites and their assessment are listed in the plan in Appendix III and are given here for the reader's convenience.

Knowledge	*Assessment Example*
1. Pupils can represent addition facts.	Pupils can use counters or drawings to show addition facts.
2. Pupils show mastery of addition facts.	Paper-and-pencil test of 100 facts; 91 (of 100) correct in 3 minutes.
3. Pupils can solve story problems involving addition given orally.	Pupils solve addition story problems.
4. Pupils can name a set of any number to 10 as $1(n)$ or $n(1)$.	Class discussion: Say: We know that 10 ones is one 10. What is 3 ones? One 5? What is a number name for ////? and so on. Paper-and-pencil test: Match drawings and words.
5. $(N)S = S(N)$	Piagetian test of multiequivalence. (Appendix I.)
6. Pupils can represent a number by joining sets each with the same number of objects.	Show three 2-bead sets. What number of beads have you shown? Or show two sets with 3 beads each. What number of beads is that?
7. Intuitive understanding of multiples.	Clapping hard and soft; skip counting.

The language heard, life's experiences, and the learning activities provided contribute to children's prerequisite understanding. For example, teachers use language to emphasize that a set of several objects can be thought of as a "one." The teacher points to a set and says, "a 3-bead set," "a 4-counter set," or "a 2-block set." Objects children see and use at home and at play are also helpful in developing prerequisite knowledge: a 3-wheeler (tricycle), 4 legs on a table, 3-legged stools, 4 wheels on a car, and the like. Children can discuss these objects with emphasis on N to 1, such as 4 wheels on 1 car. Pupils can skip-count legs or wheels as the teacher displays pictures of tables, cars, and the like. "Puzzles" can be created, such as: How many legs on 5 3-legged stools? A big garage has 6 cars; a man polishes the wheels on Monday; how many wheels does he polish on Monday? Children can draw diagrams and count to obtain answers.

Skip counting is learned for "fun" and to solve class problems. For example, skip counting can be used to find how many window panes are in the classroom windows. Other skip-counting possibilities are: chairs at each table, crayons in boxes, feet under a table, shoes in the room, and ears that can hear the rain. Books can be made illustrating "The 2s of Me" (hands, feet, eyes, and so on).

Three activities to develop the grouping notion and skip counting are:

1. Bodily movements: Bend 4 to the left, 4 to the right, ... Head moves 3 forward, 3 back, ... Low and loud counting can accompany the movements to emphasize the multiple, as 1, 2, 3, <u>4</u>, 5, 6, 7, <u>8</u>, ...

2. Making designs using strips of the same length: Children can make 2-strip or 3-strip designs, and so on (Figure 6-15). Squared paper can also be used.

3. The now very familiar games FISH, RUM-MY, SMILING FACE, and WAR with new

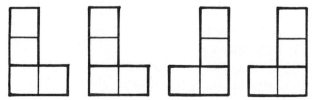

FIGURE 6-15. Example of a design made by using 2-strip cards.

names will help children recognize that different patterns can display the same number. For example . . . . . and : : both show 6.

Concepts of even numbers (divisible by 2) and odd numbers (not divisible by 2) can be introduced to develop prerequisite understanding for multiplication. Activity suggestions are:

1. Have children use red Cuisenaire rods or 2-strip cards to show all the numbers they can to 20 (Figure 6-16a gives examples). Ask: "What do you notice about the numbers you can make with these materials? What have you found out about numbers?"

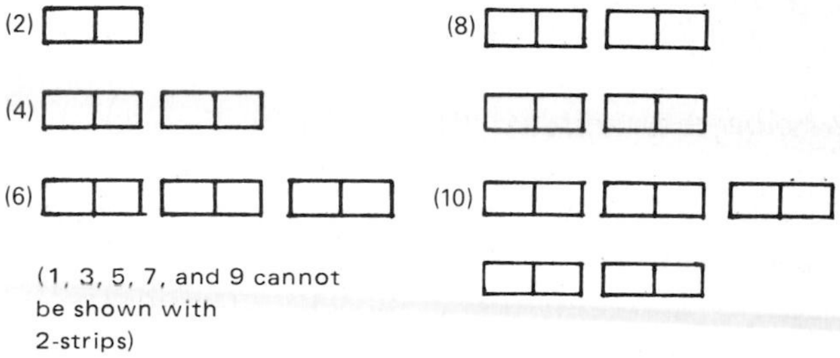

(2) ☐☐   (8) ☐☐ ☐☐

(4) ☐☐ ☐☐   ☐☐ ☐☐

(6) ☐☐ ☐☐ ☐☐   (10) ☐☐ ☐☐ ☐☐

(1, 3, 5, 7, and 9 cannot be shown with 2-strips)   ☐☐ ☐☐

FIGURE 6-16a. Using 2-strip cards to show even numbers.

2. Ask pupils to show all the numbers they can to 20 using sets of 2 counters (Figure 6-16b gives examples). Then say: "What is happening? Give the numbers that you have shown with sets of 2 counters. Predict other numbers you think you could show with sets of 2. Use counters to show these numbers. Did you make a good prediction? Why or why not?"

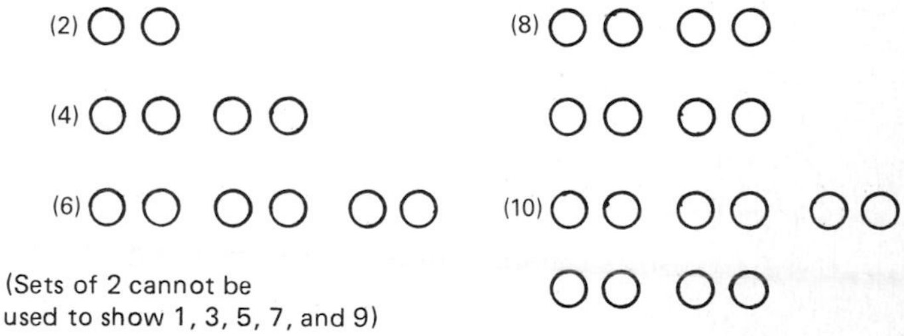

(2) ○○   (8) ○○ ○○

(4) ○○ ○○   ○○ ○○

(6) ○○ ○○ ○○   (10) ○○ ○○ ○○

(Sets of 2 cannot be used to show 1, 3, 5, 7, and 9)   ○○ ○○

FIGURE 6-16b. Using sets of 2 counters to show even numbers.

3. Have pupils use squared paper to show all the numbers they can to 20 by outlining sets of 2 squares (Figure 6-16c gives examples of pupils' work). Ask children to write numerals for the numbers they have shown. After the task is completed, say:

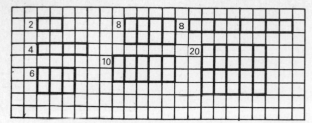

FIGURE 6-16c.   Using sets of 2 squares to show even numbers.

"What is going on? Look at the numerals. What do you notice? What other numbers can be shown using 2 squares? Write the numerals for these numbers. How will you know what to write? Check yourself by using squared paper to show a few numbers for the numerals you have written."

After children gain an intuitive grasp of the concept of even and odd numbers, the teacher helps them discuss the meanings they have acquired and use the words "even" and "odd numbers." Children are encouraged to think of examples of even and odd numbers in everyday life—for example, finding partners for class activities or the number of items in a package (socks, candy, gum, and so on). After studying division, children decide that even numbers are divisible by 2 and develop definitions of even and odd numbers.

Constructing the Concept of Multiplication

The instructional objective of this phase of learning-teaching multiplication is to guide learners to abstract the multiplication concept from joining sets of equal size. This interpretation begins the study of multiplication because children are more capable of internalizing ideas from actions than from manipulation of symbols. Some capable learners may be able to grasp the multiplication concept from relating multiplication to repeated addition, but most learners

need to relate actions to number ideas and then later to explore the relation of repeated addition to multiplication.

Teachers emphasize joining sets of equal size in many activities during the prerequisite-understanding phase. The next task is to help children "pull out" the number ideas implicit in their previous experiences. The reader is referred to the plan in Appendix III for examples of introductory lessons and suggestions for extending and consolidating conceptual knowledge. Further ideas are given in the next section.

Extending and Consolidating Knowledge of the Multiplication Concept

Children who can show that multiplication refers to the joining of sets of equal size begin the *generation of facts* under a teacher's guidance or independently. They use objects, rods, skip counting, number lines, number strips, or repeated addition (Figure 6-17). Learners generate facts to 5 × 5 (often in tables), study them, and later generate and study the facts to 9 × 9. Basic fact listings with illustrations are made into books. While learners are producing facts, they learn the generalizations listed below.

The commutative and distributive properties and the zero and factor-is-one rules are useful in generating facts and are introduced before learners complete their books for the 100 multiplication facts. An inductive lesson plan to introduce the distributive property is given in Box 6-6. The distributive property of multiplication over addition is the key to developing multiplication computation rules for use with numbers greater than 10 and is therefore emphasized in instruction.

As children show understanding of the multiplication concept and begin to generate facts, they complete activities and solve problems to extend and consolidate knowledge. Some are

	Example	*Generalization*
a.	$5 \times 3 = 3 \times 5$	Commutative property
b.	$5 \times (3 \times 2) = (5 \times 3) \times 2$	Associative property
c.	$2 \times (5 + 1) = (2 \times 5) + (2 \times 1)$	Distributive property of multiplication over addition
d.	$4 \times 0 = 0$	Zero rule for multiplication
e.	$8 \times 1 = 8$	Factor-is-one rule
f.	$3 \times 4 = 12$ $12 = 3 \times 4$	Symmetry property

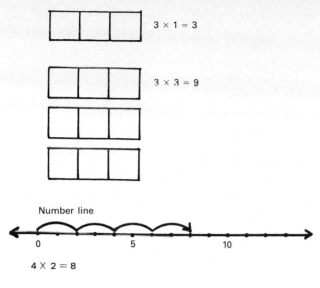

FIGURE 6-17.   Examples of pupils' work to generate facts.

listed below. Teachers can adapt many of these to create new activities and give variety to lessons and independent study.

1. Multiplication patterns on the circle. Draw a circle and write the numerals 0 through 9 at equal intervals around the circle. Say the facts for a table and connect the numerals designating the ones numbers in the products (Figure 6-18a). Various patterns result. The displays help learners recognize the patterns in products in multiplication tables.

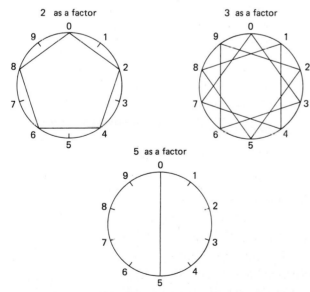

FIGURE 6-18a.   Circle diagrams showing patterns in multiplication tables.

2. Use squared paper to discover patterns in tables (Figure 6-18b).

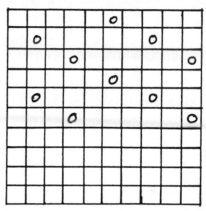

Pattern in table with 4 as a factor

Pattern in table with 6 as a factor

FIGURE 6-18b.   Squared-paper diagrams showing patterns in multiplication tables.

3. "On Your Toes" questions:
    a. Is the product of an even number times an even number ever an odd number (upper grades)?
    b. What can you discover about the product of odd and even numbers? An odd and an odd number (upper grades)?
    c. Why are odd numbers called "odd" (upper grades)?
    d. What number(s) from 1 to 100 is (are) the product(s) of the greatest number of basic facts? The least?
    e. In which decade do the greatest number of basic-fact products fall? The least?

4. Finger multiplication for use with factors greater than 5 (a fun activity). Fingers up to begin. Subtract a factor from 10 and lower the fingers on a hand the number of the remainder. Repeat for the other hand.

BOX 6-6. SAMPLE LESSON: INTRODUCING THE DISTRIBUTIVE PROPERTY OF MULTIPLICATION OVER ADDITION (GRADE 3)

1. Boys and girls, a long time ago a child told me she did not need to learn any multiplication fact greater than 5 × 5. I said I didn't believe that, and she would have to show me. She said she would. This is what she said to convince me.

    5 × 6 is 5 × 5 added to 5 × 1. The product is 25 + 5 = 30.

    4 × 8 is 4 × 5 added to 4 × 3. The product is 20 + 12 = 32.

    3 × 9 is 3 × 5 added to 3 × 4. The product is 15 + 12 = 27.

    5 × 7 is 5 × 5 added to 5 × 2. The product is 25 + 10 = 35.

    What do you think? Does it work? How does it work? (Teacher may need to help pupils realize the second factor is thought of as a sum and each addend is used as a factor with the first factor. The teacher could say: How can we name 6 as a sum? 8? 9? 7? Does that give us a clue to help figure out what the girl was doing? How?)

2. We can call this rule, think-the-parts. Mathematicians call it the distributive property. Let's look at a diagram to understand it better.

5 + 1	5 + 3	5 + 4	5 + 2
..... .	....	....	....
..... .	....	....	....
5	4	3	5 ....
..... .	....		....
..... .			....

    Study these diagrams. How do they show renaming one factor? (They show how to think about one factor as a sum.) Let's study each diagram and tell about it. ... Make a diagram for 4 × 6 and think how to use this rule to get the product. Repeat for 4 × 7.

3. We can write this rule in sentences this way:

    5 × 6 = 5 × (5 + 1) = (5 × 5) + (5 × 1) = 25 + 5 = 30

    4 × 8 = 4 × (5 + 3) = (4 × 5) + (4 × 3) = 20 + 12 = 32

    3 × 9 = 3 × (5 + 4) = (3 × 5) + (3 × 4) = 15 + 12 = 27

    5 × 7 = 5 × (5 + 2) = (5 × 5) + (5 × 2) = 25 + 10 = 35

    Study these sentences. We will talk about how they explain thinking products using this rule. (Pupils will give their ideas in their own words.)

4. Let's write our rule on the chalkboard. We call it the think-the-parts rule. You can call it the distributive property if you wish. (The rule should be similar to: Think one factor as a sum. Multiply each addend by the other factor. Add those products. You can write a sentence this way: 5 × 8 = 5 × (5 + 3) = 25 + 15 = 40.)

5. Try our rule on: 4 × 9 = N; 5 × 9 = N; 3 × 8 = N. Use paper and pencil if you wish. Let's talk about what we did. ... How can this rule help you? ...

6. Some of you might like to figure out how to use our rule on examples like 6 × 6 = N. We will discuss what you have figured out in a few days. Using a diagram can help you.

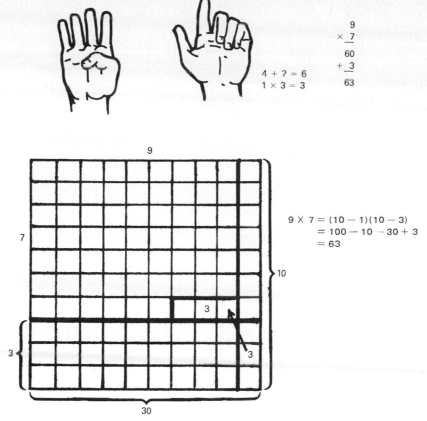

FIGURE 6-19. Example of finger multiplication for 9 × 7.

The sum of the "up" fingers gives the 10s of the product. The product of the "down" fingers on one hand and the "down" fingers on the other hand gives the 1s of the product. (See Figure 6-19.) The diagrams in the figure explain the procedure at a level children can comprehend. For the teacher the logic of finger multiplication is illustrated as follows: $7 \times 9 = (10-3)(10-1) = 100 - 30 - 10 + 3 = 63$.

5. The games FISH, RUMMY, BINGO, DOMINOES, and WAR are played with multiplication facts.

6. Complete assignments such as:
   a. How many facts can you make from the factors 2, 3, 4 each used at least one time (upper grades)?
   b. What common factors are named in facts with products (upper grades):

       18, 4, 10?

       16, 8, 12?

       9, 27, 18?

   c. What basic-fact products have 2 in the ones place? (Answer: 2, 12, 32, 42, 72.) What are the factors of these products?

   d. Complete these sentences.

       $3 \times 7 = (\underline{\quad} \times 10) + \underline{\quad}$

       $4 \times 9 = 4 (\underline{\quad} + \underline{\quad})$

       $4 \times 3 \underline{\quad} 3 \times 4$

       $5(7) = 5(\underline{\quad}) + 5(\underline{\quad})$

   e. How can 5×5 be used to think new facts? Discussion of pupils' work follows completion of assignment.

7. Oral or written work involving skip counting with predicting: What is the first number in the 40s you will reach in counting by 4s? What is the first number in the 50s you will reach in counting by 3s? What is the last number in the 60s you will reach in counting by 5s?

   As noted in parentheses, some of the activities given are useful in extending and consolidating understanding of multiplication in the upper grades. Gifted learners in primary or middle grades could be challenged by activities such as these.

Before children begin division, they should have immediate recall of the multiplication facts to 5 × 5 and be in the process of mastering the facts through 9. Teachers evaluate progress of learners before they introduce division facts. Gifted learners, however, could learn multiplication and division facts together.

LEARNING AND TEACHING DIVISION

Meaning of Division

Division is the inverse of multiplication. If $a \times b = c$, then $c \div a = b$ and $c \div b = a$.

In a division sentence the names for the numbers are:

$$8 \quad \div \quad 2 \quad = \quad 4$$

dividend ÷ divisor = quotient

(product) ÷ (factor) = (missing factor)

Division is often difficult for children. They must be given enough time to internalize the division concept and memorize the facts. Even though children understand and can retrieve addition, subtraction, and multiplication facts, recall of division facts is not immediate for most children. They must have experiences that stress the meaning of division and the rehearsal of facts. Learning division is discussed in this section in terms of the subtopics used in the other sections.

Division is interpreted in five ways: (1) measurement situation, (2) partitive situation, (3) repeated subtraction, (4) missing factor, and (5) ratio (Figure 6-20).

The first two interpretations relate division to set separation. A **measurement situation** involves the separation of a set into subsets, each with the same given number of elements: If 12 objects are separated into subsets each with 4 elements, how many subsets will result? A verbal problem that describes a measurement situation is: The teacher has 16 crayons. If each child receives 4 crayons, how many children will have crayons?

The **partitive situation** deals with the separation of a set into a given number of subsets, each with the same number of elements: If 8 objects are divided into 2 subsets, each with the same number of elements, how many elements

(1) $8 \div 4 = 2$
Measurement interpretation: How many 4s = 8? Two 4s = 8.

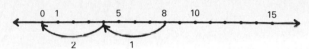

(2) $8 \div 4 = 2$
Partitive interpretation: If 8 is divided into 4 equivalent sets, what is the number of each set? 2

(3) $8 \div 4 = 2$
How many 4s = 8? Use repeated subtraction.

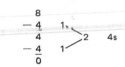

(4)   N × 4 = 8 can be written 8 ÷ 4 = N because multiplication and division are inverse operations.

(5)   Ratio interpretation:

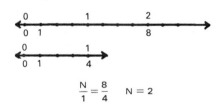

$$\frac{N}{1} = \frac{8}{4} \quad N = 2$$

FIGURE 6-20.   Various interpretations of division.

are in each subset? A verbal problem involving the partitive situation is: Jane has 15 Christmas seals. She wants to put the same number on each of 5 envelopes. How many will she glue on each envelope?

The **repeated-subtraction interpretation** of division relates division and subtraction. It can be used to help learners find the answer to questions such as: How many 6s equals 12?

$$
\begin{array}{r}
12 \\
- \ 6 \\
\hline
6 \\
- \ 6 \\
\hline
0
\end{array}
$$

Repeated subtraction enables a learner to find the answer in a measurement division situation using numbers rather than sets.

The **missing-factor interpretation** helps learners relate division and multiplication: How many 4s equals 8? ($N \times 4 = 8$.) Many children and adults find this approach for learning division easier than the $8 \div 4 = N$ format.

The **ratio interpretation** is a how-many-times comparison: 18 is how many times greater than 9? A verbal problem involving ratio comparison is: Fred is 10 years old. Jim is 5 years old. Fred is how many times older than Jim? This interpretation of division is not taught until the late elementary school years or the junior high school grades.

Prerequisite Understanding for Division

Before beginning the study of division, teachers consider learners' prerequisite knowledge and attitudes toward learning. Children must have achieved success in their work in addition, subtraction, and multiplication to set high expectations for their learning of division. Chil-

dren who know they have not done well in mathematics generally do not "try harder" to learn division. Therefore, we recommend that division not be introduced until learners have made satisfactory progress in learning the other operations and are confident of their ability to succeed in learning division.

The list below gives the knowledge to be attained and examples of assessment questions.

If children do not show readiness to begin division, the activities and games discussed earlier can be adapted and reintroduced. Several new games are:

EVEN SHARE. Children play in groups of two to six. There is a score card for each child. A stack of 24 to 36 cards displaying arrays of 3, 4, 5, 6, 8, 9, 10, 12, or 15 objects is in front of the players with cards face down. Children take turns picking a card from the top of the stack. As a player picks a card, the child to the right says: "Share evenly with 2 (or 3, 4, or 5)." The player with the array card says: "I can share . . . (the number of objects in the array) with . . . (the number given). Each will get . . . ." Or, "I cannot share . . . with . . . ." If the others agree that the statement is correct,

Knowledge	*Assessment Example*
1. A number can be represented by the union of equivalent sets.	Here are some strip cards (or rods) showing sets of 2, 3, 4, 5, and 6. Make a set to show 8, 12, 15, 10. (Observe the child's performance to determine understanding and confidence. Note any trial-and-error behavior.)
2. A number can be represented by removing subsets from a set.	Here is an array of 12 (14, 10, 16). How many sets of 3 counters (2, 5, 4 counters) can you make? What did you think to answer my question?
3. Manipulate objects to partition a given set into a designated number of subsets that are equivalent.	Here are 8 (6, 10, 12) pieces of candy. Show how 2 (3, 5, 4) children would share the candy evenly.
4. In one minute can recall 30 (of 33) correct facts for addition and subtraction; satisfactory progress in multiplication facts to 5×5; showing progress in learning multiplication facts 6–9.	Paper-and-pencil test.
5. Story problems involving addition, subtraction, and multiplication are solved correctly.	Story problems given orally or in writing.

the player makes tallies on his or her card corresponding to the number each would receive. If there is not an "even share" possible, no tallies are made. The array cards that have been played are put in a discard stack. The player with the most tallies when the playing stack is depleted wins.

HOP TO ZERO. The game is for two children. Each child has a number line to 30 on a sheet of acetate. The marks made by a player on the acetate should be erasable so the number line can be reused. There are 20 cards face down in front of the players. The cards give directions such as: Hop from 20 by 5s. Or, Hop from 13 by 4s. Following the directions may or may not enable a player to reach zero. The players take cards at the same time, and they mark the number lines according to the directions. The players check each other's work. If a player hops to 0, he or she gets a point. If the directions are written so that a player does not reach 0, he or she gets no point. The cards that have been played are laid aside. When the stack of playing cards is depleted, the game ends. The player with the most points wins. (Players may pick up counters to indicate points.)

FROGS IN THE POND. Two to four players have a supply of frog-shaped markers in the frog cage (small box). Each player has a playing board showing a path to 40 (number line) leading to a blue pond (zero on the number line). The direction cards (20–25) are face down in front of the players. The players take cards in turn. The cards give directions such as: Jump frog from 9 by 4s to the pond. Or, jump frog from 16 by 2s to the pond. The player reads his or her card, takes a frog marker, and jumps the frog (by 2s, 3s, 4s, or 5s) as directed, skip-counting as the frog jumps. If the frog lands in the pond (0), it stays there. If the frog cannot get to the pond, it goes back into the frog cage. After a card is read, it is laid aside. When the playing card stack is depleted, the player with the most frogs in his or her pond wins.

Constructing the Concept of Division

The measurement interpretation of division is used to introduce learners to the concept of division and the basic facts. A lesson plan to use in the introduction is given in Box 6-7. The measurement interpretation is used because it is the easiest to represent with concrete objects: learners can manipulate objects or rods in ways that parallel this meaning of division and begin to abstract the division concept.

In the introductory lesson both forms for reading and writing facts were mentioned, but one was emphasized. It is recommended that pupils have an awareness of both forms from the beginning, because they may converse with other children and with parents who may use the form not emphasized. At no time should pupils be completely unfamiliar with the variety of language forms that are used with the division concept. Since the "how many . . . " language conveys the meaning of the measurement situation used in the introductory lesson, that language is emphasized in beginning lessons. Partitive language is used more frequently as children are introduced to partitive situations and are able to recall both language forms for discussing division.

When children can show the meaning of division facts with materials, they are ready for instruction at the next phase.

Extending and Consolidating Knowledge of the Division Concept

Pupils begin to extend understanding of division by generating facts for division-fact books. Soon after this activity is undertaken, learners study the repeated subtraction and inverse-operation interpretations of division to assist them in their work of generating all the division facts. The facts to $25 \div 5 = N$ are studied first; pupils generate the facts, use activities, and employ the test-study-retest procedure. The facts with dividends to 81 are emphasized after learners have had the opportunity for work with the easy division facts.

The *inverse* nature of multiplication and division is an important understanding. It is developed as learners work with generating basic facts. A lesson to introduce this idea can begin with the questions: Can we use our multiplication books to help us write and remember division facts? How? Children explain their ideas and are asked to use objects or diagrams to show what they mean. Pupils are encouraged to use multiplication tables to produce division facts.

Some learners begin to verbalize division questions, such as $20 \div 4 = N$: What number times 4 equals 20? Or, 4 times what number equals 20? This is noted and commended. The missing-factor mathematical sentence ($N \times 4 = 20$; $4 \times N = 20$) is related to this language. All learners are helped to recognize the sentence as a division sentence. If some pupils do not spontaneously use the missing-factor language, teachers can say, "I know a child who says the division-fact question this way: What number times 8 equals 24? What do you think of it? Why? . . . You can use it if you like. It really helps some people with division."

BOX 6-7. *SAMPLE LESSON: INTRODUCING DIVISION (GRADE 3)*

1. Boys and girls, today we are going to learn another way to think about numbers. It is division. You should be pleased that you know so much that you can learn about division.

2. (Pass out a sheet of paper with arrays as shown here. Each pupil is also given a scissors.

```
. . . .   X X X X X   O O O   Z Z
. . . .   X X X X X   O O O   Z Z
. . . .   X X X X X   O O O   Z Z
          X X X X X   O O O   Z Z
                      O O O   Z Z
                              Z Z )
```

3. Look at the first array of dots. How many dots are in the array? (12.) Use your scissors to find how many 4-dot sets show 12 dots. What have you found out? (There are three 4-dot sets in an array of 12.) How did you discover this? (Cut out 4-dot sets.)

4. (Use same questioning sequence for the other arrays.)

5. To find the answers to all my questions what did you do? Think of as many ways as you can to tell about what you did and what you thought. (Cut out . . . Took apart . . . Removed . . . Separated . . . sets of the same size from the array.)

6. Everything you have said makes us think about separating sets of the same size from a group of objects. When we think about only the numbers in this kind of task, we are thinking division. We write the division fact one of two ways:

$$4\overline{)12}^{3} \quad \text{or} \quad 12 \div 4 = 3$$

For either fact, we can say: How many 4s = 12? Three 4s = 12, or 12 divided by 4 = 3. For today we will use the first way to write the fact. We will read it: How many 4s equals 12? Three 4s equals 12.

7. Let's write the facts for the other three examples we worked with this morning and read them.

8. Make up a division fact and share it with your neighbor. You may need to use the counters in your desk. When you finish sharing, make up another one and share. (After pupils have worked independently for a short time, they share their facts with the group. Each is written on the board, read, and shown with counters.)

9. Boys and girls, this is a great day! You have learned about the last kind of facts in mathematics. This is a day to remember.

The partitive interpretation of division is introduced after learners demonstrate that they can use the measurement idea to solve division story problems. If pupils can differentiate addition, subtraction, multiplication, and measurement ideas of division in solving story problems, they are ready for the new notion of partitive division situations. Problems and objects are used in the introduction to stress the "equal sharing" concept.

Division is neither commutative nor associative. Children are introduced to these ideas as appropriate to their level of learning. Children who must spend considerable time understanding the division concept, generating facts, and memorizing them would not have time in the middle grades to study all the mathematical ideas related to division that would be taught to children who conceptualize quickly.

The generalizations learned are listed below, together with examples.

The distributive property of division over addition is the basis for division computation rules. However, these rules can be explained in terms of repeated subtraction. Pupils are taught the distributive property of division in the middle grades if warranted by their ability and interest in mathematics. The zero rule is useful as a tool for remembering facts and is introduced as soon as possible. Intuitive understanding of the symmetry property is encouraged.

Exercises to extend understanding are patterned after the following assignments. Story problems are also used.

1. Which number(s) between 10 and 90 is (are) the dividend(s) in the most basic facts? (Answer: 12, 18, and 24.)

2. Which number(s) from 1 to 9 is (are) the quotient(s) in the most facts? (Answer: They are all the same—a quotient 9 times.)

3. Which numbers between 10 and 90 are dividends for only one basic fact? (Answer: 25, 49, 64, and 81.)

4. Put these dividends in groups so that all in a group belong together:

$$42 \quad 16 \quad 35 \quad 32 \quad 56 \quad 20 \quad 8 \quad 14$$

Pupils should spend time studying division facts using the test-study-retest procedure and adaptations of activities and games mentioned in connection with the other operations. While learners are studying facts, division with remainders is introduced.

Division with remainders occurs when the dividend is not a multiple of the divisor—for example, $2\overline{)13}$. The concept can be introduced by giving learners four examples of "uneven division" with the direction to find the answers using counters, number lines, or thinking. After learners have worked a short time, the teacher asks, "What's going on here? What do you notice?" Pupils' replies and further teacher questions help learners recognize that: (1) the examples are not basic facts; (2) basic facts can be used to obtain a quotient, but a number will be "left over"; (3) the answer considered correct is the one in which the number "left over" is smaller than the divisor in the example; and (4) the form used is:

$$\begin{array}{r} 5r2 \\ 3\overline{)17} \\ -15 \\ \hline 2 \end{array}$$

or,

$$\begin{array}{r} 5 \\ 3\overline{)17} \\ -15 \\ \hline 2 \end{array}$$

if learners cannot do the calculations mentally.

Example	*Generalization*
a. $12 \div 4 = (8 + 4) \div 4$ $= (8 \div 4) + (4 \div 4)$ $= 2 + 1$ $= 3$	Distributive property of division over addition
b. $0 \div 5 = 0$	Zero rule for division
c. $10 \div 5 = 2$ $2 = 10 \div 5$	Symmetry property

The remainder in "uneven division" can be interpreted in different ways, depending on the question asked. In a partitive situation, the quotient is a number in mixed form. (Jan has 7 cookies. She shares them evenly with a friend. How many does each get? $3\frac{1}{2}$.) In a measurement situation, the remainder is a whole number but must be interpreted in light of the problem situation. (Nine people are going on a scout trip. A car holds 5 people. How many cars will be needed? Not 1 car with four people remaining! The sensible answer is 2 cars.) For most children the first task is to understand an "uneven division" example. Later, when dealing with story problems, the interpretations of the remainder are emphasized.

In applications, division is often "inexact." Therefore, children must have help in mastering "uneven division." The games, HOP TO ZERO and FROG IN THE POND discussed for developing readiness can be adapted for practice in giving answers in "uneven division" exercises. Good study exercises are: (1) What basic fact comes to mind when you think each sentence? Write it below the mathematical sentence: $17 \div 8 = N$; $15 \div 2 = N$; $29 \div 7 = N$. (2) What different numbers can be given for N in $N \div 4$ to make it a division-with-remainder question? Children should also write story problems for division with remainders.

REINTRODUCTION TO THE OPERATIONS

Children are reintroduced to the four operations after they initially learn these concepts. Forgetting is a common experience, and review of meanings and basic facts is necessary. Furthermore, reintroduction deepens understanding. In one sense, the extending and consolidating phase continues for many years. Understanding is enriched as the operations are studied in new settings and used to solve new problems.

Usually the operations that have been learned in previous years are reintroduced after summer vacation and when children demonstrate they have forgotten meanings and facts. Children are also reintroduced to operations when they study computation. For example, when children study addition, subtraction, multiplication, and division with fractions, they reconsider the meanings of the operations.

This section gives suggestions for reintroducing the meanings of the operations and for guiding learners to study for recall of the facts.

There are several approaches to helping children *reconstruct the meaning* of an operation. One way is to suggest pupils use *materials to illustrate the solutions to story problems.* Working with materials helps many learners reexamine the sense of an operation. Discussion between two learners or among a small group of children working with the teacher helps pupils recreate concepts of operations as they use materials to solve problems.

Children who have never made *fact books* can engage in this activity as a reintroduction to the meaning of an operation. Teachers with whom the author has worked report that this activity has been very successful in reintroducing an operation.

Comparing operations is an excellent way to reintroduce the concepts. There are at least three ways to design lessons to compare operations: (1) Assign verbal problems to be classified by operations involved. Questions asked include: How are these problems alike? Different? What helped you decide? (2) Ask learners to classify diagrams such as number lines according to the operations represented. This approach provides an opportunity for upper-grade learners both to use materials and to compare the meanings of the operations. (3) Learners discuss and compare the meanings of the operations using teacher-prepared questions. Questions are similar to: What operation is related to addition? How? (Subtraction or multiplication, depending on explanation.) If you forget how to divide, what can you do? If you forgot all the basic facts except those for one operation, which operation would you choose not to forget? Why?

Review of basic facts employs direct study techniques such as the test-study-retest procedures. The study-plan aspect of the procedure is used particularly with facts shown on a test to have been forgotten. Children are also guided to assume responsibility for relearning the basic facts. To assist children to set and fulfill expectations, teachers provide opportunities for them to make charts of their objectives and their progress in learning basic facts.

The games mentioned previously in this chapter can be adapted to include basic facts for the four operations. FISH, RUMMY, SMILING FACE, WAR, DOMINOES, and BOARD AND DICE (SPINNER) games are all easily adapted to include facts for all operations. Another approach to reviewing basic facts in games is to provide learners with opportunities to pair numbers to obtain a sum, difference, product, or quotient according to the demands of the game situation. Several games of this type are described below.

RED AND WHITE. The materials for this game consist of red cards and white cards. Each of the 40–75 white cards has a red numeral from 0 to 9. Each of the 39 or more red cards shows a white numeral: 0, 1, 2, 3, 4, 5, 6, 7, 8, 9, 10, 11, 12, 13, 14, 15, 16, 17, 18, 20, 21, 24, 25, 27, 28, 30, 32, 35, 36, 40, 42, 45, 48, 49, 54, 56, 63, 72, or 81. Two to six children play. The number of white and red cards is adjusted accordingly. Each player receives white cards; the others are in the draw stack, face down. The red cards are face down beside the draw stack. The players take turns turning a red card over. The first player who uses the numbers shown on 2 of his or her cards to make a fact question answered by the number shown on the red card takes the red card and lays the 2 cards aside. If no player can make the number, all players draw another card from the draw stack. The game continues until a player is out of cards. The player with the most red cards at the end of the game wins.

ISLAND LANDINGS. Each player has markers representing his or her boats. The playing board consists of free-form islands (25–50), each showing a numeral. (The numerals used are the same as on the red cards in RED AND WHITE.) Two to six children play. Children take turns tossing two dice. If a player can use the numbers shown on the dice to make a number shown by a numeral on an island, he or she lands a boat on the island. When a player has boats on 10 islands, the game ends and that player is the winner. (The first boat on an island claims the island. No other boat may land on the island.)

BASIC FACTS FUN. Basic-fact cards as shown in Figure 6-21 are used in this game. Two children shuffle the cards, divide them, and take turns displaying a card and giving the answers. If a player can give all the facts on the card, he or she keeps the card. If not, the card is put in a separate stack. When the basic-fact cards have all been tried, the player with the most cards wins.

Teachers have major responsibilities for helping learners set attainable objectives for memorizing facts, providing suitable learning activities, and encouraging and supporting children in their efforts. The children, however, must exert the effort required to learn. Learners are helped to realize that their achievement is related to their effort.

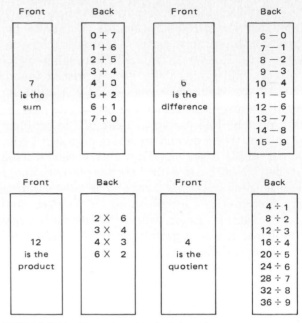

FIGURE 6-21. Examples of basic-fact cards.

SUMMARY

An instructional design for the four fundamental operations has been presented in this chapter. The design is based on cognitive theories of concept learning and follows the three-phase learning-teaching sequence. The teacher's first step in implementing the design is to insure pupils have developed prerequisite understanding for the study of a number operation. Next, teachers guide learners to construct the meaning of an operation by abstracting number ideas from the manipulation of sets of objects. When learners grasp the meaning of an operation, they generate facts by applying their understanding of the concept. To insure that concepts are internalized and can be applied to life situations, learners study the generalizations for an operation, learn various interpretations of the operation, solve problems, and study for recall. A variety of cognitive processes are encouraged in the activities and games designed to further the development of meaning and recall.

As learning the fundamental operations is crucial to the further study of mathematics and other subjects, children are helped to understand these number concepts and remember the basic facts. Teachers help learners set expectations for their learning. They encourage them to exert effort to learn, and they are supportive of children's work. In guiding learners to attain knowledge of the operations, teachers evaluate to determine individual differences in cognitive processes and achievement. They take these differences into account in planning learning experiences. They also attend to pupils' differing motivations for learning. This chapter has many suggestions for lessons, activities, and games to aid teachers in their work.

STUDY QUESTIONS

1. Ask at least three teachers how they feel about pupils' counting to obtain answers to basic-fact questions. Do you agree with them? Why or why not? What are the implications of your ideas for teaching elementary school children?

2. Discuss with other students the reasons for having children make basic-fact books for each of the operations. Do you anticipate any problems in this activity? Why or why not? How would you solve them?

3. Write a lesson for introducing the missing-addend concept, using an inductive procedure. (For the procedure to be inductive, what criteria must be met?) Exchange your plan with another student and explain why your plan uses an inductive procedure.

4. Make a board-and-dice game to review the basic facts for any or all of the operations. As you plan the activity, ask yourself what comprehension can be deepened along with rehearsal.

5. How would you determine whether or not children have an intuitive understanding of subtraction? (Any of the interpretations of subtraction will do.) If they do not, what learning activities would you plan for them? Compare your ideas with those of another student.

6. Write a lesson plan using an inductive or deductive questioning method and materials to teach the associative property of multiplication. (This property is often called the grouping rule.) Compare your plan with that of another student. How are the plans alike? Different?

7. Which approach for reintroduction of an operation do you think would be most motivating to learners? Why? Do other students agree with you? Why or why not?

8. How would you plan for children to set expectations for learning addition? Division? Are these two plans alike? Why or why not?

REFERENCES

Davis, Edward J., "Suggestions for Teaching the Basic Facts of Arithmetic," in *Developing Computational Skills*, 1978 Yearbook of the National Council of Teachers of Mathematics, eds. Marilyn N. Suydam and Robert E. Reys. Reston, VA: The National Council of Teachers of Mathematics, Inc., 1978.

Horak, Virginia M., and Willis J. Horak, "The Versatile Hundred Board," *Arithmetic Teacher*, 30, no. 2 (October 1982), 10-16.

Lazerick, Beth E., "Mastering Basic Facts of Addition: An Alternate Strategy," *Arithmetic Teacher*, 28, no. 7 (March 1981), 20-24.

Nuffield Foundation, *Mathematics Begins*. New York: John Wiley, 1967.

Rathmell, Edward C., "Using Thinking Strategies to Teach the Basic Facts," in *Developing Computational Skills*, 1978 Yearbook of the National Council of Teachers of Mathematics, eds. Marilyn N. Suydam and Robert E. Reys. Reston, VA: The National Council of Teachers of Mathematics, Inc., 1978.

Underhill, Bob, *Teaching Elementary School Mathematics*, 3d ed., chaps. 8, 10. Columbus, OH: Charles E. Merrill Publishing Company, 1981.

7 LEARNING AND TEACHING COMPUTATION RULES FOR WHOLE NUMBERS

Computation rules for whole numbers, called **algorithms**, are procedures that give a standard (decimal) numeral for an indicated sum, difference, product, or quotient in which at least one of the addends or factors is greater than 10. Algorithms are shortcuts for proofs (Boxes 7-1a and 7-1b). The first section of this chapter is an overview of teaching and learning algorithms for whole numbers. Other sections discuss computation rules for addition, subtraction, multiplication, and division.

OVERVIEW

An effective use of a computation rule to obtain a standard numeral requires that the steps be carried out routinely. However, routine manipulations, as noted by Skemp (1971), are not rote processes that lack meaning. Persons performing routine manipulations *comprehend* the process and can explain its meaning at any time.

Computation rules are based on certain relations among concepts and properties. When children understand an algorithm, they comprehend, at least in an informal way, the rationale of the procedure. During middle childhood many children are able to think logically, although their logic is not rigorous. They can comprehend the reasons for the steps in an algorithm and then use concrete and graphic materials to verify their ideas. Learning in the enactive and iconic modes can give credence to conclusions attained by reasoning, as well as aid in forming concepts and generalizations. In the late primary and postprimary years, an interplay among modes of assimilation can become as important in learning as the enactive, iconic, and symbolic sequence of incorporating information.

Chapter 13 discusses using hand-held calculators in computation. Intelligent use of the hand-held calculator depends on grasping the meaning of the rules and attaining certain skills in computing. These learning-teaching responsibilities are discussed in this chapter.

From a learning point of view, computation rules are generalizations. Therefore the plan for learning concepts and generalizations applies to algorithms. Using the three-phase instructional sequence to learn and teach computation rules is discussed in general terms in the remainder of this section. Later sections of this chapter deal specifically with algorithms for each operation.

Developing Prerequisite Understanding

Comprehending and using computation rules depends on relating certain previously acquired understandings and skills. Before beginning the learning-teaching sequence for an algorithm, teachers assess knowledge in five areas: (1) understanding of the meaning of an operation; (2) comprehension and mastery of the basic facts for the operation; (3) comprehension of base-10 and place-value concepts and renaming of numbers using these concepts; (4) mental calculation involving multiples of powers of 10 and estimation; and (5) knowledge of concepts and properties relevant to the algorithms for the operation. These prerequisite understandings are discussed in turn.

*BOX 7-1a. ADDITION AND SUBTRACTION ALGORITHMS:
SHORT AND LONG FORMS AND RATIONALES*

Addition Algorithms

Short Form

$$\begin{array}{r} 46 \\ + 48 \\ \hline 94 \end{array}$$

Long Form

$$\begin{array}{r} 46 \\ + 48 \\ \hline 14 \\ + 80 \\ \hline 94 \end{array}$$

Rationale (Proof)

$46 = 40 + 6$	By expanded notation
$+ 48 = 40 + 8$	By expanded notation
$\qquad\quad 80 + 14$	By knowledge of facts and decimal notation
$= 80 + (10 + 4)$	By expanded notation
$= (80 + 10) + 4$	By the associative property
$= 90 + 4$	By knowledge of facts and decimal notation
$= 94$	By decimal notation

Subtraction Algorithms

Short Form

$$\begin{array}{r} 94 \\ - 48 \\ \hline 46 \end{array}$$

Long Form

$$\begin{array}{r} {}^{8}\cancel{9}\,{}^{1}4 \\ - \quad 4\ 8 \\ \hline 6 \\ + \quad 4\ 0 \\ \hline 4\ 6 \end{array}$$

Rationale (Proof)

$94 =$	$(90 + 4) =$	$(80 + 14)$	By expanded notation and renaming
$- 48 = $	$- (40 + 8) =$	$- (40 + 8)$	By expanded notation
	$=$	$40 + 6$	By knowledge of facts and decimal notation
	$=$	46	By decimal notation

Understanding the *meaning* of an operation gives meaning to algorithms for that operation. Of course, prior knowledge of the operation is enriched by learning computation rules, but if children cannot attach meaning to an operation, instruction in computation rarely enables them to construct the concept of the operation. Understanding an operation therefore precedes the study of algorithms for that operation. If assessment demonstrates that pupils do not have knowledge of an operation, the operation is reintroduced before work with computation rules for it is undertaken.

Without immediate *recall* of the basic facts, learners cannot use algorithms expeditiously. The basic facts must be used as tools, effortlessly and without hesitation. Children should not experience failure in computation because they do not know the facts. Previous chapters have stressed instruction to insure mastery of basic facts. Children may need further study of facts before they learn the algorithms.

Learning *base 10 and place values* and renaming numbers using these concepts was discussed in Chapter 5. The activities to enable children to learn renaming are usually used

---

BOX 7-1b. MULTIPLICATION AND DIVISION ALGORITHMS: SHORT AND LONG FORMS AND RATIONALES

Multiplication Algorithms

Short Form	Rationale (Proof)

$$
\begin{array}{r} 12 \\ \times\ 4 \\ \hline 48 \end{array}
$$

$4 \times 12 =$

$(10 + 2)$ By expanded notation
$\underline{\times\ 4}$

$\underline{40 + 8} =$ By the distributive property of multiplication over addition, knowledge of facts, and decimal notation

Long Form

$$
\begin{array}{r} 12 \\ \times\ 4 \\ \hline 8 \\ +\ 40 \\ \hline 48 \end{array}
$$

48   By decimal notation

Division Algorithms

Short Form	Rationale (Proof)

$$
\begin{array}{r} 12 \\ 4\overline{)48} \end{array}
$$

$\dfrac{48}{4} =$

Long Form

$$
4\overline{)48}
$$

$$
\begin{array}{r} -40 \quad 10 \\ \hline 8 \\ -8 \ +\ 2 \\ \hline 0 \quad 12 \end{array}
$$

$\dfrac{40 + 8}{4} =$ By expanded notation

$\dfrac{40}{4} + \dfrac{8}{4} =$ By the distributive property of division over addition

$10 + 2 =$ By knowledge of facts and decimal notation

12 By decimal notation

---

again just prior to introduction of algorithms for an operation.

Skill in *mental computation* with multiples of powers of 10 and estimation are important prerequisites for studying computation. Mental calculation is required in many computations. Estimating before computing gives meaning to the process and enables a learner to provide his or her own feedback and to self-correct, when necessary. Mental computation and estimation are emphasized in the middle grades and reintroduced if necessary in the upper grades. If children cannot mentally compute and estimate, the introduction of algorithms is delayed and

mental computation with multiples of powers of 10 and estimation are reintroduced. In Chapter 5 we have given suggestions for instruction in these areas. Additional activities for multiplication and division mental computation and estimation will be given in this chapter.

The *properties* for the operations are introduced during the extension phase of the teaching of any number operation. This has been discussed in earlier chapters. A comprehension of the commutative and associative properties of addition and multiplication and the distributive property of multiplication over addition enhances the meaning of computational procedures. Children should have been given opportunities to learn and use these properties, at least intuitively, when developing facts. If they did not have these opportunities, teachers introduce the properties before computation rules are to be learned and taught. It is also expected children will be familiar with the concept of inverse operations and know that addition-subtraction and multiplication-division are inverse operations.

Constructing Computation Rules

Computation rules for whole numbers are usually introduced during grades three and four. Addition and subtraction algorithms are first studied in grade three; multiplication and division, in grade four.

Instruction for constructing computation rules stresses the *meanings* of algorithms. Children are guided to relate prior learning to achieve meaning. Whenever possible, questions and comments guide children to make inferences to comprehend algorithms.

If learners cannot do relational thinking and make inferences, teachers use materials to give learners an intuitive understanding of the steps in the algorithm. Children develop meaning by manipulating objects or studying pictures and use numerals and symbols to make records of actions and observations. Teachers help these learners develop the logical sense of algorithms at a later time.

To guide all learners to understand computation rules, teachers frequently begin lessons by asking children to classify and compare examples of computational exercises in terms of "old" and "new" learning. Teachers can ask learners to list what they know. The material that has been learned in any mode is reviewed so that it can be reorganized to give meaning to new rules. Inductive and deductive instructional procedures are used to help learners bring ideas into new relationships. The long (extended) algorithms are always presented in introductory lessons as meaningful records of thought or action.

During the time learners are developing the meaning of algorithms, concrete and graphic materials are often used to give them opportunities to expand awareness. The abacus and squared paper are especially helpful materials for representing the steps in algorithms.

Before moving to activities to extend and consolidate learning, teachers determine if children can give reasons for steps in a computation rule as well as use the rule to complete 2 to 5 exercises correctly. For example, a child could explain that to compute in an addition exercise it is necessary to work with 1s and 10s separately and then add the partial sums. Some children demonstrate comprehension using materials.

Extending and Consolidating Knowledge

At least nine approaches to extending learning and consolidating knowledge of algorithms are used by teachers for one or more operations:

1. Guide learners to find checks for their solutions.
2. Introduce shortcut (standard) algorithms to be used in place of the extended algorithms first presented.
3. Extend rules to use with examples involving sums of multiples of higher powers of 10.
4. Give experiences with different algorithms.
5. Help learners find approaches to completing computations with missing figures.
6. Use real-life problems that involve the computations being learned to complete solutions.
7. Continue to use materials in ways that enable learners to make translations among concrete, graphic, and symbolic representations of ideas.
8. Assign a limited number of exercises for practice of standard algorithms with emphasis on estimation, accuracy, and checking. (Mastery is 9 of 10 examples correct in a number of minutes that is too few for pupils to count basic fact answers.)
9. Provide learners with opportunities to write examples in working with algorithms and to share their examples.

In the sections that follow, instruction for each operation employing the three-phase instructional sequence will be discussed.

LEARNING AND TEACHING ADDITION COMPUTATION

In learning and teaching addition computation with paper and pencil, the examples always include addends that are greater than 10. The examples in which one addend is less than 10 (such as $19 + 3 = N$) are learned as mental calculations. Pupils are also urged to compute mentally when one addend is a multiple of a power of 10 and the other a sum of multiples of powers of 10 (for example, $300 + 341 = N$). Initial learning of paper-and-pencil addition computation is with 10s plus 1s, in which the sum of the 1s is less than 10 (for example, $23 + 42$). Pupils next study sums in which the sum of the 1s is greater than 10 (such as $48 + 23 = N$), and renaming 1s as 10 plus 1s is required. Later lessons introduce finding sums in which the addends are 100s and the sum of the 1s, 10s, or both is greater than 10 (for example, $235 + 128 = N$; $342 + 271 = N$; and $658 + 148 = N$), and renaming is required. Exercises with more than two addends (column addition) are also studied. This section deals with developing prerequisite understanding, constructing computation rules, and extending and consolidating knowledge of addition computation.

Developing Prerequisite Understanding for Addition Computation

Teachers do not begin instruction in addition computation if learners do not have prerequisite knowledge: understanding of the meaning of addition, immediate recall of basic addition facts, understanding of base and place values and of renaming numbers using these concepts, skill in mental addition with multiples of powers of 10 and estimation of sums, and an intuitive understanding that the order and grouping of addends (commutative and associative properties) do not affect sums. Teachers assess to determine learners' knowledge of prerequisites. *Assessment* is usually in the form of tests. The prerequisite concepts and skills are reintroduced if pupils show they have forgotten them.

Prerequisite understanding for addition computation (particularly column addition) also includes skill in adding by endings. Adding by endings refers to mental computation when one addend is less than 10 and the other is greater than 10. The sum of the 1s may be less than 10 (for example, $16 + 2 = N$; $30 + 4 = N$) or equal to or greater than 10 (for example, $34 + 6 = N$; $13 + 9 = N$). Adding by endings is also called **higher-decade addition,** without or with bridging the 10s. Children should develop skill in higher-decade addition, because such skill is required in computing with whole numbers and fractional numbers. It is introduced prior to computation in which the addends are sums of 10s plus 1s.

The computational procedure for higher-decade addition is less demanding if a rule is used: The 1s in the sum are equal to the 1s in the basic fact used to compute the higher-decade addition answer; the 10(s) in the sum are equal to or one greater than the 10(s) in the greater addend. For example, $35 + 3 = N$, think $8 + 30 = 38$; $39 + 9 = N$, think $8 + 40 = 48$.

A lesson to teach either type of higher-decade addition often includes recognizing patterns in endings, such as $2 + 5 = 7$, $12 + 5 = 17$, $22 + 5 = 27$, $32 + 5 = 37$, ..., $92 + 5 = 97$. If children say the sentences in unison in a rhythmic pattern, they usually recognize the importance of focusing on the basic fact and the 10 given or the 10 one greater than given. Materials can also be used to illustrate that in higher-decade addition examples, the 10(s) in the sum are either the same or one greater than the 10(s) of an addend. The abacus can be used effectively to represent the rule (Figure 7-1).

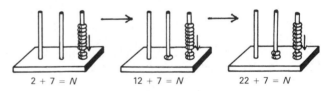

$2 + 7 = N$ $12 + 7 = N$ $22 + 7 = N$

What is the same? Different?

FIGURE 7-1. Using an abacus for the study of the higher-decade addition rule.

Some learners prefer the "making of tens" method for higher-decade addition with bridging: $45 + 8 = 45 + (5 + 3) = (45 + 5) + 3 = 50 + 3$. This series of steps can be introduced to children in an inductive lesson. The comment is made that while it seems longer, some children like it better.

Higher-decade addition is learned as a mental process; its practice stresses writing sums to exercises given orally. Team work in which children help each other learn by using a sheet of examples with answers prepared by the teacher or pupils is one approach to rehearsal. Children can also use an hourglass egg timer with the examples sheet, covering the answer and working to "Beat the Timer." The old games can now include higher-decade addition examples. Children should be helped to set expectations for achievement in higher-decade addition and be given recognition when they have fulfilled their expectations.

Constructing Addition Computation Rules

This phase of instruction stresses the meaning of the steps in the algorithm. Many children can create meaning by reasoning informally about the procedures. They verify their ideas as they work with materials. Some children, however, will learn the algorithm using materials to develop the steps. The simplest computational exercises are studied first; these involve 10s plus 1s, but not renaming of 1s: $35 + 14 = N$. Next, examples requiring renaming are introduced: $49 + 28 = N$. Long algorithms are always used in this phase.

To *introduce the addition algorithm*, a teacher chooses study material so that learners' previous learning is evident to them and they can readily reorganize it to construct new ideas. A teaching sequence that enables learners to infer new ideas from previous knowledge is given in Box 7-2. As noted in the lesson sequence, follow-up work enables children to translate ideas to other modes of learning. Some learners, of course, begin with materials. Figure 7-2 shows how addition algorithms are represented with materials.

Another follow-up lesson helps learners consider the commutative property and addition computation. To begin such a lesson, the teacher can say: "Girls and boys, you have written a rule for addition of large numbers that works very well. We have used the abacus and other materials to show using the rule. When we used the abacus, I noticed that someone worked with tens first. Is that O.K.? Let's talk about it." Sub-

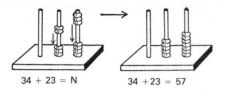

34 + 23 = N   34 + 23 = 57

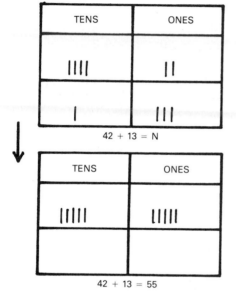

TENS	ONES
||||	||
|	|||

42 + 13 = N

TENS	ONES
|||||	|||||

42 + 13 = 55

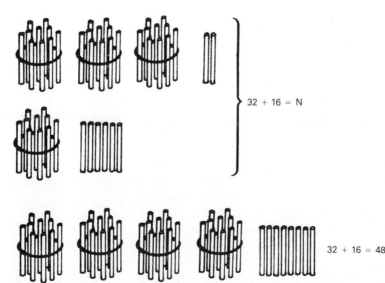

32 + 16 = N

32 + 16 = 48

FIGURE 7-2.   Using materials to show addition with no renaming.

BOX 7-2. SAMPLE LESSON: INTRODUCING ADDITION ALGORITHM (GRADE 3)

1. Boys and girls, today we have some new examples to study. I think you will find it very exciting to figure out how to complete these exercises.

2. I have written some examples on the board. The same exercises are on the paper I gave you. Some you have seen before and know how to give the sums. Others are new to you. Let's read them. . . .

    Please put a circle around the new type of addition exercises. Think about the other exercises. Are they like the new ones in any way?

$$
\begin{array}{cccccc}
34 \ (60) & 30 & 4 & 23 \ (50) & 20 & 3 \\
+\ 32 & +\ 30 & +\ 2 & +\ 34 & +\ 30 & +\ 4 \\
\hline
\end{array}
$$

$$
\begin{array}{cccccc}
62 \ (70) & 60 & 2 & 43 \ (60) & 40 & 3 \\
+\ 13 & +\ 10 & +\ 3 & +\ 23 & +\ 20 & +\ 3 \\
\hline
\end{array}
$$

    (Teacher circulates while learners complete task.) Jim, please circle the exercises on the board that are new to us. Tell us why you decided what to circle. (We have never added tens and ones together before.)

3. Yes. Write estimates for the circled examples. (See numerals in parentheses.) Then look at those you can do. Do they give an idea of how to do the new kind of exercise? (Well, 34 is 30 + 4 and 32 is 30 + 2. It makes sense to add the tens and ones and get the sum for the new examples.)

    (If learners are not able to classify examples, an alternate approach is to examine each example in turn. After the "new learning" has been identified, point to the first three examples and say: What do you notice about these? Do they go together in any way? The line of questioning helps learners construct ideas so they can respond as in the parentheses above.)

4. Good thinking! That's the way to do it. Because you know the meaning of 34 and 32, you can use what you know about adding tens and ones.

5. Let's name 34 and 32 to show the tens and ones meaning. Please give the expanded names. I'll write them on the board. (Teacher writes.

$$
\begin{array}{l}
3\,4 = 3\,0 + 4 \\
+\ 3\,2 = 3\,0 + 2) \\
\hline
\end{array}
$$

    Write this on your paper and complete what you know. Jane, tell us what you did. (I added the tens and the ones.) Please write the sums on the board. What is a standard name for 60 + 6? (66.) Tom, please write that where it belongs.

$$
\begin{array}{l}
3\,4 = 3\,0 + 4 \\
+\ 3\,2 = 3\,0 + 2 \\
\hline
6\,0 + 6 = 66
\end{array}
$$

    Was your estimate O.K.? (Yes, it was 60.)

6. Please do

$$
\begin{array}{r}
23 \\
+\ 34 \\
\end{array}
$$

on your paper. (Class member records work on the board, first noting estimate.)

7. You may be saying to yourself: That is a lot of work! I will show you a shortcut. Notice we still think tens and ones parts, add the parts, and then add the part sums together.

$$
\begin{array}{r}
34 \\
+\ 32 \\
\hline
6 \\
+\ 60 \\
\hline
66 \\
\end{array}
\qquad
\begin{array}{r}
23 \\
+\ 34 \\
\hline
7 \\
+\ 50 \\
\hline
57 \\
\end{array}
$$

How do you explain this shortcut? Why does it give a sensible answer? (Several pupils tell in their own words that it shows thinking ones and tens, adding the ones and the tens separately and then together, but that there is no rewriting in expanded form.)

8. Do the last two examples using this shortcut. Note your estimates. Then talk over with your neighbor the meaning of what you have done. Make up a rule for how to complete these exercises.

9. Let us discuss our ideas about a rule. . . . Lottie, please say our rule so that I can write it on the board. (To add tens and ones numbers: add the ones and write the sum in the ones place. Add the tens and write the sum as tens. Add the two sums to get the total.)

10. You are good at thinking about mathematics. You can figure out answers to new exercises. Tomorrow we will study our rule using the abacus.

sequent discussion helps learners understand that the accepted order is to add 1s, then 10s, but that the sum of the 10s could be determined first.

After mastering addition algorithms in which no renaming of ones is required, children learn addition computation with *renaming of ones*. Some suggestions on how to teach this type of computation are:

1. Learners examine examples with addends 10s plus 1s and involving renaming and no renaming; they classify examples into what they have studied and what is new. They estimate sums. Learners consider the examples in which the sum of the 1s is greater than 9. They recall that numbers greater than 9 can be thought of as 1s or 10(s) + 1s. They observe that the place-value system facilitates renaming 1s as 10(s) + 1s. Discussion focuses on the ideas: Think the 1s and 10s parts. Add 1s; write the sum in the 10s and 1s places. Add 10s; write the sum in the 10s and 1s places. Add the partial sums. The children write the steps in the long addition algorithm:

$$
\begin{array}{r}
47 \\
+\ 39 \\
\hline
16 \\
+\ 70 \\
\hline
86 \\
\end{array}
$$

2. Learners use materials to verify (or, with some children, construct) the procedure (Figure 7-3).

3. Gifted learners can discuss use of the associative property in addition algorithms (Box 7-1).

You will observe that the use of the long algorithm helps learners understand what they are doing. Furthermore, the long algorithm enables children to deal with the renaming step without difficulty; renaming is implicit in the place-value scheme. Abbreviated (standard) algorithms are not introduced until the next phase of instruction.

Extending and Consolidating Knowledge of Addition Computation

This phase of instruction gives learners further opportunities to use cognitive processes to deepen understanding and attain computational skill. The list below summarizes instructional objectives and activities during this phase.

1. Guide learners to find checks for solutions. Children consider changing the order of addends as a way to check solutions. The use of good estimates in checking is discussed. (After learning subtraction computation, pupils check using the idea of inverse operations.)

2. Introduce abbreviated algorithms so learners have the option of using the long or short forms. Mention that some steps can be performed mentally. Model the thought processes involved and the numeral placement in the standard algorithm to help learners adopt the arbitrary procedure. Follow modeling with a class discussion of the steps. Help pupils use materials to illustrate the procedure. Guide learners to use "crutches" in renaming if they need to do so:

$$\begin{array}{r} {}^1 59 \\ +78 \\ \hline 137 \end{array}$$

3. Provide opportunities for learners to extend computation rules when addends are less than 100 to rules for finding sums when addends are greater than 100. Help learners classify and compare "old" and "new" examples. Ask learners to infer from what they know to find solutions for the new examples. Guide children to formulate a rule that stresses adding multiples of like powers of 10: 1s, 10s, or 100s (later 1000s, and so on). Have learners verify ideas using materials, particularly the abacus and place-value frame. Continue emphasizing estimation.

4. Help learners establish expectations of achievement and provide opportunities for them to meet expectations of good estimations and accurate computations. Keep drill periods short to discourage dawdling. (Learners are expected to compute correct sums in a few examples; 9 of 10 correct with no counting is considered mastery. Pupils need not operate like machines, speedily turning out a great many correct computations.)

5. Give real-life problems involving numbers greater than 10 for individual or group study.

6. Encourage children to work with missing-figures computations by suggesting they can be "mathematics detectives." An example is:

$$\begin{array}{r} 4\ \underline{} \\ 8 \\ \underline{} \\ \hline 9\ 6 \end{array}$$

(Problems of this kind give learners opportunities to engage in reversible thought because addition and subtraction are both used in solving the problems.) Ask the "mathematics detectives" to share solutions.

7. Have learners write exercises for others to complete. Those who produce the examples supply the solutions. (This assignment helps develop awareness of renaming in addition.) Two children can work together on such an activity. A practice sheet for a group can have "Jenny's examples," and so on. This is a great way to motivate learners.

8. Ask learners to count by a number 10 or less. Begin with either a multiple or a nonmultiple of the number. Continue for several decades. Predicting the last number to be counted in a certain decade can be included in this exercise. For example: (1)

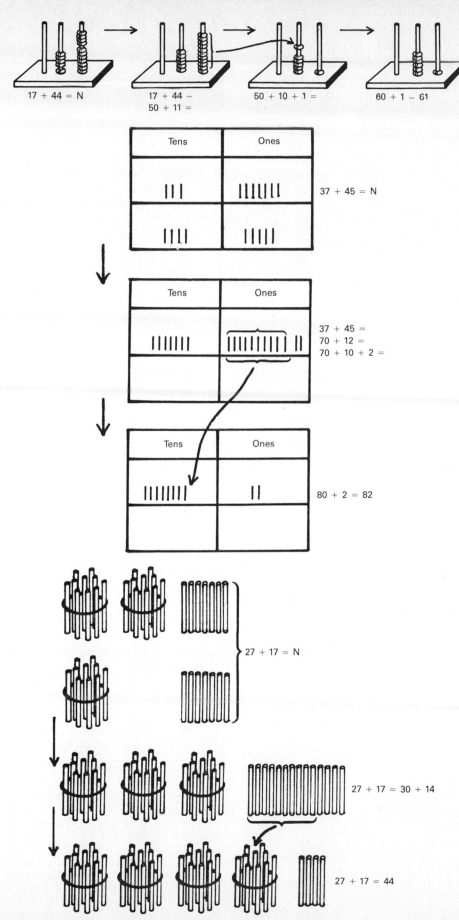

FIGURE 7-3. Using materials to show addition with renaming.

count by 4s; begin with 24 and continue until you reach the 70s; (2) count by 5s; begin with 16 and continue until you reach the 60s; (3) count by 3s; begin with 30; stop with the first number in the 70s; what will that number be? Why? Children can work in teams to perform this kind of counting. A direction sheet with answers will aid team work. This approach to counting enables learners to study higher-decade addition in a different setting.

9. Provide lessons in column addition. Have learners hypothesize about the procedure and use materials to test their ideas. Progressively more difficult examples are:

$$
\begin{array}{cccc}
6 & 21 & 7 & 47 \\
+\,3 & +\,32 & +\,8 & +\,53 \\
\hline
2 & 46 & 6 & 64 \\
 & & 4 & 98 \\
\hline
\end{array}
$$

In the first two examples only basic facts are used. The easiest type, the first example, could have been introduced when children were extending and consolidating knowledge of basic facts. Examples similar to the other exercises are introduced when learners extend understanding of algorithms. (The last two examples involve higher-decade addition. Higher-decade addition should be learned before column addition like that in the last two examples is introduced.) Children should have opportunities to work with column addition because it is a prerequisite for multiplication computation using the long algorithm. Furthermore, the solution of many problems requires such computation.

The extending and consolidating phase for addition computation extends over several years. An understanding of algorithms is usually developed in grade three. The activities suggested in this section are used thereafter when appropriate to the maturity of learners.

LEARNING AND TEACHING SUBTRACTION COMPUTATION

Subtraction computation rules can be more difficult for children to learn than those for addition. Sufficient time and a variety of activities should be given so that learners can construct the rules and extend and consolidate understanding.

Most authorities advocate the use of the **decomposition method** when renaming the minuend is required:

$$
\begin{array}{rl}
81 = & (70 + 11) \\
-\,15 = & -\,(10 + \ 5) \\
\hline
& 60 + \ 6 = 66
\end{array}
$$

This method can more easily be represented by materials than the **equal-addition method**:

$$
\begin{array}{rl}
81 = & (80 + 11) \\
-\,15 = & -\,(20 + \ 5) \\
\hline
& 60 + \ 6 = 66
\end{array}
$$

The initial instructional activities discussed below teach the decomposition method. The equal-addition method is often introduced during the extension phase.

Developing Prerequisite Understanding for Subtraction Computation

Children are not expected to learn computation rules for subtraction until they demonstrate attainment of several prerequisites: knowledge of the interpretations of subtraction; mastery of the basic facts; grasp of base-10 and place-value concepts, including renaming numbers; and skill in mental subtraction involving multiples of powers of 10 and estimation of differences. During the time just prior to introduction of subtraction algorithms, children often learn renaming numbers as 10(s) plus the sum of 10 plus 1s: $(45 = 30 + 15)$ and also begin higher-decade subtraction.

Renaming in terms of 10s plus the sum of 10 plus 1s is a prerequisite knowledge for subtraction algorithms in which renaming is necessary. A need-to-know situation for this learning is created by the introduction of a new game.

SPECIAL RENAMING. To play this game children use two types of cards. The first type are player cards on which numerals are written in standard form (for example 37) or as indicated sums giving the "special" renaming (for example, 20 + 17). Half the player cards have numerals in standard form, the other half have indicated sums. The second type are caller cards on which are written the standard form and indicated sums (such as 37 = 20 + 17). Three to six children play. Each child has 7 player cards. The caller cards (their number depends on how many play) are face down in the center of the playing area. Children take turns being the caller and choosing a caller card. The caller says, "Finish this sentence." He or she chooses one side of the equation on the card to read (for example, 37). The player who can read the correct answer from one of his or her cards to complete the sentence does so and takes the caller card, putting it with the player card just read. The next caller continues in the same manner. The game ends when a child is out of player cards. The winner has the most books of caller cards with player cards.

To play the game children need to know how to rename numbers in terms of 10s plus the sum of 10 plus 1s. This is learned by using the abacus or place-value frame. The teacher says, "To play our new game, SPECIAL RENAMING, we have to be able to rename numbers a new way. Learning to play this game will help us with subtraction. Here are some sentences showing the new renaming.

$$54 = 40 + 14$$
$$46 = 30 + 16$$
$$23 = 10 + 13$$
$$75 = 60 + 15$$

We can use the place-value tally frames I am passing out to find out why these sentences are true. Let us do the first one together (Figure 7-4 is an illustration of what children do with the place-value tally frame). Show 54. What can you do to show that $54 = 40 + 14$? Why?"

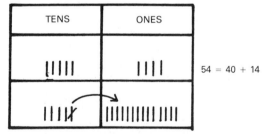

FIGURE 7-4. Place-value tally frame to show Special Renaming activity.

The pupil activity and teacher questioning continue in a similar manner for each equation. The children are next asked to look for patterns. The teacher says, "How are all these alike? How are they different?" Examining the equations and manipulating the place-value tally frames helps learners make the observation that the number is renamed as a 10s number, one 10 less than the given number, plus the sum of 10 plus 1s. Pupils state this idea in their own words, and each child writes a few equations to illustrate the concept. These are shared with the group.

The teacher gives the SPECIAL RENAMING rules at the end of this lesson. The children decide if they are ready to play the game or if they need more rehearsal.

Higher-decade subtraction is the inverse of higher-decade addition. There are four types of higher-decade subtraction:

1. $65 - 62 = 3$ Minuend and subtrahend in the same decade; difference is 1s.

2. $65 - 59 = 6$ Minuend and subtrahend in adjacent decades; difference is 1s.

3. $68 - 7 = 61$ Minuend is a 10s plus 1s number; subtrahend is a 1s number; difference is in the same decade as the minuend.

4. $61 - 8 = 53$ Minuend is a 10s plus 1s number, subtrahend is a 1s number; difference in decade 1 less than minuend.

Whether children should be able to do higher-decade subtraction mentally is a question to which not much attention has been directed. We believe children should be given the opportunity to learn to compute mentally in as many situations as possible. Higher-decade subtraction types 1 and 3 above are not difficult to do mentally and are quickly learned. Pupils should not be led to believe they need paper and pencil to find differences in examples in which no renaming is necessary. This kind of higher-decade subtraction should be introduced to learners before they do any paper-and-pencil subtraction computation. The higher-decade subtraction with renaming (types 2 and 4) can be introduced before or after paper-and-pencil computation is introduced, but it could be several weeks before pupils master the task. Attention to the patterns in 1s and 10s helps pupils form rules for finding differences.

Inductive procedures can be used to introduce higher-decade subtraction. Children look for patterns in series such as $6 - 4 = 2$, $16 - 14 = 2$, $26 - 24 = 2$, $36 - 34 = 2$, ..., $96 - 94 = 2$. Teacher questions include: What do you notice? What is alike here? Why? What rule can we make up for this kind of subtraction? The patterns in the 10s and 1s can also be inferred from a display of examples children make on the number line (Figure 7-5).

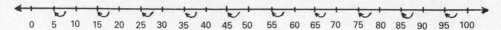

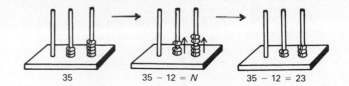

FIGURE 7-5. Number line showing 8 — 3 = 5, 18 — 3 = 15, . . . , 98 — 3 = 95.

Follow-up activities include the old games (FISH, RUMMY, SMILING FACE, WAR, and BINGO) with playing cards that show higher-decade subtraction (and addition) questions and answers. Exercise sheets giving the answers for feedback can be used by two pupils to help each other learn. An individual can use the exercise sheets alone by covering an answer, thinking it, and checking his or her response. As with higher-decade addition, the hourglass egg timer can be used to encourage practice.

Constructing Subtraction Computation Rules

Children who understand the meaning of subtraction, have good recall of the facts, and can estimate remainders and understand that an addition computation exercise is carried out by "thinking the 10s and 1s parts" are introduced to the subtraction algorithm in a lesson appropriate to their level of cognitive maturity. For children who are capable of relating prior learning to arrive at new conclusions, the plan to introduce subtraction with *no renaming* is similar to the plan to introduce addition given in Box 7-2. After children build the rule, they illustrate it using the abacus, place-value tally frame or chart, or sticks (Figure 7-6). Children who have difficulty with relational thinking begin with materials. They develop the computation rule by making records of their actions. All children use the long algorithm in initial work with subtraction computation to aid comprehension.

$$
\begin{array}{r}
69 \\
- 13 \\
\hline
6 \\
+ 50 \\
\hline
56
\end{array}
$$

Competency in subtraction computation with no renaming is followed by an introduction to subtraction with *renaming*. The introduction of this new learning is often delayed several weeks while children learn addition with renaming. Boxes 7-3a and 7-3b each give a sequence for introducing the algorithm. One sequence would be appropriate for learners who are capable of relational thinking and can make

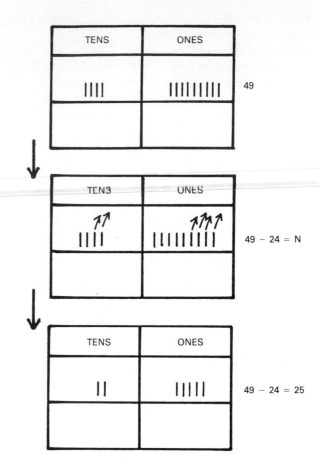

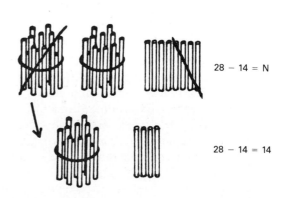

FIGURE 7-6. Using materials to show subtraction with no renaming.

BOX 7-3a. *SAMPLE LESSON: INTRODUCING SUBTRACTION ALGORITHM*
            WITH RENAMING (GRADE 3)

1. Boys and girls, you are very good at subtraction. I am sure you will enjoy figuring
    out a new kind of example today. Look at the examples on the board. Let's read
    them. . . . How are the ones in the first row different from those in the second
    row?

$$\begin{array}{cccc}
46 & 79 & 85 & 57 \\
-23 & -57 & -24 & -14 \\
\hline
\end{array}$$

$$\begin{array}{cccc}
43\ (20) & 77\ (20) & 84\ (60) & 54\ (40) \\
-26 & -59 & -25 & -17 \\
\hline
\end{array}$$

(The ones numbers are turned around. The smaller number is on the top.)

2. Can you use what you know to do the subtraction examples in the second row?
    (No, the bigger number has always been on the top.)

3. Well, we can make our estimates. What shall I write beside the examples? (See nu-
    merals in parentheses.)

4. To help us with the computation, I will rewrite the examples. Notice what I do.
    Think about what it means. I will pass out a paper that shows what I have written
    on the board. Please write the estimates on your paper.

$$\begin{array}{llll}
43 = (30 + 13) & 77 = (60 + 17) & 84 = (70 + 14) & 54 = (40 + 14) \\
-26 = -(20 + 6) & -59 = -(50 + 9) & -25 = -(20 + 5) & -17 = -(10 + 7) \\
\hline
\end{array}$$

5. Let's look at the first one. What do you notice? How can you explain it? (43 is the
    same as 30 + 13. We learned that before. That's in the Special Renaming Game.
    Now we can subtract!) How does renaming help with subtraction? (We can subtract
    the ones. We have a basic fact.) Please finish the subtraction. Was your estimate
    close? (Yes.) What is the difference? (17.)

6. Let's discuss the other examples. What do you notice in all of them? What's going
    on here? Why? (Teacher and pupils discuss the need for renaming, the use of basic
    facts in the ones part, and renaming of the minuend in a special way. Many children
    are asked to give their ideas in their own words.)

7. Girls and boys, you think very well about this kind of example. Please finish the
    computation in the last three examples on the board. . . . Remember to check
    with the estimates. . . . (Teacher circulates to observe pupils' work.)

8. Let's write a rule for what we have done. (Estimate first. If the ones in the larger
    number is smaller than the ones in the smaller number, rename the larger number
    the special way. Then subtract. Write the answer in the regular way. Check with
    your estimate.)

9. Good. To learn more about this kind of example, write two exercises, find the dif-
    ferences, and explain what you did to your neighbor. I have some papers that give
    the forms to use, but there are blanks where you write the numerals. I think the
    forms will help you. Jane, please pass out these papers. (The forms are:

$$\begin{array}{l}
= (\underline{} + \underline{}) \quad (\ ) \\
-\underline{} = -(\underline{} + \underline{}) \\
\hline
 + =)
\end{array}$$

10. Let's share some of what we have done with all our group. Tom, Sue, Terry, Pam, and Dave, please write one of your examples on the board. Then you can tell us about it. . . .

11. Are there any questions about what we have been talking about? . . .

12. You figured out how to do a new kind of example today. You should be proud of that. Tomorrow we will use the abacus to think about our rule.

inferences by abstracting from examples. The other sequence is appropriate for children who have less ability to reason and rely more on intuitive understanding developed from using materials (Figure 7-7).

Whenever children use expanded notation to clarify meaning, they are given the notational format. (Notice this in the lessons in Boxes 7-3a and 7-3b.) In the introductory lessons children are to think about renaming in subtraction, not the niceties of a record scheme. Therefore they are given the format to use in their work. Soon thereafter they are shown the long algorithm and use it in computation.

Lessons emphasize that learners estimate before computing. Estimation gives meaning to the process; it enables learners to evaluate their own efforts. Without the ability to estimate, children use computation rules in mechanical ways.

When learners can complete subtraction computational exercises with renaming using the long form, they are ready to extend and consolidate knowledge.

Extending and Consolidating Knowledge of Subtraction Computation

The objectives and procedures of this phase of learning-teaching are similar to those for the same phase of addition computation. During grades three to six, all learners have opportunities to expand their understanding of subtraction algorithms and develop computational skill. Pupils:

1. Study addition check for solutions.
2. Are introduced to abbreviated (standard) algorithms which involve (a) memory or (b) the use of "crutches":

    (a) $\begin{array}{r} 8\ 4 \\ -\ 4\ 7 \\ \hline 3\ 7 \end{array}$ (b) $\begin{array}{r} {}^{7}\!8{}^{1}\!4 \\ -\ 4\ 7 \\ \hline 3\ 7 \end{array}$

3. Use inference to extend the computation rules to numbers equal to or greater than 100.

4. Extend expectations of mastery to subtraction computation. The expectation is to complete 9 out of 10 examples correctly, with no counting of differences.

5. Study real-life problems involving large numbers and subtraction computation.

6. Solve missing-figure problems:

    $$\begin{array}{r} \underline{}\ 1 \\ -\ 3\ \underline{} \\ \hline 4\ 2 \end{array}$$

7. Write exercises for others. Production of examples is an important aspect of concept and rule learning.

8. Count backward by a number less than 10 beginning with a number greater than 20 that is or is not a multiple of the "counting" number. For example: (1) Count backward by 6s beginning with 42. (2) Count by 5s backward from 72. Go as far as you can. (3) Count by 4s beginning with 50. What number will be given first in the 20s? Why do you think that? (Higher-decade subtraction is practiced in this approach to counting.)

9. Work with examples in which the minuend is 100s or 1000s—for example,

    $$\begin{array}{r} 300 \\ -\ 198 \\ \hline \end{array}$$

    In this example 300 is renamed 200 + 90 + 10 or 290 + 10. If possible, inductive or deductive procedures are used to enable learners to extend their concept of renaming to this situation. Materials are used to verify or construct a rule for dealing with this type of exercise.

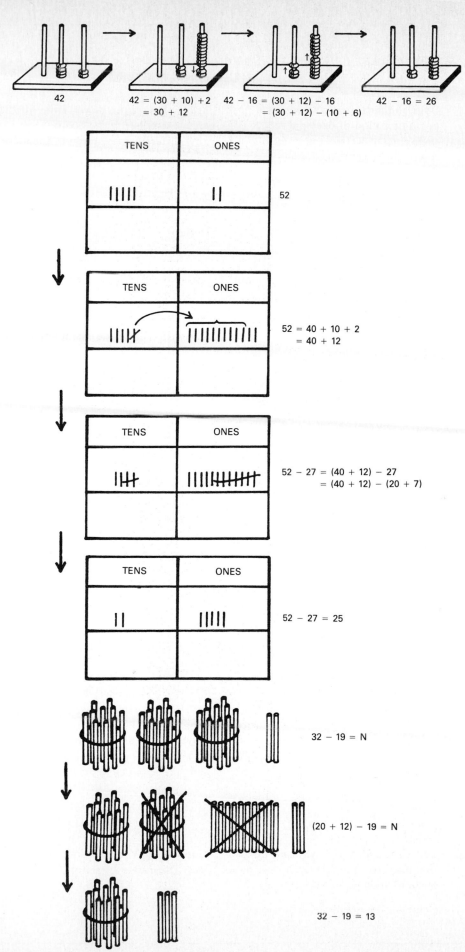

FIGURE 7-7. Using materials to show subtraction with renaming.

BOX 7-3b. SAMPLE LESSON: DEVELOPING INTUITIVE COMPREHENSION
OF SUBTRACTION ALGORITHM WITH RENAMING (GRADE 3)

1. Boys and girls, you are very good at subtraction. I am sure you will enjoy figuring out a new kind of example today. Look at the examples on the board. Let's read them. ... How are the ones in the first row different from those in the second row?

$$
\begin{array}{cccc}
46 & 79 & 85 & 57 \\
-23 & -57 & -24 & -14 \\
\end{array}
$$

$$
\begin{array}{cccc}
43\ (20) & 77\ (20) & 84\ (60) & 54\ (40) \\
-26 & -59 & -25 & -17 \\
\end{array}
$$

(The ones numbers are turned around. The smaller number is on the top.)

2. Can you use what you know to do the subtraction examples in the second row? (No, the bigger number has always been on the top.)

3. Well, we can make our estimates. What shall I write beside the examples? (See numerals in parentheses.)

4. We can use the abacus to find the difference. Jack, please pass out the abacuses. ... How would we begin? (Show 43 on the abacus.) How did you do that? (4 rings in the tens place, 3 in the ones place.)

5. What is the next step? (Take away 26.) Show how to do that. (There aren't enough ones!) What do you have? (Tens.) Is there any way you could use a ten? (Well, one ten is ten ones, so we could change a ring in the tens place for ten in the ones place.) Very good thinking. Do it. And finish the exercise. (If no pupil comes to this conclusion, the teacher can say: Watch what I am doing, and make the exchange. The children discuss what they have seen the teacher do, what it means, and how this will help find the answer. They then carry out the action using their own abacuses.)

6. Sherrie, please tell us what you did and what you have for the answer. ... Good thinking.

7. Let's make a record of what we have done. As you explain it, I will make a record on the board.

$$
\begin{array}{rl}
43 = & (30 + 13) \\
-26 = & -(20 +\ 6) \\
\hline
& 10 +\ 7\ = 17 \\
\end{array}
$$

8. What about the estimate we have written here? (It's O.K.) Yes, it is.

9. I have a paper with the exercises on the board written down and with blank spaces to help you make a record of work with the abacus. Please do the work on the abacus and use these papers to make records.* I'll come around to talk with you about your work or answer your questions. Don't forget the estimates. (The sheets have notations in this form:

$$
\begin{array}{rl}
77 = & (\_ + \_)\ (\ ) \\
-59 = & -(\_ + \_) \\
\hline
& \_\_\_\_\ ) \\
\end{array}
$$

10. Let's talk about what we have done. ... Good work. You have done the work on the abacuses and kept your records very well. This new subtraction was not hard for you. Soon we will write a rule.

*The group may work together on each example.

Some children are introduced to the equal-addition method of subtraction. The introduction is designed as an inductive or modeling procedure. The rationale of the method is not easy to understand. An example to illustrate the logic is:

$$64 - 37 = (60 + 4) - (30 + 7) + (10 - 10)$$
$$= (60 + 10 + 4) - (30 + 10 + 7)$$
$$= (60 + 14) - (40 + 7)$$
$$= 20 + 7$$
$$= 27$$

The reader will observe that an addition of 0 (10 − 10), renaming, and frequent use of the associative and commutative properties are the basis for the equal-addition method. Children may be helped to understand: We add 10 to the minuend and 10 to the subtrahend; the 10 in the subtrahend is soon subtracted; 10 minus 10 is really 0. While this explanation may not be entirely satisfactory, it can give learners the idea that there are reasons for the method which they will comprehend fully at a later time. Using the method with estimation precludes totally meaningless manipulation, and the method has been found to be an easy one for some children. Therefore, its introduction should be seriously considered for some learners.

Addition and subtraction as inverse operations can be examined with numbers greater than 10. Such a study often gives gifted learners an exciting insight into number relations. To guide pupils, teachers use an inductive or deductive questioning method. Using a deductive method, the teacher begins by saying: What do we know about addition and subtraction? ... Let's use that idea to write some subtraction equations related to these addition equations (34 + 92 = 126, 66 + 57 = 123, and so on). Children use the inverse-operations concept to write subtraction equations and continue by writing addition equations from subtraction equations.

The teacher later gives related equations with either the addition or subtraction equation solved and the related equation with a missing addend or sum. The children use the solved equation to find the missing addend or sum. No computation is involved. For example:

Given: 35 + 77 = 112 96 − 28 = 68 49 − 16 = 33

Find N: 112 − 77 = N N + 28 = 96 33 + 16 = N

Children can write their own pairs of related equations and share them with others. For verification the teacher can suggest using materials, such as the abacus. The old games can be changed to include related equations involving addends greater than 10.

When children show achievement in subtraction computation and have used some of the activities for extending and consolidating knowledge, they are ready to begin the study of multiplication computation.

LEARNING AND TEACHING MULTIPLICATION COMPUTATION

Computation rules for multiplication are usually introduced in grade four. Children initially learn to compute when one factor is less than 10 and the other factor is a sum of 10s plus 1s without and with renaming (22 × 4 = N; 45 × 7 = N.) Later both factors are sums of 10s plus 1s. In this section the three-phase instructional sequence is again the basis of the discussion.

Developing Prerequisite Understanding for Multiplication Computation

Before introducing multiplication computation rules, teachers *assess* children's (1) knowledge of the meaning of multiplication, (2) recall of the multiplication basic facts, (3) skill in mental computation with multiples of powers of 10 and estimation of products, and (4) knowledge of properties. If children have not attained the necessary prerequisite abilities in these areas, the topics are reintroduced. Mental computation and estimation, in particular, often need to be reintroduced before the algorithms are presented.

Inductive procedures are important in *reintroducing mental computation* with multiples of powers of 10 and estimation. In mental computation the teacher can present pictures of children thinking products (Figure 7-8). The questions to ask are similar to: What is going on here? What are the children thinking? Why can they think that? What would you do to think that way? ... Make up an example and ask your neighbor to think the answer. Take turns. Discuss how you did it.

Children can review the rules by using materials to find solutions. The abacus is especially useful in helping pupils visualize solutions. Chil-

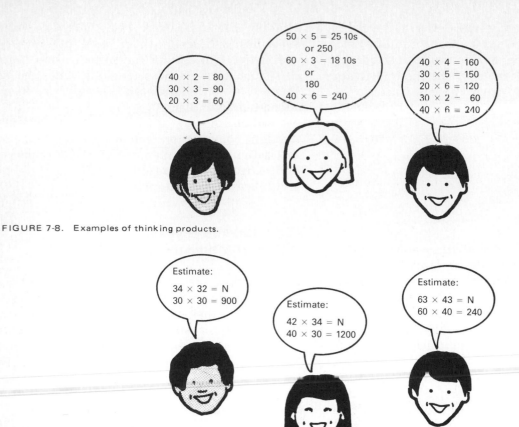

FIGURE 7-8.   Examples of thinking products.

FIGURE 7-9.   Examples of estimating products.

dren can examine the mathematical sense of a rule. For example, they note that:

$$30 \times 20 = 3 \times 10 \times 2 \times 10 = 2 \times 3 \times 10 \times 10$$
$$= 6 \times 100 = 600$$

Gifted learners can examine the use of the commutative and associative properties in the computation.

   Some children will need practice activities to reestablish skill in mental multiplication. Games and team practice are again used by children to gain skill in mentally computing products when factors are multiples of powers of 10.

   Reintroduction (or introduction) of estimation begins with rounding down. Picture characters can again be used to present examples for inductive teaching (Figure 7-9). When learners observe patterns, they can construct rules. In a deductive procedure, the picture character can give the rule and learners can construct examples (Figure 7-10). Later rules for rounding down or up are stressed.

   After initial instruction in estimation, frequent rehearsal with a variety of examples is necessary to develop competency. All the old games can be revised for estimation in computation. Children match estimates and exercises. Card games, board-and-dice games, and board-and-spinner games can be used. In games children usually will check each other's mental work so that answers need not be supplied. However, an answer sheet can be made available to help learners when disagreements occur. Learners should also assume responsibility for practice by teaming up with a partner for cooperative learning.

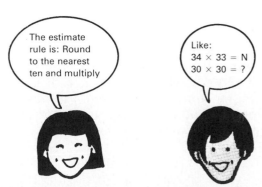

FIGURE 7-10.   Using a rule to estimate products.

Constructing Multiplication Computation Rules

Children learn the meaning of multiplication computation as they relate prior learnings to construct new rules. Teachers help children draw together their knowledge of multiplication, estimation, basic facts, base-10 and place-value concepts, the distributive property of multiplication over addition, and extended algorithms in addition and subtraction.

Children begin their study with algorithms in which one factor is less than 10 and the other factor is a sum of 10s plus 1s with *no renaming* required. Teachers can use inductive questioning methods so pupils can infer the rule from observations of examples, or they can use deductive methods. A deductive sequence is given in Box 7-4. Introductory lessons always employ long algorithms:

$$\begin{array}{r} 23 \\ \times\ 2 \\ \hline 6 \\ +\ 40 \\ \hline 46 \end{array}$$

Lessons that give learners opportunities to use materials to illustrate and verify a rule follow lessons that guide learners to use mental processes to comprehend the algorithm. Some learners, however, begin with materials. The abacus and squared paper are especially useful for representing ideas. Squared-paper diagrams illustrate the partial products and so give a good visual representation of partial products as well as the final product (Figure 7-11). The use of repeated addition to complete multiplication exercises is also discussed.

The extended algorithm introduced with examples in which there is no renaming is adapted very readily to examples with *renaming*. Pupils make the transition to renaming readily when the extended algorithm has previously been studied. An example is:

$$\begin{array}{r} 15 \\ \times\ 5 \\ \hline 25 \\ +\ 50 \\ \hline 75 \end{array}$$

Discussion with learners emphasizes the use of place value to assist them in thinking about 10s and 1s in multiplication.

Multiplication in which both factors are greater than 10 and at least one factor is a sum of 10s plus 1s is introduced in an inductive or deductive sequence. Examples used in lessons are like the following:

(a)
$$\begin{array}{r} 78 \\ \times\ 30 \\ \hline 240 \\ +\ 2100 \\ \hline 2340 \end{array}$$

(b)
$$\begin{array}{r} 65 \\ \times\ 21 \\ \hline 5 \\ 60 \\ 100 \\ +\ 1200 \\ \hline 1365 \end{array}$$

The use of the distributive property in (a) and (b) is discussed with learners who are able to follow the logic. Gifted learners should have opportunities for developing these ideas:

(a) $30 \times 78 = 30(70 + 8)$
$$= (30 \times 70) + (30 \times 8)$$
$$= 2100 + 240$$
$$= 2340$$

(b) $(21 \times 65) = (20 + 1) \times (60 + 5)$
$$= (20 \times 60) + (20 \times 5)$$
$$\qquad + (1 \times 60) + (1 \times 5)$$
$$= 1200 + 100 + 60 + 5$$
$$= 1365$$

Once again to illustrate the computation rule and to give visual representation to the partial products in the algorithm, learners use squared paper to translate the rule into a picture of the process (Figure 7-12). Pupils can also discuss what the product means in terms of repeated addition to deepen their comprehension (for example, 21×65 means using 65 as an addend 21 times).

When children can use long algorithms to complete a multiplication exercise accurately and explain in their own words what they are doing, teachers provide opportunities for extending and consolidating knowledge.

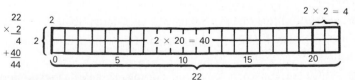

FIGURE 7-11. Diagram showing product and partial products.

*BOX 7-4. SAMPLE LESSON: INTRODUCING MULTIPLICATION ALGORITHM
(GRADE 4)*

1. Boys and girls, today we have some new multiplication exercises to study. I know you will be able to make a rule for these exercises. They are like this:

$$\begin{array}{cccc} 42 \ (80) & 32 \ (90) & 23 \ (40) & 21 \ (80) \\ \times \ 2 & \times \ 3 & \times \ 2 & \times \ 4 \end{array}$$

Let's read them. . . .

2. To help us, we can think of what we know about multiplication. What are some things we know? (We can estimate the answers.) Let's estimate the answer to begin. I will write the estimates beside the exercises. (See numerals in parentheses.)

3. How did we find the estimates? (Use the tens and ones: $2 \times 40 = 80$; $3 \times 30 = 90$; and so on.) Good.

    What part of the exercises are the same as our estimates? (Oh, the tens part!)

    Yes, we can do that part.

4. What else do we know? Look at the ones. (That's a basic fact.) Yes, it is, and you know the basic facts very well.

5. You will recall in multiplication we can multiply by parts. Remember what we learned about 5(4)? . . . Yes, $5 \times 4 = (5 \times 2) + (5 \times 2) = 10 + 10 = 20$.

    What parts do we have in this exercise? (The tens and ones.)

6. Thinking our exercise in equation form can help us. I will write it on the board. Let's discuss it. . . .

$$2(42) = 2(40 + 2) = (2 \times 40) + (2 \times 2)$$
$$= 80 + 4 = 84$$

7. When we use a short vertical form we think the ones part first. Why can we change the order? (The order rule.) What is the ones product? (4.) Notice that I write 4 in the ones place. What is the ones and tens product? (80.) Notice I write 80 below "4." What do we do now? (Add the two products.)

$$\begin{array}{r} 42 \\ \times \ 2 \\ \hline 4 \\ + \ 80 \\ \hline 84 \end{array}$$

Our estimate was good, wasn't it? (80 is O.K.)

8. Let's review what we did by doing the next one. . . .

9. Please do the last two yourselves. . . . Joan, please put the third one on the board. Don, please put the last one on the board. Tell us how you computed. . . . Good. We call these products (pointing) partial products. Say "partial." . . . It means part.

10. Look at our estimates for the last three. What do you think? (The estimates are good.) Yes.

11. Now we can write a rule for what we have studied today about multiplication.

    (Estimate the product. Multiply the ones; multiply the ones and tens. Add the partial products. Check your estimate.)

12. Girls and boys, do you know what you did today? You figured out a rule for multiplication examples that you have never done before. That's terrific! Tomorrow we will study this multiplication with the abacus. That will be interesting also.

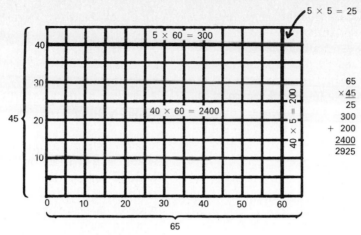

FIGURE 7-12. Diagram showing product and partial products.

Extending and Consolidating Knowledge of Multiplication Computation

This phase of instruction helps learners gain greater insight into computation and develop computational skill in exercises with factors less than 100. (The widespread use of the hand held calculator suggests that learners should not often compute when factors are greater than 100.) The following outline lists instructional objectives and activities during this phase.

1. Abbreviated (standard) algorithms in which mental calculation is employed are introduced. As mentioned previously, this kind of mental manipulation depends on skill in higher-decade addition. Examples of abbreviated algorithms are:

$$\begin{array}{r} 56 \\ \times\ 6 \\ \hline 336 \end{array} \qquad \begin{array}{r} 48 \\ \times\ 27 \\ \hline 336 \\ +\ 960 \\ \hline 1296 \end{array} \qquad \begin{array}{r} 56 \\ \times\ 35 \\ \hline 280 \\ +\ 168 \\ \hline 1960 \end{array}$$

(Higher-decade addition is used in each example. Where?) To teach the standard algorithms, teachers use modeling, inductive, or deductive procedures to help learners grasp patterns and the sequence of steps.

2. Checks for multiplication computation before the introduction of division computation are limited. Estimation is, of course, still used and provides a general check. Pupils often check computation by changing the order of the factors and repeating the computation.

3. Other algorithms for multiplication can be introduced to enrich understanding and provide for consolidation. Some learners may find them so acceptable that they will adopt them for their personal use. The lattice method and the doubling and halving method are given in Figures 7-13 and 7-14, respectively.

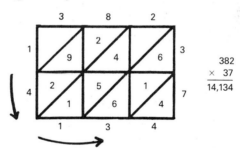

FIGURE 7-13. The lattice method for multiplication.

  a. Make lattice (squares with diagonals).
  b. Place factors (top and side).
  c. Multiply (each product in a square).
  d. Add on diagonals (begin at right).
  e. Read product (see arrows).

  a. Halve 24 . . . (discard remainders).
  b. Double 18 . . . .
  c. Cross out even numbers in a and the corresponding numbers in b.
  d. Add numbers remaining in b for product.

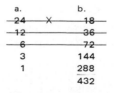

a.		b.
~~24~~	×	~~18~~
~~12~~		~~36~~
~~6~~		~~72~~
3		144
1		288
		432

24 × 18 = 432

FIGURE 7-14. The halving and doubling method for multiplication.

4. Short practice periods are used to enable learners to rehearse steps in the algorithms and develop skill in accurate computation. Expectancies are set by learners and teachers cooperatively. Meeting expectancies is cause for celebration! Individual records of progress toward goals help maintain effort.

5. Missing-figure exercises can motivate some learners. An example is:

$$
\begin{array}{r}
7\ \_\_ \\
\times\ 3\ 2 \\
\hline
1\ 5\ 6 \\
+\ \_\_\ \_\_\ 4 \\
\hline
4\ 9\ \_\_
\end{array}
$$

Writing these exercises provides an opportunity for problem solving and involves several cognitive processes. Learners can team up to write and solve these puzzles.

6. Real-life problems studied by learners now require multiplication computation for solution. Pupils are encouraged to bring problems from life outside school for solutions by different groups of children in the class.

7. Pupils are given opportunities to infer from their knowledge of multiplication with factors less than 100 to multiplication with factors greater than 100. Though learners are not expected to spend long periods of time with computations involving large numbers, a study of the meaning of exercises in which factors are greater than 100 will help learners extend their understanding of the multiplication algorithms. An excellent lesson is to examine the meaning of each partial product in these computations.

8. Estimation abilities are extended by some children to include using the rule "annex a zero to multiply by 10." Extending this rule, multiplying by powers of 10 becomes a process of counting or adding the numbers of zeros in the factors to determine the zeros in the product. Lessons to develop the sense of this procedure precede an emphasis on using this rule in estimation. These lessons stress the nature of the decimal place-value system.

The extending and consolidating phase for multiplication computation spans at least the second semester of grade four and grade five. When pupils show progress in multiplication computation, they begin division computation. However, activities for multiplication continue to be assigned.

LEARNING AND TEACHING DIVISION COMPUTATION

Division computation rules are used when the divisor is less than or greater than 10 and the dividend is less than or greater than 10 times the divisor. (If the divisor is less than 10 and the dividend is less than 10 times the divisor, basic facts are used and an algorithm is not required.) Division algorithms involve determining partial quotients, which are added to obtain a quotient in decimal form.

The basis for the division algorithm is the distributive property of division over addition. An example is:

$$
\begin{aligned}
\frac{3922}{74} &= \frac{3700 + 222}{74} \\
&= \frac{3700}{74} + \frac{222}{74} \\
&= 50\ +\ 3 \\
&= 53
\end{aligned}
$$

The division algorithm uses a "backward method" to obtain and use multiples of the divisor: determine partial quotients in turn; multiply each partial quotient and the divisor (50×74; 3×74) to obtain multiples of the divisor; repeatedly subtract multiples of the divisor to obtain new partial dividends to compare with multiples of the divisor. The example above is completed using the algorithm:

$$
\begin{array}{r}
53 \\
74\overline{)3922} \\
-\ 3700 \\
\hline
222 \\
-\ 222 \\
\hline
0
\end{array}
$$

Both long- and short-form algorithms involve the subtractive process, which can be explained by the distributive property of division over addition. In the extended algorithm best estimates are used successively and more computational work is shown. The short form involves more mental manipulation and relies on the place-value system to keep track of powers of

10 involved in the calculation (Box 7-1). The long algorithm is used in beginning lessons. The short form is adopted later by those who are capable of the mental manipulations required.

Division algorithms are often difficult for children to understand and remember. The learning and teaching can be made easier, however, if children have background understanding and are guided to integrate previous knowledge as they study the algorithm.

Developing Prerequisite Understanding for Division Computation

Readiness to learn division algorithms includes understanding the meanings of division (especially, repeated subtraction), mastery of the basic division facts, knowledge of base 10 and place value including renaming numbers, and division mental calculation with multiples of powers of 10 and estimation when the dividend is greater than 10 and the divisor is either less than or greater than 10. Children should also have had experiences to develop skill in recognizing when a division exercise involves basic-fact division with a remainder; this was discussed under the topic "Division with Remainders" in Chapter 6. The other readiness understandings and skills have been discussed in several previous chapters. Review of all the prerequisite learnings is necessary before beginning instruction in division algorithm. For most learners, a reintroduction to mental calculation with multiples of powers of 10 and estimation will be required.

Reintroduction to mental calculation with multiples of powers of 10 includes finding quotients when the dividend is 10s or 100s and the divisor is 1s, 10s, or 100s. Examples are: (a) $60 \div 3 = 20$, (b) $60 \div 20 = 3$, (c) $600 \div 2 = 300$, (d) $600 \div 20 = 30$, and (e) $600 \div 200 = 3$.

Children review rules by relating multiplication and division. They work with materials such as squared paper and the abacus to give visual representation to solutions found using the rules. Counting backward by 10s or 100s or using repeated subtraction to find solutions can give meaning to the rules.

To create an interest in relearning mental division with multiples of powers of 10, a new game, THINK BIG, is introduced. The game is an adaptation of BINGO. The game cards show quotients; the caller cards are division questions, such as those illustrated in the left members of the equations in (a) to (e) above. Some of the other old games can also be revised to deal with division mental computation. Children can use exercise practice sheets in teams of two to help each other learn.

A reintroduction to division mental computation with multiples of powers of 10 is followed by a reintroduction of *estimation* in division. To begin, examples such as the following are studied by learners:

$$64 \div 21 = N \qquad \text{Estimate, 3}$$
$$62 \div 2 = N \qquad \text{Estimate, 30}$$
$$810 \div 21 = N \qquad \text{Estimate, 40}$$
$$1409 \div 72 = N \qquad \text{Estimate, 20}$$

It will be observed that these examples involve rounding down. Later examples will require rounding up or rounding one number up, the other down, for good estimates.

Lessons to reintroduce or introduce division estimation help learners focus on the steps in the process using what they know. Children know estimation in multiplication and they can do mental division with multiples of powers of 10. They can therefore be asked to think about what they have learned and to suggest how to estimate in division. Several examples can be used by children in explaining the process they would use to estimate. In teaching division estimation, teachers can tell the class that in division computation estimation is more important than in the other operations with large numbers. Expectations for achievement are set in class discussions.

Card games and board games can be adapted to motivate learning estimation in division. Individual or partner practice is also used to give learners sufficient opportunities to develop skill in estimation. Exercise sheets with answers or cards with answers can be used by a child individually or two together (one is the "teacher," the other the "learner"). Large-group practice and games for more than 6 players are not used, because an individual wastes time waiting for his or her turn. (Children rarely rehearse when another has a turn.)

Children can be supported in their efforts to learn by receiving recognition when, by a combination of luck and ability, they achieve in estimation games. For example, if the RUMMY GAME is adapted to estimation, the winner of a game could get 100 points, the losers, 50 each. During a week or two children would have opportunities to play the estimation games. The children who accumulate 1000 points are "Estimation Champs of the Week," and their names (or pictures) are displayed in a prominent place. (Children also have opportunities to review addition with numbers to 1000 as they keep records of scores.)

When teachers ascertain that learners have developed understanding and skill in prerequisite learnings, they introduce the division algorithm. Children are not taught the division algorithm until they have developed the prerequisite knowledge, because if they are lacking in understandings and skills they cannot relate them to attain new insights.

Constructing Division Computation Rules

Initial study of division computation rules is limited to examples in which the divisor is less than 10. Children learn that the division algorithm is a series of steps involving division, multiplication, and subtraction. Deductive or inductive methods guide pupils to comprehend, construct, and use the computation rule. A deductive questioning lesson to introduce the division algorithm is given in Box 7-5. Some learners use intuitive ideas developed from working with materials to comprehend the steps.

Follow-up lessons give learners opportunities to review the thought process involved and make translations using materials (Figure 7-15). Later, study is extended to examples in which the divisor is a multiple of 10 and the dividend is a sum of 100s plus 10s and a multiple of the divisor—for example, $40\overline{)880}$. The computation rule is extended to these examples. In all computational work, estimation continues to be stressed as the first step.

When children can find correct quotients and can explain the sense of the process, they are given experiences to extend and consolidate knowledge.

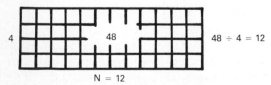

FIGURE 7-15. Using materials to show division computation.

Extending and Consolidating Knowledge of Division Computation

Following an introduction to division algorithms, learners study division computation in which more mental manipulation is required than initially. The new examples increase in complexity: subtraction is required in the 100s ($40\overline{)960}$); the dividend is not a multiple of the divisor and there is a remainder ($81\overline{)1128}$); the first partial quotient may be too low if the divisor is rounded up ($26\overline{)1066}$); or the first partial quotient may be too high if the divisor is rounded down ($32\overline{)606}$). Children learn that the first partial quotient is a "trial" quotient and various decisions may need to be made: discard the first quotient, or, if the first partial quotient is too low, "keep going."

Inductive or deductive questioning methods are used with examples, or the teacher can model thinking to present the material. Whenever possible, children use inference to extend their learning. Materials are used to enable learners to verify ideas in situations where objects or diagrams are practical to study. Estimation continues to be emphasized as the first step, a check of the estimation as the last step.

The long algorithm can be used by learners for several years. Some children will always use this form. However, children who have ability to process a number of items mentally should be introduced to the standard algorithm. Learners are guided to grasp the meaning of the standard form insofar as possible by considering that place value tells powers of 10. The thinking accompanying an example can be:

Thinking Division Using the Standard Algorithm

```
    32   (30)
24)768
  − 72
    48
  − 48
     0
```

Estimate: 30 is quotient;
think $7 \div 2 = N$;
the fact is $6 \div 2 = 3$;
3×24 is tens,
place 3 above 6;
multiply 3×24, write product under 76;
subtract, bring down 8;
$4 \div 2 = 2$;
write 2 in the ones' place;
multiply 2×24, write product and subtract;
no remainder.
Check estimate; O.K.

*BOX 7-5. SAMPLE LESSON: INTRODUCING THE DIVISION ALGORITHM
              (GRADE 4)*

1. Girls and boys, we have a new learning in division today. We are making splendid progress in learning division. The new exercises are like this:

$$4\overline{)84} \quad 3\overline{)63} \quad 2\overline{)86} \quad 3\overline{)96}$$

Let's begin by reading the exercises.

2. To help us, we should think what we know about division. I'll make a list on the board as you explain what you know. (Teacher may need to ask probing questions, such as: What do you know about . . . ?)

    What We Know About Division

    a. Estimating quotients. [What is the estimated quotient in the first one? (20.) How did you find it? (We thought $80 \div 4 = 20$.) Good.]

    b. What division means. (Like, in the first example, How many 4s = 84, or 84 divided into 4 equal-size parts.)

    c. We can find the quotient by subtracting.

3. That is an excellent list. Let's put these ideas together to find how to do the division examples. (We could subtract.) O.K., let's try that. You learned that when you studied the basic facts.

$$
\begin{array}{rl}
(\quad 84 & \\
-\ 4 & 1 \\
\hline
80 & \\
-\ 4 & 2 \\
\hline
76 & . \\
. & . \\
. & \\
0 & {}^{21}) \\
\end{array}
$$

(That's too long. I got 21. It takes forever. There must be an easier way.)

4. There is an easier way to subtract fast. I'll help you figure it out. Whenever we work with large numbers, we think of the parts. What parts do we think about? (Tens and ones.) Yes.

5. Look at the first example. Think about tens in the dividend. Estimation will help you. What is the estimate? (20.) How did you find that? ($80 \div 4 = 20$.) Good. Instead of subtracting one 4, you can subtract 20 4s. Notice what I write and think what it means.

$$
\begin{array}{r}
4\overline{)84} \\
-80 \quad 20 \\
\hline
\end{array}
$$

(It tells $4 \times 20 = 80$, and you wrote 80 below the 84 to subtract. That's easy!)

6. That's right; it is easy. What part of the dividend do we have left to divide by 4? (4.) How do we know that? (We subtracted 80 from 84 and have 4 left.) What do you think you do now? (Subtract one more 4.) Yes, first you divide $4 \div 4 = 1$.

Multiply 4 × 1 = 4 and subtract. We write it like this.

```
  4)84
  −80      20
   ‾‾
    4
  − 4    +  1
   ‾‾      ‾‾
    0      21
```

Look at what I have written. Where are the partial quotients? Where is the final quotient? Where is a partial dividend? Why do we have a partial dividend? How did we find the partial dividend? (Children point and explain their ideas in answer to the questions.)

7.   Please take paper and pencil. We will do the next three examples. (The children complete the last three examples above. The teacher continues to question learners to insure they estimate the quotients, use the estimates as the first partial quotients, know multiplying and subtracting are necessary to find partial dividends, and check their estimates. The focus in discussion is that this method is fast subtraction and that estimating helps with finding the first partial quotient.)

8.   Good work. Let us study what we have done and make a list of ideas to keep in mind when we do long division. What do we always do first? (Estimate!) Yes, I'll write that to begin our list.

In Division We Remember To:

	1. Estimate the quotient first.
How can we use the estimated quotient?	2. Use the estimated quotient as the first partial quotient.
What next?	3. Multiply the partial quotient and the divisor, then subtract the product from the dividend.
Then?	4. The new dividend is divided by the divisor. Go to step 3.
Then?	5. Add partial quotients.
Last?	6. Check estimation.

9.   That is the list that will help you remember how to think in these division exercises. Tomorrow we will learn some more about these exercises. You have gone a long way today. Girls and boys, you are good in mathematics!

Other objectives and activities for extending and consolidating knowledge of division computation are:

1.   Division is checked by multiplying the quotient and the divisor to obtain the dividend. (Division and multiplication are inverse operations.) All computation should be checked.

2.   Children are encouraged to bring real-life experiences involving division estimation or division computation to class to share with others. A bulletin board can highlight these contributions.

3.   Missing-figure problems can be used to encourage relational thinking. For example:

```
      1 __
  __ 6)1008
     −  56
       ‾‾‾‾
         8
```

Children can write and share missing-figure problems.

4. Estimations can be extended to 100s and 1000s. Learners can consider the reason why an equal number of zeros are "dropped" in both dividend and divisor to simplify the estimation; for example:

$$\frac{9865}{531} = \frac{10,000}{500}$$

$$\frac{10,000}{500} \div \frac{100}{100} = \frac{10,0\not{0}\not{0}}{5\not{0}\not{0}} = 20$$

5. The inverse relation between multiplication and division is reviewed using numbers greater than 10. Children, especially gifted learners, can apply what they know about related multiplication and division facts to write related equations with large numbers. For example:

Given	*Pupils Write*
17 × 23 = 391	391 ÷ 23 = 17
888 ÷ 74 = 12	12 × 74 = 888

Equations with a missing factor, product, quotient, divisor, or dividend can be studied by those who are able to write division equations for multiplication equations and multiplication equations for division equations when the numbers are greater than 10.

6. Practice is kept short, and children are encouraged to obtain correct quotients that have been checked for accuracy. The objective is for children to know how to use the division algorithm and to understand what they are doing. Nine of 10 examples correct with no counting defines mastery.

7. Problems include division computation.

The concepts of **prime and composite numbers** can be introduced as children extend and consolidate knowledge of division algorithms. Every number except 1 is either prime (divisible only by itself and 1) or composite (divisible by itself, 1, and one or more prime numbers). While gifted learners often find the topic of prime and composite numbers intriguing and enjoy finding long lists of prime numbers, all children need to develop skill in finding the prime factors of numbers. The study of prime and composite numbers helps children develop this skill. Children begin the study of prime and composite numbers in grade four or five. Instructional suggestions are:

1. To help learners gain an intuitive understanding of prime and composite numbers, ask them to use counters or squared paper to make every array possible for each number from 2 to 26. Box 7-6 shows arrays for 4, 8, 11, 12, 13, 16, and 20. Children will observe that some numbers can be shown by more than one array and some cannot.
2. When children have been introduced to division algorithms with divisors less than 10, they can construct the concepts of prime and composite numbers. Two approaches are:
   a. Find all the divisors of each number from 2 to 100. Record the findings. (No divisor can be divisible by any other number than itself and 1.) Observe the two categories of numbers in the record of work.
   b. Make the Sieve of Eratosthenes (Figure 7-16). This approach was invented in ancient times by Eratosthenes. A 100-square is used with numerals from 1 to 100 written in individual squares. First the numerals for numbers divisible by 2 are crossed out with a crayon and 2 is circled, next the numerals for numbers divisible by 3 are crossed out with another colored crayon and 3 is circled, and so forth,

1	2	3	~~4~~	5	~~6~~	7	~~8~~	~~9~~	~~10~~
11	~~12~~	13	~~14~~	~~15~~	~~16~~	17	~~18~~	19	~~20~~
~~21~~	~~22~~	23	~~24~~	~~25~~	~~26~~	~~27~~	~~28~~	29	~~30~~
31	~~32~~	~~33~~	~~34~~	~~35~~	~~36~~	37	~~38~~	~~39~~	~~40~~
41	~~42~~	43	~~44~~	~~45~~	~~46~~	47	~~48~~	~~49~~	~~50~~
~~51~~	~~52~~	53	~~54~~	~~55~~	~~56~~	~~57~~	~~58~~	59	~~60~~
61	~~62~~	~~63~~	~~64~~	~~65~~	~~66~~	67	~~68~~	~~69~~	~~70~~
71	~~72~~	73	~~74~~	~~75~~	~~76~~	~~77~~	~~78~~	79	~~80~~
~~81~~	~~82~~	83	~~84~~	~~85~~	~~86~~	~~87~~	~~88~~	89	~~90~~
~~91~~	~~92~~	~~93~~	~~94~~	~~95~~	~~96~~	97	~~98~~	~~99~~	~~100~~

FIGURE 7-16. Sieve of Eratosthenes.

BOX 7-6.   ARRAYS FOR PRIME AND COMPOSITE NUMBERS

```
X X      X        X X      X        X        X X      X X X X      X
X X      X        X X      X        X        X X      X X X X      X
         X        X X      X        X        X X      X X X X      X
         X        X X      X        X        X X                   X
                           X        X        X X                   X
                           X        X        X X                   X
                           X        X                             X
                           X        X                             X
                                    X                             X
                                    X                             X
                                    X                             X
                                                                  X

         4                 8        11                            12
```

```
X        X X X X      X X      X        X X X X X      X X      X
X·       X X X X      X X      X        X X X X X      X X      X
X        X X X X      X X      X        X X X X X      X )(     X
X        X X X )(     X X      X        X X X X X      X X      X
X                     X X      X                       X X      X
X                     X X      X                       X X      X
X                     X X      X                       X X      X
X                     X X      X                       X X      X
X                             X                       X X      X
X                             X                       X X      X
X                             X                               X
X                             X                               X
X                             X                               X
                              X                               X
                              X                               X
                              X                               X
                                                              X
                                                              X
                                                              X
                                                              X

13                            16                              20
```

using numbers that have not yet been found to be multiples. The sieve is completed by circling all numerals for numbers that are not multiples of other numbers. Pupils observe the two categories in the diagram: numerals crossed out and numerals circled. (The number 1 is a separate category and neither prime nor composite.)

After noting the two categories using either initial activity, children describe the characteristics of the numbers in each category and learn the words *prime* and *composite*.

3. Next children are helped to find a method for determining if a number is prime or composite. Say: What numbers are prime? Composite? People for over two thousand years have asked these questions. What is

your idea for a method to determine prime numbers? This introduction can motivate many children to learn a method for determining which numbers are prime and which are products of primes.

Children who have constructed the concepts of prime and composite numbers often infer a "trial-and-error" method. One or more in a class usually say, "Try to divide the number by 2, 3, 5, ..." Children use their method with several numbers. (If no pupil suggests the method, the teacher can model the procedure. Children observe, explain, and use the modeled procedure.)

The "trial-and-error" approach to determining if a number is prime or composite gives insight into the structure of numbers and is often used. Another approach is the "factor-tree" method (Figure 7-17). Teachers introduce this method with the comment that it can help learn prime factorization. Factoring begins at the top of the "tree" and follows along the "branches," showing, whenever possible, factors of factors. The process always gives the prime factors of composites when it is completed, or it shows a number is prime.

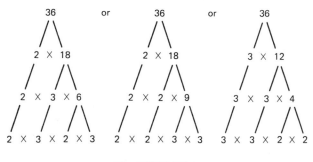

$$36 = 2 \times 2 \times 3 \times 3$$

FIGURE 7-17. Factor trees for 36.

4. Motivating activities follow an introduction to finding prime and composite numbers. Teachers ask: What are the prime numbers in the first 500 numbers? How many do you think we can find? Two activities are follow-up to these questions.

   a. Suggest children prepare a bulletin board display for prime numbers. Pupils post numerals for prime numbers they have discovered together with their names or initials. Note how the list lengthens, and refer to class hy-

potheses regarding how many primes to 500.

   b. Talk about Goldbach's Conjecture. Tell the class that Christian Goldbach in 1742 discovered that even numbers greater than 2 can be found by adding only two primes. For example, $2 + 2 = 4, 3 + 3 = 6; 3 + 5 = 8$ and $5 + 5 = 10$. Many children will enjoy adding pairs of prime numbers to explore this idea. (*Note:* There is no formal proof for this rule, so it is still known as Goldbach's Conjecture. However, no exception has yet been found!) Some way should be found for children to share their examples of Goldbach's Conjecture. Again the bulletin board or a mathematics reporting time could be used to highlight pupils' work.

5. Exponents can be introduced to some learners. Children learn that an exponent is a symbol above and to the right of a numeral that stands for a number called the base. The exponent indicates how many times the base is to be used as a factor—for example, $4^5 = 4 \times 4 \times 4 \times 4 \times 4$.

Skill in determining prime numbers and prime factors of composite numbers is useful in working with fractional numbers. Understanding of prime and composite numbers also gives knowledge of the multiplicative structure of numbers and increases children's power to deal with quantitative situations.

Children are given many opportunities to study prime and composite numbers. Learning experiences emphasize mental calculation rather than paper-and-pencil work. By the end of the elementary school children are expected to have immediate recall of the prime numbers to 50.

Knowledge of prime and composite numbers is extended to include concepts of **least common multiple (LCM)** and **greatest common factor (GCF)**. The LCM of two or more numbers is the smallest number that is a multiple of the numbers. For example, 10, 20, 30, . . . are common multiples of 2 and 5, but 10 is the LCM. The GCF of two or more numbers is the largest number that is a factor of both numbers. For example, 4 is the GCF of 12 and 16. Procedures for finding the LCM and GCF are:

To find the LCM of two or more numbers, find the prime factors of each number; the

LCM is the product of the prime factors with the highest powers. For example, to find the LCM of 72 and 48, determine their prime factors:

$$72 = 2 \times 2 \times 2 \times 3 \times 3 = 2^3 \times 3^2$$
$$48 = 2 \times 2 \times 2 \times 2 \times 3 = 2^4 \times 3$$

The LCM of 72 and 48 is $2 \times 2 \times 2 \times 2 \times 3 \times 3 = 2^4 \times 3^2 = 144$.

To find the GCF of two or more numbers, find their prime factors. The GCF is the product of prime factors common to the numbers. For example, 72 and 48 have $2 \times 2 \times 2 \times 3$ in common; the GCF is $2^3 \times 3 = 24$.

Children who are capable learners of elementary school mathematics should have opportunities to study LCM and GCF. Other children can study this topic if they are interested in doing so and will expend the effort required to achieve understanding and skill.

The LCM and GCF can be used in working with fractional numbers. This is discussed in the next chapter.

SUMMARY

The focus of this chapter has been guiding learners to use inference in arriving at new meanings. Children learn logical thinking over a long period of time. During the middle and late elementary school years, children are given more and more experiences to reason informally about mathematical ideas. Learning algorithms provides excellent opportunities to guide learners to use inference to attain new knowledge. Materials are used to verify rules and visualize solutions. Learners who cannot use inference employ materials to develop rules. The chapter has also discussed procedures to insure that meanings pupils form will be retained.

Instruction attends to prerequisite understanding, particularly estimation skills; supports learners in their efforts to construct the meaning of algorithms; and encourages learners to extend and consolidate their knowledge to the extent possible. Extending and consolidating experiences should be motivating and, whenever possible, learner-selected. Learners should develop insights into number relations and develop abilities to use those insights in a variety of situations.

STUDY QUESTIONS

1. Ask 4 children in grade five or six how they mentally compute sums and products with multiples of powers of 10. What can you conclude from their replies?

2. Plan an inductive questioning sequence to teach renaming 10s as 100s plus 10s (for example, 34 10s is 340). Include the use of materials. Compare your plan with that of another student. How are they alike? Different? Why?

3. Survey 5 adults outside of class in regard to their use of adding by endings (without and with bridging 10s). Discuss your findings with other members of the class. What are the implications of your findings for teaching adding by endings?

4. Assume children in your third-grade class can explain the reasons for renaming 1s as 10 plus 1s in an addition example (such as $28 + 46 = N$). What other rules would you expect pupils could infer from this knowledge of renaming? Why?

5. Plan a deductive questioning lesson to teach renaming in subtraction when the minuend is a multiple of a power of 10 (for example, $700 - 456 = N$).

6. Ask several adults and children to explain the rationale for computational records similar to:

$$
\begin{array}{r}
39 \\
\times\ 47 \\
\hline
273 \\
+\ 1560 \\
\hline
1833 \\
\end{array}
$$

Compare their explanations. What reasons can you give for similarities and differences in their responses?

7. Outline knowledge that is prerequisite to learning estimation of products between 100 and 1000.

8. Write two objectives for gifted learners to extend their knowledge of multiplication and division computation.

REFERENCES

Atweh, Bill, "Developing Mental Arithmetic," in *Mathematics for the Middle Grades (5-9)*, 1982 Yearbook of the National Council of Teachers of Mathematics, eds. Linda Silvey and James R. Smart. Reston, VA: The National Council of Teachers of Mathematics, Inc., 1982.

Hamrick, Katherine B., and William D. McKillip, "How Computational Skills Contribute to the Meaningful Learning of Arithmetic," in *Developing Computational Skills*, 1978 Yearbook of the National Council of Teachers of Mathematics, eds. Marilyn N. Suydam and Robert E. Reys. Reston, VA: The National Council of Teachers of Mathematics, Inc., 1978.

Hazekamp, Donald W., "Teaching Multiplication and Division Algorithms," in *Developing Computational Skills*, 1978 Yearbook of the National Council of Teachers of Mathematics, eds. Marilyn N. Suydam and Robert E. Reys. Reston, VA: The National Council of Teachers of Mathematics, Inc., 1978.

Hohlfeld, Joe, "An Inductive Approach to Prime Factors," *Arithmetic Teacher*, 29, no. 4 (December 1981), 28-29.

Kennedy, Leonard M., *Guiding Children's Learning of Mathematics*, 4th ed., chaps. 8, 10. Belmont, CA: Wadsworth Publishing Company, 1984.

Robold, Alice I., "Patterns in Multiples," *Arithmetic Teacher*, 29, no. 8 (April 1982), 21-23.

Skemp, Richard R., *The Psychology of Learning Mathematics*. New York: Penguin Books, Ltd., 1971.

8 LEARNING AND TEACHING FRACTIONAL-NUMBER AND RATIO CONCEPTS

Mathematics educators do not agree on the terminology children should use for numbers expressed in the form $\frac{a}{b}$, in which b is not 0. Some educators advise calling them **rational numbers** to introduce the language and concepts of mathematics to learners as soon as possible. Other educators suggest referring to these numbers as **fractional numbers** or **fractions** to help children grasp the idea of division implicit in the concept. Furthermore, the numerals for fractional (rational) numbers are called either fractions or fractional numerals. We will use *fractional number* to refer to the number concept and *fraction* to refer to the numeral. However, to avoid wordiness, occasionally this distinction will not be made.

Fractions have two interpretations: (1) *A fraction can represent a quotient.* A fractional number gives a solution when division of whole numbers is undefined (for example, $\frac{1}{2}, \frac{3}{4}$); whole numbers can also be considered fractional numbers and written as fractions (for example, $\frac{4}{2}$ and $\frac{6}{1}$). (2) *A fraction can represent a ratio or relative comparison between two numbers* (for example, $\frac{1}{4}$ can mean 1 compared to 4).

The three phase learning-teaching sequence applies to fractional numbers as well as other topics and is the basis for the discussion in this chapter. The first three sections deal with the fraction-as-a-quotient interpretation. The fourth section discusses understanding ratio, proportion, and probability. The final section is a brief summary.

DEVELOPING PREREQUISITE UNDERSTANDING FOR FRACTIONAL-NUMBER CONCEPTS

An intuitive understanding of the partitive notion of division is prerequisite to forming concepts of fractional numbers as quotients. Certain whole-part relations are implicit in this meaning of division: The whole is exhausted; that is, the parts combine to form the whole. The parts are equal in number or congruent. A child's awareness of these ideas is assessed using a Piagetian task. The child is asked to cut a "cake"—paper or clay—so that each of two or more dolls will receive an equal share. (This test is described fully in Appendix I.) The child's responses to this test help the teacher determine which objectives and activities to emphasize in instruction.

Children who have an intuitive understanding of whole-part ideas, as revealed by success with the Piagetian "cake" task, are guided to develop other understandings during this instructional phase. A fractional number is named using two numbers. Pupils know intuitively it can be renamed. Pupils engage in a variety of learning experiences with concrete and graphic materials to form these ideas. Children who have not developed fundamental whole-part ideas related to fractional numbers participate in many of the same activities, but the teacher guides them to become aware of the whole-part concepts embedded in the activities. Learning experiences during the prerequisite phase of instruction include folding, cutting, and coloring; designing; classifying; picturing; and playing games. Often these activities involve problem solving.

Folding, Cutting, and Coloring

Many classroom assignments in different subjects involve folding paper in halves or fourths. Young children fold drawing paper for use in illustrating the parts and sequence of stories they hear, read, or create. They fold paper for phonic books, number books, and science or social studies illustrations. Children fold and cut paper for fun activities to create figures such as hearts, trees, Christmas ornaments, lace, and the like. Often children can be asked to color or decorate a fractional part of these figures (Figure 8-1). As children engage in these activities, teachers ask questions such as the following:

How does your paper look after you folded the corners together? How did it look before you folded it? What has changed? What do we call each part? What do you notice about your heart?

You have decorated each part of your ornament in a different way. Tell us what you did. What do you notice about the shapes of the parts you decorated? What do you notice about the whole?

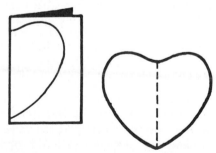

FIGURE 8-1. Folding and cutting to show one-half.

Designing

Parquetry pieces can be placed to make a design, with halves, fourths, or thirds shown by different colored pieces. In beginning work of

this kind, children can cover a model with parquetry blocks to obtain fractional parts using different colors. Later, children can be asked to create designs of several colors so that the designs show fractional numbers such as halves, fourths, or thirds. Gifted learners can create somewhat complex designs (Figure 8-2) to illustrate renaming fractional numbers. (Such designs would also provide a motivating reintroduction to fractional numbers in the upper grades.) Children share what they have created and explain the fractional numbers displayed in their designs.

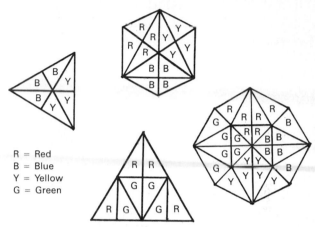

FIGURE 8-2. Parquetry block designs showing fractional numbers and renaming.

Shapes partitioned and colored to show fractional numbers can also be used in patterning. These designs can be used for decoration on items used by the children, such as place mats.

Classifying

Children should be given opportunities to classify figures according to the fractional numbers shown; that is, children put representations of halves, fourths, or thirds in separate piles or boxes. The activity directions are: Put all the cards together that belong together in some way. Children can also sort by separating figures displaying fractional numbers from figures that do not show fractional numbers (Figure 8-3). After completing these activities, children should have opportunities to explain the reasons for their classifications.

Fraction cutouts made from plastic, wood, or cardboard are often used to show fractional numbers. Generally they are fractional parts of

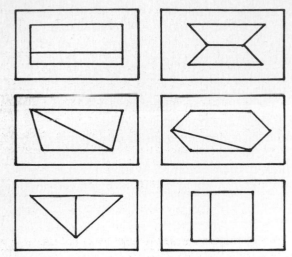

FIGURE 8-3.   Figure cards for classifying.

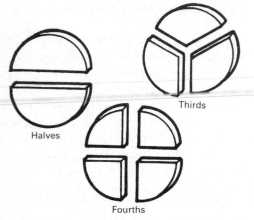

FIGURE 8-4.   Fraction cutouts.

circular or rectangular regions (Figure 8-4). They are supplied by the teacher for pupil use. Pupils can compare and classify pieces.

Picturing

Children can experiment with Cuisenaire rods and fraction strips (laminated cardboard) to create "pictures" of fractions (Figure 8-5). In working with Cuisenaire rods, it is necessary first to establish how 1 will be represented. If chil-

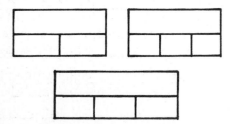

FIGURE 8-5.   Examples of fraction strips to represent fractional numbers.

dren cannot disregard the whole numbers associated with the rods, they cannot be used to represent fractional numbers.

Squared paper can also be used by learners to explore different representations of fractional numbers (Figure 8-6). Figures can be outlined on the paper and fractional parts shaded in a variety of ways to make fraction "pictures." Many different representations are possible and can give an intuitive understanding of the renaming of fractional numbers.

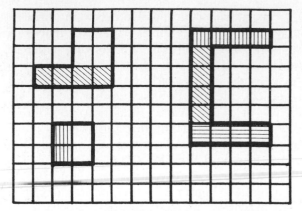

FIGURE 8-6.   Examples of squared paper diagrams to represent fractional numbers.

Playing Games

The development of fractional-number concepts is fostered as children play games. The old games, FISH, RUMMY, SMILING FACE, BINGO, and DOMINOES, are adapted to match figures showing representations of $\frac{1}{2}$, $\frac{1}{4}$, and $\frac{1}{3}$. The directions for a new game, FRAC-SPIN, are:

> Two children play the game. Each child has a game sheet with dittoed figures and a spinner, as shown in Figure 8-7. At the same time, each child spins his or her spinner and circles a figure on his or her game sheet to show the fractional number indicated by the spinner. If no figure can be found on the game sheet, the child must "pass." The winner is the child who is able to circle every figure on his or her sheet before the other child.

As children work at their tasks and games, teachers ask questions to help them develop an intuitive awareness of fractional numbers. The questions are asked so that the answers will indicate a child's grasp of certain concepts: the whole has a given number of parts; each part covers the same amount of surface; the fractional number being represented has a name and can be shown in different ways.

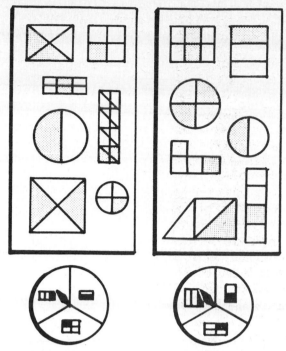

FIGURE 8-7. Game boards and spinners for Frac-Spin game.

Children are ready to advance in their study when they are successful in the Piagetian task that deals with fractional numbers, can illustrate halves and fourths by folding paper or making "pictures," and can classify a set of cards showing halves, thirds, and fourths into appropriate subsets. Most children attain these understandings by the end of grade one or early in grade two.

CONSTRUCTING A CONCEPT OF FRACTIONAL NUMBERS

A concept of fractional numbers is constructed as children abstract from their experiences and become aware that the two numbers comprising a fractional number have distinct meanings: The first number tells the number of parts being considered and the second number tells how many equal-size parts make up the whole. As children construct this concept, they learn to write fractions. A sample lesson for introducing the concept and the fractional-number symbol is given in Box 8-1.

Learning Experiences

Activities, problems, and games help learners internalize the concept of fractional num-

bers and develop skill in writing fractions. Activities emphasize the generation of examples not represented previously in instruction (for example, folding paper to show eighths and naming each fractional part as $\frac{1}{8}$). While labeling diagrams representing fractional numbers new to learners is also a learning task assigned to children, the production of examples is stressed because it enables learners to infer examples rather than react to those created by another.

Problem solving with fractional numbers is an important aspect of this phase of instruction. An example of a problem is: If twelve children share a birthday cake equally, what fractional part of the cake does each get? Children can make up problems such as this one and ask others to find the solutions.

Games that aid in constructing the concept of fractional numbers are variations of the old games. The games now include figures representing fractional numbers and fractions to match with the figures. Fractional numbers other than $\frac{1}{2}$, $\frac{1}{4}$, and $\frac{1}{3}$ are used. To build the concept, children need experience with many fractional numbers: $\frac{1}{5}$s, $\frac{1}{10}$s, $\frac{1}{6}$s, $\frac{1}{12}$s, and $\frac{1}{8}$s are used frequently in the games.

When children can write a fraction for each of several fractional numbers shown by drawings and can produce a drawing or fold paper to explain the meaning of each of several fractions, they move to the next phase of instruction: extending and consolidating knowledge.

EXTENDING AND CONSOLIDATING KNOWLEDGE OF FRACTIONAL NUMBERS

After learners grasp the part-of-a-whole meaning of fractional numbers and use their understanding in working with many examples, they study related ideas to enrich the meaning of fractional numbers and develop intuitive understanding of topics to be introduced later. During this instructional phase children learn ideas of non-unit fractions (for example, $\frac{3}{4}$); partitioning-of-a-set concept; the counting of fractional numbers; number-line representation of fractional numbers; comparing and ordering; equivalent fractions; partitioning a fractional number; indicated-division concept; and problem solving with fractional numbers.

BOX 8-1. SAMPLE LESSON: GUIDING LEARNERS TO CONSTRUCT THE CONCEPT OF FRACTIONAL NUMBERS (GRADE 2)

1. Boys and girls, I have some figures on the overhead. You have seen these figures before. Today we are going to learn more about them.

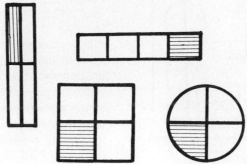

2. What do you know about these figures? (They show fourths. Each has four parts that are the same. One part is shaded. The square shows one-fourth. The circle shows one-fourth.)

3. Yes, you know all those things. We can write one-fourth this way: $\frac{1}{4}$. Look at this numeral. Think about what it tells you. (The "4" says fourths. The "1" says one of the four, and so on.) Yes. This numeral says, "Think about one of four equal-size parts of a figure." Write $\frac{1}{4}$ in the air. Think about what it means.

4. Now look at these figures.

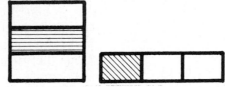

    What do you know about them? (They show thirds. Each figure has three equal parts. One part out of the three is shaded.)

5. Yes. Think about how to write $\frac{1}{3}$. Think about what it means. How can we write one-third? (If no child grasps the rule, say: Let me begin. I will write $\frac{1}{3}$. Please read what I have written.)

6. Yes, $\frac{1}{3}$ is the fraction. Think about what it means. Look at the figures to help you. (It means to think about one of the three equal parts.)

7. Let's write $\frac{1}{3}$ in the air. Think about what it means as you write it. John, tell us what you are thinking. . . .

8. Look at the last set of figures.
    What do they show? (One-halves. Each has two equal parts. One part is shaded.)

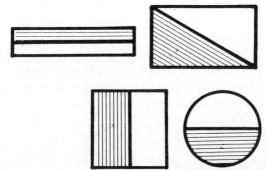

9. These figures show halves. When we think about one-half we think about one of two equal-size parts of a drawing. How do you write one-half? (If no one grasps the rule the teacher says, What goes below the line? Why? What goes above the line? Why?) Write $\frac{1}{2}$ in the air. Think about what it means. The word "halves" does not tell as much as the word "fourths." We must remember we are thinking about 2 equal-size parts in a figure. One-half means one of the two equal-size parts. Think that to yourself. Close your eyes and make a picture of $\frac{1}{2}$. Tony, tell us about your mind picture. . . .

10. Good. Let's solve a puzzle now. Please look at the chart. (Display chart showing figures partitioned into fifths.) What do you notice on this chart? What would we call the part shaded in the first figure? (Oh, one-fifth!) . . .

11. Great! Why? (Several pupils give their reasons.) Write one-fifth . . . .

12. Boys and girls, today you have learned about fractions. Let's review the fractions we have learned. Terry, please write one fraction we learned today on the board. Tell us what it means. Look at the figures on the board to help you. (Repeat for other fractions.)

13. Everyone will receive a sheet with figures showing fractional numbers ($\frac{1}{3}$, $\frac{1}{4}$, $\frac{1}{2}$, $\frac{1}{5}$, $\frac{1}{6}$). Take a few minutes to write the fractions that explain the drawings. . . . Choose a partner. Take turns explaining what you wrote and why.

14. Let's all discuss what we have done. Gretchen, tell us about the first figure. (The class discusses the fraction for the fractional number displayed in each figure.)

15. Good. You have thought carefully and learned a very important idea today. You have learned what fractions mean. How do you feel? (Happy, and so on.)

Nonunit Fractions

During the time learners are developing intuitive understanding and constructing the concept of fractional numbers, most work with fractional numbers represented by figures in which only one of the congruent parts is shaded. The fractions are in the form: $1/b$. They are unit fractions.

After children grasp the concept of unit fractions, they learn about nonunit fractions through the study of figures in which more than one of the congruent parts is to be considered. Teachers can introduce the idea by saying, "Let's do some coloring of figures that show fourths. Please begin with the first figure. Color one-fourth blue. Color one-fourth red. How many fourths are colored? How do you think we would write a fraction for two-fourths? Why do you think that? Look at the second figure. Color three-fourths green. What did you do? Why? Write three-fourths on your paper. What did you write? Why?"

Learners can continue by working with partners. They take turns representing different fractional numbers on figures supplied by the teacher and writing the corresponding fractions. They can also use squared paper to produce illustrations for nonunit fractions. Counting and adding are used by children as they identify nonunit fractions and represent them.

In these lessons the words **numerator, denominator,** and **terms** are introduced. Children learn that the *numerator* is the number represented above the bar in a fraction and the *denominator* the number represented below the bar. The word *terms* is used to indicate the numerator and denominator.

Partitioning-of-a-Set Concept

Soon after children are introduced to unit and nonunit fractions associated with regions partitioned into congruent parts, they are introduced to relating fractions to sets partitioned into equivalent subsets. An instructional sequence to develop this concept is given in Box 8-2.

Instruction dealing with the partitioning-of-a-set concept next includes consideration of

BOX 8-2.   SAMPLE LESSON: GUIDING LEARNERS TO CONSTRUCT THE PARTITIONING-OF-A-SET CONCEPT (GRADE 3)

1.   To learn more about fractional numbers, let us first think about how we name the fractional part each gets when a whole is divided equally. If three share a small pie equally, what fractional number does each receive? ($\frac{1}{3}$.) If four share equally? ($\frac{1}{4}$.) Two—and so on.

2.   Good. Now let's think about sharing a set of holiday presents. If there are two children in the family, what fractional number should each get? ($\frac{1}{2}$.) Here is a picture of 6 presents. How many is $\frac{1}{2}$ for each child? (3.) Yes, $\frac{1}{2}$ of 6 is 3. I'll write that on the board. Let's look at some other examples. (Teacher shows 8, 9, and 12 drawings in turn that represent presents and asks the following questions.)

Here is a set of 8 presents for four children to share equally. How many does each get? (2.) Please show it. What fractional number did each get? ($\frac{1}{4}$.) Why? I'll write $\frac{1}{4}$ of 8 is 2.

This set of 9 is for three children. How many does each get? (3.) Please show it. What fractional number does each get? Why? I'll write $\frac{1}{3}$ of 9 is 3.

The last drawing shows 12 presents. If there are two children to share equally, how many does each get? (6.) Please show it. What fractional number is that? Why? I'll write that down. $\frac{1}{2}$ of 12 is 6.

3.   Let us look at what we have been thinking:

$$\frac{1}{2} \text{ of 6 is 3.}$$

$$\frac{1}{4} \text{ of 8 is 2.}$$

$$\frac{1}{3} \text{ of 9 is 3.}$$

$$\frac{1}{2} \text{ of 12 is 6.}$$

If you did not have the pictures to study, how could you use some number facts to help you get the answer? (The teacher may have to prompt with: Think what fact goes with these numbers: 6, 2, 3; 8, 4, 2; . . . ? Oh, you can use division.)

4.   Good. You divide. Look at the fraction. You can think, divide by the number shown below the bar. The bar is another way to give the direction to divide. Let's do a few examples before we go on. The teacher writes on the board.

$\frac{1}{4}$ of 16 is ___

$\frac{1}{3}$ of 12 is ___

$\frac{1}{5}$ of 10 is ___

$\frac{1}{6}$ of 12 is ___

$\frac{1}{2}$ of 16 is ___

Let's do the first one together. What is the answer and why? (It is $16 \div 4 = 4$.) Let's make a drawing to illustrate that. Tell about it. (Divide 16 into four equal parts. Then notice $\frac{1}{4}$ of 16 is 4.) Good. Neighbors take turns completing the other exercises. Give answers and make drawings to explain what you have done.

The teacher circulates among children to note the work done and give guidance whenever necessary.

5. Let's review what we have done. . . . Good thinking. Tony, please tell us what we have learned today. (How to find fractional numbers of sets.) Yes!

more than one of the equivalent subsets of a set (for example, $\frac{2}{3}$ of 6). Children examine objects or pictures to develop the idea that the number of more than one equivalent subset of a set is found by determining the number of one of the equivalent subsets and multiplying or skip counting to find the number of two or more. Objects and pictures are always used in the primary grades to clarify these ideas.

Counting

Counting by fractional numbers helps many learners. It develops an intuitive understanding of addition, subtraction, and certain interpretations of multiplication and division with fractions.

The lesson to learn counting by fractional numbers can begin when each child in a group folds a piece of paper into fourths. The teacher can say, "Oh, let's see how many fourths we have. Let's count them together. As we count your fourths, hold them up." The children then say, "One-fourth, two-fourths, three-fourths, . . . , thirty-two fourths." The activity continues by asking the class to count halves, thirds, fifths,

and so on. The teacher can have a box of cutouts to use in the counting. The summary questions are: How is counting by fractional numbers like counting by whole numbers? How is it different?

As children count using fraction cutouts and as they label number lines, the equality $a/a = 1$ is emphasized. This idea is important for attaining meaning in later work with fractional numbers. An intuitive understanding of the concept $a/a = 1$ is built as children work with objects and graphic materials.

Number Lines

Work with number lines to represent fractional numbers usually begins in grade four and follows several years of work with number lines to show whole numbers. Initial lessons in using number lines to represent fractional numbers help learners infer from what they know about number lines and fractional numbers to (1) label fractional number lines and (2) represent given fractional numbers on number lines. To guide learners to label number lines to illustrate, for example, $\frac{1}{4}$s, a teacher can display a number

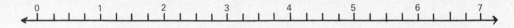

FIGURE 8-8a. Number line with segments.

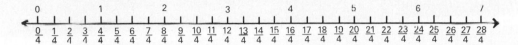

FIGURE 8-8b. A number line labeled with fractions.

line with whole numbers represented and each line segment representing 1 divided into 4 congruent line segments. Teacher comments and questions are similar to, "Let's look at this number line (Figure 8-8a). Is it different in some way from the number lines we have used before? How? What do you think we can name these small line segments? Why? Let's count them. Let's label them (Figure 8-8b). I have a sheet of other number lines. Please think about how the fractions can be written on them. Discuss what you are doing with a neighbor, if that is helpful to you."

Follow-up lessons give learners opportunities to show fractional numbers on number lines by writing fractions at points to indicate line segments representing the fractional numbers (Figure 8-9). In working with number lines to represent fractional numbers, children must be guided to develop the habit of beginning by writing the numerals 0 and 1 at the appropriate points on the number line.

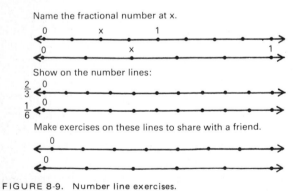

FIGURE 8-9. Number line exercises.

Improper fractions (f/b, in which $f > b$) and numerals in mixed form ($n\ a/b$, in which n, a, and b are counting numbers and a "$+$" sign between n and a/b is assumed) are introduced when children are counting fractional numbers and labeling number lines. Children count and make records of their counting using both improper and mixed numeral forms to develop an

intuitive understanding of equivalent fractions representing numbers greater than 1.

Rules for determining equivalent fractions stated as improper fractions or numerals in mixed form are learned after children are introduced to addition of fractional numbers. This topic is discussed in the next chapter. It can be introduced meaningfully, however, only if learners have had many experiences with objects and graphics that illustrate the idea prior to the introduction of formal rules.

Comparing and Ordering Fractional Numbers

The ability to compare and order fractional numbers is prerequisite to estimation in fractional-number computation and to evaluation of problem solutions involving fractional numbers. Therefore, it is emphasized in instruction.

Beginning lessons in comparing fractional numbers employ different fraction cutouts of congruent wholes. Children compare the size of parts by superimposing them (Figure 8-10). They discuss the meaning of their observations: some parts fit exactly on other parts; some do not. The teacher encourages the children to explain their observations. They are helped to conclude that two fractions can be equivalent or not equivalent.

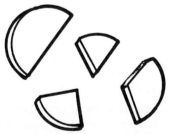

FIGURE 8-10. Fraction cutouts for studying equivalent fractions.

In subsequent lessons children study records of comparisons of fractional numbers that they have developed using fraction cutouts, fraction strips, or number lines. The lesson is planned so that only unit fractions are involved. Through a study of examples, children develop the rule: When the numerator in each of two fractions is 1, the larger fractional number is named by the fraction with the smaller denominator. (For example, $\frac{1}{3}$ is greater than $\frac{1}{4}$.) Number lines can be used to verify this rule. The old game WAR is now played with unit fractions.

Ordering of fractional numbers follows work with comparing fractional numbers. Children can be given a set of fractional numbers named by fractions with numerators of 1 and told to use what they know about comparing fractional numbers to put them in order from smallest to largest. After completing the task, children discuss how they went about the task. Work with ordering fractional numbers includes showing a set of ordered fractional numbers on a number line.

Comparing and ordering with nonunit fractions is studied after children are introduced to equivalent fractions. However, in their work with fraction cutouts and number lines, many children develop an awareness of the relations between numbers given by nonunit fractions, such as $\frac{2}{3}$ and $\frac{3}{4}$. Such understanding should be encouraged.

Equivalent Fractions

Finding equivalent fractions is a major learning requirement. Children must develop understanding and skill for working with equivalent fractions before computation with fractional numbers is emphasized to provide for success in computation.

If pupils' comments indicate they have developed intuitive understanding of equivalent fractions through activities such as discussed previously, teachers introduce the concept in a lesson in which pupils use rods or fraction cutouts of congruent wholes. The children experiment to find which congruent regions (such as $\frac{1}{4}$s) can be joined and superimposed on another region (such as $\frac{1}{2}$) (Figure 8-11). The lesson is introduced with the question: What equal-size fraction cutouts can be joined so that they cover the same surface as one larger cutout? After pupils make discoveries, the teacher says, "Let us make a record of what we have found. How would we do this?" Subsequent discussion leads learners to conclude: When the two sets of frac-

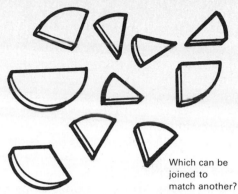

Which can be joined to match another?

FIGURE 8-11. Fraction cutouts for finding equivalent fractions.

tion cutouts cover the same surface, the fractions are equivalent. A record is made using an equals sign.

Another activity makes use of number lines, with congruent line segments representing units in number lines, for $\frac{1}{2}$s, $\frac{1}{4}$s, $\frac{1}{3}$s, $\frac{1}{6}$s, $\frac{1}{8}$s, and $\frac{1}{12}$s. Children label points on the lines and find as many equivalent fractions as they can by examining the number lines (Figure 8-12). Cuisenaire rods or fraction strips can also be used.

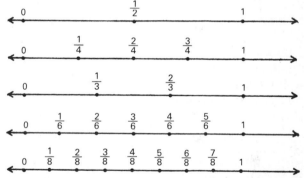

FIGURE 8-12. Number lines for comparing fractional numbers.

After children develop an understanding of equivalent fractions by working with materials, they study pairs of equivalent fractions and infer the rule: To find equivalent fractions, multiply (or divide) the numerator and the denominator of a given fraction by the same nonzero number. After inferring from examples and stating the rule, children are helped to deepen their understanding of the reasons for the rule. The teacher guides children to use their previous knowledge—multiplication by 1 does not change the value of a number—to conclude that since $a/a = 1$, multiplying (or dividing) the numerator and denominator of a fraction by the same number does not change the value of the number.

Children produce examples of the rule to consolidate the learning. They can differentiate examples from nonexamples the teacher provides.

While children are studying equivalent fractions, they should make books illustrating equivalent fractions with drawings of fraction cutouts (these can be prepared by the teacher for pupil shading), fraction strips, squared paper diagrams, or number lines. The books also give the pupils' statement of the rule for finding equivalent fractions and many examples of the rule. When children learn to find missing terms, examples of these exercises are included in the book.

To help children gain immediate recall of commonly used equivalent fractions, the old games can be played. A book is now made up of two cards that give equivalent fractions. Children can make the cards for these games to provide practice in generating equivalent fractions and to give opportunity for contributing to classroom learning experiences.

Making designs to illustrate equivalent fractions is another activity useful for helping learners deepen their understanding of equivalent fractions. Children should create designs whenever possible. In some cases teachers may wish to supply outlines that are readily converted to designs (Figures 8-13a and 8-13b; see also Figure 8-2).

The study of equivalent fractions is followed by work in finding *missing terms* in statements of equivalent fractions—for example, $2/3 = 4/N$. The rule is: Note which corresponding terms (numerators or denominators) are given in both fractions; divide the larger number by the smaller. Use the quotient as a factor (or divisor) with the other given term to find the missing term. For example, $4/N = 8/10$, $4/5 = 8/10$.

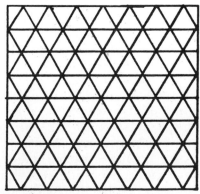

FIGURE 8-13a. Design pattern paper.

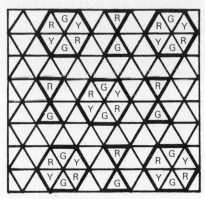

FIGURE 8-13b. Design showing thirds or sixths and halves.

This rule can be introduced in an inductive questioning sequence. (How?) A deductive questioning sequence can also be used; learners generate examples after a question-and-answer procedure in which they are guided to use reasoning to determine the rule. A deductive questioning sequence is given in Box 8-3.

While studying equivalent fractions, children learn to recognize fractions in **lowest terms**. A fraction is in lowest terms if the numerator and denominator have no common divisor other than 1. To introduce the concept, children can be asked to sort fractions such as $\frac{2}{4}, \frac{1}{2}, \frac{3}{4}, \frac{2}{3}, \frac{4}{6}$, and $\frac{6}{8}$ into two groups so that all fractions in a group are alike in some way. Pupils are guided to recognize that one group ($\frac{1}{2}, \frac{2}{3}$, and $\frac{3}{4}$) contains fractions that are in lowest terms (no renaming possible) while the other group ($\frac{2}{4}, \frac{4}{6}$, and $\frac{6}{8}$) is made up of fractions that can be simplified—that is, given in lowest terms. Discussion clarifies that nature of fractions in lowest terms, fractions not in lowest terms, and procedure for simplifying fractions.

To simplify a fraction, children can use the greatest common factor (GCF) as a divisor of the numerator and denominator.

$$\frac{27}{36} = \frac{3 \times 3 \times 3}{3 \times 3 \times 2 \times 2}, \qquad \frac{27 \div (3 \times 3)}{36 \div (3 \times 3)} = \frac{3}{4}$$

The GCF is 3×3; the numerator and denominator are divided by 3×3 to determine that $\frac{27}{36}$ in lowest terms is $\frac{3}{4}$.

An alternate approach to simplifying fractions is a systematic trial-and-error procedure: Try the factors of the numerator (other than 1) in order, beginning with the largest, as divisors of the denominator. For example, to simplify

BOX 8-3. *SAMPLE LESSON: INTRODUCING THE RULE*
         FOR FINDING A MISSING TERM (GRADE 4)

1. Let us look at a new type of exercise today and figure out a rule for finding the missing term. You usually can figure out new rules easily. These are exercises like those we are going to be studying.

$$\frac{3}{4} = \frac{6}{N}$$

$$\frac{2}{5} = \frac{6}{N}$$

$$\frac{1}{4} = \frac{4}{N}$$

2. Let's begin by recalling what we know about finding equivalent fractions. (To find an equivalent fraction, multiply the numerator and denominator of the given fraction by the same number.) Yes.

3. Look at the exercises on the chalkboard. What do you notice about them? (One term is missing in the equivalent fraction.)

4. Let's figure out how we can find the missing term. What number is given in the equivalent fraction that might help us? (The numerator.)

5. How was the first numerator obtained? (Pointing to 6.) What was the given numerator multiplied by? (2.) How did you find that number? (I just looked at it. You can divide 6 by 3.)

6. How does knowing that $3 \times 2 = 6$ help us find N? (Multiply 4 by 2. N is 8.) Correct.

7. John, review for us how we found N. (Divide the given numerators. Use the quotient as a factor with the given denominator to find the missing term.)

8. Yes. Try that rule with the next exercise. What is N? (15.)

9. O.K. Sally, tell us how you find N. ($6 \div 2 = 3; 3 \times 5 = 15$.)

10. Please do the next exercise. I will put some others on the board for you to study. After you do them, think what you have found out.

$$\frac{1}{2} = \frac{N}{6}$$

$$\frac{3}{5} = \frac{N}{10}$$

$$\frac{4}{7} = \frac{N}{14}$$

11. Let's give the answers first. The last one in the first list? (16.) The three in the second list? (3, 6, 8.) Good. How are those in the first and second lists different? (The denominators are missing in the first list. The numerators are missing in the second list.) What about the rule? How is it the same for all these exercises? (Divide the terms that are given. They can be numerators or denominators. Use the quotient as a factor with the other given term to find the missing term.) Good. I'll write that rule on the board.

12. I have a few more exercises on the board. How do they differ from what you have been studying?

$$\frac{2}{N} = \frac{8}{12}$$

$$\frac{1}{N} = \frac{3}{15}$$

$$\frac{3}{N} = \frac{12}{16}$$

(Oh, the missing term is in the first fraction.) Yes. Work with your rule to see how it can be revised for this type exercise. Discuss your ideas with a neighbor.

13. What have you found out? (The rule is almost the same, except at the end you divide instead of multiply.)

14. O.K. How do you know whether to multiply or divide by the quotient you get when you divide the missing terms? (If N should be smaller, divide; if N should be larger, multiply.) Does that make sense to everyone? Who else would like to say the rules in their own words? . . . I'll revise the second part of our rule to include these new exercises: Use the quotient as a factor or divisor with the other given term to find the missing term.

15. Make up some exercises. Write down the answers. I'll tell you to give your exercises to a neighbor in a few minutes. Solve your neighbor's exercises and discuss your answers.

16. I have been observing that you have written good exercises and solved your neighbor's exercises correctly. Good work. You learned an important rule today. To help you keep it in mind, please solve the 10 exercises on this sheet. The answers will be posted for you to check your work. If you have any difficulties, talk with me about them.

$\frac{8}{12}$, try 8, 4, and 2 as divisors of 12 until a divisor is determined; 4 is the divisor of 8 and 12. For improper fractions, divisors of the denominator are tried as divisors of the numerator. To learn a rule for simplifying fractions, pupils under the guidance of the teacher note what is required, recall what they know that is relevant to the situation, and construct the rule using inference.

Another rule to be learned as children explore ideas about equivalent fractions is that for finding least common denominators (LCD). The rule children learn depends on their developmental levels and prior experience. Children can determine the least common denominator of two or more fractions by finding the least common multiple (LCM). For example:

a. $\frac{5}{6}, \frac{3}{8}$

b. $\dfrac{5}{2 \times 3}, \dfrac{3}{2 \times 2 \times 2}$

c. $\dfrac{(5)(2 \times 2)}{(2 \times 3)(2 \times 2)}, \dfrac{(3) \times (3)}{(2 \times 2 \times 2) \times (3)}$

d. $\dfrac{20}{24}, \dfrac{9}{24}$

The LCM of 6 and 8 is $2 \times 2 \times 2 \times 3$. In step c, $\frac{5}{6}$ is multiplied by $(2 \times 2)/(2 \times 2)$ and $\frac{3}{8}$ is multiplied by $\frac{3}{3}$ to obtain equivalent fractions with the LCM (24) as the least common denominator.

A less formal approach (trial and error with multiples) can be used, particularly by children who find the rule for finding the LCM difficult to remember. The trial-and-error method rules are:

1. Note if the larger denominator is a multiple

of the smaller denominator. If it is, use the larger denominator as the least common denominator.

2. If the larger denominator is not a multiple of the smaller denominator, multiply the larger denominator by 2, 3, 4, . . . until a product results that is a multiple of the smaller denominator. Use that number as the least common denominator.

To learn either rule, children can observe examples of the steps and infer the rule. Discussion of the sense of the rules follows. A deductive questioning method can also be used. In the course of either type lesson, children should be helped to recognize that the product of the denominators may be the least common denominator. However, it may be just a common denominator and cumbersome to use to find the missing numerators.

To consolidate knowledge, children complete sets of examples; they also write examples. If learners have immediate recall of basic facts and grasp the meaning of a rule, a large amount of time spent in completing exercises is often not necessary for them to develop skill in using the rule.

Comparing and ordering fractional numbers should be reintroduced after learners study equivalent fractions. Children are guided to infer: If the numerators are equal, the larger fractional number is named by the fraction with the smaller denominator—for example, $\frac{3}{5}, \frac{3}{7}$. If the denominators are equal, the numerators are compared—for example, $\frac{5}{6}, \frac{4}{6}$.

The rules for equivalency and nonequivalency can be introduced to capable learners:

$$\text{For } \frac{a}{b} \text{ and } \frac{c}{d}$$

$$\text{if } a \times d = b \times c, \text{ then } \frac{a}{b} = \frac{c}{d}$$

$$\text{if } a \times d > b \times c, \text{ then } \frac{a}{b} > \frac{c}{d}$$

$$\text{if } a \times d < b \times c, \text{ then } \frac{a}{b} < \frac{c}{d}$$

They can infer the rules by examining examples.

The study of these rules can help gifted learners grasp the notion that the rules are short-cuts for comparing fractional numbers. The longer approach is comparing the numerators of the fractions after obtaining their respective equivalent fractions with common denominators. For example, $\frac{2}{3} > \frac{3}{5}$ because $2 \times 5 > 3 \times 3$. The longer approach is: $\frac{2}{3} = \frac{10}{15}$ and $\frac{3}{5} = \frac{9}{15}$; $\frac{10}{15} > \frac{9}{15}$, so $\frac{2}{3} > \frac{3}{5}$.

Partitioning a Fractional Number

Before children begin the study of computation with fractional numbers, an intuitive understanding of multiplication by a fraction is developed through problem-solving experiences. Children are asked to use materials to solve problems such as: John asked his mother for one-half of the last one-fourth of his favorite chocolate pie. She said, "OK, take it." How much of the whole pie did he get? After solving the problem and others like it, children discuss the meaning of what they have done. Discussion helps reemphasize the importance of the number 1 in working with fractions.

Children later make up problems involving partitioning a fractional number. These problems can be devised and solved cooperatively, or the children can find the solution for problems written by others.

Indicated-division Concept

Prior to computation with fractional numbers, children learn that fractional numbers give the solution to problems such as: Mother has 3 yards of ribbon to use in making neckbows each of the same length for her 4 daughters. What length of ribbon does each girl receive? The solution is 3 yards shared equally among 4 girls—$\frac{3}{4}$. Children can show this by folding a length of paper 3 yards long into 4 pieces. A discussion of the activity and further measuring brings out that $(1)\frac{3}{4} = \frac{3}{4}(1)$. Children have many opportunities to solve this type of problem to develop an intuitive understanding of the relation, $1(a/b) = a/b(1)$.

Problem Solving

Problem solving has been suggested to help children learn fractional-number concepts at every phase of the learning-teaching sequence:

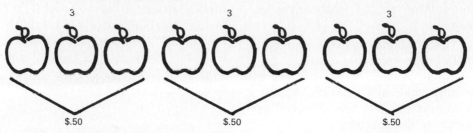

FIGURE 8-14.   Illustration of a many-to-many correspondence.

developing prerequisite understanding, constructing the concept, and extending and consolidating knowledge. The problems can be nonapplied or applied.

Examples of problems for the last instructional phase are: Make a design showing $\frac{1}{2}$s and $\frac{1}{3}$s; find the missing terms so that the fractions are equivalent—?/9, 2/?, 6/?. To extend awareness of life problems, children can make a bulletin of applied problems that involve fractional numbers.

UNDERSTANDING RATIOS, PROPORTIONS, AND PROBABILITY

Ratio and Proportion

A **ratio** is a relation between two numbers; the relation involves a "how many times" comparison. For example, the ratio 4 to 2 is the quotient $4 \div 2$; 4 is two times greater than 2. A fraction is used to express a ratio: the ratio 4/2 is read 4 to 2.

Statements of equivalent ratios are called **proportions.** Many problems deal with proportional relations. ($a/b = c/d$; a is to b as c is to d.) An example is:

Jack wants to buy 12 apples for friends at his Halloween party. He can get 4 for 75¢. How much money does he need for the 12 apples?

$$\left(\frac{4}{75} = \frac{12}{x} \right)$$

Ratio problems are solved by many mature learners using proportions. Concrete or graphic materials or division and multiplication can also be used to solve the problems. Materials can show the many-to-one, one-to-many, or many-to-many correspondences implicit in the proportional relation. Figure 8-14 shows a many-to-many correspondence.

As children use materials and diagrams to solve proportion problems, they develop an intuitive understanding of the concept. An *intuitive understanding* is prerequisite to constructing the concept of proportional relations and using rules to find missing terms in proportions.

When learners demonstrate an intuitive awareness of ratio and proportion by using materials and diagrams to solve problems and show they have developed ideas and skills related to fractions, formal instruction in ratio and proportion can begin. Children are helped to *construct the concept* of ratio and proportion, describe and name their ideas, and use proportions to *solve problems.* These learnings are introduced in grade six or junior high school.

In introductory lessons teachers guide learners to:

1. Give ratios to explain numerical aspects of certain experiences. Some examples are: 3 crackers to 1 child, 1 nickel to 5 pennies, 1 week to 7 days, and 2 shoes to 1 child. Children learn to write fractions to represent ratios as they construct the ratio concept.

2. Solve proportional problems using materials or diagrams.

3. Recognize that the problems solved involve proportional relations (a compares to b as c compares to d). Discuss the meaning of proportional relations in the problems.

4. Examine solutions, especially tables (Figure 8-15) to find patterns.

I want to give every child in my class a stick of bubble gum. It costs 5 sticks for 23¢. How much will 30 sticks cost?

Gum Sticks	5	10	15	20	25	30
Cost	$.23	$.46	$.69	$.92	$1.15	$1.38

FIGURE 8-15. Table to aid in the solution of a proportion problem.

5. Relate their observations of patterns to what they know about equivalent fractions.

6. Conclude that proportional problems can be solved by finding missing terms in statements of equivalent fractions.

7. Use the rules for finding missing terms in equivalent fractions to solve problems involving proportions.

The cross-products rule for finding missing terms in equivalent fractions is introduced when children grasp the concepts of proportion and can use equivalent-fraction rules for finding missing terms. Teachers tell children there is a simpler rule and many will want to use it. For example:

$$\frac{2}{9} = \frac{8}{N}$$

$$2N = 9 \times 8$$

$$N = \frac{9 \times 8}{2}$$

$$= 36$$

If children have been introduced to the cross-products rule for comparing fractions ($ad = bc$ if $a/b = c/d$), they use this rule to develop the idea of solving proportions together with the notion of the inverse relation between multiplication and division. If children do not know the cross-products rule for comparing equivalent fractions, they study examples of the use of the cross-products rule ($1/2 = 3/6$; $1 \times 6 = 2 \times 3$), and they decide how to apply the rule to finding missing terms in equivalent fractions.

After learning how to solve for missing terms in equivalent fractions, children have many opportunities to solve problems involving proportions. They compare and classify problems according to what is unknown; they write, solve, and share problems involving proportional relations. They also can collect examples of problems in real life for a bulletin board display.

Ratio problems can often relate to a child's life. For example:

Greg wants a dog. He is told he can have a dog if he makes enough money to pay for it selling papers. All he knows is that dog food costs $8 for 50 pounds. What will a little dog eat? What will it cost? How many papers must he sell to pay for the dog's food? Does a dog need more than food?

The research, analysis, and discussion involved in solving such a problem will help children understand the relevance of mathematics and proportion, in particular, to life.

Probability

The concept of probability is related to the study of ratio. **Probability** is the likelihood of the occurrence of an event. It is stated as a ratio of the chance of success to the chance of success plus chance of failure of the event's taking place. For example, if a bag contains 10 white marbles and 10 green marbles, the bag contains 20 marbles, half white and half green. If a child draws a marble from the bag without looking in the bag, the probability of getting a green marble is $\frac{1}{2}$:

$$\frac{\text{chance of getting green marble (10)}}{\text{chance of getting green marble (10)} + \text{chance of getting white marble (10)}} = \frac{10}{20} = \frac{1}{2}$$

Probability is understood in an *intuitive* way by children when they exclaim, "I might win a prize in the PTA drawing if I put my name in the box." Intuitive ideas of the use of ratio in probability are developed in activities such as:

1. Let children observe you put different colored chips or marbles in a fish bowl or bag. Tell them that you will ask a blindfolded child to draw one object. Have the class members each write down or state what colored object will be drawn from the bowl. Chips (marbles) to use at different times include:

   1 red and 1 white
   5 red and 5 blue
   20 blue and 10 yellow

After children state their hypotheses, let them explain why they named a particular color. Then have a blindfolded child draw a chip (marble). Again discuss the meaning of pupils' observations.

2. Have a blindfolded child take chips (marbles) from the bowl (bag) repeatedly. Always return the removed object before the next draw. Keep a record of what is drawn. Discuss the record in terms of the number and ratio of each color of object to that of the set of objects in the bowl.

3. Have groups of two children toss a coin and keep a record of the number of heads and number of tails that result. Before they begin, they can hypothesize what will happen. Combine the records of all children participating in the investigation. Discuss the record in terms of the ratio 1/2.

4. Children in a group can each toss a die and keep a record of their tosses. The records can be combined and patterns observed. Discuss the probability of tossing the number shown on any face of the die before the children begin. Have children study the combined records, noting the ratio of each number actually appearing to the total number of tosses. (Is the ratio close to 1/6?) Discuss reasons for the ratios observed.

An intuitive understanding of probability is an appropriate objective for many elementary school children. Gifted learners can pursue the topic further if they are interested in doing so.

SUMMARY

Learning and teaching fractional-number and ratio concepts was discussed in this chapter. The fractional-number concepts and rules described in the first three sections are studied by learners prior to work with computation of fractional numbers. Before children construct rules for computation, they have learning experiences to build an understanding of fractional numbers, fractions, and equivalent fractions. The discussion stressed giving learners opportunities to use fraction cutouts, number lines, and other materials to explore ideas. It also emphasized helping learners use informal logic to extend prior

knowledge. Ideas for problem solving were also suggested. Developing the meaning of ratio, proportion, and probability was discussed in the fourth section. The importance of intuitive understanding of these concepts was stressed.

STUDY QUESTIONS

1. Use the Piagetian task (Appendix I) to assess children's understanding of fractional-number concepts. If possible, include primary, middle, and upper grade children in your assessment. What conclusions can be drawn from the assessment results?

2. Plan an independent study activity involving the use of materials to develop the meaning of fractional numbers.

3. Work with Cuisenaire rods, number lines, or fraction strips to demonstrate that

$$\frac{a}{b}(1) = a\left(\frac{1}{b}\right)$$

When should this idea be emphasized with learners? Why?

4. Plan a game to help children develop understanding of equivalent fractions.

5. Plan a lesson to teach the ordering of fractional numbers represented by nonunit fractions.

6. Have a small-group discussion about your experiences using the GCF in simplifying fractions and the LCM in finding lowest common denominators in addition or subtraction of fractional numbers. Have one member of your small group summarize your discussion for presentation to the whole class. What are the implications of the group summaries presented to the class?

7. Consider the learning objectives children should have attained before they begin the study of computation with fractions. Write an assessment activity to evaluate the attainment of these objectives by learners.

8. How would you introduce the ratio concept to children in grade five?

REFERENCES

Brown, Christopher N., "Fractions on Grid Paper," *Arithmetic Teacher*, 27, no. 5 (January 1979), 8-10.

Copeland, Richard W., *How Children Learn Mathematics*, 3d ed., chap. 11. New York: Macmillan Publishing Co., Inc., 1979.

Madell, Robert L., "Children Can Understand Mathematics," *Arithmetic Teacher*, 29, no. 5 (January 1982), 18-21.

Nelson, Rebecca S., and Donald R. Whitaker, "Another Use for Geoboards," *Arithmetic Teacher*, 30, no. 8 (April 1983), 34-37.

Post, Thomas R., "Fractions: Results and Implications from National Assessment," *Arithmetic Teacher*, 28, no. 9 (May 1981), 26-31.

Schminke, Clarence W., and Enoch Dumas, *Math Activities for Child Development*, 3d ed., chap. 6. Boston: Allyn and Bacon, Inc., 1981.

9 LEARNING AND TEACHING COMPUTATION RULES FOR FRACTIONAL NUMBERS

Learning computation rules for fractional numbers is an objective in several grades. Addition and subtraction computation with fractions is usually introduced in grade four; multiplication and division, in grade five. Extending and consolidating knowledge of the operations for fractional numbers is often emphasized after the rules for all the operations have been constructed. The organization of this chapter reflects this approach. The first four sections discuss prerequisite understanding and constructing computation rules for each operation; the fifth section describes activities for extending and consolidating knowledge of all the operations; the final section is a brief summary.

COMPUTATION RULES FOR ADDITION OF FRACTIONAL NUMBERS

The addition rule for fractional numbers [$a/c + b/c = (a + b)/c$] is used with two-step examples (such as $\frac{2}{5} + \frac{1}{5} = N$) and many-step examples ($14\frac{3}{4} + 28\frac{5}{6} = N$). In learning to deal with different examples, children are guided to relate prior knowledge and to use cognitive processes to develop understanding. The use of materials also plays a major role in constructing rules. The sense of sums continues to be emphasized.

Developing Prerequisite Understanding

All the learnings discussed in Chapter 8 to extend and consolidate understanding of fractional numbers can be considered prerequisite to the study of addition computation with fractions. Of particular significance, however, is an ability to count with unit and nonunit fractions and a knowledge of equivalent fractions. Teachers *assess* children's achievement by asking them to count by fractional numbers and give equivalent fractions. The evaluation activity includes pupils' explanations of the meanings they have of counting and equivalent fractions. Pupils should also have knowledge of the meaning of addition of whole numbers and immediate recall of the basic addition facts to begin addition with fractions.

Children who have prerequisite understandings relate their prior learnings to develop an immediate awareness of the meaning of addition of fractional numbers. They also work with concrete and graphic materials. An initial activity is for each pupil to make a chart to review the meaning of addition of whole numbers (Box 9-1a). This chart is used to prepare a companion chart for addition of fractional numbers. Children begin the fraction chart by substituting fractional numbers for whole numbers in their story examples and equations. They find sums using fraction cutouts, number lines, and counting (Figure 9-1). As they continue with the chart project, they have many opportunities to discuss the meaning of addition of fractional numbers.

$$\frac{1}{3} + \frac{1}{3} = \frac{2}{3}$$

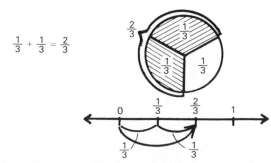

FIGURE 9-1. Finding sums.

BOX 9-1a. *EXAMPLE OF A PUPIL'S CHART:*
  WHAT I KNOW ABOUT ADDITION OF WHOLE NUMBERS

Operation: Addition

Meaning	Story Examples	Mathematical Sentences
Joining	5 cakes and 5 cakes are 10 cakes.	$5 + 5 = \underline{10}$
Putting together	Sally used 2 cups of flour for a cake and 1 cup for muffins. She used 3 cups in her baking.	$2 + 1 = \underline{3}$

BOX 9-1b. *EXAMPLE OF A PUPIL'S CHART:*
  THE MEANING OF ADDITION OF FRACTIONAL NUMBERS

Operation: Addition

Meaning	Story Examples	Mathematical Sentences
Joining	A boy ate $\frac{1}{4}$ of a cake and his sister ate another $\frac{1}{4}$. They ate $\frac{2}{4}$ of the cake.	$\frac{1}{4} + \frac{1}{4} = \underline{\frac{2}{4}}$
Putting together	Sally used $\frac{1}{3}$ cup flour for a little cake and $\frac{1}{3}$ for muffins. She used $\frac{2}{3}$ cup flour in her baking.	$\frac{1}{3} + \frac{1}{3} = \underline{\frac{2}{3}}$

The old matching-type games are employed during this phase. A book contains an addition equation and a representation of the sum using pictures or number lines.

When pupils' written work and oral discussions indicate that they grasp the idea of joining fractional parts of wholes and can relate addition of fractional numbers to this idea, they construct the rule for addition of fractional numbers.

Constructing the Addition Computation Rules for Fractional Numbers

The computation rule for addition with fractions having like denominators is studied first: Add the numerators for the numerator and use the common denominator for the denominator of the sum. The rule is formed by learners from an examination of examples they have written for their charts or worked with as they played instructional games. As they note patterns in examples, learners infer the rule. They discuss the sense of the rule as they respond to the question: Why do we add the numerators and not the denominators? They complete exercises for addition with fractions having like denominators and verify a few of the sums using materials such as squared paper (Figure 9-2).

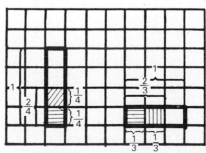

FIGURE 9-2. Using squared paper diagrams to show sums.

A rule for addition with fractions having unlike denominators is constructed by learners when they can use the rule for like denominators with confidence. A sample lesson is given in Box 9-2.

Stating sums in lowest terms is introduced after children demonstrate competency in finding sums with fractions when denominators are like or unlike. Children have learned renaming in lowest terms during the introduction to fractional numbers and fractions. They use this learning to rename sums in lowest terms.

Children who demonstrate achievement in using the rule for addition of fractional numbers when denominators are like or unlike and who can also give sums in lowest terms are ready to learn addition computation with *improper fractions* and *mixed numerals*. Renaming rules are learned first.

The *renaming rule for improper fractions* is: Divide the numerator by the denominator to obtain a whole number plus a fractional number. To learn the rule, children study examples such as: $\frac{5}{4} = N$, $\frac{3}{2} = N$, $\frac{4}{3} = N$, and $\frac{7}{6} = N$. They find sums using squared paper and number lines and

---

BOX 9-2.   SAMPLE LESSON: INTRODUCING THE RULE FOR ADDITION WITH FRACTIONS HAVING UNLIKE DENOMINATORS (GRADE 4)

1. Today we will use our rule for adding with fractions having like denominators to learn about adding with fractions having unlike denominators. Let's review our rule. . . .

2. I have written some examples on the chalkboard. How do these examples differ? (In the first group the fractions have common denominators; in the second list, they do not.)

$$\frac{1}{4} \qquad \frac{1}{8} \qquad\qquad \frac{1}{2} \qquad \frac{1}{4}$$
$$+ \qquad + \qquad\qquad + \qquad +$$
$$\frac{1}{4} \qquad \frac{1}{8} \qquad\qquad \frac{1}{4} \qquad \frac{1}{8}$$

3. What does our rule say about the denominators in fractions? (They must be like.)

4. What must we do? (Make the fractions have like denominators.) You have learned how to do that. Review it for us, Sam. . . .

5. Let's use what we know to find equivalent fractions. Then we can add. We can do several together on the chalkboard. (Teacher and class complete two examples. They note if answers are sensible.)

$$\frac{1}{2} = \frac{2}{4} \qquad\qquad\qquad \frac{1}{4} = \frac{2}{8}$$
$$+ \qquad\qquad\qquad\qquad\qquad +$$
$$\frac{1}{4} = \frac{1}{4} \qquad\qquad\qquad \frac{1}{8} = \frac{1}{8}$$
$$\frac{3}{4} \qquad\qquad\qquad\qquad \frac{3}{8}$$

6. Use your study paper to do others I will write on the chalkboard. (Teacher writes on the chalkboard:

$$\begin{array}{ccc}
\dfrac{1}{3} & \dfrac{1}{4} & \dfrac{2}{5} \\[4pt]
+ & + & + \\[4pt]
\dfrac{1}{6} & \dfrac{3}{8} & \dfrac{1}{10}
\end{array}\;\Big)$$

7. Let's share with each other how we thought to find these sums. . . .

8. It will help us understand our rule if we use number lines to find the sums. Please use the number lines I will pass to you to find the sums in the first two examples with unlike denominators.

9. Dawn, explain to us how you thought about doing the first example on the number line. (I labeled the line in fourths because I decided to show only the fourths. I can rename $\frac{1}{2}$ as $\frac{2}{4}$ to show $\frac{1}{2} + \frac{1}{4}$. The answer is $\frac{3}{4}$. That is a sensible answer because the sum would be less than 1.) Good. Please show your work on the number line I have made on the chalkboard. (The group discusses several more examples and shows sums on chalkboard number lines. The sense of answers is stressed.)

10. Let's write our rule for addition of fractional numbers to include what we have learned today. . . .

11. Super. Please complete the 8 examples on page 199 of your textbook. They are similar to what we have done today.

NOTE: For some learners, examples in which one denominator is not a multiple of the other denominator could be studied in the introductory lesson. Denominators can be multiplied to find a common denominator. Later some learners find the LCD by using the LCM (Chapter 8).

discuss their work (Figure 9-3). They are helped to translate what they have done into mathematical sentences such as:

$$\frac{5}{4} = \frac{4+1}{4} = \frac{4}{4} + \frac{1}{4} = 1 + \frac{1}{4} = 1\frac{1}{4}$$

After equations for several study examples are written on the chalkboard, the teacher says: "What do you notice about these examples? What operations are used? Why?" Children observe that division and addition are involved. Those who have studied the distributive property of division over addition are guided to relate it to the examples in developing the rule. Many children will use the knowledge that a fractional number is an indicated division to grasp the meaning of the rule. All learners use graphic materials to verify their rule. They also learn that the plus sign is not shown in a mixed numeral.

Mental computation in which a basic fact is used in division (for example, $\frac{15}{4} = 3\frac{3}{4}$) is emphasized in assignments. Pupils are helped

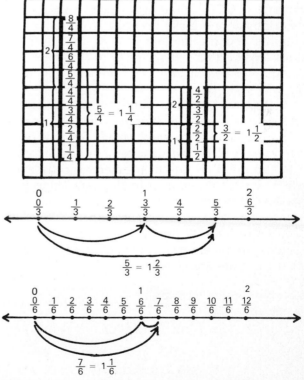

FIGURE 9-3. Showing equivalent fractions with materials.

to relate renaming with improper fractions to whole-number division with remainders.

To express *mixed numerals as improper fractions*, children—with guidance as required—also use materials and find paper-and-pencil solutions such as:

$$1\frac{1}{3} = \frac{3}{3} + \frac{1}{3} = \frac{3+1}{3} = \frac{4}{3}$$

The mathematical process of renaming the whole number as a fractional number and adding the two fractional numbers is a long procedure; learners generally welcome the shortcut rule. The *renaming rule for mixed numerals* is: Add the product of the denominator times the whole number to the numerator of the fraction to obtain the numerator of the equivalent fraction; the denominator is the same as that of the given fraction.

The rule is formulated by inferring from examples of the long form for finding solutions. Children's attention is directed to the fraction in which the numerator is a sum—for example:

$$\frac{3+1}{3}$$

They are asked to study this fraction in several examples, think about how each number was determined, and make up a rule to find the numerator and the denominator of the improper fraction. Further questions and comments by the teacher help learners comprehend and write the rule.

Children are given opportunities to use the rule as they work with examples and play games. Mental calculation is emphasized, for it is often required in work with fractional numbers. Special attention is given to mental calculation when the whole number in the expression is 1, because subtraction computation of fractional numbers involves this computation.

Addition with fractions in mixed form can require no renaming or renaming of the sum. The two types are:

A. *No Renaming of Sum*

$$12\frac{1}{6} = 12\frac{2}{12}$$
$$24\frac{1}{4} = 24\frac{3}{12}$$
$$\overline{}$$
$$36\frac{5}{12}$$

B. *Renaming of Sum*

$$12\frac{5}{6} = 12\frac{10}{12}$$
$$24\frac{3}{4} = 24\frac{9}{12}$$
$$\overline{}$$
$$36\frac{19}{12} = 36 + 1 + \frac{7}{12}$$
$$= 37\frac{7}{12}$$

To deal with type B, children must have ability in mental calculation. (Where?) Therefore, as mentioned previously, mental calculation involving improper fractions and mixed numerals has high priority in instructional programs. It is fostered by using individual and partner practice and the old games requiring matching. An effective motivation device is giving learners opportunities to graph progress in tests that they request when they feel their study has led to improvement.

Mental processing is more demanding in a situation in which renaming is required in both the whole- and fractional-number computations. The child must be able to differentiate between renaming a fractional number using a fractional name for 1 and using base-10 concepts when renaming whole numbers. For example:

$$15\frac{3}{4} = 15\frac{6}{8}$$
$$27\frac{5}{8} = 27\frac{5}{8}$$
$$\overline{}$$
$$42\frac{11}{8}$$
$$= 42 + 1\frac{3}{8}$$
$$= 43\frac{3}{8}$$

Computation of this kind requires sustained attention as well as knowledge of rules and skill in mental calculation. Teachers help learners develop these abilities by providing support and encouragement as well as appropriate learning experiences.

In all addition computation with fractions, teachers emphasize the need to estimate before computing and to check sums. Estimating sums involves thinking if the sum should be less than or greater than a fractional number, such as $\frac{1}{2}$, or a whole number.

COMPUTATION RULES FOR SUBTRACTION OF FRACTIONAL NUMBERS

The rules for addition and subtraction of fractional numbers show their inverse relation; therefore, the instructional phases for subtraction usually closely follow those for addition.

Developing Prerequisite Understanding

Pupils should be able to count backward with unit and nonunit fractions and understand equivalent fractions to begin the study of computational rules for subtraction of fractional numbers. Children must also understand subtraction of whole numbers and have immediate recall of basic subtraction facts. Initial lessons involve making charts (Boxes 9-3a and 9-3b) similar to those made by pupils when they began the study of addition computation with fractions. Materials are used to find solutions to examples in the charts (Figure 9-4).

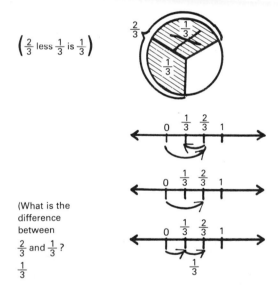

FIGURE 9-4. Finding differences.

Constructing the Subtraction Computation Rules for Fractional Numbers

Subtraction with fractions having like denominators is introduced soon after addition with fractions having like denominators. Pupils are given subtraction exercises (for example, $\frac{5}{7} - \frac{3}{7} = N$) with the direction: Think what you know about addition, subtraction, and fractional numbers to complete these exercises. Children should be able to relate their prior learning to

complete such exercises. After time spent in independent or team study, children have opportunities to exchange ideas about how they completed their work. Diagrams are drawn to verify solutions (Figure 9-5).

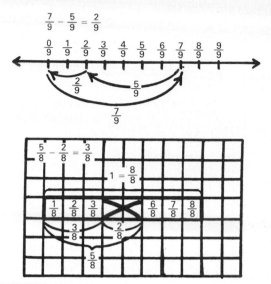

FIGURE 9-5. Using materials to show differences.

Next a *rule for subtraction with fractions having like denominators* is formulated by learners: Subtract numerators; use the common denominator in the difference.

Subtraction with fractions having *unlike denominators* is less difficult for children if they have developed a good understanding of the process in addition computation of finding equivalent fractions to obtain like denominators. Many children should be given the opportunity to complete exercises such as $\frac{5}{8} - \frac{1}{4} = N$ and $\frac{3}{4} - \frac{1}{12} = N$ before teacher-directed lessons are presented. This procedure gives learners opportunities to use cognitive processes of relating and inferring in a problem-solving situation. A discussion after pupils have worked on the exercises provides opportunities for clarifying the procedure and writing the rule for subtraction computation with fractions having unlike denominators.

Number lines are used with examples to verify the rule (Figure 9-6). Estimating the difference in terms of a fractional or whole number and checking the estimate continues to be a learning objective.

Activities to insure understanding and memory of the rules for subtraction with fractions having like or unlike denominators include exercises for pupils to complete and games to

---

BOX 9-3a. *EXAMPLE OF A PUPIL'S CHART:*
WHAT I KNOW ABOUT SUBTRACTION OF WHOLE NUMBERS

Operation: Subtraction

Meaning	*Story Examples*	*Mathematical Sentences*
Take away	If I eat 3 of my 5 cookies, I have 2 left.	$5 - 3 = \underline{2}$
Comparing	11 pies are 2 more than 9 pies.	$11 - 9 = \underline{2}$
Missing addend	Sister baked 12 rolls. Father ate some. 9 were left. Father ate 3.	$12 - \underline{3} = 9$

BOX 9-3b. *EXAMPLE OF A PUPIL'S CHART:*
THE MEANING OF SUBTRACTION OF FRACTIONAL NUMBERS

Operation: Subtraction

Meaning	*Story Examples*	*Mathematical Sentences*
Take away	If I eat $\frac{1}{2}$ of a cookie, I have $\frac{1}{2}$ left.	$1 - \frac{1}{2} = \frac{1}{2}$
Comparing	$\frac{1}{2}$ of a pie is $\frac{1}{4}$ bigger than $\frac{1}{4}$ of a pie.	$\frac{1}{2} - \frac{1}{4} = \frac{1}{4}$
Missing addend	Sue baked one pan of rolls. Tom ate some. $\frac{3}{4}$ of the pan was left. Tom ate $\frac{1}{4}$ of the pan of rolls.	$1 - \underline{\frac{1}{4}} = \frac{3}{4}$

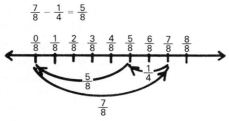

FIGURE 9-6. Using a number line to show a difference.

play. Children also have opportunities to write exercises; these should be completed by other children in the class. The child who wrote the exercises can participate in verifying their correct completion.

After children learn addition computation with numerals in mixed form, they are introduced to subtraction with *mixed numerals.* Learners usually easily construct the rule for subtraction with mixed numerals in which the fractional number in the minuend is greater than the fractional number in the subtrahend ($3\frac{5}{8} - 1\frac{3}{8} = N$). Pupils need more guidance, however, when the fractional number in the minuend is less than the fractional number in the subtrahend. In these exercises *renaming* is required: the minuend whole number is 1 less; 1 is renamed as a fractional number and added to the lesser fractional number to make subtraction possible.

$$
\begin{array}{r}
9\frac{1}{5} = \quad 8\frac{6}{5} \\
-4\frac{2}{5} = -(4\frac{2}{5}) \\
\hline
4\frac{4}{5}
\end{array}
$$

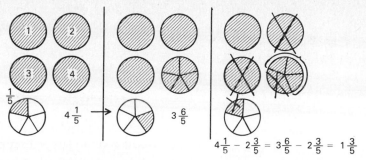

$$4\tfrac{1}{5} - 2\tfrac{3}{5} = 3\tfrac{6}{5} - 2\tfrac{3}{5} = 1\tfrac{3}{5}$$

FIGURE 9-7.   Using materials to show a difference.

If the fractions have unlike denominators, further computation is required to find equivalent fractions with like denominators.

To teach subtraction involving renaming of the minuend, teachers begin with examples in which the minuend is 1 plus a fractional number and the subtrahend is a fractional number, such as $1\tfrac{1}{3} - \tfrac{2}{3} = N$. Learners are asked how these examples differ from those they have previously studied. They are helped to conclude that renaming of the minuend as an improper fraction is required. Children are guided to recall what they know about expressing mixed numerals as improper fractions and to use this learning in the new examples. Mental computation is stressed.

After gaining skill in computation in which the minuend is 1 plus a fractional number, children work with more difficult examples, such as $4\tfrac{1}{5} - 2\tfrac{3}{5}$. Pupils are guided to use prior learning to solve these examples and to use materials to verify thinking (Figure 9-7). Rewriting the minuend as a sum in which one addend is the number 1 helps many learners:

$$
\begin{array}{ll}
4\tfrac{1}{5} = & 3 + 1 + \tfrac{1}{5} = \quad 3 + \tfrac{6}{5} \\
-\,2\tfrac{3}{5} = & -(2 + \quad \tfrac{3}{5}) = -(2 + \tfrac{3}{5}) \\
\hline
& \qquad\qquad 1 + \tfrac{3}{5} = 1\tfrac{3}{5}
\end{array}
$$

Children adopt the short form when they can do the intermediate steps mentally:

$$
\begin{array}{r}
4\tfrac{1}{5} \\
-\,2\tfrac{3}{5} \\
\hline
1\tfrac{3}{5}
\end{array}
$$

Subsequent lessons include exercises with more computational steps, such as:

$$
\begin{array}{r}
41\tfrac{1}{6} \\
-\,19\tfrac{1}{4} \\
\hline
\end{array}
$$

In completing computational exercises with many steps, children are encouraged to make records using as little or as much mental calculation as they find necessary to complete the exercise.

A.   *Little mental calculation*

$$
\begin{array}{llll}
41\tfrac{1}{6} = & 41\tfrac{2}{12} = 40 + 1 + \tfrac{2}{12} = & 40\tfrac{14}{12} \\
-\,19\tfrac{1}{4} = & -(19\tfrac{3}{12}) = & = -(19\tfrac{3}{12}) \\
\hline
& & \quad\quad 21\tfrac{11}{12}
\end{array}
$$

B.   *Maximum mental calculation*

$$
\begin{array}{ll}
41\tfrac{1}{6} = & 40\tfrac{14}{12} \\
-\,19\tfrac{1}{4} = & -(19\tfrac{3}{12}) \\
\hline
& \quad 21\tfrac{11}{12}
\end{array}
$$

Estimating and checking for sensible answers continues to be emphasized.

Learning activities to enable learners to internalize both addition and subtraction computation with fractions includes playing games and making books. A new game is COVER-UP. The materials used are two white circular regions for each of 2-4 players; a spinner labeled with the fractions $\frac{1}{2}$, $\frac{1}{4}$, $\frac{1}{3}$, $\frac{1}{6}$, and $\frac{1}{8}$; and several fraction cutouts representing each of these fractional numbers (Figure 9-8). Each player in turn flips the spinner, selects the cutout designated, and places it on his or her circular region, if possible. The first player who covers his or her regions wins.

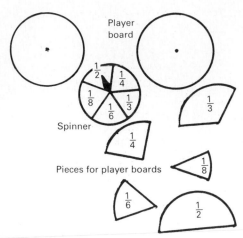

FIGURE 9-8.   Materials for Cover-up game

Children can make individual books that explain computation rules and show examples. Number lines illustrate some examples. These books provide good summaries of work accomplished and meanings achieved. They can be shared with another class.

Children learn addition and subtraction computation during grades four and five. Some courses of study introduce multiplication computation with fractions after learners give evidence of satisfactory progress in learning addition and subtraction computation with fractions having like or unlike denominators, but have not yet worked with mixed numerals.

COMPUTATION RULES FOR MULTIPLICATION OF FRACTIONAL NUMBERS

The rule for multiplication of fractional numbers is easy for most children to learn: Multiply the numerators to obtain the numerator of the fraction for the product; multiply the denominators to obtain the denominator of the fraction for the product ($a/b \times c/d = ac/bd$). However, a product can be interpreted in several ways, and many children have difficulty interpreting problem situations involving multiplication when one or more factors is a fractional number. Therefore, the meaning of the product is emphasized as children develop prerequisite understanding and construct the rule for multiplication of fractional numbers.

Developing Prerequisite Understanding

Prerequisite understanding for multiplication of fractional numbers includes: immediate recall of multiplication basic facts; an understanding of the repeated-addition interpretation of multiplication of whole numbers; knowledge of the partition interpretation of division; an understanding of the fractional-number ideas discussed in Chapter 8; and satisfactory progress in learning computation rules for addition and subtraction of fractional numbers. When teachers ascertain children have these prerequisite understandings and skills, they guide them to relate prior learnings to develop meanings for multiplication of fractional numbers.

The initial experience to develop awareness of the meaning of multiplication of fractional numbers is constructing charts. The first chart reviews the meaning of multiplication with whole numbers (Box 9-4a). The second chart relates whole-number operations to multiplication of fractional numbers (Box 9-4b). The repeated-addition interpretation of multiplication of fractional numbers is developed as children substitute fractional numbers in story examples and equations for whole numbers and use materials to solve their equations.

Pupils soon become aware that the repeated-addition interpretation of multiplication must have a whole number as the first factor (multiplier); if the first or both factors are fractional numbers, the sentence must be interpreted as a partitioning situation (Figure 9-9). The teacher guides children to use the word *of* in these sentences to clarify the partition interpretation. The chart is expanded to include this meaning. Children continue to write and solve story and number examples and use materials to find products until the teacher ascertains they have an understanding of the meaning of multiplication of fractional numbers and can solve problems using concrete or graphic aids.

Constructing the Multiplication Computation Rule for Fractional Numbers

The rule is probably most effectively introduced in the situation in which both factors are fractional numbers. A lesson sequence is given in Box 9-5. Helping learners extend the rule to

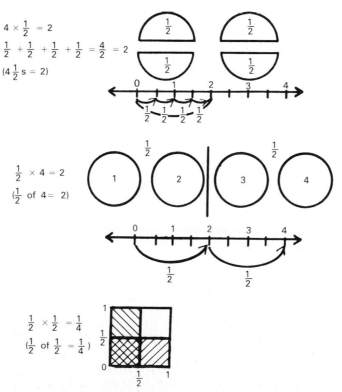

$$4 \times \frac{1}{2} = 2$$
$$\frac{1}{2} + \frac{1}{2} + \frac{1}{2} + \frac{1}{2} = \frac{4}{2} = 2$$
$$(4 \tfrac{1}{2} \text{s} = 2)$$

$$\frac{1}{2} \times 4 = 2$$
$$(\frac{1}{2} \text{ of } 4 = 2)$$

$$\frac{1}{2} \times \frac{1}{2} = \frac{1}{4}$$
$$(\frac{1}{2} \text{ of } \frac{1}{2} = \frac{1}{4})$$

FIGURE 9-9. Using materials to show meanings of multiplication with fractions.

BOX 9-5. SAMPLE LESSON: INTRODUCING THE COMPUTATION RULE FOR MULTIPLICATION OF FRACTIONAL NUMBERS (GRADE 5)

1. Boys and girls, you are really ready to learn the computation rule for multiplication of fractional numbers. You have shown you know the meaning of multiplication of fractional numbers. Please use the squared paper I will pass to you to find the products in these sentences. You recall you have done this before. Any questions? . . . (Answers in parentheses are not shown until later.)

$$\frac{3}{4} \times \frac{1}{2} = N\left(\frac{3}{8}\right) \qquad\qquad \frac{1}{3} \times \frac{1}{3} = N\left(\frac{1}{9}\right)$$

$$\frac{1}{2} \times \frac{3}{5} = N\left(\frac{3}{10}\right) \qquad\qquad \frac{1}{3} \times \frac{2}{5} = N\left(\frac{2}{15}\right)$$

Pupils make diagrams such as:

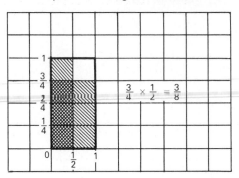 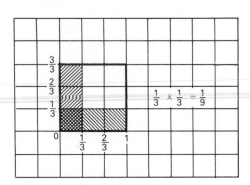

2. Let us write our answers for these examples. Don, Carol, Ted, and Sally, erase N and write the product. Tell us the meanings of the answers. ($\frac{3}{4} \times \frac{1}{2}$ means to find $\frac{3}{4}$ of $\frac{1}{2}$. That is less than $\frac{1}{2}$. It is $\frac{3}{8}$. The diagram shows 1 is $\frac{8}{8}$, and 3 squares are shaded twice. . . .)

3. Good. If we look at the answers, a rule for multiplication of fractional numbers is easy to formulate. (Oh, the rule is multiply the numerators for the numerator of the product; multiply the denominators for the denominator of the product!)

4. Great thinking! Let's check out each example together to test the rule. . . .

5. How would this rule be used if one factor is a whole number? Look at

$$\frac{1}{2} \times 4 = N$$

We know a rule for multiplication of fractional numbers. What can we do? (Write 4 as $\frac{4}{1}$. That makes a fraction.) O.K. Do these in the same way. Always think about the sense of your answer.

$$\frac{2}{3} \times 6 = N \qquad \frac{1}{4} \times 8 = N \qquad \frac{3}{5} \times 10 = N$$

6. Let's discuss what we have done. Tell your answer and why it is sensible. . . .

7. That was not a hard rule to learn. A little practice and you will remember it forever! Please complete the exercises on the study sheet I will pass to you. Remember to check for sensible answers.

BOX 9-6a. EXAMPLE OF A PUPIL'S CHART:
WHAT I KNOW ABOUT DIVISION OF WHOLE NUMBERS

Operation: Division

Meaning	*Story Examples*	*Mathematical Sentences*
Sharing	Mother shares 6 cupcakes equally with 3 children. Each gets 2 cupcakes.	$6 \div 3 = \underline{2}$
Repeated subtraction	Mother has 6 pies to give to neighbors. If each neighbor gets 2 pies, 3 neighbors get pies.	$6 \div 2 = \underline{3}$

BOX 9-6b. EXAMPLE OF A PUPIL'S CHART:
THE MEANING OF DIVISION OF FRACTIONAL NUMBERS

Operation: Division

Meaning	*Story Examples*	*Mathematical Sentences*
Sharing	Mother says 3 children can share $\frac{3}{4}$ of a pie. Each gets $\frac{1}{4}$.	$\frac{3}{4} \div 3 = \underline{\frac{1}{4}}$
Repeated subtraction	Mother has $\frac{5}{6}$ of a pie. If each person gets $\frac{1}{6}$ of a pie, 5 people will get pie to eat.	$\frac{5}{6} \div \frac{1}{6} = \underline{5}$

the case in which one factor is a whole number (Steps 5–7) is optional in the introductory lesson.

Later lessons deal with examples in which the fractions for the products are in mixed form, such as $\frac{3}{5} \times 8 = \frac{24}{5} = 4\frac{4}{5}$. Such examples require mental calculation to avoid excessive pencil-and-paper computation. Mental computation has been stressed in learning each topic. If children have not had a program emphasizing immediate recall of facts and mental calculation, the teacher in grade five or six should plan a special unit to enable learners to develop these competencies.

Estimating fractional-number products in terms of fractional numbers or nearest whole numbers is emphasized as pupils develop skill in computation. Children learn that the sense of products should always be evaluated.

COMPUTATION RULES FOR DIVISION OF FRACTIONAL NUMBERS

Many children and adults remember the *invert-the-divisor-and-multiply rule* but grasp little of the rationale for it. They also have difficulty deciding whether or not to use division to solve problems involving fractional numbers. A cognitive approach to instruction guides children to understand the rule and the various meanings of division of fractional numbers and gain skill.

Developing Prerequisite Understanding

If children demonstrate they understand the meaning of multiplication of fractional numbers, they begin the study of division of fractional numbers. They construct two charts to compare the meanings of division of whole numbers and fractional numbers (Boxes 9-6a and 9-6b). They use their whole-number examples

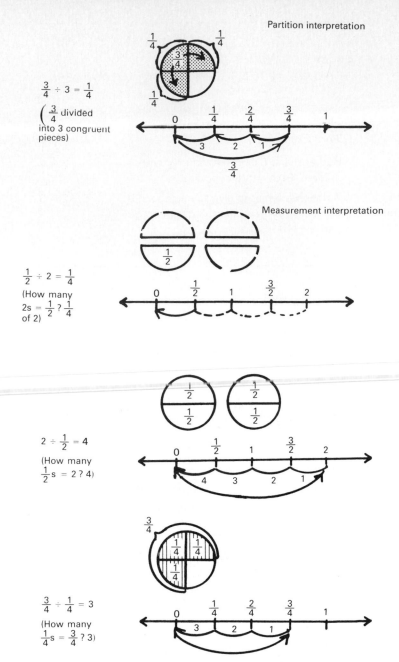

FIGURE 9-10. Using materials to show meanings of division with fractions.

to write fractional-number examples and solve equations using materials (Figure 9-10). They are helped to notice that the sharing interpretation of division is possible only when the divisor is a whole number; the measurement interpretation of division, however, can include fractional numbers as dividends, divisors, or both. After children have developed the meanings of division of fractional numbers and can use materials to find quotients when fractional numbers are dividends, divisors, or both, they are guided to construct rules for division of fractional numbers.

Constructing the Division Computation Rules for Fractional Numbers

There are three approaches for finding quotients when fractional numbers are involved:

1. *Common-denominator rule.* After the fractions in the expression are given as equivalent fractions with common denominators, the numerator of the dividend is divided by the numerator of the divisor to obtain the quotient.

$$\frac{3}{4} \div \frac{1}{3} = \frac{9}{12} \div \frac{4}{12} = \frac{9}{4} = 2\frac{1}{4}$$

2. *Invert-the-divisor-and-multiply rule.*

$$\frac{3}{4} \div \frac{1}{3} = \frac{3}{4} \times \frac{3}{1} = \frac{9}{4} = 2\frac{1}{4}$$

3. *Simplification-of-complex-fraction approach.*

$$\frac{\frac{3}{4}}{\frac{1}{3}} = \frac{\frac{3}{4} \times \frac{3}{1}}{\frac{1}{3} \times \frac{3}{1}} = \frac{\frac{9}{4}}{1} = \frac{9}{4} = 2\frac{1}{4}$$

Both 2 and 3 make use of the reciprocal-of-a-number concept. (Two numbers are said to be **reciprocals** of each other if their product equals 1. For example, $\frac{1}{5}$ is the reciprocal of 5 and 5 is the reciprocal of $\frac{1}{5}$). Rule 2 is a shortcut for the simplification-of-a-complex-fraction approach.

Any of the computational rules can be used to introduce children to division of fractional numbers. When any rule is introduced, certain *instructional guidelines* are taken into account by teachers to facilitate children's learning. These are discussed briefly.

When introducing the *common-denominator rule*, teachers use examples in which fractions have like denominators. After pupils construct the rule, they examine its use when denominators are unlike.

Teachers choose one of three sequences to introduce the *invert-the-divisor-and-multiply rule.*

1. An inductive sequence which includes only examples with whole-number dividends and unit fractions as divisors, such as $4 \div \frac{1}{2}$. Number-line solutions (based on the repeated-subtraction interpretation of division) or repeated subtraction are suggested to children. The pattern of solutions leads to the conclusion: Use reciprocals to find solutions (Figure 9-11). Further discussion helps clarify the invert-the-divisor-and-multiply rule. The rule is then used with examples in which fractions are also non-unit and are in any position in the exercise. The sense of solutions is stressed.

2. A deductive sequence which makes use of examples with fractions as dividends and

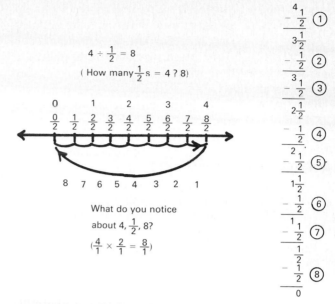

$$4 \div \frac{1}{2} = 8$$

(How many $\frac{1}{2}$s = 4 ? 8)

What do you notice about 4, $\frac{1}{2}$, 8?

$(\frac{4}{1} \times \frac{2}{1} = \frac{8}{1})$

FIGURE 9-11. Solutions for a division-with-fractions question.

whole numbers divisors, such as $\frac{2}{3} \div 2$. Questions posed to learners help them recall that to divide a number by 2 means to find $\frac{1}{2}$ of that number. Continuing with this line of thought, $\frac{2}{3} \div 2$ becomes $\frac{1}{2} \times \frac{2}{3}$. (The reciprocal of 2 is used.) Several examples are discussed in this way. Because learners know that the order of factors can be changed without changing the product, they are able to comprehend that the position of the reciprocal of the divisor need not be changed from that in a given example. A variety of examples enables learners to internalize the rule.

3. The common-denominator method as the rationale for the invert-the-divisor-and-multiply rule. This approach can be used with children capable of following the logic of the approach. For example:

$$\frac{3}{4} \div \frac{1}{3} = \left(\frac{3 \times 3}{3 \times 4}\right) \div \left(\frac{4 \times 1}{4 \times 3}\right) \quad \text{Multiplication by 1}$$

$$= \frac{3 \times 3 \div 4 \times 1}{12 \div 12} \quad \text{Computation}$$

$$= \frac{3 \times 3 \div 4}{1} \quad \text{Computation}$$

$$= \frac{3}{1} \times \frac{3}{4} \quad \text{Notation}$$

$$= \frac{3}{4} \times \frac{3}{1} \quad \text{Commutative property}$$

The *simplification-of-complex-fractions* approach can be explored with capable learners. It too is a rationale for the *invert-the-divisor-and-multiply rule*. It can be used to explain this rule to children who can comprehend the reasoning involved.

As children learn one or more rules for division of fractional numbers, estimating and the sense of quotients continue to be emphasized. Children also continue to review the repeated-subtraction and partition interpretations of division of fractional numbers to provide a background for analyzing problems.

Children can play games and make fraction books for multiplication and division to help them clarify the differences in these operations for fractional numbers. Word exercises (for example: What number equals $\frac{1}{3}$ of 8? How many $\frac{2}{3}$s is 12?) and subsequent discussion of pupils' solutions also aid the development of meaning.

EXTENDING AND CONSOLIDATING KNOWLEDGE

The major topics emphasized during the phase of extending and consolidating knowledge of fractional-number computation are: (1) comparing and ordering, (2) new shortcuts in computation, (3) the properties of the operations, and (4) problem solving beyond that required when an operation for fractional numbers was introduced. Some of the activities described in this section could be used as pupils develop competency in using computation rules. Others could serve as reintroduction to fractional-number computation or be of interest to gifted learners.

Comparing and Ordering

To estimate when fractional numbers are involved in computation, one determines how a sum, difference, product, or quotient compares with familiar fractional numbers, such as $\frac{1}{2}$, or with whole numbers. This process is stressed as computation rules are formulated. Abilities can be extended, however, by activities for comparing and ordering. Games and exercises to help learners strengthen relational thinking with fractional numbers include:

The old games are used, but now the game rule is that the winning cards display two numbers in a comparison relation or three or four indicated numbers in an order relation. For example, if the rule is: Match numbers in a greater-than (or less-than) relation, matches could include: 1 with $\frac{1}{2} + \frac{1}{4}$, $\frac{5}{4} \times 3$ with 2, and $25 \times \frac{1}{2}$ with 10. (The player is required to state the relationship between the numbers shown in his or her books.) If the rule is: Order three sums, cards could show: $\frac{1}{4} + \frac{1}{2}$, $\frac{3}{4} + \frac{3}{4}$, $\frac{5}{4} + \frac{7}{8}$. WAR is played with some cards in a stack showing 1 or 2.

FRAC-COMPARE, a spinner game, consists of cards, a spinner, and a cup of beans. The rules for four to six players are:

Each player gets 7 cards, such as those shown in Figure 9-12. Players spin in turn. After a spin a player tries to finish the inequality partially shown on one of his or her cards by using the number given by the spin. If successful, he or she gets a bean from the bean cup. The game is over when one player is out of cards. The winner has the most beans.

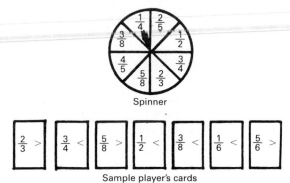

Spinner

Sample player's cards

FIGURE 9-12. Materials for the Frac-Compare game.

Exercises encouraging generativity require learners to write sums, products, differences, or quotients that are less or greater than given numbers. For example, a child could write:

$$\frac{1}{4} + \frac{1}{4} < 1$$

$$\frac{4}{3} + \frac{1}{3} > 1$$

For this exercise, children can work in teams of two, completing the task and checking the other team person's work. Gifted learners can write examples such as:

$$1 < \frac{3}{4} + \frac{3}{4} < 2$$

Exercises requiring decisions about inequality can be used for summary and evaluation purposes, as well as for individual or group study.

For example, children can be asked to write inequality signs on the lines:

$$\frac{2}{3} + \frac{2}{3} \underline{\quad} 2$$

$$\frac{6}{5} - \frac{1}{4} \underline{\quad} 1$$

$$5 \times \frac{1}{2} \underline{\quad} 4$$

$$\frac{3}{4} \times \frac{3}{4} \underline{\quad} 1$$

In estimating and checking computations, children carry out various mental calculations involving comparing or ordering numbers. Providing time for children to discuss the mental calculation they used will help all children develop strategies for estimating and checking fractional-number computations.

Computational Shortcuts

Many computational shortcuts have been devised. This section discusses only widely used, easy, and efficient manipulations: cancellation and two numerator-denominator rules.

Cancellation in multiplication and division computation involves dividing a numerator and a denominator by the same number prior to finding products or quotients. The procedure is used after the mathematical sentence is in the form of a product. Examples are:

$$\frac{3}{4} \times \frac{2}{9} = \frac{\overset{1}{\cancel{3}}}{\underset{2}{\cancel{4}}} \times \frac{\overset{1}{\cancel{2}}}{\underset{3}{\cancel{9}}} = \frac{1}{6}, \qquad \frac{3}{8} \div \frac{1}{2} = \frac{3}{\underset{4}{\cancel{8}}} \times \frac{\overset{1}{\cancel{2}}}{1} = \frac{3}{4}$$

The reasonableness of the procedure is shown by rearranging factors and dividing the numerator and denominator by the same number (dividing by 1). For example:

$$\frac{3}{4} \times \frac{2}{9} = \frac{3 \times 2}{4 \times 9} = \frac{2 \times 3}{4 \times 9} = \frac{(2 \div 2)}{(4 \div 2)} \times \frac{(3 \div 3)}{(9 \div 3)} = \frac{1}{2} \times \frac{1}{3} = \frac{1}{6}$$

The logic of the procedure should be discussed with learners who can profit from such a discussion. All children can compare several examples using both methods, cancellation and renaming the final answer. For example:

$$\frac{\overset{1}{\cancel{3}}}{\underset{2}{\cancel{8}}} \times \frac{\overset{1}{\cancel{4}}}{\underset{3}{\cancel{9}}} = \frac{1}{6} \quad \text{or} \quad \frac{3}{8} \times \frac{4}{9} = \frac{12}{72} = \frac{1}{6}$$

Children should use cancellation in a few examples to "try out" the procedure. In subsequent work, they choose whether to use cancellation or not. The teacher, however, knowing its usefulness in later mathematical study, encourages children to adopt it as soon as possible.

Numerator-denominator rules include one for addition and one for division. In addition, if the numerators are 1, the numerator of the sum is the sum of the denominators and the denominator of the sum is the product of the denominators. For example:

$$\frac{1}{3} + \frac{1}{5} = \frac{8}{15}$$

This rule is derived by studying examples and noting what steps may be deleted or rearranged in the computation.

$$\frac{1}{3} + \frac{1}{5} = \left(\frac{1}{3} \times \frac{5}{5}\right) + \left(\frac{1}{5} \times \frac{3}{3}\right) = \frac{5}{15} + \frac{3}{15} = \frac{8}{15}$$

Why this rule can be used only when the numerators of the addends are 1 should be investigated by learners as they study examples.

A cross-products rule for division can be learned as a shortcut; for example:

$$\frac{2}{5} \div \frac{1}{8} = \frac{16}{5} = 3\frac{1}{5} \quad \begin{array}{l} \text{is found by multiplying} \\ 2 \times 8 \text{ and } 5 \times 1. \end{array}$$

In general terms:

$$\frac{a}{b} \div \frac{c}{d} = \frac{a \times d}{b \times c}$$

This rule can be rationalized by noting it is a shortcut for the invert-the-divisor-and-multiply rule. The same numbers are used together as factors, but no rewriting of the divisor is necessary.

The Properties of the Operations

The commutative, associative, and distributive properties are reviewed as children extend their understanding of fractional-number computation. Learners investigate whether or not the properties hold for addition and multiplication of fractional numbers.

A lesson can begin with a question, such as, "Do you think the commutative property of addition of whole numbers can be extended to fractional numbers? How could we find out?" Children study examples by finding sums and verifying solutions on the number line. Follow-up discussion affirms that the property is valid for fractional-number computation. Other properties are similarly studied.

Extending awareness of the properties of operations with whole numbers to fractional numbers is most appropriate for capable learners. They generally are motivated by a spirit of curiosity and enjoy relational thinking.

Problem Solving

Problems involving fractional numbers are used to help children develop an understanding of the interpretations of the operations for fractional numbers in the first two phases of instruction. Problems continue to be an important part of learning during the extension and consolidation phases. Children should write problems as well as solve problems written by others. Especially helpful to many learners is the knowledge that whole numbers can often be substituted for fractional numbers to clarify the meaning of problems. Other suggestions given in Chapter 3 for learning problem solving are also used when children extend problem-solving abilities to problems with fractional numbers.

SUMMARY

This chapter has emphasized that building computation rules for fractional numbers provides opportunities for children to construct knowledge from prior learnings. Pupils are guided to use cognitive processes, particularly inference, to arrive at new insights. The use of concrete and graphic materials to help children review and develop knowledge was also stressed. Mental computation as an aspect of fractional number computations was discussed. Many activities were described to help learners reconsider prior knowledge, construct rules, and efficiently use computation rules for fractional numbers.

STUDY QUESTIONS

1. List the steps involved in completing an addition example with fractions having unlike denominators that requires giving the sum in lowest terms. Ask a child to explain his or her thinking in completing such an example. How does your list compare with the child's report of steps used?

2. Plan an independent study activity to help learners develop mental computational skill in giving fractions in improper form as equivalent fractions in mixed form (for example, $\frac{11}{6} = 1\frac{5}{6}$).

3. Plan a game UNCOVER for subtraction of fractional numbers similar to COVER-UP described in this chapter for addition of fractional numbers.

4. Discuss the cognitive processes children engage in as they make the charts suggested in this chapter for introducing multiplication of fractional numbers.

5. Write 10 word questions for learners to answer using materials to help them extend meanings of all four operations for fractional numbers. (For example, 9 is equal to how many $\frac{2}{3}$s? How much less is $\frac{3}{5}$ than $\frac{5}{8}$?)

6. How would you introduce the rule for division of fractional numbers? What are your reasons for your answer to this question?

7. Plan a lesson to help learners develop an understanding of cancellation in computation. What questioning method seems most appropriate for use in this lesson? Why?

8. Write an independent study activity for capable children to use to develop a numerator-denominator rule.

REFERENCES

Nuffield Foundation, *Computation and Structure: 5.* New York: John Wiley & Sons, Inc., 1972.

Post, Thomas R., Merlyn J. Behr, and Richard Lesh, "Interpretations of Rational Number Concepts," in *Mathematics for the Middle Grades (5–9)*, 1982 Yearbook of the National Council of Teachers of Mathematics, eds. Linda Silvey and James R. Smart. Reston, VA: The National Council of Teachers of Mathematics, Inc., 1982.

Rudnitsky, Alan N., Priscilla Drickamer, and Roberta Handy, "Talking Mathematics with Children," *Arithmetic Teacher*, 28, no. 8 (April 1981), 14–17.

Schminke, Clarence W., and Enoch Dumas, *Math Activities for Child Involvement*, 3d ed., chap. 6. Boston: Allyn and Bacon, Inc., 1981.

Thompson, Charles, "Teaching Division of Fractions with Understanding," *Arithmetic Teacher*, 27, no. 5 (January 1979), 24–27.

Usiskin, Zalmon P., "The Future of Fractions," *Arithmetic Teacher*, 27, no. 5 (January 1979), 18–20.

10 LEARNING AND TEACHING DECIMAL FRACTIONS AND PERCENT

The study of decimal fractions and percent enables learners to extend their understanding of base-10, place-value, and fraction concepts and to clarify ideas discussed in social studies and science lessons. Out-of-school activities are also often more meaningful if decimal and percent concepts can be used to explain experience. The meaning of decimal fractions and computation with decimals are usually studied in grades five and six. Percent concepts are introduced in grade six and extended in junior and senior high school.

This chapter is divided into four sections: studying decimals, computation with decimals, comprehending percent and solving percent problems, and a summary.

STUDYING DECIMALS

Decimals are fractions whose denominators are powers of 10; place-value notation is used in writing decimals (decimal fractions) rather than the common-fraction form which uses numerals above and below a fraction bar (Figure 10-1). The place-value notation for fractions has advantages; it is faster and permits computation with place-value algorithms.

The study of decimal fractions involves attaining a number of objectives. Children learn to interpret decimals, as well as develop skill in reading and writing decimals. They study decimal place values. Children also learn to compare, order, and round decimals. Meeting these objec-

Decimal Place Values								
10,000	1000	100	10	1.	$\frac{1}{10}$	$\frac{1}{100}$	$\frac{1}{1000}$	$\frac{1}{10,000}$
10,000	1000	100	10	1.	.1	.01	.001	.0001
10^4	10^3	10^2	10^1	10^0	$\left(\frac{1}{10}\right)^1$	$\left(\frac{1}{10}\right)^2$	$\left(\frac{1}{10}\right)^3$	$\left(\frac{1}{10}\right)^4$
ten-thousands	thousands	hundreds	tens	ones	tenths	hundredths	thousandths	ten-thousandths

FIGURE 10-1. Decimal place-value chart.

tives is discussed in terms of developing prerequisite understanding, constructing decimal concepts, and extending and consolidating knowledge. Frequent reference is made in this section to activities with concrete and graphic materials because of their usefulness to pupils in forming concepts.

Developing Prerequisite Understanding

Before introducing decimals to learners, teachers ascertain that children have constructed the concept of fractional numbers, can interpret common fractions, and understand base-10 and place-value concepts. Prerequisite knowledge and assessment examples are listed on p. 184.

Knowledge		*Assessment Examples*	
1.	Representation of fractional numbers.	1.	Show $\frac{1}{2}$, $\frac{2}{10}$, and so forth on the number line. Explain your work. (Or teacher notes pupil's labels on number lines.)
2.	Meaning of fractions.	2.	What words are used for the numbers given by numerals above and below the fraction bar? What does the numerator tell? The denominator? (A matching test can be used in this assessment.)
3.	Knowledge of base 10.	3.	In counting, how many different number words are used? Why? How do you continue counting when you have used those number words? (When you get to 10, start all over again.) Display sticks grouped by 10s and many single sticks. Say: Show 100 as fast as possible. (Does pupil use 10s?)
4.	Understanding of place value.	4.	Say: Write three hundred seventy-two as a decimal numeral. . . . How did you know what to do? Write 782 and say: What does this mean? (Note pupil's reference to value of each place.)

If learners demonstrate knowledge of the above prerequisites, teachers help them develop further readiness by studying *patterns in counting fractions whose denominators are powers of 10*; children are helped to notice the base-10 scheme of counting to 10 and starting all over again. To introduce counting with fractions whose denominators are powers of 10, teachers can say, "Let's count by tenths today. You have counted by halves, thirds, and other fractional numbers. How do we count by fifths? . . . Why can you say *one* instead of *five-fifths*? Now let's count by tenths: one-tenth, two-tenths, three-tenths, . . . , ten-tenths. What is another name for ten-tenths? . . . Yes, one. Let's keep going. . . ."

Children count several times by 10ths, stopping each time at 3 or 4. The teacher continues the lesson by asking children to think how counting by 10ths is like and different from counting by 1s. Children are guided to note the base-10 counting pattern in both counting sequences.

Children who grasp how the base-10 concept is extended to counting by 10ths can later examine the base-10 pattern in counting by 100ths. When learners show an awareness of patterns in counting by 10ths and 100ths, they begin to construct ideas of decimal fractions.

Constructing Concepts of Decimal Fractions

When considered as representing fractional numbers, decimals are interpreted in two ways:

1. A decimal can mean 10ths, 100ths, or other power-of-10 fractional parts of a unit; for example, $.3 = 3 \times .1$.

2. A decimal can mean an indicated division, for example, $.3 = 3 \div 10 = .1 \times 3$.

As children form concepts of decimals, they study these interpretations, develop skill in reading and writing decimals, and learn the meaning of each place in a decimal.

The *fractional-part-of-a-unit interpretation of decimals* is studied first. Children work with diagrams showing 1s, 10ths, and 100ths (Figure 10-2). Beginning activities are with 10ths. Children who learn mathematics easily study 100ths soon thereafter. Children who require more time to develop concepts are not introduced to 100ths until they demonstrate understanding of 10ths and gain skill in reading and writing 10ths.

To introduce the fractional-part-of-a-unit idea, the teacher asks children to show the meaning of fractions such as $\frac{1}{10}$, $\frac{3}{10}$, and $\frac{7}{10}$ by

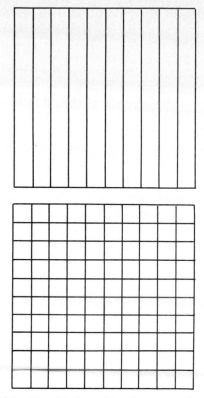

FIGURE 10-2. Materials for making diagrams to show decimals.

coloring 10ths of figures that are partitioned into 10 congruent sections. The teacher says that there are two ways to write the fractions that tell what children have colored. The children talk about the common-fraction form, which they have already learned. The teacher models writing and reading decimal fractions. The children write decimals and common fractions on their figures. They read both common and decimal fractions. They discuss how common and decimal fractions are alike and different.

Follow-up activities include shading 10ths of figures and naming the fractional parts of figures shaded by others to show 10ths. Number lines displaying 10ths are also studied. Children can use Unifix cubes or Cuisenaire rods to represent 10ths. Decimals should be written to describe work done. Sometimes children write both decimal and common fractions to label their work. The introduction to decimals also includes writing decimals from dictation and reading decimals written by others.

In all graphic representations for 10ths, the unit is highlighted. Children are frequently asked to point out what represents 1. Using materials, they are helped to form the idea that .1 means one-tenth of 1.

As children study 10ths, they are introduced to mixed decimals such as 6.5. They study the meaning of these numerals by examining and producing diagrams showing 1s plus 10ths. They learn to read and write mixed decimals by observing the teacher model the process. They notice the use of the word *and* to refer to the decimal point, and they use *and* in reading these decimals; for example, they read 6.5 as six and five tenths.

The sequence for studying 100ths is similar to that for 10ths. The teacher leads children to generate examples using squared-paper (10 × 10) diagrams. They discuss the use of common fractions to explain shaded parts (100ths) of their figures. The teacher models writing and reading decimal fractions that correspond to the common fractions. Children write decimals for 100ths. Other examples are produced or studied by learners in subsequent lessons. They often use number lines showing 10ths and 100ths. Children write decimals from dictation and work with mixed decimals. Children can also write a series of decimals, such as .22, . . . , .37, and discuss how they knew what to do.

As children work with materials showing 100ths, they are guided to observe that .10 = .1. They discuss the meaning of this observation and sometimes write statements of equivalent decimals on their diagrams (Figure 10-3).

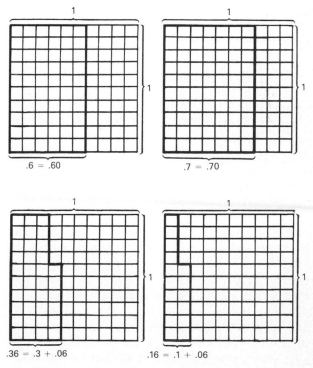

FIGURE 10-3. Diagrams showing 100ths.

A gamelike activity to develop understanding is a variation of BUZZ: Children count in order; at multiples of 100ths (say, .20) the person counting gives the equivalent fraction (.2). At 100 100ths, the counter can say O N E. (All children can also clap on 10ths.)

Four games to help children learn about 10ths or 100ths are:

GET ONE, for a group of four or five players. Materials for use in the game are a spinner showing decimals .1, .2, .3, and .5; a unit bar or square region with 10 congruent sections for each player (player's board); and 40 pieces (labeled .1), each the same size as one section of a player's board. The players spin the spinner in turn and take as many pieces as indicated by the spinner. The first player to cover his or her board wins. (If a player's draw requires him or her to show more than 10 10ths, he or she must discard that draw's pieces. To win, the player must use pieces drawn to cover his or her board with only 10 pieces.)

THIS IS ONE. This game uses a 10 × 10 playing board and an arrow winding from the upper left-hand square to the bottom right-hand square. The words *This Is One* are written on the face of the board. Each of four players has a special colored token. Children choose cards from the stack in the center of the playing area. Each card gives directions to move along the arrow a certain number of 100ths (for example, .02, .12, or .08). The player who first completes the arrow route wins.

WRITE ON, a game for two to six players. Up to 30 cards are prepared with decimals written in words or represented in illustrations. A blackboard (or sheet of paper) is given to the players. The cards are laid face down on the playing area. The player designated to begin picks up a card, reads it, and writes the decimal on the blackboard. If the players agree it is correct, the player keeps the card; if not, the player discards it. When the stack of cards is depleted, the player with the most cards wins.

DECIMAL BINGO, a game for a small group. Ask pupils to make the cards and player boards using decimals. The game rules are the same as for BINGO.

Children who can show that decimals can be interpreted as 10ths or 100ths of a unit are helped to understand that *a decimal can represent an indicated division*. Some questions and discussions used to introduce the idea are:

1. A group of children is making ten puppets. Each puppet has a small neckbow. The group has 2 meters of ribbon to use. What part of the ribbon does each puppet get?

(The teacher helps children understand that the problem can be solved by thinking 2 divided by 10 or $\frac{1}{10}$ of 2. A diagram is used to illustrate this meaning. Figure 10-4a shows a solution to the problem and illustrates that .2 means .1 of 2 or .2 of 1.)

2. There are three delicious cakes at a party: chocolate, coconut, and orange. The ten people at the party decide to each have a piece of each cake. However, they want each one to get the same amount. How much does each person get? Draw a diagram to show your thinking. (Children draw the cakes and make the cuts to answer the question. They should be helped to observe that 3 divided by 10 can be .1 × 3 or .3 × 1, as shown in Figure 10-4b: Each person gets .1 of 3, which is the same as .3 of 1.)

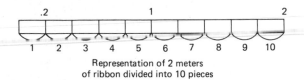

Representation of 2 meters
of ribbon divided into 10 pieces

(a)

FIGURE 10-4a. Showing a meaning of a decimal.

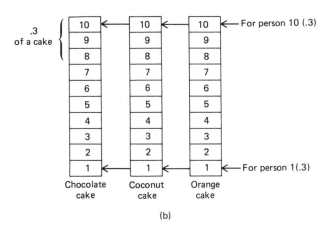

(b)

FIGURE 10-4b. Showing a meaning of a decimal.

Over a period of time, children solve problems, study diagrams, and engage in discussions to enable them to distinguish between the two fractional-number meanings that can be given to decimals. Knowledge of the two interpretations helps children grasp the meaning of problems involving decimals as well as understand decimals.

When children can show the meaning of 10ths and 100ths using proportional material, they study the meaning of decimals using non-

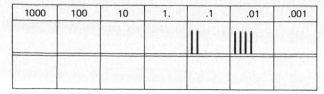

1000	100	10	1.	.1	.01	.001
				II	IIII	

Place value chart with sticks showing   .24

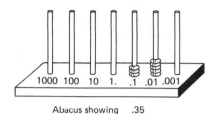

Abacus showing   .35

FIGURE 10-5. Nonproportional   materials   for   representing decimals.

proportional material, such as place-value charts or abacuses (Figure 10-5). Work with nonproportional material precedes the study of decimal places. While both place-value charts and abacuses are used in the classroom, the discussion that follows deals only with abacuses to avoid repetition of instructional procedures. However, place-value charts could be used in any of the activities.

To participate actively in lessons involving abacuses if three-dimensional abacuses are not available, each child should have a dittoed paper-and-pencil abacus and beans to place on the posts to represent numbers. The abacuses first used by children to study decimals should have four posts, labeled 100, 10, 1., and .1. The labeling of the posts is pointed out to children. They are also told to notice that 1 is the center of the system and the decimal point shows the ones place. Children then use beans to show decimals on their abacuses. They are sometimes asked to image a diagram showing 10ths as they work with abacuses. (A diagram can also be displayed.) Initial work is limited to showing .1, . . . , .9.

In a following lesson, children are asked to place 10 objects (beans or rings) on the 10ths post. The teacher then says, "When we use the abacus to show ones or tens, we have a rule that tells how many beans should go on a post. What is that rule? . . . Yes, only 9 beans on a post. What do we do when we get 10 on the ones post? . . . Yes, put 1 bean on the tens post. We use that rule with tenths, too. So what do we do now? What is 10 tenths? . . . Yes, 1. Show that on your abacus. . . . Have we ever talked about 10 tenths and 1 being equal? . . .

Yes, when we counted and worked with common fractions, or when we used squared-paper diagrams. Let's make a record of what we have done: 10 .1s = 1. We can write that this way, $10 \times .1 = 1$. Why?"

Children next are given abacuses with five posts, labeled 100, 10, 1., .1, .01. They learn to show 100ths numbers on the abacus and are helped to relate representing 100ths on the abacus to representing 100ths with proportional materials. The introductory lessons deal with .01 to .09, but soon children are helped to show .11, . . . , .99 on their abacuses. They discuss what can be done when 10 objects are on the 100ths post: Replace 10 objects on the 100ths post with 1 object on the 10ths post. They have many opportunities to use abacuses to demonstrate renaming numbers (.13 = .1 + .03; 1.89 = 1 + .8 + .09) and to discuss their work. They can make records of what is shown on the abacus. When children can state how they will show 100ths on the abacus before they carry out the task, they are ready to work with the meaning of places in decimals.

A teacher can begin a lesson on *places in decimals* by saying, "You know about the meaning of places in numerals for whole numbers. Let's review the names of these places. Look at the numerals on the chalkboard: 563, 54, 300. What do you know about the names of the places in these numerals? . . . What do these names tell us? Think what we might call places in decimals as you study these numerals. Remembering how to show decimals on the abacus will help you: 1.3, .4, 3.7, and .9. Let's talk about why we said ones place and tenths place. . . ."

Later, children name the places in decimals for 100ths (.21, .11, .59, and .78) and discuss their meaning. The teacher then says, "We can write math sentences to tell the meaning of place value. I'll begin some math sentences for you. Please work in teams of two to finish these sentences."

$$.44 = \underline{\hspace{1cm}} + .04$$
$$.23 = \underline{\hspace{1cm}} + .03$$
$$.69 = \underline{\hspace{1cm}} + .09$$

Some children may complete these sentences using expanded notation—for example, .44 = .4 + .04. Other children may write .44 = .40 + .04. The teacher helps children recognize that either sentence gives the meaning of the decimal. They are *equivalent statements*. If children do not use expanded notation (expanded form), the teacher introduces it saying: "Would this be correct? Why? Remember our work with the abacus." The teacher also helps children who used expanded form examine the meaning of examples, such as $.44 = .40 + .04 = .4 + .04$. In the same or a following lesson, the term *expanded notation* or *expanded form* is introduced. Later, numerals such as 3.9 are written in expanded form.

Children who can show the meaning of decimals using proportional materials and non-proportional materials, who can explain the meaning of decimal places, and who can write decimals in both standard- and expanded-form study topics to extend and consolidate knowledge of decimals.

Extending and Consolidating Knowledge

Children extend and consolidate knowledge of decimals as they: (1) extend the meaning of decimals to 1000ths, 10,000ths, . . . ; (2) compare decimals; (3) order decimals; (4) extend place-value concepts; and (5) round decimals. Promoting each of these learnings is discussed in turn.

To begin the *study of 1000ths*, the teacher says, "Boys and girls, you know about tenths and hundredths. You are ready to learn more about decimals. To begin, let's review what we know. What decimals have we studied? . . . Yes, tenths and hundredths. What probably comes next in the sequence? . . . Yes, thousandths. Why? . . . What do you think one-thousandth means? Yes, one-thousandth of one. Let's use meter sticks to study thousandths. Each two people will have a meter stick. Study it to find out about thousandths. . . . " Children note that a millimeter is $\frac{1}{1000}$ of a meter and discuss lengths such as $\frac{5}{1000}$ of a meter.

Later, the teacher says, "Let's figure out how to write thousandths. Please read silently what I am writing on the chalkboard:

$$1000, 100, 10, 1., .1, .01$$

Let's read these together. What comes next? How would we write one-thousandth? Why? . . . " If no pupil infers that the next decimal is .001, the teacher models writing and reading .001. The children discuss their observations, the

meaning of .001, and copy the teacher's work. Children continue their study by writing decimals for 1000ths from dictation and reading decimals for 1000ths. They refer to the meter stick or image the size of pieces if each 100th in a diagram is partitioned into 10 congruent sections. The abacus is also used to represent 1000ths, and children are helped to relate representing 1000ths on the abacus to expanded notation (for example, $.444 = .4 + .04 + .004$).

Lessons to introduce 10,000ths, 100,000ths, . . . , are presented later. Children use abacuses and inference to grasp the meaning of decimals that cannot be satisfactorily represented with proportional materials.

Learning to compare decimals includes working with equivalent decimals and non-equivalent decimals. Children were introduced to *equivalent decimals* as they formed concepts of 10ths and 100ths. Learning experiences now enrich and extend concepts of equivalent decimals.

An activity to further understanding is:

Study the following decimals. Put them in groups so that the decimals in a group are alike in value. You can use common fractions to help solve the problem. Use a red crayon to circle the decimals in one group, a blue crayon for another group, and so on.

3.1 .7   .31 .700 .450 .70 .060 3.10
.6 .310 .07 .60   .06   .45 .070 .600

After pupils have finished the assignment, the teacher asks, "How did you know what to do? What did you think to group the decimals?" During the discussion that focuses on the answers to these questions, children explain how using equivalent common fractions helped them with the problem ($\frac{7}{10} = \frac{70}{100}$).

In the same or following lesson, the children are helped to form a *rule for determining equivalent decimals*: To find a decimal equivalent to a given decimal, annex zeroes to the right of the given decimal. In constructing and verifying the rule, diagrams or common fractions are again used. Pupils employ the rule to complete exercises and later in comparing nonequivalent decimals. Work with equivalent decimals includes exercises with mixed decimals, such as 4.71.

An independent study activity for two children is:

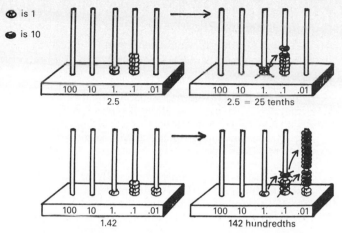

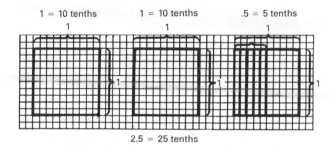

FIGURE 10-6a. An abacus showing equivalent decimals.

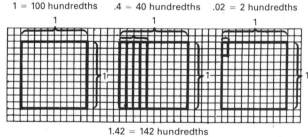

FIGURE 10-6b. Squared paper showing equivalent decimals.

$$2.5 = 2\frac{5}{10} = \frac{25}{10} = 25 \text{ tenths}$$

$$1.42 = 1\frac{42}{100} = \frac{142}{100} = 142 \text{ hundredths}$$

FIGURE 10-6c. Using common fractions to show equivalent decimals.

Work with a partner and take turns showing examples in Part 1 below on the abacus, squared paper, or with common fractions. What patterns do you notice? (Figures 10-6a, b, and c show pupils' work.) Try to think the answers in Part 2 before you show them on the abacus. When you finish the examples, make up a rule. Write some examples of your own for your partner.

Part 1

2.5 = 25 tenths

1.42 = 142 hundredths

14 tenths = 1.4

224 hundredths = 2.24

Part 2

16 tenths =____.

421 hundredths =____.

2.6 =_____tenths

4.31 =_____hundredths

Children who understand equivalent decimals extend their understanding to *nonequivalent decimals* and have many experiences comparing such decimals. When beginning work, the teacher can ask children to find the "different" decimal in a group of two equivalent decimals and one greater or less than the other two—for example, .45, .4, .40. Children discuss their answers and give reasons for their responses. Children who learn mathematics slowly can use the abacus to aid in solving this problem.

It is easier for most children to compare decimals if they first name all decimals to be compared in the same power of 10. For example, to compare .78 and .8, children would think .78 and .80 before deciding which decimal represents the greater number. Teachers help pupils use this procedure, for while some children may not always find renaming necessary, it enables many learners to compare decimals correctly.

Learning activities with nonequivalent decimals include: (1) Use the $>$ and $<$ symbols with decimals. (2) Count from one decimal to another to demonstrate their difference and how they compare. (3) Use the abacus to show how nonequivalent decimals can be increased or decreased so they are equivalent. Gifted learners may be able to solve this problem without the aid of the abacus. (4) Think and write a decimal greater or less than a given decimal. This activity can be carried out with a partner, one writing a decimal and the other deciding if it is greater than or less than the given decimal.

Activities and games for comparing decimals are used with small groups or individuals to provide for individual differences. Some suggestions are:

Ask pupils to make a bulletin board or charts of the use of decimals in their lives and the lives of those around them. Examples to use are: rainfall, sports records, oil consumption per nation, and inflation rates. Discuss the findings shown on the bulletin board or charts.

A variation of WRITE ON (discussed earlier) can be used with a small group or teams of two pupils. Decimals on the cards are to be written by the pupils as equivalent decimals (for example, if the card shows .50, the pupil writes .5; if the card shows .52, the pupil writes .520).

EQUIVALENT, a game for two to four players. Cards are prepared showing 10ths, 100ths, or 1000ths in words or decimals. The cards are face down in the center of the playing area. Players take cards in turn. After picking a card, a player reads what is written on the card and gives another name for the number (for example, sixteen tenths = one and six tenths, or 160 hundredths). If the other players agree about the equivalent fractions, the player holding the card may keep it. When the cards are depleted, the player with the most cards wins.

UP IT, a game for four to seven players. Each player receives 5 to 7 cards. Each card has a decimal written on it. Players in turn choose one of their cards and say, "Up It." If another player can show a card with a decimal greater than the decimal named, he or she gets both cards. If no one can produce a card with a decimal greater than the one named, the player lays the card down as his or her own. The game ends when a player has no more cards. The winner has the most cards. (The players will soon learn to name the greatest decimal in their hands!)

The old games, FISH, RUMMY, SMILING FACE, and WAR can be adapted for comparing decimals.

Comparing decimals is readiness for *ordering decimals*. When children can compare decimals, they are asked to order a set of decimals. Less difficult tasks precede more difficult ones. Pupils first order 10ths (for example, .8, .5, .7, and .2), next 100ths (.16, .18, .04, and .09), and then 10ths and 100ths (.9, .05, .89, and .03). Later 1000ths and mixed decimals are included. After each type of set is ordered, children discuss what they did, explaining to each other the thought processes used to complete the task. Sharing strategies helps many children understand how to order decimals. The teacher insures that during the discussion following ordering decimals with different power-of-10 values, pupils become aware of the usefulness of the strategy of renaming all decimals in a set so that they have the same decimal value (all 10ths, 100ths, . . .). This strategy is particularly help-

ful if children have difficulty knowing how to begin an ordering task.

A game for children to play as they study ordering decimals is ORDER, ORDER! I SAY ORDER! for two to six players:

Thirty to 40 cards are prepared for use by the players. Each card has three decimals (in words) that are to be ordered by the player drawing the card. The first player draws a card from the stack of cards face down in the playing area. He or she reads the decimals and displays the card so that it can be seen by the other players. He or she gives the decimals in order (from greatest to least or least to greatest). (A slate may be provided for the player to use to write the decimals in order.) If a player says: "Order, order, . . . " and the first player cannot explain why his or her order is correct, the challenging player gets the card. If no player says: "Order, order, . . . ," the first player keeps the card. When the stack is depleted, the player with the most cards wins.

Extending understanding of the *place-value system* can follow work with ordering decimals. The lesson can begin with the request to order from greatest to least: 100, .1, 10, .01, 1. When children have completed the ordering task, the teacher asks, "What decimal comes next? . . . Why? What rule do we use to think the next decimal?" The children are helped to state a rule similar to: Take $\frac{1}{10}$ of a number in the list to find the next number.

The teacher then writes 11.111 and says, "How does our rule help explain the meaning of what I have written on the chalkboard?" Other questions asked can include: How does the value of the number given by the 1 in the left-hand place compare to the value of the number given by the numeral in the next place? How much greater is the number given by the numeral in the second place from the left than the number given by the numeral in the third place from the left? What is going on here? What pattern do you notice? (The abacus can be used to show the pattern.)

When children can state the idea that *each place indicates a value 10 times greater (or less) than the value of the place adjacent to it* and use examples to illustrate their ideas, the teacher concludes they have a grasp of the meaning of the place-value system. Children are then helped to make a record of their ideas in writing, for example, 111.111 = 1(10 × 10) + 1(10) + 1 + 1(.1) + 1(.01) + 1(.001). They write other examples to consolidate knowledge of the meaning of the place-value system. Children who are capable of more abstract thinking can use exponential notation:

$$777.777 = 7(10)^2 + 7(10)^1 + 7(10)^0$$
$$+ 7(\tfrac{1}{10})^1 + 7(\tfrac{1}{10})^2 + 7(\tfrac{1}{10})^3$$

Children who can compare and order decimals have attained background for learning to *round decimals*. An inductive approach can be used to introduce rounding decimals. Children first review the meaning of rounding numbers and give a few examples of rounding whole numbers. They next study examples, such as:

.43 rounds to .4

.56 rounds to .6

.79 rounds to .8

.23 rounds to .2

Patterns in the examples are studied and discussed. Number lines can be used to help children explain the patterns observed. Pupils conclude their study of examples by composing a *rule for rounding decimals*, such as: Round hundredths to the nearest tenth; round *up* if the number shown in the hundredths place is 5 or more, and round *down* if it is less than 5.

A deductive plan can also be used to introduce rounding decimals. Pupils first discuss rounding whole numbers: the purpose of rounding and how to think to round whole numbers. They then use their knowledge of rounding whole numbers and of the meaning of decimals to infer how to round 100ths to 10ths. They discuss their ideas of rounding 100ths and also produce several examples, such as .47 rounds to .5. Number lines showing 10ths and 100ths can be used to clarify ideas presented during the discussion. A rule for rounding decimals is written by the group to summarize the lesson.

In subsequent lessons, children work with examples of rounding 100ths to 10ths. For practice, they can be asked to write several decimals that round to a given decimal—for example: Write 3 decimals that round to .7; think rounding up and rounding down to do this exercise. Pupils can write decimals for a partner to round; together they can evaluate responses.

Later, children study rounding 1000ths and mixed decimals such as 5.9. The teacher continues to assign independent study experiences to further understanding and provide practice. These can be adaptations for decimals of activi-

ties and games described in Chapter 5 for learning rounding whole numbers. Another game is COVER IT:

> The game is for four to six players. Each player has a board with 10 squares in a row. In the squares are written 1, .9, .8, . . . , .1. Thirty to 40 cards placed face down in the center of the playing area give numerals for numbers that are the sum of 10ths plus 100ths—for example, .62. Players draw a card each in turn, round to 1 or 10ths, and cover the square showing that numeral with a token. The first player to cover all his or her squares is the winner.

COMPUTATION WITH DECIMALS

Computation with decimals is a two-step procedure: (1) compute as for whole numbers, and (2) assign the sum, difference, product, or quotient a decimal value. Mathematical ideas are the basis for this two-step procedure for each of the operations, as shown in the following examples:

Addition

$.3 + .3 = 3(.1) + 3(.1)$	Renaming
$= (3 + 3)(.1)$	Distributive property of multiplication over addition
$= 6(.1)$	Addition fact
$= .6$	Renaming

Subtraction

$.6 - .3 = 6(.1) - 3(.1)$	Renaming
$= (6 - 3)(.1)$	Distributive property of multiplication over subtraction
$= 3(.1)$	Subtraction fact
$= .3$	Renaming

Multiplication

$.3 \times .3 = 3(.1) \times 3(.1)$	Renaming
$= (3 \times 3) \times (.1 \times .1)$	Associative and commutative properties of multiplication
$= 9 \times .01$	Multiplication fact and knowledge of base 10
$= .09$	Renaming

Division

$$\frac{.09}{.3} = \frac{9(.01)}{3(.1)} \quad \text{Renaming}$$

$$= 3(.1) \quad \text{Division fact and knowledge of base 10}$$

$$= .3 \quad \text{Renaming}$$

Elementary school children usually do not study the rationale for the two-step procedure but develop an intuitive understanding of the mathematical basis for the algorithms as they construct computation rules. Gifted learners may be introduced to the reasoning involved by discussing examples such as those given above.

This section discusses (1) addition and subtraction computation with decimal fractions and (2) multiplication and division computation with decimal fractions. The three-phase instructional sequence is used as the framework in describing instruction. Special emphasis is given in the discussion to guiding children to relate prior knowledge to build new concepts.

Addition and Subtraction Computation with Decimal Fractions

To learn *addition computation* with decimals, children must grasp the meaning of addition of whole and fractional numbers and have skill in whole-number addition computation, both with and without renaming. Children who demonstrate this prior learning as well as show an understanding of decimals are introduced to addition computation with decimals.

The study of addition computation with decimal fractions begins with developing abilities to compute mentally with 10ths, 100ths, and 1000ths and to estimate decimal sums. These abilities are prerequisite to studying paper-and-pencil computation. A lesson to introduce *mental computation* with 10ths or 100ths as addends is given in Box 10-1. The procedure followed in the lesson enables learners to use inference to arrive at new knowledge. Children are guided to infer the rule for mental computation with decimal fractions from knowledge of whole-number addition and the meaning of decimals.

Children who can estimate whole-number sums, can round numbers represented by decimals, and can mentally compute sums when addends are 10ths, 100ths, or 1000ths are ready to *estimate sums that involve decimals.*

An introductory lesson helps learners relate prior learnings to understand the new task. An inductive or deductive method can be used in the lesson. (How?)

To give practice with estimation, the old games (FISH, RUMMY, and SMILING FACE) can be revised to include indicated-sum cards (such as .32 + .22) and estimated-sum cards (such as .50 or .5). A book would contain one of each. The game WRITE ON, outlined earlier in this chapter, can also be adapted to estimating sums.

The next step is *constructing the computation rule*. Lessons begin with a display of examples, such as:

.34	.45	.62	.27
+ .14	+ .34	+ .19	+ .34

Children estimate answers and make records of their estimates. The teacher then asks, "In what way do these examples differ from the whole-number sums we have computed in the past?" The children respond that the examples are for adding, but with decimals, not whole numbers. The teacher then reminds children that they estimate and compute mentally with decimals. He or she suggests a review of mental computation procedures to help with paper-and-pencil computation. As they review, children are guided to recall that in mental computation they compute as for whole numbers and then decide the decimal value of the sum. This value is the same as the value of each addend. The use of two steps is emphasized.

The teacher next suggests using abacuses to find the sums in the given exercises. As children find sums using their abacuses, they observe that determining the place value of the sum is separate from joining objects on the posts; again two steps are involved.

Their observations lead the class to compose the two-step rule: Add using basic facts as for whole numbers; decide the value of the addends and give the sum the same value—10ths, 100ths, or 1000ths. A few examples are completed using the rule.

Later, children consider how to simplify their rule by noting the number of decimal places in each addend and in the sum. The children conclude it is the same number and revise their rule to state this idea.

Another learning activity is rewriting decimal-fraction addition exercises in common-

BOX 10-1.   *SAMPLE LESSON: INTRODUCING MENTAL COMPUTATION*
(ADDITION) WITH DECIMAL FRACTIONS (GRADE 6)

1.   Boys and girls, this morning we are going to study a new topic, mental computation with tenths and other decimals. You know many things that you can use to learn this new skill. Look at the list of examples on the board, think what they mean, and mentally compute the sums for as many exercises as you can. Think about what you know to help yourself.

$$3 + 3 = N \ (6)$$
$$30 + 30 = N \ (60)$$
$$300 + 300 = N \ (600)$$
$$3000 + 3000 = N \ (6000)$$
$$.3 + .3 = N \ (.6)$$
$$.03 + .03 = N \ (.06)$$
$$.003 + .003 = N \ (.006)$$

As you say the answers, I'll write them in place of the Ns. (See numerals in parentheses.)

Some of these sums you have never been asked to think before. How did you know them? What did you think? (Well, tens plus tens are tens, hundreds plus hundreds are hundreds, and so on, so tenths plus tenths must be tenths, hundredths plus hundredths must be hundredths, and so on. I thought $3 + 3 = 6$ and then thought the decimal value of the sum. . . .)

2.   Very good thinking! I will write that rule on the board: Think the addition fact; then give the sum the decimal value of the addends. How can we show that rule is sensible? (Use common fractions, the abacus, or squared-paper diagrams.)

O.K., let's do that. I have abacuses for you and some squared paper. Use either kind of material or common fractions to check the rule. . . . Let's show what we have done and explain our work. Why does our rule make sense? (Pupils discuss meaning of the rule using examples:)

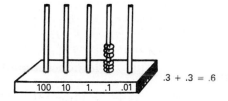

$$.3 + .3 = .6$$

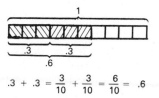

$$.3 + .3 = \frac{3}{10} + \frac{3}{10} = \frac{6}{10} = .6$$

3.   I have written some other examples on the board. If you want help to get started doing these examples or want to check yourself, you can use materials. Try to think answers as often as you can before using materials. Remember your rule.

$$(1) \quad .8 + .1 = N \ (.9)$$
$$(2) \quad .4 + .3 = N \ (.7)$$
$$(3) \quad .5 + .6 = N \ (1.1)$$
$$(4) \quad .4 + .8 = N \ (1.2)$$

4.   Let's talk about the first two examples. (They are easy. Just add and think tenths.) What about the third example? (I knew it was 11 tenths. Then I remembered the game EQUIVALENT. I thought, you can rename 11 tenths 1 and 1 tenth.)

Great thinking! What about the last one? (You do the same thing: $4 + 8 = 12$, think 12 tenths and rename 12 tenths as 1 and 2 tenths.)

You have all used what you know to learn something new. That is the best way to learn mathematics.

5.   Now do these using your rule.

$$.06 + .02 = N$$
$$.04 + .03 = N$$
$$.07 + .05 = N$$
$$.06 + .06 = N$$

The class discusses the sums, giving reasons to explain why they are correct.

6.   Make up exercises and ask a partner the sums. Don't write them. We can do our work mentally and orally. We know how to use quiet voices so everyone can work without interruption. . . .

7.   Let's review what we learned today and how we will remember the new rule we have formed. . . .

fraction form and computing with common fractions. Children are guided through questioning (What do you notice?) to observe that the denominators of the addends must be like and that the denominator of the sum is the same as that of each addend. This observation is related to the class rule, which states that the number of decimal places in the sum is the same as the number of places in each addend. Reference to prior work with addition involving common fractions helps many learners give more meaning to the rule they have constructed.

When children demonstrate ability to add with decimals and understand whole-number and fractional-number subtraction, they are guided to use their knowledge to learn *subtraction computation* with decimals. The first learning objective is prerequisite understanding: mental computation of differences and estimation.

Teachers help learners relate addition and subtraction to learn *mental subtraction* with 10ths, 100ths, or 1000ths. Children are guided to recall their addition rule for mental computation and rephrase it for subtraction: Use basic subtraction facts. Then remember 10ths minus 10ths equals 10ths, 100ths minus 100ths equal 100ths, and so on. Because of previous work in renaming decimals, children can deal with examples such as $1.6 - .9 = N$ by thinking: 1.6 is 16 tenths.

Verification of the mental computation rule should include using squared-paper diagrams, common fractions, and the abacus to show subtraction with decimals (Figure 10-7). Children deepen their understanding of the rule as they work with materials.

Estimation of differences involving decimal fractions is studied next. Pupils use what they know about addition estimation with decimals to develop rules for subtraction estimation. To develop skill, children can play a BINGO game adapted for estimation of differences. Also useful for practice is a number line or board game. Line segments or stepping stones are labeled in 10ths on the playing surface. The game cards, which players draw, show indicated differences (such as $.45 - .23$). The estimated difference is the distance a player can move on the line or along the stepping-stone path (Figure 10-8).

When constructing the rule for subtraction with decimals, learners study examples such as:

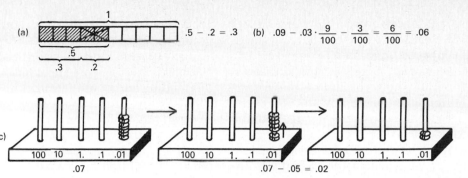

(a) .5 − .2 = .3   (b) $.09 - .03 \cdot \frac{9}{100} - \frac{3}{100} = \frac{6}{100} = .06$

FIGURE 10-7. Showing subtraction with decimals.

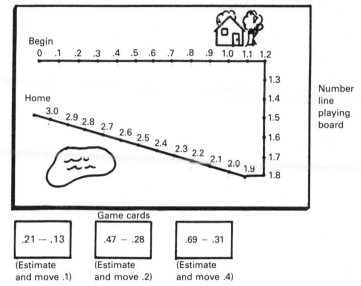

Number line playing board

FIGURE 10-8. Materials for a subtraction estimation game.

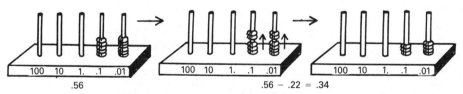

FIGURE 10-9. Using an abacus to show subtraction with decimals.

.66	.74	.86	.92
− .23	− .51	− .44	− .83

The teacher's directions are, "Estimate the differences. Then think what you know about addition computation with decimals and what you know about subtraction." After reviewing with learners what they remember, the teacher guides pupils to form a *rule for subtraction with decimals*: Compute as for whole numbers. Place the decimal point so that the difference has as many decimal places as the minuend or the subtrahend. The rule is used to find the differences in the examples being studied. The computed differences are checked with the estimated differences.

In a later lesson the common-fraction form is used and the subtraction computation rules for common and decimal fractions are compared. Materials such as the abacus can also be used to give further meaning to the algorithm (Figure 10-9).

Extending and consolidating activities for addition or subtraction include working with **ragged decimals**—decimals with different numbers of places (such as .34 + .5). Generally the procedure is to annex zeros. This rule will be meaningful to learners if they have studied equivalent decimals as suggested in the previous section of this chapter. Children should discuss the reasons for annexing zeros and conclude that the procedure tends to insure that the computation will be correct because the decimal points are more easily "lined up" than when ragged decimals are used. Children in the elementary school usually do not explore the idea of significant digits that arises in connection with computation with numbers derived from measuring.

The addition and subtraction rules constructed by learners state that the algorithm for whole numbers is used in the first step in decimal computation; the fractional value is determined in the last step by the placement of the decimal point. Therefore, *renaming partial sums* (for example, 100ths as 10ths) or *renaming minuends* (10ths as 100ths) is not required and is not a part of instruction for most children. It can be included as a lesson for extension, particularly with gifted learners. (Children do study renaming of decimals and use it in mental computation; for example: 6 10ths plus 7 10ths equals 13 10ths or 1 and 3 10ths. This aspect of instruction was discussed previously.)

As children use whole-number algorithms as the first step in addition and subtraction with decimal fractions, renaming situations should present no problems. If they can use algorithms for whole numbers, children usually do not need much practice to remember how to use the addition and subtraction algorithms for decimal fractions when either no renaming or renaming is required.

Problems involving addition and subtraction computation with decimals are included in the extending and consolidating phase of instruction. The problems often involve measurements in metric units. It is good to encourage children to find real-life problems that deal with decimals. Parents can contribute problems from their lives to help relate school and out-of-school experiences.

Multiplication and Division Computation with Decimal Fractions

Learning multiplication and division with decimal fractions involves developing the meaning of the operations with decimals, mental computation with 10ths and 100ths, estimation, and formation and use of the computation rules. In this section, multiplication computation is discussed first, then division computation. Both multiplication and division computation with decimal fractions are included in suggestions for extending and consolidating knowledge.

Study of *multiplication with decimals* is begun when children know decimal concepts, grasp multiplication of whole and fractional numbers, and can compute whole-number products. If children have attained this prior knowledge, learning multiplication with decimal fractions begins with developing prerequisites: meaning, mental computation, and estimation. An introductory lesson to develop *meaning and mental computation rules* uses examples such as:

1. $3 \times .3 = N$
2. $2 \times .4 = N$
3. $.2 \times .3 = N$
4. $.1 \times .5 = N$

The children are asked to think about the sense of these multiplication sentences. They conclude that the first two can be interpreted as repeated addition and the last two involve partitioning. The teacher helps learners restate the third and fourth examples as:

.2 of .3 is N

.1 of .5 is N

The boys and girls discuss how to obtain the products for all examples and decide that the common-fraction form or the use of squared-paper diagrams would be possible for each example. Repeated addition is useful for only the first two. Individually, or in teams, children find the products [Figure 10-10 shows (1) and (3) above]. The equations children write are:

$3 \times .3 = .9$

$2 \times .4 = .8$

$.2 \times .3 = .06$

$.1 \times .5 = .05$

An examination of the equations and attention to common-fraction and material solutions help learners notice these patterns: 1s times 10ths equals 10ths and 10ths times 10ths equals 100ths. They decide that the rule for mental computation is: Use multiplication facts and then think the decimal value of the product using the patterns.

$$3 \times .3 = \frac{3}{10} + \frac{3}{10} + \frac{3}{10} = \frac{9}{10} = .9$$

$$3 \times .3 = .3 + .3 + .3 = .9$$

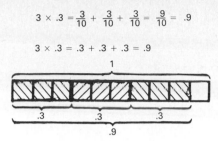

$$.2 \times .3 = \frac{2}{10} \times \frac{3}{10} = \frac{6}{100} = .06$$

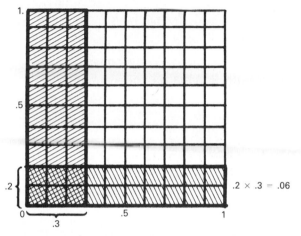

FIGURE 10-10. Showing multiplication with decimals.

Their rule is written on the board and later transferred to a chart. Pupils use their rule to find solutions mentally to other exercises. They work in a small-group setting or in teams of two. So that pupils will have opportunities to review renaming in multiplication, the teacher soon includes examples in which the products can be renamed. Using the common-fraction form helps some learners in their review (for example:

$$3 \times .8 = \frac{3}{1} \times \frac{8}{10}$$
$$= \frac{24}{10} = 2\frac{4}{10}$$
$$= 2.4\ )$$

Examples used include:

$$6 \times .4 = N$$
$$7 \times .8 = N$$
$$.5 \times .4 = N$$
$$.5 \times .8 = N$$

The study of *estimation* follows mental computation. Children round to the nearest value and compute mentally when factors are 1s, 10ths, or 100ths. They are asked to recall prior learnings and to make inferences to construct estimation rules for multiplication with decimals. Of special significance is children's previous development of the patterns relating values of factors to values of products. For practice, children can play the old games adapted to estimation for multiplication with decimals or use study sheets in team work.

Children next *construct the computation rule*: Multiply as for whole numbers; add (or count) the number of decimal places in the first factor and the number of decimal places in the second factor to determine the number of decimal places in the product. Learners construct the rule by observing examples of products computed mentally using the generalizations they have developed. (One times 10ths equals 10ths and 10ths times 10ths equals 100ths.) They are helped to decide that in decimal computation the first step is to compute as for whole numbers and then place the decimal point in the product. They observe that adding (or counting) the number of places in the factors to determine the number of places in the product is a good shortcut and eliminates thinking the generalizations each time. Work with common and decimal fractions (such as $\frac{3}{10} \times \frac{2}{100} = \frac{6}{1000}$; $.3 \times .02 = .006$) extends understanding of the rule.

After forming the rule for multiplication with decimal fractions, children practice its use in solving exercises so they can retrieve it whenever necessary. Teachers continue to remind pupils to estimate before computing and to check the computed product with the estimate.

Division computation with decimal fractions is often said to be difficult for children. Perhaps it is difficult because children do not have retrievable knowledge to use to construct meaning and to develop skill in using the algorithm. Before learners turn their attention to division computation with decimals, they must have developed *prerequisite learnings*: the meaning of division for whole and fractional numbers, immediate recall of division facts, competency in using the division algorithm for whole numbers, and understanding of decimals. Teachers assess for these learnings before beginning division computation with decimals.

Meaning, mental calculation, and estimation are also prerequisite to study of division computation with decimals. Teachers first help children *interpret* division equations involving decimals. Examples are studied and interpretations given—for example:

.8 ÷ 2 = .4   means .8 divided into two same-size parts. The quotient means .4 in each part.

.9 ÷ .3 = 3   means how many .3 equals .9. The quotient says three .3 equals .9.

.06 ÷ .2 = .3   means how many .2 equals .06. The quotient says .3 of .2 equals .06.

To insure that pupils understand the meaning of such examples, teachers ask learners to use squared-paper diagrams (or number lines) to represent the several interpretations (Figure 10-11).

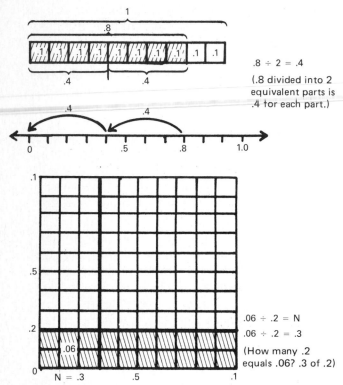

.8 ÷ 2 = .4

(.8 divided into 2 equivalent parts is .4 for each part.)

.06 ÷ .2 = N
.06 ÷ .2 = .3
(How many .2 equals .06? .3 of .2)

N = .3

FIGURE 10-11.   Diagrams showing division with decimals.

In a subsequent lesson the interpretations of division with decimals are reexamined, and children are helped to relate division and multiplication with decimals to aid in their construction of rules for *mental computation*. The teacher can say, "How can we write these division questions we studied yesterday as multiplication questions? . . . Now let's write multiplication questions as division questions." The teacher's list and the pupils' work are as follows:

Teacher's List	*Pupils' Work*
.20 × 2 = .40	.40 ÷ 2 = .20
.2 × 4 = .8	.8 ÷ 4 = .2
40 × .2 = 8	8 ÷ .2 = 40
4 × .2 = .8	.8 ÷ .2 = 4
.4 × .2 = .08	.08 ÷ .2 = .4

Pupils discuss these examples and use them to generate the *rule for division computation with decimals*: Use the basic facts to divide; to give the quotient a decimal value, think:

Hundredths divided by 1s equals 100ths.
Tenths divided by 1s equals 10ths.
Ones divided by 10ths equals 10s.
Tenths divided by 10ths equals 1s.
Hundredths divided by 10ths equals 10ths.

Materials can be used to verify the rule.

In some examples the dividend must be renamed to complete the computation. For example, 2 ÷ .5 = 4 means 20 10ths divided by 5 10ths equals 4 (10ths divided by 10ths equals 1s); and .4 ÷ .8 = .5 means 40 100ths divided by 8 10ths equals 5 10ths (100ths divided by 10ths equals 10ths). Other exercises can require renaming of the quotient. For example, .44 ÷ .4 = 1.1 means 44 100ths divided by 4 10ths equals 11 10ths or 1.1 (100ths divided by 10ths equals 10ths). Such mental computation examples with renaming are not used in mental computation exercises for children until they have developed a mature understanding of decimal relations.

Practice of mental division computation with decimals is pursued by children as they use study sheets or play games. The study sheets give division questions with quotients. Two children use a study sheet, one asking the question and the other answering. Halfway through the sheet, the children change roles. Games children play include those described previously for learning mental computation but now adapted for division computation with decimals.

Estimation of quotients in division with decimals emphasizes rounding divisors to 1s or 10ths; dividends to 1s, 10ths, or 100ths. The mental computation rule is then used. With practice, children who have had a program that insured mastery of prerequisite learnings will be able to develop skill in estimating quotients.

Computation rules involving division with decimals are constructed by learners when they understand the meaning of division with decimals and can estimate some quotients. The first rule taught refers to division when the divisor is a whole number and the dividend is a decimal. Children explain the meaning of equations such as:

$$.8 \div 2 = N$$
$$.6 \div 2 = N$$
$$.44 \div 4 = N$$
$$.66 \div 3 = N$$

They estimate and find solutions using thinking, squared-paper diagrams, or number lines (see diagrams in Figure 10-11). Pupils next study their work to formulate the rule: Divide as for whole numbers. Decide where to place the decimal point: when the divisor is a whole number and the dividend is a decimal, the quotient has the same number of places (same value) as the dividend. Later pupils use their rule in a few practice exercises to insure it will be remembered. The need to estimate in practice exercises is stressed by the teacher.

A sample lesson for division of decimals when both the divisor and dividend are decimals is given in Box 10-2. Practice exercises soon include divisors that are 1s, 10ths, or 100ths. When children develop skill in division with decimals (8 out of 10 completed without error), they are introduced to exercises requiring the annexation of zeros to obtain quotients. Inductive lessons are often used to help learners understand the process. Pupils study examples and infer the procedure. The rationale is then discussed. Examples of exercises used in one or more lessons are:

$$9.1 \div 2.8 = N$$

$$
\begin{array}{r}
3.2\,5 \\
2.8\,\overline{)9.1\,0\,0} \\
-8\,4 \\
\hline
7\,0 \\
-5\,6 \\
\hline
1\,4\,0 \\
-1\,4\,0 \\
\hline
0
\end{array}
$$

$$.819 \div .23 = N$$

$$
\begin{array}{r}
3.5\,6\,0 \\
.23\,\overline{)\,.81\,.9\,0\,0} \\
6\,9 \\
\hline
1\,2\,9 \\
-1\,1\,5 \\
\hline
1\,4\,0 \\
-1\,3\,8 \\
\hline
2\,0 \\
-0\,0 \\
\hline
2\,0
\end{array}
$$

If the division process does not terminate, pupils learn to round the quotient to the same number of places as in the dividend or the divisor, choosing whichever has the least number of places.

Extending and consolidating experiences for multiplication and division with decimals include extending ideas of different representations for a number, learning high-level rules for mental computation, and solving problems. Examples of learning experiences are:

1. *Extending ideas of representing numbers*

    a. Determining same values but different forms for large numbers—for example, 2,300,000 is 2.3 million. Many graphs and current event articles use the latter form. Finding examples of numbers given by numerals and words will introduce children to these ideas. Next, they compute (for example, 4.2 million: $4.2 \times 1,000,000 = 4,200,000$) and study their results for patterns, such as 100,000s are 10ths of millions. The patterns are discussed; examples with common fractions can be studied $[(1/10) \times 1,000,000 = 100,000]$. Pupils form rules and generate other examples. This activity is especially suitable for children who learn mathematics easily.

    b. Working with decimal names for common fractions. Children who understand annexing zeros to dividends are asked to recall that the bar in a common fraction means divide. They conclude that a division such as $\frac{5}{8}$ can be carried out:

BOX 10-2. *SAMPLE LESSON: INTRODUCING DIVISION WITH DECIMALS*
            IN DIVISOR AND DIVIDEND (GRADE 6)

1. Yesterday we learned how to divide when the divisor is a whole number and the dividend is a decimal. Let's review this rule. . . . Let's all do this computation using paper and pencil:

$$7\overline{)9.1}$$

Sue, tell us what you thought, and write the quotient on the chalkboard. Did anyone think another way? Are there any questions?

2. I have written some division examples on the board. What do you notice about them? (Divisors and dividends have decimal points.)

$$\overset{(20)}{.4\overline{)8.64}} \qquad \overset{(2)}{.3\overline{).6}} \qquad \overset{(20)}{.3\overline{)6.96}}$$

3. Let's estimate quotients. (See numerals in parentheses.) Now I will rewrite the examples in fraction form to help us figure out the rule.

$$\frac{8.64}{.4} \qquad \frac{.6}{.3} \qquad \frac{6.96}{.3}$$

What kind of division computation with decimals do we know? (We can divide when the divisor is a whole number and the dividend is a decimal.)

How can we rename each expression so the divisor is a whole number? (Multiply the dividend and the divisor by 10.) Use your paper and pencil to do that. Notice what happens to the decimal point in the divisor and in the dividend.

When we multiply by 10, what happens to the decimal point? (The decimal point moves one place to the right.) Yes, moving the decimal point in the dividend and the divisor one place to the right multiplies both numbers by 10 and renames the expression. Moving the decimal point one place to the right is a shortcut for multiplying by 10. Finish your division. Let's discuss our work. . . . How were our estimates? (O.K.) Let's discuss what to do when divisors are hundredths. . . .

Let's make a rule now. The divisor must be a whole number. How do we rename in this kind of exercise? What is the shortcut? (Move the decimal point in the divisor and the dividend the same number of places to the right.)

What do we do next to find the quotient? (Divide and give the quotient the same number of decimal places as the dividend.)

Let's write the rule on the board (pupils and teacher cooperatively compose the rule, and a pupil or the teacher writes it on the board): First estimate. To divide when the divisor is a decimal, move the decimal point in the divisor so that the number becomes a whole number. Move the decimal point in the dividend the same number of places to the right. Divide and place the decimal point so that the quotient has the same number of places as the dividend. Check the estimate.

4. Let's all work the same example using the rule. What is the estimate? (2.) Use your paper and pencil as we do it together. (Use other examples as needed by group.)

$$.4\overline{).72} \qquad \overset{1.8}{(\ \underset{\wedge}{.4}\overline{)\underset{\wedge}{7.2}}\ )}$$

5. Now find the quotients in these examples. Remember to estimate. Then use the rule on the board.

$$\overset{(.2)}{.5\overline{)\,.105}} \qquad \overset{(1)}{.6\overline{)\,.612}} \qquad \overset{(3)}{1.8\overline{)\,5.76}} \qquad \overset{(10)}{.7\overline{)\,8.4}}$$

6. Let's review what we have done. What are the estimates? (See numerals in parentheses.) What are the quotients? (.21, 1.02, 3.2, 12.) Are the estimates O.K.? (Yes.) Please explain how you found the first quotient. ... The second? ... What did you think when you moved the decimal point one place to the right in the divisor and the dividend? (It is multiplying the divisor and dividend by ten.)

7. Study the rule on the board. After you study it, I will erase some words and ask you to fill them in.

8. Cover your eyes. (Erase the words "same.") What words did I erase? ... Why are they very important words? ...

9. Say the rule to yourself. Neighbors then take turns saying the rule to each other.

10. Look at the work I've put on the board while you were practicing the rule:

$$\overset{2.2}{.4\overline{)\,8.8}} \qquad \overset{8.3}{.4\overline{)\,3.5.2}} \qquad \overset{2\,1.}{.6\overline{)\,12.6}}$$

Let's check to find which exercises are correct or incorrect. How do we always check our results? (Look at the estimate. Multiply the quotient and the divisor to obtain the dividend.) Yes. ... (The second one should be 8.8.) Why? ...

11. Your assignment is to complete with no errors the first 5 exercises on page 198 of your textbook. Remember to estimate and use multiplication to check yourself. Raise your hand if you need help. (Pupils do assignment.)

12. I noticed everyone learned the rule. This is what we expected, isn't it!

$$\begin{array}{r} .6\,2\,5 \\ 8\overline{)5.0\,0\,0} \\ -4\,8 \\ \hline 2\,0 \\ -1\,6 \\ \hline 4\,0 \\ -4\,0 \\ \hline \end{array}$$

$$\frac{5}{8} = .625$$

Children should determine decimal fractions for $\frac{1}{2}, \frac{1}{4}, \frac{1}{6}, \frac{1}{7}, \frac{1}{8}, \frac{1}{9}, \frac{2}{3}, \frac{3}{4}$, and any other common fractions they choose. Pupils can infer from their work that some decimals terminate and some repeat. After classifying the decimals into these two groups, pupils can construct a table with entries, showing the two categories (Table 10-1).

Children are guided to set goals of remembering decimal names for certain common fractions because this knowledge is useful in many situations. Learners are given time to study those frequently used, such as $\frac{1}{2} = .5$ and $\frac{1}{4} = .25$. Adaptations of old matching games or of WRITE ON can be used to give opportunities for rehearsal.

2. *Learning high-level rules for mental computation*

High-level rules for mental computation are: (1) If a multiplier (divisor) is a whole number and a power of 10, to multiply (divide) a given number by that multiplier (divisor) move the decimal point in the given number to the right (left) the same number of places as zeros in the multiplier (divisor). (2) If a multiplier (divisor) is a decimal and a power of 10, to multiply (divide) a given number by that multiplier

Decimals for Common Fractions		
Common Fractions	Decimals	
	Terminating	Repeating
$\frac{1}{2}$	.50	
$\frac{1}{3}$		.33 . . .
$\frac{2}{3}$		.66 . . .
$\frac{1}{4}$	.25	
$\frac{3}{4}$	.75	
$\frac{1}{5}$	.20	
$\frac{2}{5}$	.40	
$\frac{3}{5}$	.60	
$\frac{4}{5}$	.80	
$\frac{1}{6}$		.166 . . .
$\frac{1}{7}$		.142857142857 . . .
$\frac{1}{8}$	.125	
$\frac{1}{9}$		.11 . . .
$\frac{1}{10}$	.10	

TABLE 10.1.   Table of decimals for common fractions

(divisor) move the decimal point in the given number to the left (right) the same number of places as places in the decimal. For example:

(1) $10 \times 34. = 340.$; $450. \div 10 = 45.$
(2) $.1 \times 45. = 4.5$; $450. \div .1 = 4500.$

These rules are very general. Children cannot construct them until they have worked with materials and constructed less general rules, such as 10ths times 10ths equals 100ths. In the elementary school gifted learners can often infer the high-level rules

and use them in mental computation. Most children, however, should not be introduced to these rules until the junior high years.

3.   *Solving problems*
Routine and nonroutine problems, applied and nonapplied, now include multiplication and division computation with decimals. Children are helped to extend their problem-solving abilities to include such computation. Of special importance is the writing of problems by pupils.

This section has discussed how learners use their knowledge of base-10 relations, place value, common fractions, and the algorithms for whole numbers to develop computational skills with decimals. The value of informal reasoning in reorganizing prior learning to attain new knowledge has been emphasized. It was suggested that materials be used to verify thinking whenever learners are capable of using prior knowledge to produce new ideas.

COMPREHENDING PERCENT AND SOLVING PERCENT PROBLEMS

The percent concept is a ratio idea: **percent** is a comparison of a number to one hundred. For example, 25 percent means 25 per 100, or 25 compared to 100. The percent symbol is %; 25% is read 25 percent. A common or decimal fraction ($\frac{25}{100}$ or .25) can also be used to express a percent. When a percent is one ratio in a proportion, the numbers have certain names:

20/100 = 140/700
20/100 (20%) is the *rate*
140 is the *percentage*
700 is the *base*

Types of Percent Problems

Three types of problems can be given for situations involving percents. Examples below are shown with the *cross-product solutions* and *finding-missing-term* solutions.

1.   The new carpeting in Tom's house was supposed to cost $2000, but Tom's Dad got 25% off the original price. What was the amount he got off? (*percentage unknown*)

Cross-product solution	Finding-missing-term solution
$\dfrac{25}{100} = \dfrac{N}{2000}$	$\dfrac{25}{100} = \dfrac{N}{2000}$
$100N = 25 \times 2000$	$\dfrac{25 \times 20}{100 \times 20} = \dfrac{N}{2000}$
$N = 500$	$N = 500$

2. Jim's parents got $500 off a carpet price that originally was $2000. What percent did they get off? (*rate unknown*)

Cross-product solution	Finding-missing-term solution
$\dfrac{N}{100} = \dfrac{500}{2000}$	$\dfrac{N}{100} = \dfrac{500}{2000}$
$2000N = 100 \times 500$	$\dfrac{N}{100} = \dfrac{500 \div 20}{2000 \div 20}$
$N = 25$	$N = 25$
Rate is 25%	Rate is 25%

3. The salesman said that $500 off on a carpet was 25% off. What was the original price? (*base unknown*)

Cross-product solution	Finding-missing-term solution
$\dfrac{25}{100} = \dfrac{500}{N}$	$\dfrac{25}{100} = \dfrac{500}{N}$
$25N = 100 \times 500$	$\dfrac{25 \times 20}{1000 \times 20} = \dfrac{500}{N}$
$N = 2000$	$2000 = N$

Percent problems can be solved by using the idea: percent of the whole (base) equals the part (percentage). The equation format for solutions is: 100ths times the whole equals the part. The above examples are solved by thinking:

1. 25% of $2000 is .25 of $2000

$$.25 \times 2000 = N$$
$$500 = N$$

2. What percent of $2000 is $500?

$$N \times 2000 = 500$$
$$N = 500 \div 2000$$
$$N = .25 \ (.25 = 25\%)$$

3. 25% of a number is $500 or .25 of a number is $500

$$.25 \times N = 500$$
$$N = 500 \div .25$$
$$N = 2000$$

Learning About Percent

Prerequisite understandings for learning and applying percent ideas are: (1) ability to analyze problems; (2) skill in writing and solving equations related to problems; and (3) understandings related to decimal or common fractions. Pupils who have these competencies can extend their mathematical knowledge by learning percent concepts and studying the three types of percent problems. Pupils who do not have readiness abilities should have instruction to develop prerequisite knowledge before being introduced to percent and percent problems.

Teachers introduce *percent concepts* by telling learners that percent is used in many situations to give meaning to events. Teachers note references to percent in social studies material, current events, and local sales. Children can collect newspaper clippings that include references to percent to help them understand its significance.

Beginning lessons stress the meaning of percent. Teachers tell children that percent means per one hundred. Pupils are shown the notation for writing percent. They examine and read examples, such as 46% and 34%. They study the meaning of the examples and are helped to restate the percents in common- and decimal-fraction form ($\frac{46}{100}$ or .46). They can use squared-paper diagrams to represent percents (Figure 10-12). They work with a few exercises which require translating from one notation to another, such as:

Write the correct numerals or symbols in the blank spaces:

$$75\% = \underline{\hspace{1cm}} / \underline{\hspace{1cm}}$$
$$\frac{36}{100} = \underline{\hspace{1cm}}\%$$
$$.25 = \underline{\hspace{1cm}}\%$$

Children also write their own examples and discuss them with a classmate.

When pupils can state percents as common

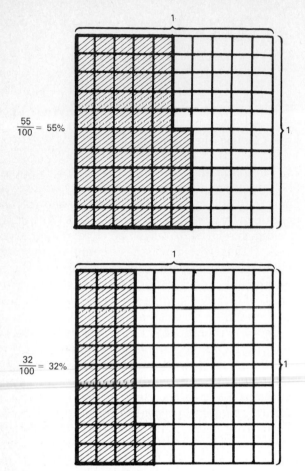

$\frac{55}{100} = 55\%$

$\frac{32}{100} = 32\%$

FIGURE 10-12.   Diagrams to represent percent.

and decimal fractions, *percent problems* are introduced. Either the proportion or multiplication approach to finding solutions is presented to learners. Learning each method is discussed briefly.

If pupils can solve ratio problems, the introduction to percent problems makes use of this prior learning to learn the *proportion approach*. The new idea that percent means *per one hundred* is stressed. Pupils analyze problems, write equations as proportions, and solve them using the cross-products or missing-term method. The first problems introduced are solved for percentages. Later the missing number in a problem is the rate or the base.

If the *multiplication approach* to solving percent problems is taught, teachers begin by presenting exercises in the "percent of" form for learners to study; for example:

25% of 400 is *N*

50% of 500 is *N*

40% of 900 is *N*

65% of 1000 is *N*

Questions teachers ask as learners examine the exercises are: What does "of" mean in mathematical language? Will the solutions be greater or less than 400, and so on? Why? What does percent mean? How can you rewrite the exercises using decimals? Using the times sign?

As learners examine the given examples and answer teacher questions, they develop examples in the form: $.25 \times 400 = N$; $.50 \times 500 = N$; and so forth. A study of the examples enables learners to state the rule:

1.   Percent of the whole equals the part

or

2.   Hundredths times the whole equals the part.

Which rule (1 or 2) is easier to use in finding solutions to the percent exercises depends on the individual. Children are encouraged to use the form most meaningful to them. (Using rule 1, of course, requires rewriting sentences to show 100ths and multiplication.) Pupils use the rule they have adopted to solve percent exercises before they learn to use the rule in solving problems. When problems are introduced, children are helped to rephrase the problem question in the format of the exercises they have studied. This enables them to use their rule to find solutions. Problems first require solutions for percentage; later the rate or base is the missing number.

Percent problems are difficult for many children to analyze, and the topic of percent often is not introduced in the elementary school but delayed until grade seven. In some curricula only problems requiring solutions for percentage are introduced in the late elementary school years; problems involving solutions for rate or base are introduced in junior high school.

SUMMARY

This chapter discussed how children are helped to use prior knowledge, materials, and cognitive processes to construct decimal and percent concepts. The first section dealt with studying decimals. The prerequisite understanding for learning decimals is knowledge of fractional numbers, common fractions, base 10, place value, and counting. Constructing decimal concepts includes studying the meaning of decimal fractions and forming ideas of decimal place values. Children extend understanding of decimals as they learn to compare, order, and round decimals. It was noted the materials are used extensively when children study decimals.

The second section outlined learning computation rules for decimals. Mental computation and estimation are studied prior to the introduction of computation with decimals. When children study computation with decimals, they learn that the algorithms involve two steps: (1) compute as for whole numbers, and (2) correctly place the decimal point. Inductive and deductive methods were described to guide children to construct computation rules. Extending and consolidating activities, including problem solving, were also discussed.

Learning percent concepts was the topic of the third section. Before studying percent, children should have developed the concept of ratio and understand multiplication with decimals. Then they learn the meaning of percent and develop ability to analyze percent problems. It was pointed out that attention to individual differences often leads to delaying the introduction of some percent topics until the junior high school years.

STUDY QUESTIONS

1. Evaluate your skill in mental calculation with decimals. If your skills need improvement, work with another student who has the same need to develop the ability mentally to calculate sums, differences, products, and quotients with 1s, 10ths, and 100ths (only in certain products and quotients). Would the activity you use be appropriate for upper-grade pupils? Why or why not?

2. Assess pupils' abilities to compare decimals. What are the implications of your results?

3. Write a lesson for learning the ordering of decimals.

4. Make a file of uses for decimals you observe in your life and of references to decimals in newspaper articles and textbooks.

5. Discuss with another student how computation rules for the operations with decimals should be taught. What methods will you employ? Why?

6. Make a list of reasons why pupils should or should not be introduced to percent problems in grade six. Share your reasons with your class. Have one member of the class summarize these reasons and their implications.

REFERENCES

Dewar, Jacqueline M., "Another Look at the Teaching of Percent," *Arithmetic Teacher*, 31, no. 7 (March 1984), 48-49.

Dollins, Anabeth, "How I Teach It: Percent," *Arithmetic Teacher*, 29, no. 2 (October 1981), 37.

Grossman, Anne S., "Decimal Notation: An Important Research Finding," *Arithmetic Teacher*, 39, no. 9 (May 1983), 32-33.

Lichtenberg, Betty K., and Donovan R. Lichtenberg, "Decimals Deserve Distinction," in *Mathematics for the Middle Grades (5-9)*, 1982 Yearbook of the National Council of Teachers of Mathematics, eds. Linda Silvey and James R. Smart. Reston, VA: The National Council of Teachers of Mathematics, Inc., 1982.

"Rational Numbers (Focus Issue)," *Arithmetic Teacher*, 31, no. 6 (February 1984).

Riedesel, C. Alan, *Teaching Elementary School Mathematics*, 3d ed., chap. 11. Englewood Cliffs, NJ: Prentice-Hall, Inc., 1980.

Zawojewski, Judith, "Initial Decimal Concepts: Are They Really So Easy?" *Arithmetic Teacher*, 30, no. 7 (March 1983), 52-56.

11 LEARNING AND TEACHING CONCEPTS OF GEOMETRY, COORDINATES, AND GRAPHING

Look almost anywhere and you see representations of space figures. The study of space leads to greater understanding of the environment, as well as giving knowledge for more advanced work in mathematics. Children study space concepts in every grade. After an informal introduction to these concepts in kindergarten and grade one (Chapter 4), children study the properties of geometric figures in the primary years and examine classes of figures in the postprimary grades. In the elementary school children also explore ideas of motion geometry, coordinates, and graphing.

The first section of this chapter is a brief review of content. Later sections discuss learning and teaching (1) concepts of geometric figures, (2) concepts of classes of geometric figures, (3) motion geometry, and (4) coordinates and graphing. A brief summary concludes the chapter.

OVERVIEW OF CONTENT

This section discusses the geometric concepts taught in the elementary school: points, curves, and lines, two-dimensional and three-dimensional figures, motions, and coordinates. The language used is appropriate for adults. Elementary school children use less technical language that is meaningful to them.

Points, Curves, and Lines

Point is an undefined term. It is considered an exact location in **space**, the set of all points.

A point has no dimension. A set of points can form an identifiable pattern or figure.

A **curve** is a set of points represented by a drawing formed without lifting one's pencil. It can be closed (with no endpoints) or open (with endpoints). It can be simple (not intersecting itself) or not simple (intersecting itself). Curves include line segments, circles, and ellipses, as well as "free-form" figures. Figure 11-1 shows categories of curves.

A **line** is a set of points that extends endlessly in both directions. It is considered to be straight. In geometry, line is an undefined term. A **line segment** lies on a line; it is formed by two specified points of the line called **endpoints** and all the points between the endpoints. A **ray** consists of a specified point of a line and all the points on one side of the given point. An **angle** consists of two rays with the same endpoint, called the **vertex** of the angle. Figure 11-2 gives examples of these figures and the symbols used to designate them.

Lines can have no or one point in common (Figure 11-3). Two lines that have no point in common are **parallel lines**. Two lines that have one point in common are **intersecting lines**. Two lines whose intersection forms four congruent (same size and shape) angles are **perpendicular** to each other. The angles are **right angles**.

Simple Closed Plane Figures

Plane is also an undefined term. It is represented by a flat surface. An intuitive idea of a plane is formed by thinking of a flat surface extending endlessly in all directions.

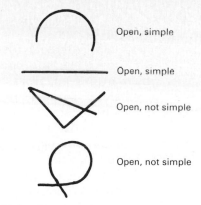

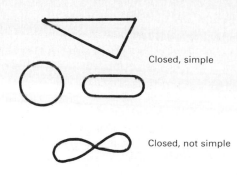

FIGURE 11-1. Curves.

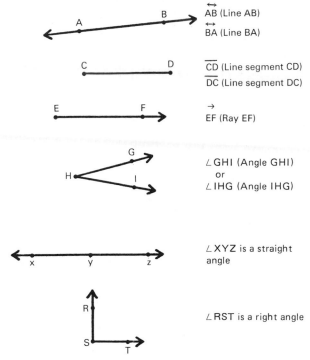

FIGURE 11-2. Line, line segments, ray, and angles.

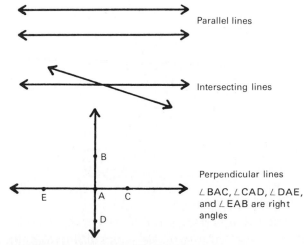

FIGURE 11-3. Parallel and intersecting lines.

A **simple closed plane figure** is a simple closed curve in one plane. Simple closed plane figures formed by the union of line segments are **polygons**. The line segments are called the **sides** of the figure; the endpoints are the **vertices**. Figure 11-4 shows various polygons.

Triangles and parallelograms are emphasized in instruction in the elementary school. **Triangles** are polygons with three sides. Different types of triangles are shown in Figure 11-5a. **Parallelograms** are quadrilaterals (four sides) with the opposite pairs of sides parallel. Figure 11-5b shows types of parallelograms. **Rectangles**

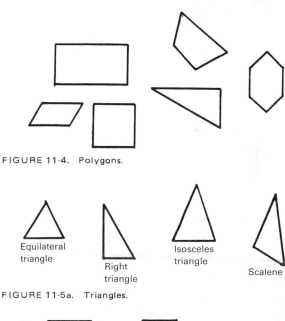

FIGURE 11-4. Polygons.

FIGURE 11-5a. Triangles.

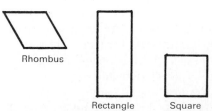

FIGURE 11-5b. Parallelograms.

are parallelograms with four right angles. **Squares** are rectangles with all sides of equal length. A **diagonal** is a line segment that connects two nonadjacent vertices of a polygon. A **regular polygon** has sides equal in length and angles of equal measure.

Circles are simple closed plane figures formed so that each point on the circle is equidistant from a given point called the **center of the circle.**

A simple closed plane figure is differentiated from the portion of the plane it bounds, the **interior** of the figure. The part of the plane bounded by a simple closed plane figure is called a **region.** The figure together with the region is two-dimensional.

Three-Dimensional Figures

Solid figures are sets of points forming simple closed surfaces and their interiors. Solid figures are three-dimensional. Physical objects such as coins are models of solid figures.

Polyhedrons, the boundaries of certain solid figures, are three-dimensional figures formed by the union of polygons and the regions they bound (Figure 11-6). The line segments are called **edges;** the regions, **faces;** and the intersections of edges, **vertices.**

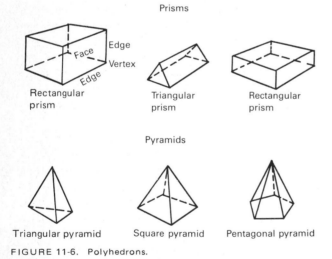

FIGURE 11-6. Polyhedrons.

A **prism** is a polyhedron with two congruent polygons and their interiors in parallel planes (the bases) and the other polygonal regions bounded by parallelograms.

A **pyramid** is a polyhedron formed by a polygon and its interior (the base) and the triangles and their interiors formed using a point

not in the interior of the polygon and each edge of the base.

Spheres, cones, and cylinders are three-dimensional figures formed by the boundaries of solid figures which are curved, at least in part (Figure 11-7). A **sphere** is formed by all the points in space that are equidistant from a point called the center. A **cone** consists of a simple closed curve and its interior and a surface formed by a line moving through all the points on the curve and a point not on the curve. A **cylinder** consists of two congruent simple closed curves in parallel planes and their interiors and a surface formed by a line moving parallel to itself through the points on the curves.

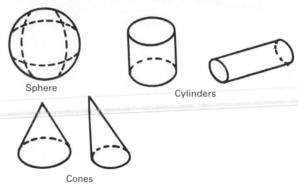

FIGURE 11-7. Sphere, cylinders, and cones.

Motion Geometry

Motions can be performed on geometric figures. **Stretching** was mentioned in Chapter 4. We can also think of a figure as being moved. Figure 11-8 shows the moves discussed in the elementary school: **slides** (translations), **turns** (rotations), and **flips** (reflections). If two figures coincide after a sequence of moves, they are said to be **congruent;** that is, they have the same size and shape.

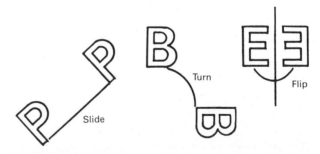

FIGURE 11-8. Motions.

Flipping a figure produces a mirror image of the figure (the two halves match one-to-one). If a figure can be divided in half and one-half

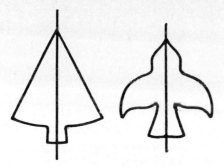

FIGURE 11-9.   Examples of line symmetry.

flipped so that it coincides with the other half, the figure is said to have *line symmetry* (Figure 11-9).

Coordinates

Coordinates relate space and numbers. A point in a plane can be located by an ordered pair of numbers called **coordinates** of the point. Perpendicular number lines, called the **x (horizontal) axis and the y (vertical) axis,** aid in locating the point (Figure 11-10). In the elementary school, Quadrant I is the focus of instruction. Negative numbers and Quadrants II, III, and IV are emphasized in junior high school.

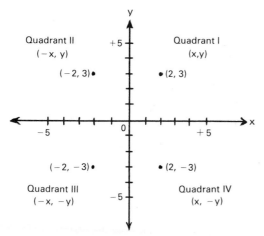

FIGURE 11-10.   Coordinates.

LEARNING AND TEACHING CONCEPTS OF GEOMETRIC FIGURES

Children in kindergarten and grade one are guided to develop prerequisite understanding of geometric figures (Chapter 4). They learn to differentiate two-dimensional and three-dimensional figures. They sometimes draw figures, such as triangles and squares. Assessment of prerequisite understanding determines if children can distinguish among figures and name the most common ones. When assessing for prerequisite understanding, teachers ask children to:

1.   Find a different object in a set of three in which two show the same figure (for example, a set of one square object and two circular objects) and name the shape chosen (whenever possible).

2.   Find an object in a set of five or more that is like a designated object [for example, find a shape (show sphere) like this on the table (show a ball, jack, two small boxes, and a block the shape of a pyramid) and name the shape chosen (whenever possible)].

When children demonstrate they have an awareness of similarities and differences among two-dimensional and three-dimensional figures and have labels for some figures, teachers plan activities to help them build on their prerequisite understandings and construct concepts of geometric figures. Children are guided to describe the attributes of figures and learn the concept words they do not yet know.

Points, Curves, and Lines

Children develop *intuitive ideas* of points, curves, and lines by walking or riding in particular paths. Reenactments of such activities and discussions related to their movements enable children to *construct concepts* of shapes of figures. A lesson to introduce these ideas is given in Box 11-1. Later lessons deal with models of points, line segments, and circles.

Activities in which children walk in pairs help pupils develop notions of parallel and intersecting lines. The words *parallel* and *intersecting* are introduced to enable children to describe what they have done. Designs that show parallel and intersecting lines can be made by children to aid in forming these concepts. (Straightedges are used by pupils in this activity.) Suggestions to image parallel and intersecting lines are given from time to time.

After children construct concepts and use words correctly to discuss their motions and drawings, activities are planned to *extend and consolidate knowledge*. One activity is for children to examine the manuscript form of letters of the alphabet and numerals to find models

BOX 11-1.   SAMPLE LESSON: DEVELOPING IDEAS
OF SHAPES OF PATHS (GRADE K OR 1)

1. Boys and girls, it is such a beautiful day; let's go outside to think about some math ideas.

2. (Outside on the playground) I have noticed that you walk, run, and ride your bikes in many different paths. Think about the shapes of paths for walking so you can show them to us. John, please show us the shape of a walking path. (Several other children demonstrate walking paths.) Soon we will all walk a path. As you walk your path, remember what you are doing so we can return to the classroom and draw our paths. There is a lot of room on the grass and blacktop so no one will be interfering with anyone else. As I tap you on the shoulder, you may begin to walk a path. When I clap my hands, please come back to this area and sit down again.

3. What different paths you thought to walk! When we return to the classroom, I will pass paper. Please draw one or more paths that you could walk. You may use a straightedge such as the side of a book, if you wish. (Class goes indoors.)

4. We have many different paths drawn. Let us walk in order by each desk to see the different paths. As you are looking at the paths we have drawn, think how some are alike or not alike.

5. What have you noticed? How are some paths alike? (Some are straight.) Will those who have drawn straight paths come up to show all the class. If only one of your paths is straight, fold your paper so only the straight path can be seen. Then come to the front to show us.

6. Let's look carefully at these straight paths. Does anyone have another way to talk about them? Have you heard other words we can use instead of straight paths? Yes, many people call these paths straight lines. Please sit down now.

7. Think about the straight lines we just saw. Close your eyes and make a picture of a straight line.

8. Will the children who have drawn paths that are not straight come up. . . . What do you notice about them? (They are round. They are like circles.) Yes. What words have you used to tell about these paths? (They are not straight; they are curved.) Yes. Will the children in the front of the room please sit down.

9. Think about the paths we have shown. Close your eyes and make a picture of a path. . . . Now make a picture of a path that is straight at first and then not straight. Good, I know you are thinking pictures of paths that are straight and not straight.

10. Let's trade papers. . . . Think about a path that is different from the one you see. Tell us what you are thinking, Tom. (I see a curve, so I am thinking a straight path.)

11. I am passing out red crayons. Draw a path that is different in shape beside each path you see.

12. Good. Every paper shows paths that are different in shape. These papers will look good on the bulletin board. They will help us remember how paths are straight or not straight. I will ask some children to help me hang them up after school. When we look at our drawings, we can think about what we learned today.

13. Tomorrow, we will discuss other ways straight paths are shown in the world. Look around you to see what you can see that shows a straight line. We will talk about what you have observed tomorrow.

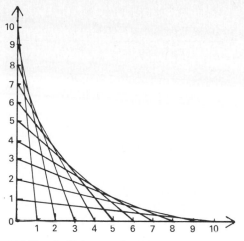

FIGURE 11-11. A stitchery project.

of open and closed curves and of points, line segments, and parallel or intersecting lines.

Weaving provides good opportunities for deepening ideas of points and curves. Weaving for children involves creating mats using string or yarn. Looms can be made from cardboard or wood and nails, or they can be purchased commercially.

Stitchery, such as embroidery, is another activity that provides opportunities to discuss points and various open or closed curves. Stitchery is also enjoyed by children. Even first or second graders can do stitchery if it is kept simple. Burlap is a good fabric to use for stitchery with young children. Designs for the stitchery are drawn on the fabric.

Stitchery involving connecting points with string to achieve a curvelike design is an interesting activity for gifted learners in the primary grades (Figure 11-11).

Polygons and Circles

Polygons and circles are studied early in the primary grades. Children build *intuitive understanding* of common figures—triangles, rectangles, squares, and circles—as they handle objects representing these figures in play and game activities (Chapter 4). To guide children to *construct concepts* of these figures, cardboard or wire frames depicting the figures are used. Such materials emphasize the figures and not the regions bounded by the figures. Beginning lessons provide opportunities to classify figure frames and to discuss the characteristics of the shapes in each category. Teachers ask children what they observe about a figure. Characteristics noted by children are:

Triangles:	Three straight sides and three corners
Rectangles:	Four straight sides and four square corners
Squares:	Four straight sides that are the same length and four square corners
Circles:	No straight sides and no corners; perfectly round (no bulges)

The teacher introduces the word *angle* to replace the child's term *corner* and encourages children to use the word *angle*.

To evaluate children's understanding of concepts, teachers ask learners to produce figures from memory. A straightedge or squared paper can be provided for evaluation exercises requiring the drawing of triangles, rectangles, or squares. Circles can be drawn freehand, but the evaluation of circles takes into account that the drawings were done without instruments.

Many activities can be used to help children *extend and consolidate* their ideas. The following activities are appropriate for children in grades two, three, or four.

1. Suggest each child make a BOOK OF FIGURES. A book can contain drawings or cutouts of common objects, such as a circular plate. Each type of figure has a section in the book. To emphasize the shape of the figure, it can be traced with a crayon. Descriptions are also included.

2. Let pupils set up a display of real-life models or a bulletin board of pictures.

3. Have pupils use geoboards to investigate figures.

4. Have pupils make designs for the front and back of their books or borders for the bulletin board. Blocks representing the shapes can be traced. By noting that the figure or its interior can be colored with crayons, the teacher helps learners differentiate between the figure and the region bounded by the figure.

5. Ask children to use three sticks to make a triangle; then a second different set of three sticks; and a third set. Say: Can a triangle have a square corner? Two square corners? What else do you notice? Do all sets make a triangle?

6. Ask children to use two sticks to make angles. Ask them what they notice about their angles. [This activity leads to the conclusion that there are straight and square (right) angles, as well as angles that are greater or less than a right angle and greater than a straight angle.]

7. Have pupils tear the angles of a triangle and place them together. Ask: What do you notice? (They form a straight angle.) (Figure 11-12.)

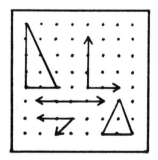

FIGURE 11-12.   Tearing paper to show a straight angle formed from angles of a triangle.

8. Suggest pupils use dot paper (Figure 11-13) or squared paper to show the discoveries made while investigating figures. Introduce words such as *equilateral triangle* and *right triangle*, so pupils can properly label their drawings.

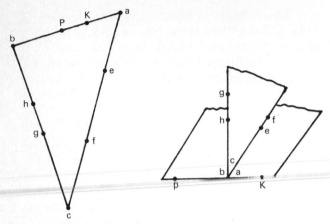

FIGURE 11-13.   Figures drawn on dot paper.

9. Have children study and name polygons with more than four sides.

10. Introduce constructions with straightedge and compass. Initial activities are exploratory. After children have time to "play around," they share their findings. They should determine how to draw circles, line segments equal in length to other line seg-

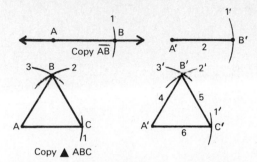

FIGURE 11-14.   Construction directions. Children follow steps in 1, 2, 3, . . . order.

ments, and triangles. (Figure 11-14 gives construction directions.) Introduce such concepts as *diameter* and *radius*.

Three-Dimensional Figures

Three-dimensional figures are first studied in kindergarten. *Intuitive awareness* of three-dimensional figures (Chapter 4) develops as children build towers, walls, houses, and other objects with large blocks and as they handle objects in the environment, such as boxes and balls. To *construct concepts* of these figures, children first sort representations of two-dimensional and three-dimensional figures. Later they classify models of spheres, cylinders, cones, prisms, and pyramids. (Wooden or plastic models are used.) Each figure is discussed in turn in one or more lessons. The shapes of the faces of polyhedrons are observed and named. The notion is explored that in certain figures two faces lie in parallel planes. Children bring in models of three-dimensional figures and discuss their distinguishing characteristics, using correct labels for parts of the objects. Children relate three-dimensional models to two-dimensional pictures of figures. When children can identify a figure from a two-dimensional picture, teachers provide *extending and consolidating* experiences. Some of these are:

1. Trace the faces of some prisms on paper. What do you notice? (How many? Do any match?)

2. Make a cone and a cylinder from sheets of paper (Figure 11-15). Describe what you have done and the results.

3. Make a bulletin board of examples of three-dimensional figures using magazine pictures. Three-dimensional objects can be included to add interest to the bulletin board.

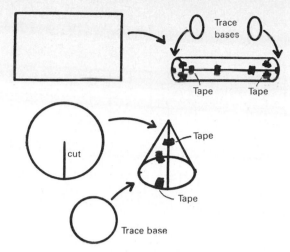

FIGURE 11-15. Directions to make a cylinder and a cone.

4. Extend the BOOK OF FIGURES to include pictures of three-dimensional figures correctly labeled.

5. Have a 3-D FIGURES FAIR. Each child decorates a paper or plastic model of a three-dimensional figure. Another grade is invited to the fair. The child who decorated the figure explains the characteristics of his or her figure to a child invited from the other class. Visiting children can walk around to hear about several figures.

LEARNING AND TEACHING CONCEPTS OF CLASSES OF GEOMETRIC FIGURES

To build concepts of classes of geometric figures, concepts of specific figures are drawn together and related. Thus, when children have no difficulty describing the distinguishing characteristics of two- and three-dimensional figures, it can be assumed that they have the prerequisite understanding for constructing concepts of classes of geometric figures.

Classes of Simple Closed Plane Figures

To guide children to *construct concepts* of classes of simple closed plane figures, teachers ask pupils in grade four or five to sort representations of triangles, rectangles, squares, and circles into two sets. The children observe that one set of figures includes circles and the other set, figures formed from line segments. The teacher gives the label *polygon* to name these latter figures. Subsequent lessons guide children to classify quadrilaterals either as parallelograms

or not parallelograms (no pair of parallel sides or one pair of parallel sides). Parallelograms are then further classified either as rectangles or not rectangles, and rectangles as squares or not squares.

Activities to help learners construct ideas of classes of simple closed plane figures include a game in which each of the three to six children playing receives seven cards. The cards are labeled with words or show diagrams of figures. The objective of the game is to create a diagram classifying figures, as in Figure 11-16. Children take turns drawing cards from a stack of cards (face down) similar to those dealt to each player. The first player to make a diagram wins, or, if all the draw cards are gone, the player with the most complete diagram wins.

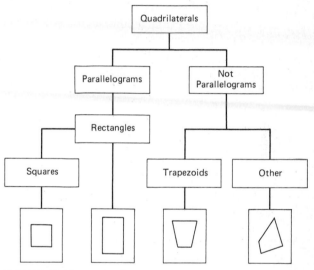

FIGURE 11-16. A classifying game.

When children have constructed concepts of classes, they demonstrate understanding by using a straightedge or compass to draw examples of circles, polygons, quadrilaterals, and other classes. They label the drawings correctly.

Activities to *extend and consolidate* knowledge enable children in the upper grades to deepen awareness of relations among figures. Activities include:

1. Make a chart listing various polygons and the number of sides and angles associated with each. What do you notice? (The number of sides and angles is the same.)

2. Tear square and rectangular objects so that the angles of each object can be placed side by side. (The angles can also be traced.) What do you notice? (The angles of each object form two straight angles.)

3. Activity 3 may be extended to other quadrilaterals and observations compared.

4. Draw lines from the center of a circle to points on the circle. Compare their lengths. What do you notice? (They are equidistant from the center of the circle.)

5. Make and solve puzzles such as: A _____ is a rectangle that is a parallelogram that is a _____ .

6. Play the old games FISH, RUMMY, and BINGO, matching descriptions and labels to make a book or a play.

7. Trace the diagonals in figures and compare them. What do you notice? (Diagonals in regular polygons are of equal length.)

8. Solve construction problems, such as copying a triangle, constructing perpendicular lines, and bisecting a line segment (Figure 11-17). Children can work in teams of two to solve these problems, sharing their ideas with other teams and the teacher until constructions are determined.

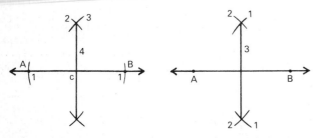

Constructing perpendicular line to $\overline{AB}$ at c with compass and straightedge

Bisecting $\overline{AB}$ with compass and straightedge

FIGURE 11-17.   Construction directions: Follow in 1, 2, 3, . . . order.

9. Solve problems such as: How many diagonals can be drawn from one vertex of a polygon? How many distinct triangles can be drawn in a polygon? (*Note:* Tables can aid in solving these problems, as in Figure 11-18.)

Number		Number	
Sides	Diagonals from One Vertex	Sides	Distinct Triangles
4	1	4	2
5	2	5	3
6	3	6	4
7	4	7	5
8	—	8	—
12	—	12	—

FIGURE 11-18.   Tables to aid in solving geometry problems.

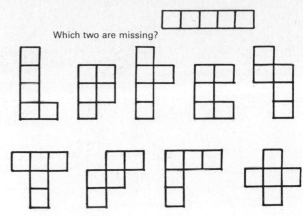

Which two are missing?

FIGURE 11-19.   Pentominoes.

10. Investigate arrangement possibilities with *polyominoes* (a set of squares connected along their edges). Find how many arrangements with none congruent to each other are possible for *monominoes*, *dominoes*, *triominoes*, *tetrominoes*, *pentominoes*, and *hexominoes* (1, 1, 2, 5, 12, and 35, respectively). Squared paper is useful to study the possible arrangements. (Figure 11-19 shows pentominoes.)

Classes of Three-Dimensional Figures

Lessons to guide the *construction of concepts* of classes of three-dimensional figures emphasize classifying figures, articulating class characteristics, and labeling classes. Whenever possible, plastic models should be used to stress that the surface comprises the figure and that the figure is separate from its interior. Children demonstrate comprehension of concepts of classes of three-dimensional figures by: (1) describing classes and differentiating them from one another, and (2) choosing examples of classes from a set of different figures and justifying their choices. They then advance their understanding through activities to *extend and consolidate* knowledge. These activities, some of which could be used earlier in forming concepts of three-dimensional figures, include:

1. Build models of polyhedrons from pipe cleaners or assemble models from cardboard polygonal regions.

2. Use covers (sometimes called nets) to make models. Use the models in a display (Figure 11-20).

3. Write *Who Am I?* questions (with answers) to share with other members of the class.

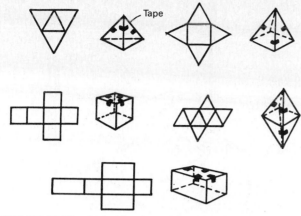

FIGURE 11-20. Covers for three-dimensional figures.

Example: What three-dimensional figure has no vertices? (Sphere, cylinder.)

4. Investigate sections of solid figures (advanced learners). Clay models are cut in this activity (Figure 11-21).

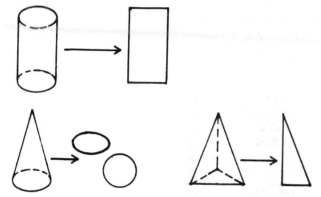

FIGURE 11-21. Cuts.

5. Study drawing three-dimensional figures in two-dimensional space. Make drawings for a book or a bulletin board showing what has been learned about perspective drawing.

6. Make a table listing the number of faces, vertices, and edges displayed by various three-dimensional figures. Use your table to find out about Euler's formula:

$$F + V - E = 2 \quad \text{(Figure 11-22)}$$

(F is number of faces, V is number of vertices, and E is number of edges.)

Solid Figure	F	V	E	Invariant
Cube	6	8	12	2
Square pyramid	5	5	8	2
Octagonal prism	10	16	24	2

FIGURE 11-22. Table to illustrate Euler's formula.

7. Classify polyhedrons as regular (all faces congruent regular polygons and the same number of edges meet at each vertex) and irregular. Look up (or infer) the names of these figures, called *Platonic solids*: *regular tetrahedron* (4 faces), *regular hexahedron* (6 faces), *regular octahedron* (8 faces), *regular dodecahedron* (12 faces), and *regular icosahedron* (20 faces) (Figure 11-23).

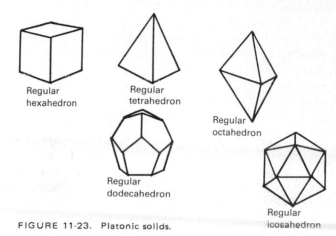

FIGURE 11-23. Platonic solids.

The instructional program outlined to enable children to create concepts of geometric figures and of classes of figures has emphasized helping learners integrate prior learning into more complex structures of knowledge. Many learning experiences have been suggested. Pupils often choose from among these learning activities to relate their interests to instruction and to have opportunities to set expectations.

LEARNING AND TEACHING MOTION GEOMETRY

Motions that can be performed on geometric figures give interesting results. Children explore flips, turns, and slides as they study mathematics and use these ideas in other subjects.

Flips and Line Symmetry

A flip (reflection) gives a figure one-half of which coincides with the other half. The figure has **line symmetry**. Line symmetry is the first concept related to motion geometry that is investigated by children in kindergarten and grade one. As they cut hearts, butterflies, or trees by folding and cutting one-half of the figure, they experience line symmetry *intuitively* (Figure 11-24).

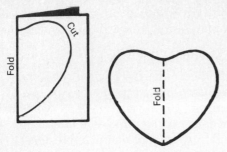

FIGURE 11-24. Folding and cutting to show line symmetry.

A lesson to enable children to *construct the concept* can begin by directing children to trace shapes, as those representing one-half a tree, to turn them over (flip-flop) and to trace again (Figure 11-25). Children can exhibit their drawings and respond to the question: What do you notice? When children point out that the two halves match each other (like they are folded together), the teacher can introduce the word *symmetrical.* Children use the word in further discussion of their work. They find objects in the room or outside that show symmetry. The symmetry in some numerals and alphabet letters is observed. Pictures are collected or drawn to be used on a bulletin board or symmetry books.

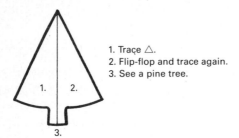

1. Trace △.
2. Flip-flop and trace again.
3. See a pine tree.

FIGURE 11-25. Tracing to show line symmetry.

Symmetry in nature should be explored sometime during the elementary grades. It is often introduced as an *extending* activity. The symmetry of pieces of fruit (apples, oranges) or of vegetables (beans, cabbage) when cut in half is fascinating to investigate. The symmetry of flowers and leaves is also a delight to explore. Flowers, however, often show point rather than line symmetry (Figure 11-26).

FIGURE 11-26. Point symmetry.

FIGURE 11-27. Using a mirror to show line symmetry.

Mirrors are also useful in studying line symmetry (Figure 11-27). Mirror cards are available commercially for use by children of all ages.

Designs often make use of symmetry. Children can study designs in real-world objects and make designs that employ symmetry. The designs can be used on book covers or for borders on bulletin boards. They can also be used to decorate presents for parents, as matchbook sewing kits or picture frames.

Turns and Slides

Turns (rotations) and slides (translations) can be explored in the late primary years by the moving of objects, such as pencils or paper dolls (Figure 11-28). Intuitive understanding develops as children observe the positions resulting from turns and slides of objects. After many experiences with moving objects, children attain concepts and are helped to explain their ideas. Children also hypothesize the arrangement of properties of figures before moving objects; they verify their hypotheses by carrying out the motions.

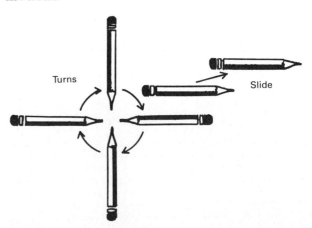

Turns

Slide

FIGURE 11-28. Turns and slide.

Activities to extend understanding include working with simple maps. Children note and discuss the effects of rotating the map 180°. In using maps in real life to observe streets from an automobile, it is often necessary to turn the map to correspond. Therefore, working with simplified or real maps together with concepts of rotation enables pupils to develop an understanding useful in life.

The study of motion geometry need not always be organized as mathematics lessons but can be integrated with art activities or social studies projects. It is a topic that enables the teacher and learners to become more aware of their environment than formerly and in so doing to enrich notions of mathematics in life.

LEARNING AND TEACHING COORDINATES AND GRAPHING

Coordinates

Coordinates relate space and number ideas. Comprehending and using coordinates requires that learners hold several thoughts in mind simultaneously and associate them in a specified way. Not until the middle years of the elementary school are most children able to carry out such mental manipulations. Therefore, coordinates are not introduced until grade four or later. However, readiness activities that employ the idea of coordinates in informal ways can be introduced in the primary grades.

An intuitive understanding of the concept of coordinates involves developing an immediate awareness that a location can be determined by means of two directions followed in order. Games that require stepping right or left and then forward or backward a given number of steps help develop the idea that position can be found by a series of ordered directions for moving.

STEPPING (or HOPPING), a playground game: Children take positions on the playground. "It" quickly moves among the players, pretending to put a penny in the hands of three children but slyly giving it to only one. Then "It" calls out a direction such as: Two steps (hops) to the right and four steps (hops) forward. All children step (hop). The child who received the penny shows it and the child nearest to him or her becomes "It." (If there is disagreement about who is closest to the penny-receiver, "It" decides.)

Classroom games to develop readiness for work with coordinates include:

FOUR TOGETHER. A game board consists of a grid of squares 8 by 8. Two rows from the bottom and two columns from the left side, red lines are drawn with zero written at their intersection; 36 cards (all possible intersections) are written with directions to move across and up—for example, across 3, up 5. Each of two to four players takes different-colored markers. The players in turn choose from the cards, which are face down in a stack near the playing board. The player reads his or her card, moves from the 0 position indicated and places his or her marker at the correct point. The first player to get four of his or her markers in a row, column, or diagonal is the winner.

FRIENDS. A game board showing city streets and blocks is made (Figure 11-29). A box of markers showing faces of children is available for the two to five players. Cards are prepared for the players that read: You have a friend on street (#) _____ in block (#) _____ . Go from home to your friend's house. Various streets and block numbers are written on the cards, insuring that all locations are included. Players should always begin at Home (zero). The players take the cards in turn from the stack, read them, and place a marker on the correct house. The child who places the last marker in a street or in a block is the winner. (This game can be adapted as a Bingo-type activity if playing cards for all players show different streets and blocks.)

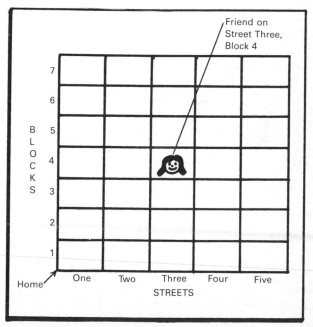

FIGURE 11-29. Game board for Friends game.

A lesson for middle-grade children to *introduce* the concept of using an ordered pair of numbers—coordinates—to locate a point in a plane begins with the teacher saying that the ideas learned in this lesson lead to many interesting activities. He or she shows two perpendicular number lines superimposed on a grid. The teacher poses the problem: How can the number lines be used to locate the point that is marked on the grid? The teacher may need to remind the class of the games they have played as a hint to use in solving this problem. Discussing how the problem is solved enables children to grasp the idea of using coordinates to locate a point in a plane. The teacher insures that the children know how to begin at the point of intersection of the lines (0) and use the horizontal and vertical axes in turn. The notation in terms of specific points such as (4, 2) is introduced. To study the concept meaning further, children can work in teams of two, using a grid with the origin (0) and the horizontal (*x*) and vertical (*y*) axes shown. Pupils take turns naming a point in terms of its coordinates and marking the point.

Using coordinates to draw a picture is another activity to enable learners to form the concept of using coordinates to locate a point in a plane (Figure 11-30).

An alternate procedure for introducing coordinates is for the teacher to model the use of coordinates and ask learners to explain what he or she is doing.

When children demonstrate that they have an understanding of the use of coordinates to locate a point, *extending and consolidating* activities are provided so learners can apply their knowledge in a variety of situations. Reading maps of various kinds in grades five and six contributes to the study of local communities and knowledge of other cities, states, and countries, as well as the study of different ways to locate positions. Some of the graphing activities discussed in the next subsection are a natural extension of work with coordinates.

Graphs

Graphs are diagrammatic representations of numerical information and relations. Because they are somewhat pictorial, they usually communicate concepts better than words. In the elementary school, graphs are found in mathematics, science, and social studies. They are often introduced during mathematics lessons. Chartlike graphs are studied in the primary grades. In later grades, children work with graphs that require more relational thinking.

Intuitive understanding of graphs develops as children construct chartlike graphs with teacher guidance. As the concept of using graphs to communicate ideas develops, children are able to make graphs with less and less teacher direction. When the graphing idea has been formed, a child or a small group can make a chart-graph independently. This occurs in grade two or three if children have had appropriate prerequisite experiences.

Extension and consolidation of the concept of graphing continues throughout the elementary school as children apply ideas of graphing to more topics and situations. If children have not had prerequisite experiences in the primary grades, teachers in the upper grades design activities that provide graphing experiences to help children develop concepts to use in interpreting graphs found in their textbooks.

Intuitive understanding of graphs begins as children make and interpret *chart-graphs* in connection with their study of the concept of inequality. For example, they can represent ideas of greater-than and less-than in the course of discussions in social studies that help class members know each other. Topics discussed include:

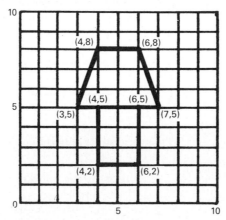

Draw line segments between
    (4,8) and (6,8)
    (3,5) and (7,5)
    (4,2) and (6,2)
    (4,2) and (4,5)
    (6,2) and (6,5)
    (3,5) and (4,8)
    (7,5) and (6,8)

    What is the
    picture?
    (a lamp)

FIGURE 11-30. Making a drawing using coordinates.

Children who are bussed or not bussed to school

Children who live in apartments or houses

Children who have pets or no pets

Children who have brothers or sisters at home (school) or no brothers or sisters at home (school)

At times children line up in rows to determine the greater (or lesser) category. Frequently they use objects (curtain rings, paper clips, or tags) that can be hung on a cup-hook chart (Figure 11-31). Each child can write his or her name on a tag to stress that it stands for a child. The one-to-one correspondence between objects and children is an important aspect of initial activities with charts. Also, only two categories are used in beginning work.

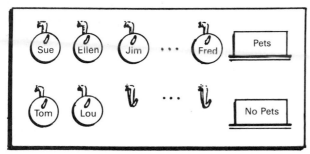

FIGURE 11-31. A cup-hook chart.

The next step is for children to use stickers or pictures instead of objects and gradually increase the number of columns (or rows) in the chart-graph (Figure 11-32). They also begin to

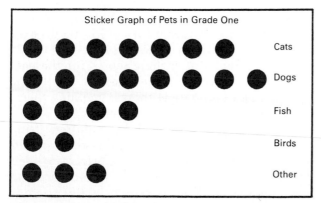

FIGURE 11-32. A sticker graph.

count and compare the numbers in categories rather than express the comparisons in general terms, such as greater-than. At this stage graphs can show:

Children's birthdays in each month

Colors of children's eyes

Children's names beginning with different alphabet letters

Different pets cared for by children

Children can be encouraged to suggest collecting and displaying other information related to their lives or school subjects; for example, birthday months of sisters and brothers.

Next children study *block graphs* prepared with squared paper and a number line along one axis (Figure 11-33). The teacher can introduce

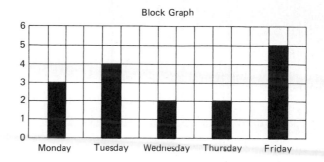

The graph shows number absent each day. Most are absent Friday.

FIGURE 11-33. A block graph.

this type of graph by showing several picture or sticker graphs previously made by the class and comparing them with block graphs communicating the same information. The teacher asks: How are these graphs alike and different? After identifying similarities and differences, the class studies reading block graphs; the children discuss counting blocks as well as using the scale. Each child makes his or her own graph with teacher guidance. Each also writes one or more sentences explaining his or her graph. They discuss and display their graphs. Later, children collect information and independently prepare their graphs or use information collected by another class member or the teacher. Examples of information to collect and graph include:

The number of trucks, cars, and motorcycles I saw from the bus while riding to school

My weekly spelling-test scores

Numbers of different trees on our school campus

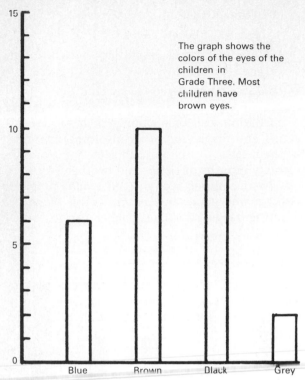

The graph shows the colors of the eyes of the children in Grade Three. Most children have brown eyes.

FIGURE 11-34. A bar graph.

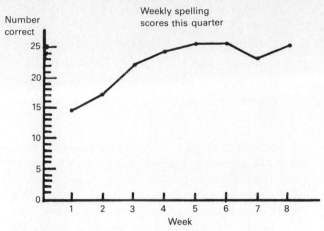

FIGURE 11-36. A line graph showing a trend.

Temperatures at each hour of the school day

Numbers of different reading books in our class

Bar graphs are studied next (Figure 11-34). Teachers guide pupils in learning that bar graphs are read by using vertical or horizontal scales. Children make bar graphs when they can read graphs by using this plan rather than counting blocks. While working with bar graphs, learners are introduced to the *line* bar graph (Figure 11-35).

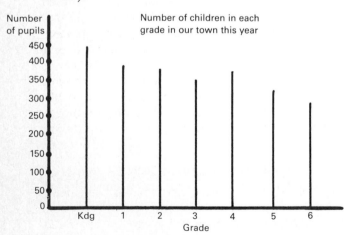

FIGURE 11-35. A line bar graph.

After many experiences with bar and line bar graphs, children study *line graphs that show trends* (Figure 11-36). In a lesson to introduce these line graphs, a bar graph and a line graph of weekly spelling-test scores can be examined by children to determine the characteristics of a line graph. Children can also discuss which they think is most effective in conveying information. After identifying the characteristics of a line graph and considering the steps in constructing one, children make line graphs. Making their own line graphs of weekly spelling-test scores enables children to internalize the concept that line graphs show trends.

An alternate approach to introducing line graphs is for the teacher to display a line graph showing spelling scores of a hypothetical student and to say, "Does this graph tell how this student is doing in spelling? How do you know? How would a person make a graph like this? How would you make a graph like this of your weekly spelling scores? What could you do with the graph?" A follow-up to the lesson is: Pupils make line graphs of spelling scores for the past six or eight weeks. Some learners can profit from listing hypothetical scores, graphing them, and interpreting the graph's meaning.

Line graphs produced by children using material from social studies and science should be emphasized in instruction. Constructing such line graphs helps children understand graphing techniques as well as concepts in the content areas—for example, population trends.

Circle graphs (Figure 11-37) are studied after children have learned about representing fractional parts of a whole with circular diagrams. Initial lessons help pupils examine circle

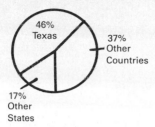

FIGURE 11-37. A circle graph.

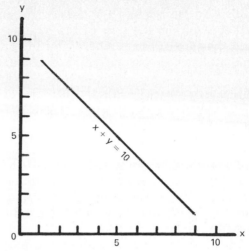

FIGURE 11-38. Graph of x + y = 10.

graphs; children discuss how information is communicated. They later produce circle graphs, often beginning with one that shows how they spend their time in a typical day. Records are first kept of hours spent on different activities, and the information is then used in constructing the graph. (If a circular region pattern divided into 24 congruent wedges is given to learners, they will be able to complete the task more successfully than if they begin with a blank circular region.) After children study percent, they can examine circle graphs that give percents for different categories. Some children can make circle graphs using percents. Gifted learners often will be challenged by the task of preparing circle graphs using data from social studies or science.

In helping children understand graphs showing real-world information, several cautions must be kept in mind: blocks must be the same size; bars must be the same width and evenly spaced; points should be connected only when trends can by hypothesized; and circle graphs must depict a whole or 100 percent.

Graphs showing mathematical ideas have been mentioned in several chapters, though they have not been labeled graphs—for example, squared-paper diagrams showing basic facts for a number or showing patterns in multiplication tables. Graphs of certain mathematical sentences are introduced in the fifth or sixth grade and often only to gifted learners (Figure 11-38). Prior to making such graphs, children will have been introduced to coordinates. A first lesson in representing a mathematical sentence with a graph can make use of any table constructed in connection with the NAME CHANGER MACHINE activity discussed in Chapter 6. The teacher can suggest using the numbers in the table as coordinates and connecting the points plotted. The lesson can end with the question: If you use a number rule to find pairs of numbers and use these numbers as coordinates to plot points for a graph, will the graph always be a line? Individuals or teams can carry out investigations and discuss their conclusions as they seek answers to this question.

Pupils' construction of graphs together with pupils' interpretations of their graphs has been emphasized in the discussion of all types of graphs. In the process of producing graphs, children learn to read and interpret graphs prepared by others. Interpreting graphs in textbooks and newspapers is not difficult for those children who have developed concepts of graphing by making graphs.

Graphs made by children, together with written commentaries, should be displayed on bulletin boards or made into books and shared. If it is to be meaningful to children, making graphs cannot be an isolated experience. The usefulness of graphing to communicate ideas must be demonstrated in the classroom if the purpose of graphing is to be learned.

As children work with graphs, the question should arise: What one number gives the most information about the data? The *average* (mean) is taught in the elementary school, while other measures of central tendency (*median* and *mode*) are usually introduced in junior or senior high school. To introduce the concept of average, the teacher can ask, "What one score would tell your parents the most about how you are doing in spelling this month? Is it fair to use the highest score? The lowest? Could we *even up* the scores? How?"

After using trial-and-error (even-up) procedures to find averages, children learn the word *average*. They are also introduced to the *rule for finding the average of a set of numbers:* Add the numbers and divide by the number of addends. To construct this rule, children are guided to examine the sum of the numbers in a set and the sum of the numbers after the process of even up has been carried out. For example:

$$7 + 5 + 9 + 3 = (7 - 1) + (5 + 1) + (9 - 3) + (3 + 3)$$
$$24 = 6 + 6 + 6 + 6$$
$$= 24$$

Pupils observe that the sums are equal. Children are helped to infer from their observation that the average can be found using a trial-and-error method of even up or an adding-and-dividing rule. After the rule has been constructed, it is used by pupils to solve exercises and problems written by the teacher and by pupils.

To extend their understanding of the concept of average, children can find the average height of the members of the class, of the boys, and of the girls; the average number in a class family; the average number of glasses of milk children drink a day; or the average number of centimeters class boys, girls, or both move in the standing (or running) broad jump. Children can graph averages of monthly spelling scores or temperatures. They often enjoy studying batting averages of baseball players or the average number of yards run in football games by favorite football players. Discussions to clarify the meaning of sports news items give children opportunities to apply mathematics to out-of-school life.

SUMMARY

A brief overview of geometric content began this chapter. Other sections described learning and teaching concepts of plane and three-dimensional figures, concepts of classes of figures, ideas from motion geometry, and concepts of coordinates and graphing. The three-phase learning-teaching sequence was used to present instructional suggestions appropriate for different levels of learning. Pupil generation of examples was stressed to insure internalization of concepts and to foster interest. The use of various cognitive processes was emphasized as well as attention to individual differences.

It was noted that learning about geometry helps children understand their environment. The study of space is also exciting. One objective of the instructional program outlined in this chapter is for children to discover the fascination of geometric concepts.

STUDY QUESTIONS

1. List the representations of geometric figures you find about you in several different environments. What conclusions do you reach as a result of this activity?

2. Discuss with other members of the class the level of conceptual development children in the elementary school should be expected to attain when studying geometry. Should formal definitions be introduced? Should children learn these definitions? What are the reasons for your answers?

3. Write an assessment activity to determine if pupils are ready to study concepts of classes of geometric figures.

4. Prepare an activity to teach the idea of turns (rotations). Begin with the objective of the activity.

5. Write a lesson to guide gifted children to learn graphing of certain mathematical sentences.

6. Plan an activity to enable children to use concepts of symmetry.

7. Write an evaluation activity for a geometric topic of your own choice. Begin with objectives for the study of the topic.

REFERENCES

Bruni, James V., "Geometry for the Intermediate Grades," *Arithmetic Teacher*, 26, no. 6 (February 1979), 17–19.

Campbell, Patricia F., "Cardboard, Rubber Bands, and Polyhedron Models," *Arithmetic Teacher*, 31, no. 2 (October 1983), 50–52.

Charles, Randall I., "Some Guidelines for Teaching Geometry Concepts," *Arithmetic Teacher*, 27, no. 8 (April 1980), 18–20.

Damarin, Suzanne K., "What Makes a Triangle," *Arithmetic Teacher*, 29, no. 1 (September 1981), 39–41.

Johnson, Elizabeth M., "Bar Graphs for First Graders," *Arithmetic Teacher*, 29, no. 4 (December 1981), 30–31.

Nibbelink, William, "Graphing for Any Grade," *Arithmetic Teacher*, 30, no. 3 (November 1982), 28–31.

Nuffield Foundation, *Pictorial Representation*. New York: John Wiley & Sons, Inc., 1967.

Thomas, Diane, "Geometry in the Middle School: Problem Solving with Trapezoids," *Arithmetic Teacher*, 26, no. 6 (February 1979), 20-21.

Troutman, Andria P., and Betty K. Lichtenberg, *Mathematics: A Good Beginning*, 2d ed., chaps. 11-12. Monterey, CA: Brooks/Cole Publishing Company, 1982.

Walter, Marion I., *Boxes, Squares and Other Things*. Reston, VA: The National Council of Teachers of Mathematics, Inc., 1970.

————, "Frame Geometry: An Example in Posing and Solving Problems," *Arithmetic Teacher*, 28, no. 2 (October 1980), 16-18.

Young, Jerry L., "Improving Spatial Abilities with Geometric Activities," *Arithmetic Teacher*, 30, no. 1 (September 1982), 38-43.

12 LEARNING AND TEACHING MEASUREMENT

Is it time to go home? How much does it cost? How far is the store? Both children and adults ask such questions. Measurement enters every life. To cope with our measurement needs, we perform routine measuring tasks and solve measurement problems. Many persons also use measurement concepts and skills to make a living.

Measuring is assigning to a property of an object, phenomenon, or set a number of units that possess the same property as the property being measured: lines are assigned linear units; surfaces, surface units; and time, time units. The units can be **standard,** those legally defined, or **nonstandard,** those arbitrarily defined and not universally accepted. Both types of units have a place in instruction.

In the elementary school children study many measurements: linear, area, volume, capacity, weight (mass), time, temperature, money, and angle. After instruction in measurement in the elementary school, children should be able to use measuring instruments, comprehend the English and metric systems of measurement, estimate measurements, calculate with measurements, use measurement formulas, and solve problems. This chapter deals with these objectives in two sections: (1) constructing and extending concepts of standard units and (2) extending the study of measurement. (Developing prerequisite understanding for the study of standard units was discussed in Chapter 4.) The final section of this chapter is a brief summary.

To learn measurement concepts and skills, pupils engage in measuring activities and think about what they have done. To encourage children to mentally manipulate experience, teachers ask questions and also insure that children have opportunities to discuss ideas with each other.

CONSTRUCTING AND EXTENDING CONCEPTS OF STANDARD UNITS

This section describes learning experiences that enable children to construct and begin to extend concepts of standard units for length, area, volume, capacity, weight (mass), temperature, money, time, and angles. Competency in measuring is also an objective of the activities described. A greater number of learning experiences is given for the study of length than for other kinds of measurement. However, these activities can be adapted to learning other measurement concepts and skills.

The **metric system (SI)** will be emphasized, along with some references to the **English system.** Because of its importance and increased use, the metric system is stressed in instruction. However, the English system is still a legal system in the United States and must also be learned by children. It should be taught after children learn about standard metric units.

Length

Before beginning the study of standard units for linear measurement, teachers ascertain that children have attained prerequisite concepts. Children should demonstrate that they can use nonstandard units in measuring linear attributes of objects. By engaging in activities such as those described in Chapter 4, children have learned to measure to the nearest unit and to use a measuring device marked off in units. They also have some awareness of the confusion resulting when nonstandard units are chosen by different individuals to measure the same object. A lesson to introduce measuring with standard metric units to children who have attained pre-requisite understandings is given in Box 12-1. Some children are ready for an introduction to metric units the second semester of grade one; most children learn about metric units in grade two. In discussing the learning of linear measure-ment, primary- and upper-grade instruction are treated separately.

After an introduction to measuring with centimeters, primary-grade children will *con-struct and extend* ideas of metric units as they: (1) measure objects, usually of their own choos-ing (this activity will require studying measuring to the nearest centimeter); (2) estimate the length of objects 25 centimeters or less; (3) use meter sticks; (4) estimate the length of objects that are about a meter.

The activities that follow are designed to reach these objectives. Activities 1 through 7 relate to objectives 1 and 2; activities 8 through 12, objectives 3 and 4. While the experiences are described for learning metric units, they can be adapted to English units if children are learn-ing about these units.

1. Have children make a CENTIMETER BOOK. Directions are: Choose objects you can measure with your 25-cm ruler. Look at home, outside, or at school. You can draw pictures of the objects, write their names, or do both pictures and names. Give the measurement beside the object or its name. Give your measurement to the near-est centimeter.

2. Suggest each can work with a friend on a poster for a centimeter bulletin board. Some ideas are: (1) Write the names of the boys (girls) in your room. Measure the length of the names. Whose name is long-est? shortest? You may decide to put them in order by length. (2) Look in your read-ing book for words that are 1 centimeter long. Write a sentence with them if you can. (3) Make some imaginary bugs that are different centimeter lengths. Write on your poster the number of centimeters long your bugs are. Decorate the bugs.

3. Assign an activity. Show the length of your fingers in centimeters this way: Spread your hand out and trace it with the other hand. Measure the length of all your fingers and write the measurement beside each finger. You may want to know if other children in the class have fingers about the same length. Ask your teacher to make a chart of the length of children's fingers. What do you notice about the measurements?

4. Have them measure some objects that will help them remember the length of 1, 3, and 10 centimeters. Say: "Use things like the width of your little finger, length and width of paper clips, and the width of your hand. Make a chart of your findings."

5. Have children play I ESTIMATE for two pupils. Directions are: Use a record sheet (Table 12-1). Write your estimate of the length of each object given on the sheet; your friend will write his or her estimates too. Then take turns measuring the objects. Note who made the most best estimates. That person wins the game. You can play this game again with different objects if you wish.

RECORD SHEET OF ESTIMATES OF LENGTHS			
Object	My Estimate	Your Estimate	Measurement
Chalkboard eraser			
Window pane			
Writing paper			
Spelling book			

TABLE 12-1. Record sheet for "I Estimate" game

6. Have three or four children play CENTI-METERS. Directions are: Use the CENTI-METERS game box of objects (about 20). (The box contains, for example, a comb, a pencil, a toothbrush, a candy bar, a cookie wrapped in plastic, a bookmarker, an eraser, or a tube of paste. It also con-tains a centimeter ruler.) The teacher names "It." He or she decides on an object and says: "It is (color, use, and so on) and is about _____ cm long (wide)." The child to the right of "It" guesses. The child who

BOX 12-1. SAMPLE LESSON: INTRODUCING METRIC UNITS TO MEASURE LENGTH (GRADE 1 OR 2)

1. Boys and girls, several times recently we have said that measuring the length of things using the width of our hand or the length of our foot was not a very good way. Why did we think that? (Our hands are not the same size; the numbers aren't the same and you don't know which one is right.)

2. That's what we decided. Does anyone know what people do to get the right measurement? (They use rulers . . . yard sticks.)

3. Yes. (If pupils do not know about these tools, the teacher says: You probably have seen someone use a ruler.) I have rulers for all of you. They are metric rulers. There are metric rulers and foot rulers. We will learn to use metric rulers first. (Children are given tagboard metric rulers each 25 centimeters long.)

4. Look at your metric ruler. What do you notice about it? (It has marks and numbers.)

5. The marks show small lengths. They are called centimeters. I am writing that word on the board. I will write cm beside centimeter. Cm is the short way to write centimeters. Say centimeter. Read (pointing) centimeter and cm. . . . Put your thumbnail against a centimeter. Is your thumbnail about one centimeter long? (Yes.) Close your eyes and picture your thumbnail centimeter.

6. How many centimeters does your metric ruler show? (25.) Move a finger along and count the centimeters. Start at the beginning. Please count together. (1 centimeter, 2 centimeters, 3 centimeters, . . . , 25 centimeters.) Good. Now do that again but this time think the numbers of centimeters in your mind. . . .

7. Close your eyes. Can you see your centimeter ruler? Picture 25 centimeters.

8. Open your eyes. What in this room is about 25 centimeters? (Our music book; the window pane; the class crayon box.)

9. Great. I have pictures of objects for you to measure with your centimeter ruler. There is a line across the object to tell you where to measure the length. Please write the measurement on the line. Before we start, let's measure the lines I have on the board. Will the last person at each table go to the board with his or her metric ruler, measure the line across the object, and write the number of centimeters. Each person at a table think if you would do it the same way as the child from your table. . . . Now each child at the board write cm after the numeral to show the measurement is centimeters. . . . (Continue with other examples.) Any questions?

10. I believe you know how to do this kind of measurement. I will pass out the study papers to you. The first one is done. Do that measurement yourself and write your measurement above the one written for you. What will it be? (The same.) Why? (Centimeters are all the same.) Good thinking.

11. After you finish your sheet, compare your answers with your math partner. What will you expect? (We will have the same measurements.) Why? (The centimeters are all the same.) O.K.

12. Let's start now. Raise your hand if you need help.

NOTE: The objects on the study paper are 5 cm, 10 cm, 4 cm, 17 cm, and 22 cm in length. At a later time children measure objects they choose and give the measurement to the nearest whole number. The first examples used by learners do not require thinking to the nearest centimeter.

is guessing (the "Guesser") the object "It" is thinking of says: "I agree (or disagree) with the length of the _____. It is _____ long." "It" measures the object with a centimeter ruler. If "It" made a good estimate, he or she gets a point. If the Guesser made a better estimate, he or she gets a point. The Guesser is the next "It." After all objects are used, each player counts his or her points. The winner has the most points.

7. Have each pupil work with a friend to carry out the activity ESTIMATE MY-SELF. Give each a ruler, string, and a record sheet (Table 12-2). Directions are: Estimate the length of the body parts given on the sheet. You may use more parts if you wish. Record your estimates. Your partner will estimate his or her body parts and record the estimates on his or her record sheet. Help each other measure using a string, and then measure the string. Record the measurements. Note how close the estimate is to the measurement. Think: Why was I close or not close?

ESTIMATE MYSELF RECORD		
Body Part (Length)	Estimate	Measurement
Nose		
Waist		
Wrist		
Arm		
Foot		
Ankle		

TABLE 12-2.   Record Sheet for Estimate Myself

8. After children show skill in using centimeter rulers, a measuring task should be undertaken that demonstrates the inadequacy of a 25-cm ruler to measure a long length, such as that of the table. Introduce the meter stick for this purpose. Each two or three children should have a meter stick. (If less than twelve are supplied to a class, ask parents to make meter tapes from sturdy cloth or oil cloth at a Materials Workshop.) Ask children to study the meter stick. They should notice that 1 meter equals 100 centimeters. Discuss this observation and talk about what can be measured with a meter stick.

9. One of the early measuring experiences with the meter stick should be measuring the heights of children. Measuring children's heights will often involve recording measurements such as a meter and centimeters. When it is seen that the meter is too short for measuring a height, ask the children what can be done. (If necessary, model the procedure and have children use the same approach.) The meaning of measurements such as 1 m 10 cm should be discussed with the class.

10. A class activity is: Use math partners on the playground. In turn, the two children make a standing and a running broad jump. The partner records the jump. When all have finished, return to the classroom and make a chart of the measurements. Ask: "What do you notice about these measurements? What is the same? Different?"

11. Estimation involving a meter should be introduced after children have learned to measure with a meter. The I ESTIMATE game can be adapted for lengths to one meter.

12. A bulletin board list of objects about a meter in length can be a cooperative class project. Help children set high expectations of the number of objects they can find. In one (two) day(s) can we together see 25 (50, 75) different objects in the world that are about a meter long? Have children decide on the goal and begin looking. Encourage creative thinking, such as: two chair seats together are about a meter long. Before they begin to look, have children close their eyes and think a meter. Ask them to show a meter with their hands and check their meter as they pass by the door, where a meter tape is fastened.

By the end of grade three, children should have developed concepts of linear measurement with centimeters and meters. They should be able to use 25-centimeter rulers and meter sticks confidently and correctly. They should be able to estimate lengths of about a meter.

During the upper grades, *children construct and extend ideas* by: (1) measuring lengths several meters long; (2) learning to use reference measurements; (3) measuring the perimeters of a variety of objects; (4) determining solutions to measurement problems; (5) working with the formula for the perimeter of a rectangle. Learning activities to attain these objectives include:

1. Suggest finding out about lengths of rooms. The activity could begin with the question: How long or wide are rooms—school room, lunch room, principal's office, hall, your living room at home, your bedroom, and so on? Let children make some estimates and then propose that they measure these rooms and make a class record. To help with the activity, meter ropes or strings can be made with a knot at the end of each meter. Children can be involved in making these tapes.

2. Emphasize *reference measurements* (an awareness of a measurement used as the basis of comparison in estimating). Have children walk 10, 50, and 100 meters on the playground and think about trips important to them that are about 10, 50, or 100 meters. Make a chart of these ideas.

3. Use reference measurements to estimate how far it is to the principal's office, nurse's station, or the kindergarten. One or more members of the class can measure the distance to help all learners refine their reference measurements.

4. Introduce kilometers (1000 meters) as units useful in measuring distances very difficult to measure with meters. Find out how far each child lives from school in kilometers (parents may be asked to help with this project). Have children compare distances.

5. Have pupils find out the distances to shopping centers or cities important in their lives. Make a chart of their findings. Have pupils suggest any relationships which may be observed in the records on the chart.

6. Generate excitement for finding out the perimeter of real objects. Ask: "How many meters is it around our classroom? Our building? Your house? Your room?" and so on. Have teams volunteer to find out these measurements. (Ask for sketches and perimeters.) Make a record and analyze it for similarities and differences. Introduce the word *perimeter* for the length of a polygon. Compare perimeters.

7. Discuss the perimeter of small objects, such as desks, tables, shoes. Have teams work on finding perimeters of these objects. Perimeters of pupils' shoes can be matched with shoe outlines and both ordered.

8. A bulletin board could be created from the reports of teams' findings, as suggested in activities 6 and 7. The board's title could be: *Which of These Perimeters Surprises You? Why?*

9. Work with perimeters of rectangles leads to calculation with measurements and involves rules and formulas. After many perimeter measurements have been made, say: "Measuring perimeters of rectangles is a lot of work. Do you need to do all that measuring?" (A diagram on the board of a perimeter pupils have found can help children conclude that only the length and width need to be measured.) More questions guide children to conclude: If two adjacent sides of a rectangle are measured, the perimeter can be found by adding the length and the width and multiplying the sum by 2. Give a few examples so learners can try out their rule. Follow up with distribution of boxes; have pupils measure two adjacent edges of their boxes, compute the perimeter, and check their work.

10. Have pupils write perimeter problems for use by small groups. If possible, have them measure objects at home or school to use in these problems.

11. When pupils can use their rule stated in words, introduce the formula $P = 2(l + w)$ (P = perimeter, l = length, w = width) for perimeter of a rectangle. Tell the group that it is convenient to write the rule in a math sentence (math rule). Write the rule in English and in equation form on the board. Ask them to compare the statements. Emphasize the meaning of the math rule. Suggest pupils try thinking the math rule to solve a few perimeter exercises. Remind them that they can use the rule stated in English words if they wish. After several exercises are completed, ask them to tell about how they used the math rule. Introduce the word *formula* for the math rule.

12. Assign exercises or use problems written by pupils (in activity 10 above) in which the perimeter is stated as, for example, 135 cm. Ask: "How can we rename 135 cm in

meters?" If no one says, "1 m 35 cm," suggest measuring this length. Say: "Is the meter stick or 25-cm ruler better to use? Why?" After measuring, the children should be able to conclude: Since a meter is 100 cm, 135 cm is 1 m 35 cm.

Learning more advanced ideas related to linear measurement, such as the circumference of a circle, is discussed in the last section of this chapter.

Area

Children are introduced to standard units of area at the end of grade three or early in grade four. Standard units are introduced only after children have had many experiences comparing regions and using nonstandard units to measure regions. To assess prerequisite understanding for the study of standard units of area, a teacher can pose a problem to third- or fourth-grade children, such as, "How would you use this piece of linoleum to find the size of our library table?" Pupils should be able to explain (and show) that the piece can be used repeatedly, with some mark being made to keep track of where the piece has already been laid, and a count made of the times the piece has been used.

In a lesson to help learners construct concepts of standard units of area, the teacher asks, "What different shapes are used to measure surfaces? Which do you think is best (triangles, rectangles, squares)? Why?" (If children cannot answer this question, they again use different figures to find area.) The teacher displays a square centimeter, tells what it is, and asks the class to think about the reason for its name. The lesson continues with the introduction of a grid 10 cm by 10 cm (*square decimeter*). The teacher asks the class why the grid would be better than the square centimeter. Sometimes during this lesson, he or she introduces the word *area* as the measure of a region.

In the same or a following lesson, pupils are each given a transparent grid 10 cm by 10 cm. (This can be made on a thermofax-type machine using acetate material for overhead projectors.) The children are asked what areas they could find with their grids. A list is made and pupils choose a number of objects to measure. Before they begin, they are asked what they will do if the grid does not cover the region

to be measured or if the grid is too large. The procedures to follow in approximation are decided upon by the class. Any procedure that results in a good approximation is included in the list. However, as pupils have studied fractional numbers by grade four, they are encouraged to combine parts of standard units whenever possible.

As pupils measure the area of regions greater than 100 cm^2, the need for a larger unit becomes apparent. The *square meter* is introduced to meet this need. Working together, pupils make square meters, either one for a group or one for each child. Pupils use the square meter to measure regions in the school and at home—for example, the floor of the classroom, the hall, or a bed mattress. A record of their measurements is displayed and the meaning of *area* discussed frequently.

An important activity is for children to determine the number of square centimeters (10,000) in a square meter by placing 100 cm^2 grids on a square meter. This experience gives learners an intuitive understanding of decimal relations in the metric system. These relations are studied systematically by many children in grade six.

As with the perimeter of a rectangle, children begin their study of the formula for the area of a rectangular region with measuring activities. This process soon becomes tedious; shortcut methods must be considered. Teacher guidance enables learners to develop understanding and skill at three levels.

1. Recognize that the area of a rectangular region may be found by determining the number of square units in a row and multiplying the number in the row by the number of rows (Figure 12-1).

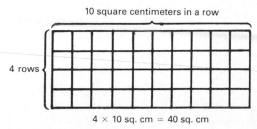

4 × 10 sq. cm = 40 sq. cm

FIGURE 12-1. Calculating area.

2. Write the rule: The area of a rectangular region equals the number of square units in a row times the number of rows.

3. Know that the formula $A = l \times w$ (A = area, l = length, and w = width) is a short-cut for the rule in words. Length is the same as the number of square units in a row; width is the same as the number of rows. (At grade six if some pupils cannot comprehend the meaning and use of a formula, they may use the rule.)

For capable learners in grade six, the study of area includes the learning of a procedure for finding the area of circular regions. This is discussed in the section on extending the study of measurement.

Experiences with the measurement of regions incorporate real-life objects, enable learners to estimate and develop reference measurements, provide opportunities for solving and writing problems, and lead by grade six to calculating the area of rectangular regions. Many experiences are patterned after those for linear measurement given earlier. They include, whenever possible, working with areas of special interest to learners: the area of a baseball or other field for athletic games, areas of swimming pools at parks, homes, or gymnasiums, the area of a sleeping bag, or the area of a tennis court. The study of area can be made vital to children if their life style is taken into consideration in the learning experiences planned for them, and they are given choices of activities to carry out.

Volume/Capacity

The activities suggested to promote prerequisite understanding for the study of volume help children grasp the notion that units of volume are used to measure other units of volume (Chapter 4). If pupils can make reasonable estimates regarding the number of small objects that will fit into a larger object, teachers introduce standard units of volume. The cubic centimeter, cubic decimeter (10 cm × 10 cm × 10 cm), and the cubic meter are units most commonly studied by elementary school children.

To introduce the cubic centimeter in grade five or six, the teacher can say, "We have measured length in units called centimeters and area in units called square centimeters. We are ready to learn about measuring the space inside objects. We will learn about metric units to measure volume. What kind of unit do we need to explain how much, for example, this box (displays a small box) holds?" As pupils respond to this question, the three-dimensional nature of volume units is emphasized and the use of the cubic centimeter noted. Each child receives one or more cubic centimeters to explore. The class considers familiar objects whose volume could be measured in cubic centimeters. Boxes are provided by the teacher, and small groups use their cubic centimeters to find the volume of the boxes. Children are encouraged to estimate before measuring. After time in groups, the class as a whole discusses what was learned. During this or a subsequent lesson the teacher inquires about the best procedure to use in finding a volume using cubic centimeters. Children are guided to conclude that the best plan is to fit a row of cubes into the box, then a layer, and repeat the process until the box is full.

As children measure the volume of boxes, they observe that the cubic centimeter is so small that using it to measure is a time-consuming process. The cubic decimeter (1000 cm^3) and the cubic meter (m^3) are introduced to make the measurement of volume less tedious. Children should cooperatively make cubes 10 × 10 × 10 centimeters from paper squared in centimeters and make a cubic meter using a wooden frame and wrapping paper. Constructing and handling these models is a valuable experience. Committees can make the models and report to the class on their appropriate use. Charts can be made to accompany the reports.

Measuring using the tools built by children continues until someone (the teacher or a child) asks the question, "What is the volume of this room?" The need for a rule to use in finding volume is obvious. Questioning by the teacher regarding the best procedure for measuring volume (make a row, a layer, and so on) enables learners to compose a rule similar to: Compute the measure of one layer by multiplying the number of rows by the number of cubic units in a row. Use that product as a factor with the number of layers in the interior of the object. (The number of layers is the height of the object.)

This rule is used by children to obtain the volume of real objects and those described in exercises written by the teacher and children (Figure 12-2). Some children will quickly see that the rule leads to the formula: $V = l \times w \times h$ (V = volume, l = length, w = width, and

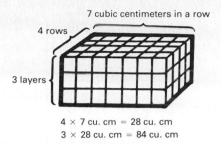

4 rows

7 cubic centimeters in a row

3 layers

4 × 7 cu. cm = 28 cu. cm
3 × 28 cu. cm = 84 cu. cm

FIGURE 12-2. Calculating volume.

h = height). Other children will continue to use the rule because of its meaningfulness to thcm.

The measurement of a continuous substance (such as liquid) is studied in every grade in the elementary school. Many life and school experiences involve such measurement—for example, drinking and cooking. In studying capacity, teaspoons, tablespoons, cups, quarts, and gallons (used in preparing food) are emphasized, as well as the milliliter, 100 milliliters, and liter. Learning about these standard units involves achieving prerequisite understanding discussed earlier and experimenting with containers to develop familiarity with the units and with common relations (2 pints = 1 quart; 1000 ml = 1 l). Children in the late primary grades use containers of water (sand, sugar) to conduct these investigations. They are encouraged to work in teams, often out of doors, and to ask each other questions concerning the investigations. Records of the experiments are made and used in solving real and contrived problems, such as: There will be 8 children at my birthday party. If each child drinks a pint of chocolate milk, how many quarts should my mother buy for the party? Children are encouraged to image and draw diagrams to solve problems of this type. In grades five and six some children write and solve equations to solve the problems.

From measuring experiences, children develop ideas of reference measurements. Questions posed by the teacher will also help children develop notions of "about a cup" or "about a liter," for example.

A useful activity to help children develop concepts of standard units and reference measurements is for the class to prepare a display of empty containers or a bulletin board of pictures of containers all labeled to indicate their capacity. Either of these activities also helps chil-

dren become increasingly aware of the use of capacity measurements in everyday life.

Weight (Mass)

Prior to work with standard units of weight (mass), pupils have had prerequisite experiences with nonstandard units of weight (mass) as described earlier in Chapter 4. The study of standard units of weight (mass) can begin with weighing each child in grade two or three. If the school scale is calibrated in kilograms and grams, the metric system is used in instruction. Otherwise, the study of weight (mass) begins with the English system. It will be assumed a metric scale is available in the school.

After children learn their weights, the teacher asks, "What is a kilogram? What is a gram?" Answers to these questions are discussed by children and investigations suggested. The investigations involve using a balance or springs scales with metric weights: 1 gram (g), 10 grams (10 g), and kilogram (kg). Children weigh such objects as paper clips, pencils, crayons, tacks, sheets of paper, and books. Objects are compared and ordered by their weights. Children can summarize their work by constructing charts to show the results of their investigations.

To form an idea of the relation of a gram to a kilogram, children are helped to recall that a kilogram is 1000 grams. They use bags of sand, flour, sugar, or rice to establish ideas of 100 grams and 1 or more kilograms. They estimate the weight of objects and check their estimations.

To extend their understanding of weight (mass), children engage in activities similar to many of those suggested for the study of length. Of particular usefulness in developing weight (mass) concepts are activities such as book making, playing estimating games, and gathering objects such as cans or boxes of food, which show weights on their labels. Some children can relate the study of weight (mass) to the study of nutrition by examining the quantity of different foods that should be eaten by children and adults daily.

Temperature

Children learn to read thermometers after they have developed an awareness of differences in temperatures. Often the thermometer is introduced in grade two. Children take turns reading the thermometer each morning and afternoon at a stated time. Both inside and outside thermometers can be read. Children set a ribbon thermometer (Figure 12-3) to correspond to the thermometers.

After a record is made of the temperatures and how the air feels (hot, cool, comfortable, and so on), many comparisons are possible: inside and outside, morning and afternoon, last

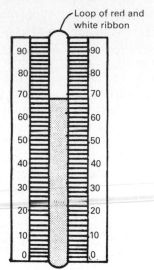

FIGURE 12-3. A ribbon thermometer.

week and this week, or this month and last month on the same day of the month. Such comparisons provide meaningful settings for comparing numbers as well as give an understanding of differences in temperatures.

The author recommends that the Fahrenheit scale be used in the primary grades if that scale is used in the media in a particular locale. Children should be able to compare their records to those given by radio, TV, or newspaper reporters. The Celsius scale is introduced first if it is commonly used in the local area. In grade five or six, children can keep records using both scales (Figure 12-4), develop an awareness of Celsius values for comfort and noncomfort, and study the relevance of the Celsius scale for industry and science (Table 12-3).

When using either the Fahrenheit or Celsius scale, there are occasions to observe temperatures recorded as negative numbers. (In warm climates, the temperatures in other parts of the country can be noted.) Using a thermometer scale to determine differences in temperatures when one or more is below zero provides

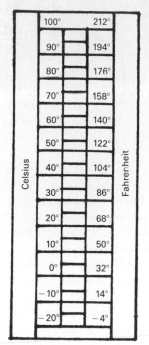

FIGURE 12-4. A thermometer with Celsius and Fahrenheit scales.

experiences to develop an intuitive awareness of subtraction with negative numbers.

A display that children organize of different kinds of thermometers, such as candy, meat, refrigerator, and clinical thermometers, extends their understanding of the usefulness of the thermometer. It can also relate life in and out of school.

Money

The major objective in studying money is for children to be able to use coins and paper money in purchasing and making change. To reach these objectives, children need the following experiences: identify coins; classify coins; state the value of coins; count the value of coins of like values (for example, dimes, quarters);

	Temperatures	
	Fahrenheit	Celsius
Water freezes	32	0
Water boils	212	100
Cold room	50	10
Cool room	68	20
Warm room	77	25
Hot room	86	30

TABLE 12-3. Comparing Fahrenheit and Celsius scales

count by 1s, 10s, and 5s (later 25s), beginning with any multiple of 5 (for example, count by 5s beginning with 35); order coins by value from largest to smallest; count the values of coins ordered from largest to smallest; use money in simulated buying and selling activities; use notation for money; and solve money problems.

Many children have had experience with money outside of school and need less instruction than those for whom the use of money is not an everyday experience. When the use of money is taught in school, real or play money should be used frequently. Work sheets involving pictures of money are less effective in learning about money than handling real or play coins and dollar bills.

Initial lessons involving money focus on the children's past experience with coins and dollar bills. Children are asked to tell what they know about money. Whenever possible, such a discussion should culminate in a chart: *What We Know About the Value of Coins*. Some activities suitable for children in primary grades to help them acquire abilities to spend small amounts of money are:

1. Ask children to be bank money sorters. Have them sort coins and place them in plastic bags.

2. When a few spare minutes are available (as while waiting in the lunch line), chorus-count by multiples of 5, beginning with a number greater than 25.

3. Play COIN COUNT. For this game use real or toy nickels and dimes. Each of six to eight children in a group gets a nickel and a dime coin. "It" (designated by the teacher to begin) picks a card from a stack of cards, each of which gives a sum of money (multiples of 5 and less than 1 dollar) and shows the card to the group. The child to the right of "It" begins counting by showing his or her nickel or dime coin and naming the coin displayed. The next child to the right must count on, using his or her nickel or dime coin, and so on. The first child to reach the sum on the "It" card gets a play dollar bill. After three rounds "It" chooses another "It." The first child to get $3 is the winner.

4. Use cards with pictures of coins and amounts to play the old games (FISH, RUMMY, SMILING FACE).

5. Play I'M RICHER—a variation of WAR. Use cards showing coins. (The child getting the larger amount gets both cards.) A variation is I'M POORER.

6. Have children set up, sell, and shop in a Discount Toy Store. The store will consist of a box of pictures of toys cut from catalogs or drawn by children. The price of the toy is written on the picture. It must be $5 or less. To play store, two children get the box of pictures and a box of play bills and coins. One begins as storekeeper and the other as buyer. (They trade roles after three purchases.) The children buy and sell using the pictures and toy money. (Children who need special help counting out money and making change can play with an aide from an upper grade.)

7. A problem for the day (provide all day to solve) can be: How many ways can you use coins to total 56¢, 43¢, and 98¢?

Computation involving sums of money is often required to solve word problems. It can be introduced when children understand money values and are learning about two- or three-digit addition, subtraction, multiplication, or division. The careful placing of the decimal point to show cents and the use of the dollar sign to show dollars can be stressed by asking a group to examine a mistake by a child last year. The lack of meaning in the example should be quickly observed by the children. Correct computation examples are also examined and their meaningfulness stressed.

Time

Learning to tell time is often difficult for young children. If experiences outside school are used in instruction, and if meaningful classroom experiences are arranged by the teacher, the task of learning to tell time can be made somewhat easier. Instruction emphasizes such experiences, and children are given time to internalize concepts embedded in the experiences.

Children are asked about times important to them when they begin the study of telling time. The times they report are shown on clocks by them or by the teacher, and later these times are shown on clocks displayed on a bulletin board. Labels beside the clocks tell the importance of the times. During the discussion, the teacher mentions times important to him or her or to class routines so that examples of *hour time* are included.

Play clocks for all the children are distributed during the following lesson. These can be made by the children from pie plates; a marked face is dittoed for each child to cut and paste on the pie plate (Figure 12-5a). They finish their clocks by writing numerals and fastening hands with a paper fastener (Figure 12-5b). (If children are to write numerals on the pie plate instead of using the ditto, the plate must be marked for placement of the numerals, or they will be incorrectly placed by most children.) Children set their clocks to correspond to some of the times shown on the bulletin board. They discuss the importance of these times.

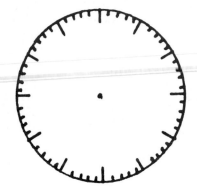

FIGURE 12-5a. A marked circular region.

FIGURE 12-5b. Pie-plate hour clock with numerals.

Children next study telling time by examining the clocks on the bulletin board that show time to the hour. The teacher asks, "What do you notice about these clocks?" (When the long hand is at 12, the hour is given by the short hand.) Children are asked to set their clocks for

hour times. Later they practice with partners using their clocks to show and read hour times.

In a subsequent lesson, children are asked to think about: What is an hour? After they share their ideas, the teacher suggests that they notice how much happens in an hour at school. To help with this, an hour caller is assigned to report when the hands on the clock show the hour. (Children take turns; the first hour caller chooses the next, and so on.) At the end of the day, children discuss what they noticed about an hour.

The discussion about hours will lead to the awareness of a need for *minute time.* (An hour is so long!) The teacher asks if anyone knows about minutes. During the discussion the information is shared that sixty minutes makes one hour; the teacher may need to give this information to the class. To experience a minute, children can watch the class wall-clock move a minute, or they can pass a small clock from child to child to observe the passing of a minute. The latter activity should be carried out when children are engaged in independent study, for it will take many minutes for all to observe minutes passing on the clock. Children later talk about what can be done in a minute. (How far can I walk? How many addition facts can I write in a minute?)

To study more about minutes, children use the clocks they made previously. They write the minute count (5, 10, . . . , 60) beside the numerals showing the hours (Figure 12-5c). They should count the minutes as they move the long hand on their clocks. It is also useful for them to close their eyes and think the minutes as they picture their clocks.

Telling time to the *hour and minutes past*

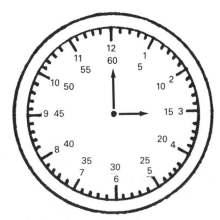

FIGURE 12-5c. Pie-plate hour and minute clock with numerals.

the hour is studied next. One difficulty children face in telling time to the hour and the minute is that the numerals on a clock are used to determine both hours and minutes. Through discussion, working with their clocks, and responding to questions about the two kinds of times shown on a clock, children are helped to overcome this difficulty. They rehearse telling time to the hour and minutes past by using their clocks in a group or with a partner. In both situations, they give times for others to set and evaluate what is done, and they set clocks for times indicated by others.

Writing and reading time is next introduced. Clock setting now involves using notation (for example, 2:45). As children are developing skill in using notation, a fun activity can be carried out: For a week or two each day have a child set an alarm clock to go off sometime during the day. (The time is known to the teacher.) Each day five children guess when the alarm will go off, set their clocks for their guesses, put their clocks on the chalkboard ledge, and write their guesses above their clocks. The child who guesses closest to the time the alarm rings sets the clock for the next day.

Later, children can use their clocks to figure out *hours before and after* a given time. After group work to clarify how times before and after a given time can be found (for example, two hours before 8 o'clock), work with a partner (with pupils using clocks and a teacher-prepared set of exercises) provides opportunities for rehearsal of this skill. A Bingo-type game, TIME BINGO, can be adapted for telling times before and after given times when children understand the procedures involved. The caller reads a phrase, such as two hours after 7:30, and children use markers on their TIME BINGO cards if they can locate that time. The winner is the one who covers a row, column, or diagonal first.

Telling time should be emphasized in grade three. During that year, most children become conservers of time and have enough experience with time to be aware of its importance in their lives.

Calendar time is studied earlier than clock time. Beginning in grade one, the day of the month and year is noted each morning and written on the chalkboard. Important days, such as birthdays and holidays, are emphasized to enrich the study of calendar time. In the primary grades, children also mark a class calendar each day. They often make individual calendars at the beginning of each month and mark their own calendars daily to learn about calendar time.

Angles

The study of angles is appropriate for some sixth-grade children. It should be preceded by exploratory activities with angles. Children should have observed the different-sized angles that can be associated with a triangle and the straight angle formed by joining the angles of a triangle.

The angles children have compared, classified, and related in geometry activities are displayed in the initial lesson on angle measurement. The teacher asks learners to tell what they know about these angles. Pupils review ideas such as: The angles associated with a triangle form a straight angle, and angles come in different sizes. The teacher next says, "Let's think about how angles could be measured. Which angle would you use to measure other angles? Decide why you made that choice. Work on this problem for a few minutes with your math partner." Class discussion follows partner discussion of a solution to the problem and examines the various solutions. Some learners will suggest using the smallest angle displayed; others will decide to use parts of a larger angle, such as one-half of a right angle. Either approach can be interpreted as a need for a unit angle measurement. The solution from antiquity—a circular angle is considered to be divided into 360 unit angles called degrees—will need to be communicated to learners. However, it is but a refinement of their own ideas, and the sense of their solutions to the problem should be noted and commended.

Children can make their own protractors for measuring and making angles before they use commercially produced protractors (Figure 12-6). The proper use of these instruments usually needs to be stressed. (The vertex of the angle must coincide with the center of the circular region used in making the protractor. A point on one ray of the angle must coincide with the point labeled "0" on the protractor.)

Children should use protractors to construct and label angles. This activity can be motivated by construction of a poster or bulletin

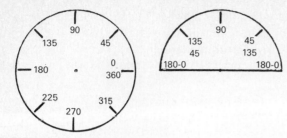

FIGURE 12-6. Cardboard protractors.

board showing observations pupils have made of angles represented in real objects (90°—table corner; 60°—sidewalk crack). Creative thinking about angles can result in drawings and a bulletin board titled *What's the Angle?* (Figure 12-7).

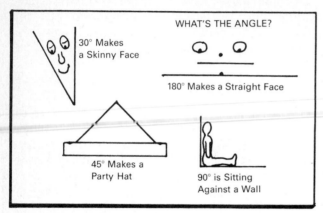

FIGURE 12-7. A bulletin board displaying imaginative use of angles.

In summary, learning measurement concepts involving length, area, volume, capacity, weight (mass), temperature, money, time, and angles has been discussed in this section. We stressed that the task of the teacher is to help learners relate and reorganize what they know to arrive at new concepts. Examples of activities to enable learners to form and extend concepts have illustrated how meaningful measurement experiences include both doing and thinking.

EXTENDING THE STUDY OF MEASUREMENT

In this section ideas useful for extending and enriching the concepts of children in grades five and six will be discussed. Some learners will not be ready to study all the topics included. Those for advanced learners will be designated as such to aid teachers in planning instruction. Topics to be discussed are perimeter and area, the metric system, and problem solving with measurement.

More on Perimeter and Area

When children can find the perimeter of a rectangle and the area of a rectangular region using rules or formulas, they are guided to construct the rules and formulas for the perimeter of a square, for the length of a circle (known as **circumference**), and for the areas of square, parallelogram, triangular, and circular regions. The rules and formulas are developed by a reexamination of what is known. Most children will study the rules and formulas for the circumference of a circle, the perimeter of a square, and the area of a square region. Advanced learners will study the formulas for the areas of parallelogram, triangular, and circular regions.

Children's first experiences with the circumference of circles are provided by an assignment to measure the length of the edges of the room wastepaper basket, coins, different-sized plates, and round tables. Metric tapes are used, and the word *circumference* is introduced as children discuss their findings. A sample lesson sequence to introduce the rule for finding the circumference of a circle is given in Box 12-2. When children can find the circumferences of circles using the rule, the formula $C = \pi d$ ($C =$ circumference, $\pi = 3.14 \ldots$, and $d =$ diameter) is developed by the group from the rule. Children choose to use the rule or the formula in subsequent work.

Children construct rules and then formulas for the perimeter of a square ($P = 4s$, $s =$ length of a side) and the area of a square region ($A \doteq s^2$) by using the rules and formulas for those measures of a rectangle and rectangular region and their knowledge that a square is a rectangle with sides equal in length.

The formula for the area of a parallelogram region ($A = b \times h$; $A =$ area, $b =$ base, and $h =$ height) is developed by learners by rearranging parts of a parallelogram region (Figure 12-8) to form a rectangular region and then applying their knowledge of the formula for a rectangular region. The labels *base* and *height* are introduced after pupils know their meaning.

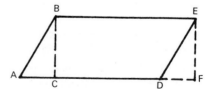

Δ ABC and Δ DEF have the same area measure.

FIGURE 12-8. Developing the formula for the area of a parallelogram region.

BOX 12-2.   SAMPLE LESSON: INTRODUCING A RULE FOR FINDING
THE CIRCUMFERENCE OF A CIRCLE (GRADE 6)

1. Boys and girls, you recall that last week we used our metric tapes to measure the rim of the wastepaper basket, the edge of a plate, the edge of a quarter, and the edge of the round table in our library center. Someone remarked that there must be a better way to find circumferences of circular objects, and of course there is. Today we will do some study to find the rule for finding the circumference of a circle. To get started, comparing diameters and circumferences will help us. I have some cardboard circular regions. Please work with your math partner to find the diameters and circumferences of the circles. You can use a meter tape to measure around the object or you can roll the object along the tape. You recall we used both approaches last week. Please keep a record of your findings on this record sheet. The sheet has columns for recording the diameters and circumferences of the five circular regions. A quick review: What is the diameter of a circle? How can we find it? (A diameter is a line segment through the center of the circle. Find the center and measure across the region.) You will notice I have indicated the center of each circle for you. (*C/D* column is included later.)

2. Your records look great:

Circle	Circumference	Diameter	*C/D*
A	25 cm	8 cm	3.13
B	18.75 cm	6 cm	3.13
C	22 cm	7 cm	3.14
D	11 cm	3.5 cm	3.14
E	12.5 cm	4 cm	3.13

   What does a record tell you about the relation between diameters and circumferences? (The circumference must be about 3 times the diameter.)

3. It looks that way. What operation could we use to determine the relation more closely? (Divide.)

4. Each team perform the division rounding to hundredths. What are your results? (3.14, 3.13.) Write them on your record sheet.

5. Does that give us a clue for a rule to find the circumference of the circle? (Oh, multiply by 3.14 or 3.13.) We will use 3.14, but the ratio is approximately 3.14. It is called "pi" and written this way: π.

6. Jack, please state the rule for us. (To find the circumference of a circle, multiply the diameter by 3.14 or π.)

7. O.K. I'll write that rule on the board.

8. I have a few more cardboard circles for us to use in trying out and checking our rule. With your math partner, measure the diameter, use our rule to find the circumference, and measure the circumference to see if your calculation is correct. Remember, you can't find tenths and hundredths of centimeters easily, so your calculations will not be the very same as your measurement.

9. What did you find out? (Our rule is O.K.) (Later children use the rule in devising the formula, $C = \pi d$.)

Children develop the formula for the area of a triangular region ($A = \frac{1}{2} b \times h$) by noting the relation of a triangular region and a parallelogram region, as shown in Figure 12-9. Subsequently, they use formulas and diagrams as necessary in writing and solving exercises such as: The base of a parallelogram is 3 cm, the height is 4 cm. What is the area of the region it bounds? Finding answers to such exercises with math partners is more productive for many learners than independent study and is frequently suggested by the teacher.

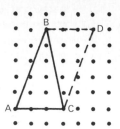

FIGURE 12-9.   Developing the formula for the area of a triangular region.

An activity resulting in new insights about the relation of perimeter and area is: record the areas for regions bounded by rectangles with different lengths and widths but the same perimeters. (For example, 3 m by 4 m and 6 m by 1 m). Squared paper is good material to use in this activity. An examination of the record reveals that the area of a rectangular region can vary with no change in the perimeter of the rectangle.

Learners develop the formula for the area of a circular region $A = \pi r^2$ (A = area; r = radius) by using their knowledge of the formula for the area of a parallelogram region and the formula for the circumference of a circle. To construct the formula, they cut a circular region and rearrange it as shown in Figure 12-10.

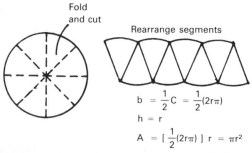

FIGURE 12-10.   Developing the formula for the area of a circular region.

The sense of the formula for the area of a circular region is fully appreciated by some learners if they examine the relation of two areas: the area of a square region formed by four square regions ($s = r$) and the area of a circular region bounded by a circle with a radius r. Squared paper can be used (Figure 12-11). Pupils observe that the area of the four square regions is greater than the area of the circular region, and they can conclude that 3.14 is a sensible approximation of the number of times the area of 1 square with side r is needed to cover the area of the circular region.

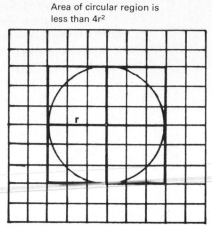

FIGURE 12-11.   The area of a circular region is less than $4r^2$.

Materials are very important in helping learners comprehend the meaning of rules and formulas. Each learner should have enough opportunities to construct and investigate examples of relationships using concrete or graphic materials so that he or she can infer rules. The formulas that are derived from rules become sensible statements of relationships if children have had concrete or pictorial experiences with examples of the generalizations.

Metric System (SI)

The approach to metric measurement that has been outlined gives children experiences with metric relations as they measure. From work with instruments such as the meter stick children learn that 100 cm measures the same length as 1 m. Many are able to state conversions (142 cm = 1 m 42 cm) after experiences with instruments.

At grade six, however, some children are able to study the metric system more systematically. The teacher can introduce the metric system by saying, "Boys and girls, you have worked with metric units for a number of years. You know many units. What units can you recall? (Meters, square centimeters, and so on.) I know you understand statements, such as 400 cm = 4 m. I think you would like to know all the units in the metric system, though you will not use some of them very often. I have a chart showing the metric system on the board (Table 12-4). What relations can be observed by studying the information on this chart?" The discussions following pupils' observations highlight base-10 relations and the relations among units for length, area, and volume. The meaning of prefixes is also studied:

milli means $\qquad \frac{1}{1000}$

centi means $\qquad \frac{1}{100}$

deci means $\qquad \frac{1}{10}$

deka means $\qquad$ 10

hecto means $\qquad$ 100

kilo means $\qquad$ 1000

Children label number lines in metric units; they reexamine a cubic centimeter block to deepen their understanding of the relation of a centimeter to a square centimeter and cubic centimeter. Of special importance in the course of these experiences is for children to image a meter displaying 1000 mm, 100 cm, and 10 dm. Imaging square and cubic units is also crucial for learning. For example, imaging a dm^3 as a cube 10 cm by 10 cm by 10 cm or a vessel filled with 1000 blocks each a cm^3 is a very important prerequisite for manipulating numbers to state relations.

TABLE 12-4. SELECTED METRIC UNITS

Linear

10 millimeters (mm)	= 1 centimeter (cm)
10 centimeters	= 1 decimeter (dm)
10 decimeters	= 1 meter (m) = 100 cm = 1000 mm
10 meters	= 1 dekameter (dkm)
10 dekameters	= 1 hectometer (hm)
10 hectometers	= 1 kilometer (km) = 1000 m

Area

100 square millimeters (mm^2)	= 1 square centimeter (cm^2)
10,000 square centimeters	= 1 square meter (m^2)
1,000,000 square meters	= 1 square kilometer (km^2)

Volume/Capacity

1,000 cubic millimeters (mm^3)	= 1 cubic centimeter (cm^3)
1,000 cubic centimeters	= 1 cubic decimeter (dm^3)
1,000 cubic decimeters	= 1 cubic meter (m^3) = 1,000,000 cm^3
10 milliliters (ml)	= 1 centiliter (cl)
10 centiliters	= 1 deciliter (dl)
10 deciliters	= 1 liter (l) = 1000 ml
1000 liters	= 1 kiloliter (kl)

Weight (Mass)

10 milligrams (mg)	= 1 centigram (cg)
10 centigrams	= 1 decigram (dg)
10 decigrams	= 1 gram (g) = 1000 mg
1000 grams	= 1 kilogram (kg)
1000 kilograms	= 1 metric ton (t)

During lessons stressing imaging, children are encouraged to talk about what they see. (*Image* would be an appropriate word to use with many sixth graders.) After imaging, children can write down what they were able to image. Comparing records gives learners further background for work with metric relations.

It is expected that learning in the enactive and iconic modes will be so meaningful that when children are asked to state computation rules, they will be able to infer them with little hesitation: to state smaller units as larger units, divide; to state larger units as smaller units, multiply. However, children should not often need these rules. To solve problems, they should be able to draw on immediate awareness of relations.

Children can also explore the relations among metric units. The relation of cubic units to units of capacity is easily grasped if a liter box is filled with 1000 cubic-centimeter blocks. A box whose volume is 1000 cm^3 (1 dm^3) can also be fitted with a plastic liner and a liter of water poured into the box. To help children grasp the relation of weight units to volume units, 1 kilogram (kg) of water is weighed in a plastic sack. Then the 1 kg of water is poured into a cubic-decimeter (1,000-cm^3) box to illustrate that it fills the box (4° Celsius at sea level).

Knowledge of metric-system relations is stressed in instruction if children can grasp the relations and use them to solve exercises and problems. The metric system is studied as a system of relations only when children have thought structures that can incorporate these ideas.

Many children will relate English and metric units as they use both to deal with measurement in and out of school. Occasionally, the teacher can ask learners what they know. Common comparisons are:

1 meter is about 39 inches.

1 kilometer is about .6 mile.

1 cup is about 250 milliliters.

1 quart is about 1 liter.

Children develop an intuitive understanding of conversions as they work with instruments calibrated in both English and metric units. Exercises requiring calculating English-metric conversions are not assigned to pupils. Class discussions are sufficient to bring them to their attention.

Problem Solving

Problem solving of all types—routine and nonroutine, applied and nonapplied—can be devised for boys and girls in the upper grades. Nonroutine problems are especially important for advanced learners. Examples of all types are:

Routine/applied: Mr. Smith's rectangular garden plot is 2 meters by 8 meters. The rabbits are eating his carrots, so he is going to put a chain-link fence around the plot. How much does he need to buy? The fence cost $200. Carrots cost $.25 a pound. How many pounds of carrots must he grow to pay for the fence? (Should he put in the fence?)

Routine/nonapplied: The perimeter of a rectangle is 19 cm. One side is 5 cm. What are the other sides?

Nonroutine/applied (for gifted learners): Space travelers have found a planet which, during one revolution around its sun, rotates on its axis 25 times. Invent clock and calendar time for this planet. Make any assumptions about the planet that you need to make.

Nonroutine/nonapplied: Use a plastic model to decide how many properties of a triangular prism you can measure.

To teach problem solving involving measurement, many of the suggestions given in Chapter 3 can be used. Of particular importance are discussions among learners as they solve problems and after they have found solutions. As a participant in group discussions, the teacher encourages children to examine alternate ways to solve problems and continues to remind them to consider the sense of solutions (look back). Pupils are also given opportunities to write problems that are used in assignments for other members of the class.

SUMMARY

This chapter has discussed learning and teaching measurement after children develop certain prerequisite understanding. The relevance of measurement to children's lives was stressed to insure that the study of measurement is meaningful. Instructional suggestions for helping pupils construct and extend concepts of standard units emphasized that learners must be involved in measuring and given assignments that require reflecting about what they have done. Of special significance are activities for imaging, comparing, ordering, and relating measurements. For children who make good progress in understanding measurement, the study of formulas and the metric system was suggested. Problem solving was stressed throughout the chapter; specific suggestions for extending concepts through problem solving were given in the last section.

STUDY QUESTIONS

1. Would you introduce the metric system of measurement before the English system? Why or why not? Discuss your ideas with other students. Do most agree or disagree with suggestions given in this chapter?

2. Plan an assessment activity to determine if children understand that it is not possible to communicate measurements meaningfully if individuals use different nonstandard units.

3. Write a lesson plan to help children learn measuring to the nearest centimeter.

4. Discuss your reference measurements with another student. How did you develop these reference measurements? What are the implications for elementary school instruction of your experiences in forming reference measurements?

5. How would you assess the meanings children have gained from the study of area measurement?

6. Write an independent study activity to help children develop the formula for the area of a parallelogram.

7. Talk with children who learn mathematics slowly and those who learn quickly about their interest in the study of measurement.

Ask them what they think is the purpose of such a study. Compare the responses of the two groups.

REFERENCES

Deloach, Ruby Haydock, "The Little Hand Tells You When," *Arithmetic Teacher*, 30, no. 2 (October 1982), 39-40.

Fennell, Francis (Skip), "The Newspaper: A Source for Application in Mathematics," *Arithmetic Teacher*, 30, no. 2 (October 1982), 22-26.

Higgins, Jon L., ed., *A Metric Handbook for Teachers*. Reston, VA: The National Council of Teachers of Mathematics, Inc., 1974.

Inskeep, James E., Jr., "Teaching Measurement to Elementary School Children," in *Measurement in School Mathematics*, 1976 Yearbook of the National Council of Teachers of Mathematics, eds. Doyal Nelson and Robert E. Reys. Reston, VA: The National Council of Teachers of Mathematics, Inc., 1976.

Leffin, Walter W., *Going Metric: Grades K-8*. Reston, VA: The National Council of Teachers of Mathematics, Inc., 1975.

Pagni, David L., "Applications in School Mathematics: Human Variability," in *Applications in School Mathematics*, 1979 Yearbook of the National Council of Teachers of Mathematics, eds. Sidney Sharron and Robert E. Reys. Reston, VA: The National Council of Teachers of Mathematics, Inc., 1979.

Riedesel, C. Alan, *Teaching Elementary School Mathematics*, 3d ed., chap. 14. Englewood Cliffs, NJ: Prentice-Hall, Inc., 1980.

Shaw, Jean M., "Meaning Metrics: Measure, Mix, Manipulate, and Mold," *Arithmetic Teacher*, 28, no. 7 (March 1981), 49-50.

Troutman, Andria P., and Betty K. Lichtenberg, *Mathematics: A Good Beginning*, 2d ed., chaps. 14-15. Monterey, CA: Brooks/Cole Publishing Company, 1982.

13

LEARNING AND TEACHING WITH CALCULATORS AND COMPUTERS

Many adults believe the hand-held calculator and the computer can make important contributions to the learning of children. The calculator is relatively inexpensive and enables learners to be mathematical—to experiment with numbers, observe patterns, and solve problems—rather than be involved in tedious computation. The computer can do this and more, but it is expensive; other hurdles also stand in the way of its contributing to the learning of children. In this chapter we will examine learning and teaching with the calculator and the computer and discuss problems connected with their use.

THE CALCULATOR

The calculator performs computations swiftly and accurately. The majority of adults in our society use calculators when adding, subtracting, multiplying, and dividing at home and at work. Using calculators, however, is more than punching keys. The operator must have a good number sense. Every output must be interpreted by answering questions such as: Is that output sensible? Is the output what I need to deal with my question?

When children use calculators to find solutions, they are guided to transfer the abilities and attitudes that have been emphasized in all previous chapters. Work with numbers must be meaningful, and solutions must always be checked for reasonableness. Gentle reminders, estimation activities, and discussions of pupils' experiences with evaluating outputs are used by teachers to help children use calculators intelligently.

The role of the calculator in learning elementary school mathematics is broader, however, than its use in knowledgeable ways to solve exercises and problems. The calculator can be used as a resource in learning concepts and generalizations. For the most part the calculator is used as a tool for extending understanding of topics discussed in earlier chapters. The remainder of this section describes using the calculator as a learning aid in elementary school mathematics instruction.

Introducing the Calculator

To enable children to use calculators as instructional aids, teachers must first provide opportunities for pupils to learn how to operate calculators. Children usually learn to use calculators in grade three or early in grade four. The devices are not introduced before children have made satisfactory progress in learning the basic facts. A good approach is to introduce the calculator by saying, "You will want to explore using the calculator before we begin to learn mathematics with it. Let's investigate what the calculator can do!"

An instruction sheet is usually provided so children will know the format for making entries in the calculator. There are two major formats. (1) Numerals and symbols are entered in equation order: 3 $\boxed{+}$ 4 $\boxed{=}$ 7. (2) Numerals are entered and then the symbols for the operations: 3 $\boxed{\text{ENTER}}$ 4 $\boxed{+}$ 7. Exploration accompanied by brief explanations of proper procedures usually enables children to use the calculator in a short period of time. While children may examine keys for inputs unknown to them, usually they subsequently ignore these keys. The teacher can say that the meaning of those inputs will be studied at a later time. Children's ability to use the calculator is, of course, evaluated before it is used as a resource in learning elementary school mathematics.

Learning and Teaching Prime and Composite Numbers

To develop an intuitive awareness of prime and composite numbers, children are asked to use their calculators to find all the divisors of each number from 2 to 100. Divisors are to be numbers divisible only by 1 and by themselves. The activity can be carried out as a class project, with a list of numbers and their divisors posted on the bulletin board. Individuals or teams can make entries in the list and initial their entries. Children should be encouraged to explain how they used their calculators to find all the divisors of a number.

As the list lengthens, children become aware of differences in entries in the list. Two sets—numbers with no divisors other than 1 and the number itself (**prime numbers**), and numbers whose divisors are prime numbers (**composite numbers**)—are observed. As children examine these categories, they *construct concepts* of prime and composite numbers. Labels for the categories are given to learners as they discuss their ideas. Children can *extend understanding* by finding primes over 100. (See also Chapter 7 for extension ideas.)

More on Estimation

The calculator can be used to develop or verify several rules for estimating products. As children work with these rules, the need for estimation in work with calculators is emphasized.

Use of the round-up or round-down rules in estimating products in which both factors are 10s plus 1s often gives large overestimates or underestimates. Rules for better estimates can be developed from work with calculators. Such activities would be appropriate for advanced learners in the upper grades.

One such rule is: When the 10s number in each factor is not less than three and the 1s greater than five, round both factors up, mentally multiply the rounded numbers, and subtract from the product a number equal to 100

times the remainder of 10 minus the lesser 1s number.

Indicated Product	Rounding-Up Rule Estimate	Better Estimate Rule	Computed Product
48 × 58	3000	50 × 60 − (100 × 2) = 2800	2784
38 × 67	2800	40 × 70 − (100 × 3) = 2500	2546
89 × 56	5400	90 × 60 − (100 × 4) = 5000	4984
78 × 56	4800	80 × 60 − (100 × 4) = 4400	4368
36 × 46	2000	40 × 50 − (100 × 4) = 1600	1656

A second rule is: When the 10s number in each factor is greater than three and the 1s less than five, round down, mentally multiply the rounded numbers, and add 100 times the greater 1s number.

Indicated Product	Rounding-Down Rule Estimate	Better Estimate Rule	Computed Product
73 × 84	5600	70 × 80 + (100 × 4) = 6000	6132
43 × 54	2000	40 × 50 + (100 × 4) = 2400	2322
62 × 84	4800	60 × 80 + (100 × 4) = 5200	5208
52 × 42	2000	50 × 40 + (100 × 2) = 2200	2184
73 × 92	6300	70 × 90 + (100 × 3) = 6600	6716

Either of these rules can be developed using inductive questioning to enable learners to examine examples, to observe patterns in the size (in hundreds) of the overestimates or underestimates, and to form the rule. The calculator can be used subsequently to verify the rule using other examples. An alternative approach is: Give children the rule and ask them to find examples using the calculator that show or do not show the rule's usefulness.

The estimation rule involving rounding one factor up and the other factor down can be studied using the calculator. Examples are:

Indicated Product	Estimate	Computed Product
42 × 37	40 × 40 = 1600	1554
86 × 54	90 × 50 = 4500	4644
22 × 66	20 × 70 = 1400	1452
74 × 46	70 × 50 = 3500	3404
81 × 58	80 × 60 = 4800	4698

Using calculators, pupils can examine estimating rules for products that involve renaming using fractional numbers:

1. When one factor is close to 25, round the other factor to a multiple of 4, divide by 4, and multiply by 100.

2. When one factor is close to 50, round the other factor to an even number, divide by 2, and multiply by 100 (Figure 13-1).

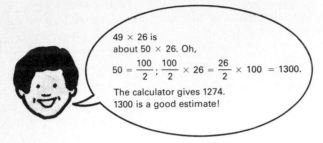

49 × 26 is about 50 × 26. Oh,

$$50 = \frac{100}{2}; \frac{100}{2} \times 26 = \frac{26}{2} \times 100 = 1300.$$

The calculator gives 1274. 1300 is a good estimate!

FIGURE 13-1. Steps in estimating.

Examples using these rules are:

Indicated Product	Estimate	Computed Product
49 × 26	$\frac{26}{2} \times 100 = 1300$	1274
24 × 39	$\frac{40}{4} \times 100 = 1000$	936
26 × 57	$\frac{60}{4} \times 100 = 1500$	1482
51 × 82	$\frac{82}{2} \times 100 = 4100$	4182
49 × 73	$\frac{72}{2} \times 100 = 3600$	3577

A successive *approximation rule* for finding the square root of a number with a calculator can be explored by some children in the upper grades. For example, the following computations using the calculator and trial and error would enable one to determine that a good approximation of the square root of 37 is 6.083:

$$6.1 \times 6.1 = 37.21$$
$$6.09 \times 6.09 = 37.0881$$
$$6.083 \times 6.083 = 37.002889$$

Children can be given examples to study and questioned about the steps used in the examples. They then generate the rule. A few children may become very interested in finding better and better approximations of the square root of a number.

Constant Arithmetic Function

The constant arithmetic function on many inexpensive calculators enables learners to *extend understanding* of place value and of the operations. If a calculator has this feature, after pressing a numeral key and an operation key, the repeated pressing of $\boxed{=}$ continues the operation with the indicated number—for example, 5 $\boxed{+}$ $\boxed{=}$ 10 $\boxed{=}$ 15 $\boxed{=}$ 20 . . . . Activities that make use of the constant arithmetic function include:

1. Suggest the pupils use the constant arithmetic function to multiply (or divide) any number by 10. Ask them to record the calculator output and report their observations of patterns. (A multiple of 10 can also be used.)

2. Have pupils use repeated addition (subtraction) to demonstrate the meaning of multiplication (division) facts or multidigit computation examples.

3. Ask pupils to look for patterns in repeated addition of 11, 12, 15, and 25.

4. Say: Decide how many times 5 must be subtracted from 55 to reach 0; 7 from 98; 25 from 100; then check with the calculator. Ask: How did you decide?

5. Suggest children study powers of numbers using calculators. Ask children to find products such as 8 × 8 × 8 × 8 × 8 × 8 × 8 × 8 = 16,777,216 and report their reactions to this assignment. During this activity pupils can be introduced to the notation for powers (raised numeral) and to the reading of the notation (9^6 is 9 to the 6th power). The constant arithmetic function can also be used with fractions to develop an awareness of the use of powers in denominators: $\frac{1}{5} \times \frac{1}{5} \times \frac{1}{5} \times \frac{1}{5} = (\frac{1}{5})^4 = .0016$.

Operations and the Calculator

A number of calculator activities enable children to *extend understanding* of the operations. Such activities are effective because pupils do not need to attend to paper-and-pencil computation. They are free to explore patterns and number relations. Mathematical learnings for children to explore, together with sample activities, are given in the following list.

1. The commutative, associative, and distributive properties and related ideas:

    a. How many ways can you arrange the addends to find the sum?

    $$19 + 17 + 11 + 18 = N \quad N = 65$$
    $$14 + 19 + 13 + 16 = N \quad N = 62$$

    Which arrangement is best for mental calculation? Why?

    b. How many ways can you arrange the factors to find the product?

    $$8 \times 5 \times 9 \times 4 = N \quad N = 1440$$
    $$2 \times 9 \times 4 \times 5 = N \quad N = 360$$

    Which arrangement is best for mental calculation? Why? Can you rearrange the words in English sentences? Why can you rearrange addends or factors in mathematical sentences?

    c. How many ways can you rearrange the numbers to find the given differences?

    $$120 - 60 - 40 - 18 = N \quad N = 2$$
    $$197 - 70 - 31 - 28 = N \quad N = 68$$

    What are your hypotheses about what is going on here? What have you learned?

    d. How many ways can you rearrange the numbers to find the given quotients?

    $$100 \div 2 \div 5 \div 10 = N \quad N = 1$$
    $$80 \div 4 \div 5 \div 2 = N \quad N = 2$$

    What are your hypotheses about what is going on here? What have you learned?

    e. Perform these computations using your calculator. Then change the placement of the parentheses. What do you notice? How do you explain your observations (Figure 13-2)?

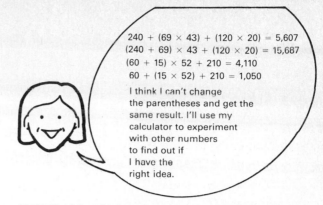

FIGURE 13-2. Thinking while using calculators.

$$240 + (69 \times 43) + (120 \times 20) = N$$
$$(60 + 15) \times 52 + 210 = N$$
$$3 + (1200 \times 4) + (24 \times 68) = N$$
$$1002 + (2 \times 56) + 65 = N$$

    f. You know a parentheses rule: Compute within parentheses first. There are other rules when parentheses are not given that tell you about the order of operations. Study these examples to learn the rule:

    $$4 + 3 \times 2 = 4 + 6$$
    $$= 10$$
    $$3 + 5 \times 2 = 3 + 10$$
    $$= 13$$
    $$4 + 6 \times 6 = 4 + 36$$
    $$= 40$$

    Which operation is performed first? Use your rule to think about the following:

    $$2 + 9 \times 2 + 6 \times 4 = 2 + 18 + 24$$
    $$= 44$$
    $$6 + 3 \times 2 + 2 \times 4 = 6 + 6 + 8$$
    $$= 20$$

    What do you notice? What is the order of operations? Write a rule. Use your rule and the calculator to solve the following and check your solutions with those given below.

    (1) $9 + 43 \times 67 + 21 + 84 \times 32 = N$
    (2) $64 + 31 \times 22 + 59 + 62 \times 19 = N$
    (3) $18 + 35 \times 66 + 27 + 86 \times 14 = N$

FIGURE 13-3. Ways to calculate.

(1) 5599

(2) 1983

(3) 3559

Tell your teacher your rule. The teacher will have a class discussion about this rule when several pupils have learned about it.

2. The inverse nature of addition/subtraction and of multiplication/division:

Solve with your calculator:

a.

$$N - 75 = 5 \qquad N \times 25 = 200$$
$$80 - N = 75 \qquad 200 \div N = 8$$
$$80 - 5 = N \qquad 200 \div 8 = N$$
$$N + 5 = 80 \qquad N \div 25 = 8$$

What do you notice? Make rules so you will not need to use trial and error. Try your rule on exercises that you write or that are written by a person also doing this exercise.

3. The structure of numbers and number relations:

a. Use your calculator to find solutions using as many approaches as you can think of (Figure 13-3). What ideas come to your mind as you think these approaches?

$$36 \times 81 = N$$
$$6150 \div 150 = N$$
$$595 + 999 = N$$
$$609 - 310 = N$$

b. Use your calculator to complete these exercises to four decimal places. Record your results. What patterns do you observe? Why do these patterns appear?

$$\frac{1}{12} = N \qquad \frac{1}{8} = N$$
$$\frac{2}{12} = N \qquad \frac{2}{8} = N$$
$$\frac{3}{12} = N \qquad \frac{3}{8} = N$$
$$\vdots \qquad \vdots$$
$$\frac{12}{12} = N \qquad \frac{8}{8} = N$$

4. Evaluating solutions:
What was the incorrect input in these (Figure 13-4)?

$$32 \times 33 = 1089$$
$$459 + 348 = 797$$
$$786 - 238 = 538$$
$$560 \div 35 = 112$$

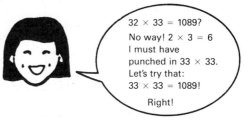

FIGURE 13-4. Checking an output.

Games

Calculator games often require devising winning strategies. In the course of determining a winning strategy, learners can develop new number meanings. A few such games are:

Variations of NIM. Two players with one calculator pick a game number and are provided with inputs allowed. These have been selected by the teacher to insure a winner is possible (for example, game number 21, inputs allowed: first-row calculator digits—1, 2, and 3; game number 57, inputs allowed: 7 and 9; game number 670, inputs allowed: 20 and 30). Players take turns inputting an allowed number and the $\boxed{+}$ key. The first player to reach the game number is the winner.

ZERO EXACTLY. This is NIM in reverse. Players begin with the game number and in turn push the $\boxed{-}$ and an allowed number until one player's input gives zero on the calculator. That player is the winner. (Negative outputs, while disregarded, can give intuitive notions of negative numbers.)

Adaptations of NIM and ZERO EXACTLY could provide for the game numbers to be large and two operations to be included (for example: game number 888; allowed numbers: 1, 2, and 10; addition and multiplication).

CALCULATE. Two players use one calculator. The first player enters a number in the calculator and says CALCULATE . . . (a second number). The second player takes as many turns inputting into the calculator as are necessary to obtain the number named by the first player. His or her score is the number of inputs. The score is recorded. He or she then inputs a number for the first player and names the number to calculate. After five turns for each player, the scores for each player are summed. The player with the lowest score is the winner of that round. Three rounds make a game. (An example of an exchange is: Player one inputs 56 and names 66. Player two inputs 10, receiving a score of 1.) It will be observed that this game can be adapted to meet individual needs very easily by stating constraints. For example, the second number must be a multiple of 10 and obtained by adding or subtracting multiples of 10 to the first number; basic facts must be used; or no first number greater than 50 can be used.

Problem Solving

Problem solving can be enhanced if pupils are permitted to use calculators when multidigit computation is involved. If real-life or textbook problems are solved using calculators in the carrying-out-of-the-plan step, learners need only focus on the making of accurate inputs. They avoid the computation usually associated with that step. Their energies can be directed toward the thought processes associated with the other steps.

Problem solving with the calculator can move beyond mundane problems, however, to deal with fascinating questions involving large numbers that both teachers and children ask. Some examples are:

1. How old will I be in the year 2000, 2002, 2020, 2022?

2. How many times does my heart beat in an hour? day? week? year? (Count how many times it beats in a minute.)

3. How many gallons of gasoline would it take to travel by car around the earth at the latitude of my city? How much would it cost? (Find out how many miles your family's car travels on a gallon of gas.)

4. How much milk do I drink in a year?

5. How many steps do I take walking to school in a week? month? year?

6. How fast can I count by ones? How long would it take to count to a million? a billion?

7. Make up problems using the *Guinness Book of Records*. Share them.

8. How many hamburgers do I eat in a year? The pupils in our class? Our school?

The calculator can foster the search for alternative solutions to problems and involve research. Examples of such problems are:

1. Joe told his Mom and Dad he needed more allowance. They asked him to make a list of expenditures he would like to make each week, month, and year so he could give them an idea of what he needed each week. They said he should make a low, high, and in-between budget for the three of them to consider. Make these budgets for Joe.

2. Joe made his budgets and decided he would not get all the money he needed for his expenditures unless he did some work. He decided to make a list of jobs and possible earnings that would supplement his allowance. Make such a list for Joe for a week, month, and year.

3. How many ways could you spend $1000? Make up three lists.

4. A person aged 10–12 needs 45–50 g of protein a day. Find how many different ways you can obtain your needed protein.

Misuse of Calculators

The teaching and learning suggestions given in this section demonstrate that the calculator can be a useful aid in elementary school mathematics instruction. It can stimulate interest in mathematics and promote the generation of number ideas. However, the calculator cannot replace the concrete and pictorial experiences necessary to develop a good number sense. Young children do not construct ideas from symbolic representations of those ideas. They form concepts by manipulating and generalizing from experiences that involve action and imaging. Calculators are being misused when they replace a thoughtful study of concrete and graphic examples of mathematical ideas. When children can generate ideas by manipulating symbolic expressions, the calculator can contribute to the formation of ideas. This occurs in the upper elementary grades. However, upper-grade learners still need experiences to promote learning in the enactive and iconic modes. Most preadolescents cannot yet rely solely on abstract thinking processes to generate meaning.

Another misuse of calculators is to ask learners to use them to check paper-and-pencil computations with large numbers. If a calculator is available, children can rightly ask, "Why do these long computations with large numbers and check with the calculator? Why not use the calculator in the first place?" There is no reasonable answer to this question. Asking children to use the calculator to check computation can make school seem irrelevant. Children know adults do not use calculators to check paper-and-pencil work. However, they will agree that outputs must be evaluated. Children know that they must decide if the output makes sense; it is important to learn to estimate.

THE COMPUTER

The Western world is rapidly becoming computerized. Computers are making contributions to industry, business, government, entertainment, and the personal lives of millions of individuals. Many believe that to function effectively in society one must be computer literate—know about computers and be able to do something with them. It is natural that educators are giving serious consideration to the use of small computers, microcomputers, in schools. In this section we will examine two approaches to using microcomputers in teaching and learning elementary school mathematics: (1) computer-assisted instruction (CAI), and (2) interactive experiences.

Computer-Assisted Instruction (CAI)

CAI makes use of tutorials of various kinds to enable students to develop a body of knowledge. Such tutorials can be used in late primary or early upper-grade years. Many are programmed *drill-and-practice* lessons. A basic fact or computational exercise is flashed on the screen and the learner uses the keyboard to make a response. Programs of this type have both positive and negative aspects.

On the positive side, rehearsal is necessary for learning, and the drill-and-practice program provides rehearsal opportunities. It is reported that drill-and-practice tutorials can be very effective with slow learners, who often profit from a patient teacher unaware of other pupils' needs. CAI can make important contributions to providing for individual differences in the amount of time needed for rehearsal.

The negative aspects of drill-and-practice lessons stem from the fact that they are only response oriented. The learner is not guided to relate number ideas as a means for attaining recall. Generally one or more incorrect responses are followed by the computer teacher's giving the correct response. The stimulus is again presented and the learner is expected to respond correctly. The learner is not encouraged to develop recall strategies based on meaningful number relations.

Furthermore, because the programmed instruction format for drill-and-practice tutorials does not guide the learner to find ways of self-help, such a lesson can be a frustrating experience. A girl sitting at a microcomputer and making no response for several minutes to the question $8 \times 7 = ?$ confided in me, "I don't know the answer and I don't want to get a bad grade." Indeed, the computer does keep track of every response, and the information is readily available to the child and the teacher. Failure as well as success is carefully recorded—not a happy prospect for a child to contemplate.

CAI tutorials can be designed as *guided practice*. To aid the child in making the response, a diagram or hint is part of the stimulus. For example, *** **** could accompany the question $3 + 4 = ?$ Problems that include hints for solution, such as "There are two steps in this problem," are another example of guided practice.

Some tutorials are written as *concept-development* activities. For example, graphics can show joining sets and the related addition facts. However, in such lessons the learner is a passive recipient of information. Pupils are not generally required to use cognitive processes to make learning experiences meaningful.

Some tutorials are designed as *games*—for example, a computer version of TIC TAC TOE using basic-fact answers as entries in the grid. Such games can be played by two or more players. Motivation is high in computer games. They also encourage children to develop strategies to win. In planning winning strategies, children learn a great deal about number relations.

It is hoped that tutorials will be available that make it possible for learners to organize and relate present and past learning to arrive at new mathematical insights. One approach would be for children to be given menus of material related to lessons or assignments. Children could choose menu entries useful to them (1) in constructing concepts or generalizations, (2) in reviewing the sense of previously studied ideas, or (3) in aiding the recall of problem-solving strategies. Tutorials of this type offer great promise for guiding the mathematical learning of children.

Interactive Experiences

The interactive-experience approach to computing engages the child in problem solving as he or she programs the microcomputer to perform a task. Writing and executing programs requires learners to carry out the problem-solving steps discussed in Chapter 3: understanding the problem, devising a plan, carrying out the plan, and looking back.

To program, however, one must know a computer language. Some children are being introduced to BASIC (Beginner's All-purpose Symbolic Instruction Code). LOGO is a computer language frequently used by elementary school children, beginning in the late primary grades. LOGO was developed by Seymour Papert, a mathematician at Massachusetts Institute of Technology. LOGO enables children to command a trianglelike figure—the turtle robot —to make lines and shapes on a video screen.

After learning a few simple commands, children can create their own pictures or designs using the problem-solving process.

Papert and his associates (1979) report research to show that children learn thinking abilities using LOGO. However, the research is based on small numbers of children, and the conclusions the researchers report are based on their observations of learners. There is a lack of statistical evidence to support the hypothesis that children learn to think by being involved in programming activities using LOGO. It is indeed too soon to pass judgment on the value of LOGO for developing cognitive abilities.

SUMMARY

Children can learn a great deal of mathematics using calculators and computers. These machines enable children to work with mathematical content in ways not possible with textbooks and paper and pencil. They can stimulate thinking processes and contribute to problem-solving abilities. Using machines is also motivating. Creative instructional activities employing the calculator and computer, such as described in this chapter, are being designed and used in the schools. These resources can help children develop mathematical meanings and thought processes. They should not be used to support instruction that lacks significance to learners.

STUDY QUESTIONS

1. What is your point of view about children's using calculators for computation related to problem solving?

2. Discuss with four or five other people the level of paper-and-pencil computational skill that children in the elementary school should attain and the role of calculators in computation. What reasons are given for various positions on these issues?

3. Include in your problem-solving file, suggested in the study questions for Chapter 3, problems to solve with calculators.

4. Ask elementary school children who work with computers their reactions to working with computers and what they have learned.

5. The professional journal *Arithmetic Teach-*

er is a resource for ideas about working with calculators and computers as well as the traditional topics of elementary school mathematics. Find an article in a recent issue of this journal on calculators or computers and share it with another student.

6. Use one of the calculator activities suggested in this chapter with a small group of upper-grade children. What are their reactions? What have you learned from this experience?

REFERENCES

Barnes, B.J., and Shirley Hill, "Should Young Children Work with Microcomputers—Logo Before Lego™," *The Computing Teacher*, 10, no. 9 (May 1983), 11-14.

Beardslee, Edward C., "Teaching Computational Skills with a Calculator," in *Developing Computational Skills*, 1978 Yearbook of the National Council of Teachers of Mathematics, eds. Marilyn N. Suydam and Robert E. Reys. Reston, VA: The National Council of Teachers of Mathematics, Inc., 1978.

Billings, Karen, "Developing Mathematical Concepts with Microcomputer Activities," *Arithmetic Teacher*, 30, no. 6 (February 1983), 18-19, 57-58.

Corbitt, Mary Kay, *Guide to Resources in Instructional Computing* (mimeographed). Reston, VA: The National Council of Teachers of Mathematics, Inc., 1982.

Duea, Joan, and others, "Problem Solving Using the Calculator," in *Problem Solving in School Mathematics*, 1980 Yearbook of the National Council of Teachers of Mathematics, eds. Stephen Krulik and Robert E. Reys. Reston, VA: The National Council of Teachers of Mathematics, Inc., 1980.

Heck, William, "Teaching Mathematics with Microcomputers: Primary Grades," *Arithmetic Teacher*, 30, no. 6 (February 1983), 27, 63-66.

Judd, Wallace, "Instructional Games with Calculators," *Arithmetic Teacher*, 23, no. 7 (November 1976), 516-18.

Kantowski, Mary Grace, "The Microcomputer and Problem Solving," *Arithmetic Teacher*, 30, no. 6 (February 1983), 20-21, 58-59.

Markuson, Carolyn, Joyce Tobias, and Tom Lough, "Logo Fever: The Computer Language Every School Is Catching," *Arithmetic Teacher*, 31, no. 1 (September 1983), 49-51.

Papert, Seymour, *Mindstorms*. New York: Basic Books, Inc., 1980.

Papert, Seymour, and others, *The Brookline LOGO Project. Final Report. Part II: Project Summary and Data Analysis*. A. I. memo no. 545. Cambridge: MIT, 1979. (ERIC Document Reproduction Service No. ED 196 423.)

Usiskin, Zalman, "One Point of View: Arithmetic in a Calculator Age," *Arithmetic Teacher*, 30, no. 9 (May 1983), 2.

Wiebe, James H., "BASIC Programming for Gifted Elementary Students," *Arithmetic Teacher*, 28, no. 7 (March 1981), 42-44.

Winter, Mary Jean, "Teaching Mathematics with Microcomputers: Middle Grades," *Arithmetic Teacher*, 30, no. 6 (February 1983), 28-29, 66.

Zemke, Suzanne, "Microcomputers and Education—Choices and Consequences," *Educational Computer*, 3, no. 2 (March/April 1983), 42-45.

Zucker, Andrew A., "The Computer in the School: A Case Study," *Phi Delta Kappan*, 63, no. 5 (January 1982), 317-319.

14 IN CONCLUSION

The Cognitive Model for Guiding Learning of Elementary School Mathematics described in Chapter 1 consists of four principles: encourage the use of cognitive processes; stress learning concepts and generalizations; emphasize intrinsic motivation; and provide for individual differences. These principles reflect two major cognitive ideas: (1) children create their own mathematical knowledge by mentally transforming learning experiences; and (2) teachers are responsible for guiding all children to attain mathematical meanings and skills.

Earlier chapters have discussed a cognitive orientation to managing instruction and to learning and teaching specific topics. This chapter reviews key concepts and instructional procedures presented previously. The principles of the Model are the basis for the discussion.

Encourage the Use of Cognitive Processes

A cognitive view of learning and teaching gives attention to the mental activities—cognitive processes—used to acquire knowledge. The cognitive processes described in Chapter 1 are: receive (attend); interpret (translate, compare, classify, and order); organize (relate, question, infer, and summarize); apply (predict, evaluate, hypothesize, and test); remember (rehearse, image, and retrieve); and solve problems.

All chapters discussed learning experiences to give children opportunities to engage in these cognitive processes. Many activities were suggested that involve comparing, classifying, ordering, relating, and inferring. Translating among modes (concrete, graphic, and symbolic) of

learning was required in many assignments. Estimating was emphasized as the first step in computation. Problem solving was discussed in every chapter.

Sample lessons also illustrated how teachers encourage learners to engage in cognitive processes. To present mathematical ideas, teachers ask learners to attend, remember, interpret, and organize. Lessons to help children learn problem solving stress remembering, organizing, and applying. In the course of a lesson, teachers sometimes model thinking to guide children to use particular mental processes.

Teachers with a cognitive orientation encourage the use of cognitive processes. They guide children to use thinking abilities as they study mathematics at all grade levels.

Stress Learning Concepts and Generalizations

Elementary school mathematics consists of number and space concepts and generalizations. The major thrust of instruction is for children to understand these concepts and generalizations and use them in problem solving.

Concepts are ideas abstracted from concrete, graphic, or symbolic examples or inferred from prior learning. To form a concept, children often work with examples until the idea is mentally constructed, described, and named. Generalizations are broad ideas formed by relating concepts. They are constructed by abstracting from examples or by inferring from previously formed ideas.

Children in the elementary school study concepts of whole and fractional numbers; the operations, addition, subtraction, multiplication, and division; base 10; and place value. Special attention is given to learning the basic facts (concept examples) because of their use in developing other mathematical ideas. Generalizations relating concepts are also studied.

Knowing concepts and generalizations helps children understand estimation. Estimation is learned before paper-and-pencil computation to enable pupils to evaluate the sense of computed answers.

The initial study of rules for paper-and-pencil computation stresses the meaning of the procedures. Later children develop skill in computing with numbers less than 100 and learn how to extend the rules to larger numbers. One purpose for studying multidigit computation is to develop a good number sense so children will be intelligent users of calculators and computers when they work with these machines.

Elementary school mathematics instruction also emphasizes basic concepts and generalizations of geometry and measurement. Geometry and measurement help link mathematics to children's daily life. Geometric ideas are represented everywhere in the world around us, and measurement is used to solve many real-life problems.

Since learning concepts and generalizations is a major objective of elementary school mathematics, a *learning-teaching sequence* for concepts and generalizations has been the basis for discussions in all chapters. The summary that follows deals with the major characteristics of the three phases of the sequence.

Studying a topic of elementary school mathematics begins with developing *prerequisite understanding*. During this phase of learning concepts and generalizations children explore concrete and graphic examples of ideas or review previously learned material. Activities with objects, pictures, or diagrams give children an immediate awareness of mathematical concepts and generalizations. Many such activities have been suggested in preceding chapters. As children progress in the study of mathematics, prerequisite understanding can be previously learned content. It is examined and relearned if necessary before new material is introduced. Games can be used at all grade levels to foster prerequisite understanding.

Teachers assess children's prerequisite knowledge before beginning instruction at the next phase. Frequently assessment activities ask children to use concrete and graphic materials to demonstrate understanding. Assessment can make use of Piagetian tasks to determine children's levels of cognitive development. If knowledge acquired previously is prerequisite to learning a concept or generalization, assessment evaluates children's recall of the prior learning. All chapters have discussed developing prerequisite understanding and assessing children's readiness to learn new material.

Constructing concepts and generalizations, the second phase of the sequence, is reorganizing what is known to create a concept or generalization and using language to describe it. Constructing a concept or generalization can be a slow process. Teachers give learners many opportunities to examine ideas by working with concrete, graphic, and symbolic examples and to use cognitive processes to form a concept or generalization. Learners demonstrate they have constructed a concept or generalization by identifying and producing examples of the idea.

The final phase of learning and teaching concepts and generalizations is *extending and consolidating* conceptual knowledge. Activities during this phase help learners develop examples of the concept or generalization in an organized way, if appropriate; study related ideas; rehearse for retention; and solve problems. Learning activities include (1) producing, as in making books and in writing exercises or problems for other children; (2) exploring patterns and relations in completing exercises; and (3) playing games. All chapters have offered a variety of activities to help learners deepen and expand understanding as well as rehearse what has been studied.

The *instructional procedures* used in all phases of the learning-teaching sequence are telling, modeling, questioning, and questioning methods. Telling is used mainly to convey arbitrary information, modeling to display thinking processes or steps in computation rules, and questioning to guide learners to form and relate ideas. The two methods, inductive and deductive questioning, have been illustrated in many lesson examples. Inductive questioning helps learners to construct ideas by inferring from examples. Deductive questioning guides learners in the process of reasoning from what is known to form new ideas.

The learning-teaching sequence was designed to insure that children internalize concepts and generalizations and develop related skills. The sequence is the framework for planning instruction.

Emphasize Intrinsic Motivation

Motivation results from both inner and outer forces. In the long run, intrinsic motivation is thought to be more reliable than extrinsic motivation. Therefore, teachers emphasize intrinsic motivation in several ways.

Teachers help children set their own expectations for learning. Standards set by learners are very effective incentives. Children persevere to meet their own objectives. Discussions were suggested as useful in encouraging pupils to examine expectations.

Teachers provide challenging and curiosity-arousing activities to stimulate interest in mathematics. Games have been described in all chapters to generate enthusiasm for study and practice. Problems were also suggested.

Teachers encourage cooperative learning because working with another child tends to encourage many learners to do their best. Teachers also help children relate effort to achievement and discourage them from thinking that outside factors are mainly responsible for success and failure.

Teachers are supportive of children's efforts and show they are interested in the progress children make in learning. Teachers also serve as models by demonstrating enthusiasm for the study of mathematics. They convey to learners that they like mathematics.

Provide for Individual Differences

Individual differences in learning mathematics are apparent to even a casual observer in a classroom. Some children quickly grasp mathematical ideas and are eager to work with challenging problems. A few are curious about the implications of ideas and examine them without being questioned by teachers or textbook writers. They ask their own mathematical questions. Other children need to study many concrete and graphic concept examples before they construct an idea. They process experiences slowly and abstract ideas only after the study of concept representations in many settings. They also need many rehearsal activities to insure recall.

Teachers make judgments about the learning objectives and experiences appropriate for different individuals on the basis of the evaluations they make of pupils' abilities and achievements. Assessment, feedback, and final evaluation are used to determine pupils' understanding, development of skill, and learning processes. Whatever their abilities to learn mathematics or their prior attainments, all children are helped to experience the joy of constructing mathematical meanings, recalling needed information, and solving problems.

Teachers stress *mastery* of what is studied to insure all learners will be able to achieve success in their future study of mathematics and to help children become confident of their ability to learn mathematics. Children at all levels of ability and achievement are expected to master content that is carefully selected for their study. Mental manipulation of mathematical ideas to the extent possible is an instructional goal for all learners. Teachers often use different methods and learning experiences for different learners to help all children attain mathematical knowledge.

Many interrelationships can be observed among the principles of the Model. Learning-teaching situations involve mathematical meanings, cognitive processes, motivations, and individual differences in unique combinations. You, the teacher, orchestrate these factors so children learn mathematics.

APPENDIX I:
GUIDE TO ASSESSMENT
OF COGNITIVE DEVELOPMENT
BASED ON PIAGETIAN TASKS

AREA: ONE-TO-ONE CORRESPONDENCE

Assessment	Age*	Materials and Procedure
Complementary sets	3–6	Use sets whose elements are related, generally by use, such as cups and saucers or dolls and clothes. One set has more elements than the other. Lay the elements of the smaller set in a row. The elements of the other set are placed at random on the table. Say: Please get enough saucers, so that there is a saucer for each cup.
Sets with like elements	3–6	Use two sets of like elements, such as beans or disks. The elements of one set may differ in color from those of the other set. One set has more elements than the other. Lay the elements of the smaller set in a row. The elements of the other set are placed at random on the table. Say: Please get enough green disks so that for every red disk there is a green disk.

AREA: CONSERVATION

Assessment	Age	Materials and Procedure
Discontinuous quantity (number)	4–7	Use sets as for one-to-one correspondence. Ask pupils to make one-to-one correspondence. Discuss: Sets have the same number. (Do not ask for a count.) Make transformations by changing arrangement of one set. Spread out the elements or push them together. Say: Does one row have more or do they have the same number? Why?

*Age to use to assess developmental stage: 1. cannot perform task and justify response
2. transition; both 1 and 3
3. can perform task and justify response

		Reestablish one-to-one correspondence and make a different transformation. Ask the same questions.
Continuous quantity	5-8	Use continuous quantity (such as liquid, sand, vermiculite). Use two identical containers and several containers of other sizes and shapes. It is useful to have several small containers that are identical in size and shape.
		Fill two containers with the same amounts. Let pupil decide that amounts are the same.
		Make a transformation of substance in one container by pouring substance into a nonidentical container. Several smaller containers may be used in the transformation.
		Say: Is there the same amount in this container as in this one (or these) or is there more in this one or in this one (or these)? Why?
		Return quantity to original containers and make a second transformation. Use the same questions.
Area	6-9	Use two identical surfaces, such as felt pieces, and small objects to place on surfaces. The surfaces represent grass; the objects, barns or houses. Place an animal on each surface. Establish that they have the same grass to eat. Continue for two more objects on each surface. Use different arrangements of objects on the two surfaces. On one surface, place objects close together. As you place objects on surfaces, make up a story about what you are doing, such as a farmer building barns in the field.
		Say: Does the cow in this field have the same amount of grass to eat as the cow in this field or does one have more? (Point to fields as you talk.) Why do you think that?
		Increase the number of objects in the fields, keeping the same number in each field but with different arrangements, and ask the questions given above.
Length	6-9	Use two strips of paper of the same length. Place strips side by side. Discuss that the lengths are the same.
		Make a transformation—for example, $\mid \ \mid$ or $\mid \ \_\_\_$
		Say: Are the strips the same length now or is one longer or is one shorter? Why?
		Vary the task by using two long strips. Cut one so that there are several short strips to compare to the long one. Follow the procedure above.
Volume	8-12	Use a set of 36 one-inch cubes (blocks); a large block 3″ by 4″ by 3″; 4 pieces of cardboard: two, 3″ by 4″; one, 3″ by 3″; and one, 3″ by 2″. Place the large block on one 3″ by 4″ cardboard.
		Say: This is a house on an island. Other people want to build houses with the same number of rooms on the other islands. How would they look? Figure it out before you begin. (Suggest beginning with the 3″ by 4″ island, to give the child a preliminary experience.) Ask: How tall will the new house be? Why? Use the other "islands." Ask the same questions.
Volume (displacement of liquid)	8-12	Use identical metal pill boxes filled with materials of different weights. The differences should be apparent from handling the boxes. Have two identical clear glass bowls filled

with water to the same levels. (Use materials in boxes that show a rise in the water level when a box is immersed in the water.)

Place one box in the water. Ask pupil to predict the water level in the second bowl when a heavier box is immersed in the water. Mark the predicted level with a rubber band. Ask for an explanation of the prediction. Place the second box in the water. Discuss pupil's observation.

Repeat with other boxes in the second bowl (use one at a time). Repeat questions as above.

Multiequivalence   6-9   Use objects or cutouts: 20 flowers, 10 identical vases, 1 large vase, and a bowl.

Ask the pupil to put a flower in each vase. Then put the 10 flowers in the large vase. Have pupil put 10 different flowers in the 10 identical vases. Place these flowers in the bowl.

Ask: Are there as many flowers in this vase as this bowl or does one have more? Why?

If pupil can conserve, ask: If we put the flowers back in the small vases, how many would be in each vase? Why?

If pupil knows there would be 2 in each vase, ask: How many would be in each vase if we had 10 more flowers? and 10 more? . . .

AREA: SERIATION

Assessment	Age	Materials and Procedure
Single series	5-7	Use 10 objects graduated in size from smallest to largest. (Suggestion: Use triangles for Christmas trees or party hats.)
		Choose 6 of the objects. Reserve 4 for insertion (below).
		Say: Please place these hats in order, beginning with the smallest.
Insertion— Single series	5-7	If pupil is successful, give him or her the remaining hats and say: Where would these go? Tell about what you have done.
Double series	5-7	Use 10 additional objects graduated in size from smallest to largest. (Suggestion: Use stars for the trees or decorations for the hats.)
		Show the pupil 6 objects from the two sets. Ask him or her to arrange them from smallest to largest so that each tree has its own star.
Insertion— Double series	5-8	If the pupil is successful with double seriation with 6 objects, show the other 4 from each series.
		Say: Where would these go? Explain what you did.

AREA: CLASSIFICATION

Assessment	Age	Materials and Procedure
Attribute discrimination	3-5	Use objects differing in several attributes.

		Ask pupil to locate object(s) with a given attribute, such as red color.
		Ask pupil to name attributes of objects.
Classifying	4-7	Use a collection of objects differing in several attributes, but only two forms of each attribute, such as red and blue forms of the color attribute.
		Say: Please put these blocks (toys, or whatever) in two piles so that everything in a pile will go together (or is alike) in some way. Tell what you did.
		After the pupil has classified in one way, make the collection again and ask the pupil to put the objects in two piles so that everything in a pile will go together in some way, but in a different way from the other time. Discuss.
		Continue until the pupil can construct no other categories for classifying.
Class inclusion	5-7	Use materials having the same composition, such as wooden beads or plastic toys. Eight to ten of the objects are one color; two objects are a different color. Discuss composition of objects.
		Ask: Are there more wooden beads or more (name color of more numerous group). Why?
All and *some*	6-11	Use pieces different in shape and with several colors for each shape. Discuss the pieces.
		Ask: Are all the squares green? Are all the green ones squares? Why? Continue with similar questions about other shapes and colors.
Hierarchical classification	6-11	Use any objects or pictures of objects that can be arranged in a hierarchy, such as flowers, roses, yellow roses, yellow rose buds.
		Say: Please put these pictures in an arrangement so that pictures that are alike go together. Explain what you did.
Multiplicative classification	5-9	Use a four-by-four table. The rows are different colors. The columns are different kinds of geometric figures. Have a collection of pieces to place in the matrix.
		Place appropriate pieces in all cells except one of the matrix. Say: Will you please place the last piece in the box. Make sure that it fits. Why did you choose that?

AREA: ORDER

Assessment	*Age*	*Materials and Procedure*
Copy a pattern	4-6	Use beads or other objects of different colors and shapes. Place 4 to 9 objects in a row or on a string.
		Say: Look at these beads. Here is a string. Make a necklace so that yours looks just like mine.
		If a pupil is successful, say: Make yours so that it is backward (or opposite) from mine. Tell what you have done.
		Place a string in a circular figure. Say: Lay the beads on this string in the same order as on mine. Tell about what you have done.
Repeat a pattern	5-8	If pupils can copy a pattern in the same linear order as the model, say: Keep the order going and make a long necklace. Tell about what you did.

AREA: QUANTITY

Assessment	Age	Materials and Procedure
Number recognition	5–7	Use cards or paper plates with disks or stars pasted on in various arrangements. Have 3-5 arrangements for each number to 9. Say: Find all the cards (plates) that have the same number. Explain what you did. If the pupil is successful, but does not use number names in his or her explanation, say: What are the names of these numbers? or How many do you have on each card? Notice if the pupil counts each group of disks. (A pupil who counts one card should know the number of the cards that he or she said had the same number.)
Number series and ordinal names	5–8	Use blocks or strips of cardboard graduated in size so that each strip in the series differs from the preceding one by a strip the size of the first one. (Graduated number blocks or rods may be used.) Say: Please put these strips in order. If the pupil is successful, say: Tell about what you have done. What do the strips look like? (Answer: A staircase.) Say, pointing to the first block: "We say this is the first strip." Point to each strip in turn. Ask the pupil to give its position name. Ask positional names in random order.
Coordination of cardinal and ordinal concepts	5–8	Use graduated number blocks. When the pupil knows the cardinal number of a set and ordinal names, say: Please put these blocks in order of a staircase. Ask: How many of the first block would it take to make the third? seventh? second?
Equality	5–8	Place 8 pieces of cutouts of candy in two arrangements: . . . . and . . . . Say: Tom could have these candies or these candies (point to each group) for himself and his friends. Which should he choose? Explain why you think that. Repeat with other arrangements of equivalent sets.
Fractional numbers	5–12	Use a piece of paper to represent a cake and supply a scissors for cutting. Round, square, or rectangular "cakes" can be used. A modeling clay cake can be used with a plastic knife. Say: Some people want to eat this cake. They asked you to help them. Cut the cake for two people so each gets the same amount. After the child has done this task, ask: If the pieces are put back together, how much cake would you have? Why do you think that? Continue with other cakes to cut for three, four, five, six or more people. Ask the same type of questions.
Pattern	6–12	Use rules involving one or two operations. Example:

N	M		S	L	
2	4		2	5	
3	5	Rule: $M = N + 2$	4	9	Rule: $L = 2S + 1$
7	9		6	13	
8	_		1	3	
10	_		5	_	
			7		

Say: What numbers go in the blanks? How do you know? (Do not ask pupils to write the rule unless they have been taught to construct equations.)

| Proportion | 10–12 | Use two drawings, one higher (or longer) than the other. Stick men, trees, cars, and the like may be drawn. Have two measuring devices. One has longer units than the other. Strings with knots to show equal units or paper clip chains may be used. |

Have students measure the large and small drawings with the measuring string or chain that has longer units. Ask the pupil to measure the large drawing with the measuring device that has shorter units. Ask him or her to predict the length of the small drawing using the device with the shorter units.

Ask: How did you figure it out? Then ask the pupil to verify his or her prediction by measuring the small drawing with the device with shorter units. (*Note:* Did the child predict by using a proportion or difference-comparison relation? If the prediction was incorrect, what was the child's response?)

(*Suggestion:* For younger children, use very simple ratios such as 3/1. Be sure that the answer cannot be correct by using observation.)

AREA: SPATIAL RELATIONS

Assessment	*Age*	*Materials and Procedure*
Positional words	4–7	Use a model of a village with toy houses, schools, shops, and streets. Ask the pupil to place a doll in the village, using position words such as: behind the school, in front of the candy store, and beside the little street. Place a doll in various positions. Ask the child to describe where it is. (*Note:* Does pupil use positional words?)
Spatial visualization	4–9	Use a cutout of a hand. Use pictures of the hand in various positions. Have a mirror available. Ask the child to choose a picture that shows the position of the cutout when: a. It has been flipped or turned over. b. It has been rotated 90°, 180°, 270°, and 360°. c. It is seen in a mirror. In each situation the child may move the cutout to check his or her choice.

Use an arrangement of objects, such as silverware and glasses or doll furniture. (The child should be able to visualize the 180° rotation.)

AREA: LOGICAL REASONING

Assessment	Age	Materials and Procedure
If/then reasoning	10–12	Ask questions which require reasoning based on an assumption. Example: If gold were as easily found as wood, what would be different in the world? Ask questions which require a pupil to explain the meaning of a proverb. Example: What does this sentence mean? A bird in the hand is worth two in the bush. Ask questions which require pupils to deduce an ordering. Example: June has lighter hair than Karen. June has darker hair than Bev. Who has the darkest hair?
Combinatorial reasoning (to determine if pupils can take into account all possible combinations)	10–12	Say: You are starting a bicycle license business. You have a machine to stamp the letters A, B, and C on licenses. Each license plate will have only three letters. How many different licenses can you make for sale?

APPENDIX II: MATHEMATICS TAUGHT IN ELEMENTARY SCHOOL BY GRADE LEVELS

GRADE	Problem Solving	Attributes of Objects; Sets	Meaning of Whole Numbers and Numerals	Introduction to Space Concepts	Geometry	Introduction to Measurement Concepts	Measurement	Base-10 and Place-Value Concepts, $N \leq 100$	Base-10 and Place-Value Concepts, $100 \leq N \leq 1000$	Base-10 and Place-Value Concepts, $N \geq 1000$	Addition and Subtraction: Facts	Addition and Subtraction: Mental Computation	Addition and Subtraction: Estimation	Addition and Subtraction: Multidigit	Multiplication and Division: Facts	Multiplication and Division: Mental Computation	Multiplication and Division: Estimation	Multiplication and Division: Multidigit	Fractions: Meaning	Fractions: Addition and Subtraction	Fractions: Multiplication and Division	Decimals: Meaning	Decimals: Addition and Subtraction	Decimals: Multiplication and Division	Ratio and Percent
Kdg.	X	X	X	X		X																			
First	X	X	X	X		X		X			X								X						
Second	X		X	X	X	X	X	X	X		X	X			X				X						
Third	X			X	X	X	X	X	X		X	X	X	X	X	X			X						
Fourth	X				X		X	X	X	X	X	X	X	X	X	X	X	X	X	X					
Fifth	X				X		X	X	X	X	X	X	X	X	X	X	X	X	X	X	X	X	X	X	
Sixth	X				X		X	X	X	X	X	X	X	X	X	X	X	X	X	X	X	X	X	X	X

X indicates grades of introduction and review.

APPENDIX III: INSTRUCTIONAL TOPIC PLAN

PLAN TITLE: INTRODUCTION TO MEANING OF MULTIPLICATION AND RECALL OF EASY FACTS

Topic Objectives

1. Pupils will understand multiplication as related to the joining of sets of equal number.

2. Pupils will show numbers to 25 in terms of sets of equal number and write basic facts to 5 × 5.

3. Pupils will count by numbers other than 1 and use skip counting in multiplication, if necessary.

4. Pupils will solve story problems using multiplication facts.

5. Pupils will recall multiplication facts to 5 × 5 = 25.

6. Pupils will set expectations for learning, in planning with teacher.

Major Prerequisites	*Assessment of Prerequisites*
1. Pupils can represent addition facts.	1. Pupils can use counters or drawing to show addition facts. Performance criterion: 95%.
2. Pupils show mastery of addition facts.	2. Paper-and-pencil test of 100 facts. Performance criterion: 91 correct in 3 minutes.
3. Pupils can solve story problems involving addition given orally.	3. Pupils will solve addition story problems. Performance criterion: 90%.
4. Pupils can name a set of any number to 10, such as $1(n)$ or $n(1)$.	4. Class discussion: Say: We know that 10 ones is one 10. What is 3 ones? one 5? What is a number name for ////? and so on. Paper-and-pencil test: Match drawings and words. Performance criterion: 90%.
5. $(N)S = S(N)$	5. Piagetian test of multiequivalence.

6. Pupils can represent a number by joining sets each with the same number of objects.

6. Show three 2-bead sets. What number of beads have you shown? Show 3 sets with 2 beads each. What number of beads is that?

7. Intuitive understanding of multiples.

7. Clapping hard and soft; skip counting.

Final Evaluation

Paper-and-pencil test with the following sections: (1) make arrays for facts, (2) rename arrays, (3) solve story problems, (4) give answers to 25 facts: 1 minute. Performance criterion for test: 90%–100%, sections 1–2; 80%–89%, sections 3–4.

Materials

Games: ARRAY RUMMY; FACT FISH; SMILING FACE; BINGO; WAR; DOMINOES. (*Note:* No more than 4 will play a game at one time.)

Unifix cubes or Cuisenaire rods

Cardboard strips

Number lines

Squared paper

Supplemental Objectives

1. To show meaning and use of commutative property of multiplication.
2. To show meaning and use of distributive property of multiplication over addition.
3. To show meaning and use of associative property of multiplication.
4. To use word "multiple" correctly.
5. To use study procedures for rehearsal.
6. To play games.

Sequence of Teaching Episodes

1. *Subordinate objective.* Pupils will relate knowledge of union of equivalent sets to number operation of multiplication. Vocabulary: multiplication; giving fact in form: $N\ ns = p$ (three 5s = 15).

Pupil activity. Teacher asks learners to: Use 3-strip cards to show 6 and 12; use 2-strip cards to show 4 and 8.

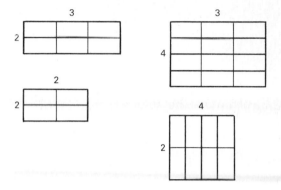

What did you do to show these numbers? (We joined the 3-strip cards . . . or the 2-strip cards.) What is true of the numbers of the cards you joined to make 6? 12? 4? 8? (The numbers of the cards are the same.) We talk about what we have shown by saying two 3s = 6; four 3s = 12; two 2s = 4; four 2s = 8. I will write these sentences on the board. When we think about numbers in this way, we are thinking multiplication. Please read the multiplication sentences with me. Show some more numbers by joining sets of equal size: Show three 3s and two 6s. Tell your neighbor what you have done. Make up a multiplication sentence. Show it with your strip cards. We will all share what we have done.

Feedback evaluation. Can pupils show a number as the joining of equivalent sets and give the multiplication sentence? Can they demonstrate understanding of a multiplication sentence by joining sets of equal size? Tell them what they have learned.

2. *Subordinate objective.* Pupils will show meaning of multiplication using sets of equal size. Vocabulary: array; standard reading of multiplication fact. Pupils will

observe that several arrays can be made for some numbers. Pupils will record findings.

Pupil activity. Give pupils sets of counters. Say: Take 8 (12, 16) counters. Ask: How many ways can you rearrange the set of 8 (12, 16) in groups of equal size? Discuss findings. Ask questions such as: What have you found out about 8? 12? 16? Point out the work of a student who has used an array. Introduce the word "array." Show how numerals are used with an array:

$$
\begin{array}{l}
4 \\
\cdots \\
3 \cdots \\
\cdots
\end{array}
$$

Introduce the standard reading of a multiplication fact (for example $3 \times 4 = 12$ is read 3 times 4 equals 12). Pupils write and read multiplication facts for 8, 12, and 16. They work with other facts and arrays.

Follow-up. Play games matching fact with array.

Feedback evaluation. Can pupils work with counters to show fact arrays? Can pupils read and write facts? Let them know what has been accomplished.

3. *Subordinate objective.* Pupils will begin to make multiplication books. Pupils will be involved in planning books insofar as possible.

Pupil activity. (1) The books will show diagrams for all facts to $5 \times 5 = 25$. Each pupil will decide organization of his or her book, if possible. (Show all facts for a number or build facts for each table 1 . . . 5.) (2) Books will show drawings or tallies arranged in sets of equal size and number lines. (3) They will give story problems for facts. (4) Pupils will make a multiplication table to 5×5 as a summary chapter. Encourage pupils to remember facts. Help them set expectations for recall. (Complete books by end of seventh episode.)

Feedback evaluation. Can pupils generate facts? Can pupils write (or tell) story problems? Can pupils explain the meaning of the summary multiplication table? Ask: What have you learned?

4. *Subordinate objective.* Pupils will continue study of multiplication facts to $5 \times 5 = 25$. Pupils will be helped to review expectations for recall and be guided in confirming expectations.

Pupil activity. Ask pupils to give some multiplication names such as 2×4 and show the multiplication facts with rods or strips. Ask them to think how many they can remember. As pupils are familiar with number names for rods, they should be able to show facts using little trial and error. Pupils work in pairs; one gives a number name, the other shows the fact, then reverse. Teach pupils to support each other in remembering.

Follow-up. Games; fact books.

Feedback evaluation. Note how readily pupils can give basic facts with and without rods or strips.

5. *Subordinate objective.* Pupils will draw rod patterns for multiplication.

Pupil activity. Pupils will continue books by making pages of rod diagrams to show some facts: Outlines of rods on squared paper are drawn. Encourage pupils to look for and report any new discoveries such as $5 \times 2 = 2 \times 5$. Discuss these findings using correct vocabulary. Review expectations for recall.

Feedback evaluation. Note number of rod arrangements in book. Note use of rods in completing page. Note pupil discoveries. Help them evaluate work.

6. *Subordinate objective.* Pupils will relate counting and repeated addition to multiplication. They will state how counting and repeated addition can help with generating multiplication facts.

Pupil activity. Review counting by 2s, 3s, and 5s. Ask: How does skip counting help with multiplication? Is skip counting like repeated addition? How? ($2 + 2 + 2 = 6$ or count 2, 4, 6.) Can you use repeated addition in making books? How? ($4 \times 5 = 5 + 5 + 5 + 5 = 20$.) Explain how to skip count to get $4 \times 2 = N$, $3 \times 3 = N$. Explain how to use repeated addition to get the same products. Which method do you prefer? Why?

Feedback evaluation. How do learners answer questions during lesson? Can they relate skip counting and repeated addition to multiplication?

7. *Subordinate objective.* Pupils will write story problems for addition and multiplication and solve problems written by others; pupils will work in teams.

Pupil activity. Discuss differences in addition story problem and multiplication story problem. Examples of each will be used to develop concept. Pupils will classify problems. Pupils will write (or tell) story problems for addition and multiplication on small sheets of paper. Pupils will exchange problems. The pupil who wrote the problem can help with the solution, if necessary.

Feedback evaluation. Collect problems. Note if problems can be solved by addition or multiplication. Have pupils put multiplication problems in books. Paper-and-pencil test of story problems. Review attainments with learners.

8. *Subordinate objective.* Pupils will be helped to review expectations. Pupils will self-check their achievement prior to final test.

Pupil activity. Pupils will take a test of 25 facts (1 minute) and 5 story problems. Fact questions correctly and incorrectly answered will be noted. Study on facts not remembered or not remembered quickly will follow self-check. Use flash cards, games, and so on.

Feedback evaluation. Confer with each pupil on his or her achievement. Devise a study plan with pupil who has low achievement. Help pupils carry out study plan.

Supplemental activities. Plan to meet individual learning needs.

Final evaluation. As outlined.

APPENDIX IV:
SUPPLIERS OF LEARNING MATERIALS

Activity Resources Company, Inc.
P.O. Box 4875
Hayward, CA 94540

Creative Publications
P.O. Box 10328
Palo Alto, CA 94304

Cuisenaire Company
  of America, Inc.
12 Church Street
Box D
New Rochelle, NY 10805

Educational Teaching Aids
159 West Kinzie Street
Chicago, IL 60610

Math Media Inc.
P.O. Box 1107
Danbury, CT 06810

McGraw-Hill Book Co.
1221 Avenue of the Americas
New York, NY 10020

INDEX